34.95

D0568475

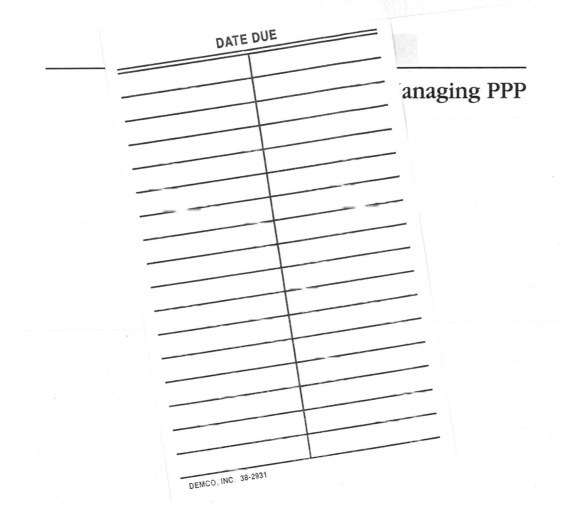

DATE DUE

anaging PPP

DEMCO, INC. 38-2931

Using and Managing PPP

Andrew Sun

O'REILLY®

Beijing · Cambridge · Farnham · Köln · Paris · Sebastopol · Taipei · Tokyo

Using and Managing PPP
by Andrew Sun

Copyright © 1999 O'Reilly & Associates, Inc. All rights reserved.
Printed in the United States of America.

Published by O'Reilly & Associates, Inc., 101 Morris Street, Sebastopol, CA 95472.

Editor: Mike Loukides

Production Editor: Mary Anne Weeks Mayo

Production Services: Nancy Crumpton

Printing History:

March 1999: First Edition.

This book is printed on acid-free paper with 85% recycled content, 15% post-consumer waste. O'Reilly & Associates is committed to using paper with the highest recycled content available consistent with high quality.

ISBN: 1-56592-321-9   [7/99]

Table of Contents

Preface .... *ix*

1. **What Is PPP?** *1*
   Early Remote Access and Networking *1*
   Serial Line Internet Protocol (SLIP) *4*
   Point-to-Point Protocol (PPP) *5*
   Open Systems Interconnect Model *6*
   What You Need to Know *8*

2. **Serial Interfaces and Modems** *10*
   Serial Interfacing *10*
   Modems *21*

3. **How PPP Works** *29*
   PPP Frame Format *30*
   PPP Connection States *35*
   Link Control Protocol *37*
   Authentication in PPP *48*
   Network Control Protocol *53*
   Internet Protocol Control Protocol *54*
   Compressed Datagram *58*
   What PPP Doesn't Provide *59*

4. **TCP/IP** *60*
   The Internet Protocol *61*
   Van Jacobson Compression *66*

IP Addresses *69*

Media Access Control Addresses *75*

Routing *78*

5. *Selecting Hardware, Software, and Services* *84*

Selecting Serial Connections *84*

PPP Hardware *88*

PPP Software *94*

6. *Dial-out PPP Setup* *103*

PPP Sign-on Procedures *104*

General PPP Setup Steps *106*

Linux PPP-2.3 .... *107*

Solaris PPP *117*

Windows 3.1 .... *128*

Windows 98 (and 95) *128*

Windows NT 4.0 Workstation *143*

7. *Dial-in PPP Setup* *155*

Dial-in PPP Architecture for Internet Access *156*

Communication Servers *158*

Linux PPP-2.3 .... *165*

Solaris PPP *172*

Windows NT 4.0 Server *178*

8. *Network Architectures Incorporating PPP* *190*

Choosing Network Architectures *190*

Proxy ARP *193*

Split Subnet *197*

Unnumbered *201*

PPP in a Subnet *204*

Multipoint PPP in a Subnet *209*

9. *Routing to PPP Connections* *213*

Routing Entries *213*

Using Default Routes *218*

Using Subnet Routes *220*

Using Host-Specific Routes *223*

Dynamic Routing Protocols *226*

10. *Domain Name System* *232*
    Domain Name System Hierarchy *233*
    Using DNS *235*
    DNS Records for PPP *236*
    Setting up DNS Name Resolution *238*
    DNS Servers *243*

11. *Customizing and Tuning PPP* *245*
    PPP Startup Options for Dial-in Servers *245*
    PPP Startup Options for Dial-out Servers *248*
    Adjustable LCP Options *250*
    Authentication Policy *257*
    Adjustable IPCP Options *260*
    Setting IP Addresses *264*
    Other Adjustable Settings *268*

12. *Authentication* *269*
    Password Authentication Protocol *270*
    Challenge Handshake Authentication Protocol *274*
    Microsoft CHAP *278*
    Authenticating Outside PPP *280*
    Call Back *283*
    Security Tokens *285*

13. *Private Networks* *289*
    Private Network Setup *290*
    Application Layer Proxies *291*
    Network Address Translation *295*

14. *Virtual Private Networking and Tunneling* *302*
    Virtual Private Network Architectures *303*
    Tunneling Protocols *306*
    Redirecting Serial Input/Output *310*
    Setting up Outgoing PPP Tunnels *313*
    Setting up Incoming PPP Tunnels *318*
    Routing with Tunnels *322*
    Network Security *326*

15. *Troubleshooting* *328*
    Troubleshooting Approaches *328*

Trace and Activity Logs *329*

Checking the Serial Connection *330*

Checking Modems *343*

Chat Script Problems *348*

PPP Failures *354*

Checking TCP/IP *371*

16. *What's New for PPP?* *383*

Communication Services *384*

Network Layer Protocols *387*

PPP Extensions *388*

Developments Relating to PPP *394*

Product Obsolescence *396*

A. *PPP Assigned Numbers* *397*

B. *Serial Interface Emulation* *410*

Index *421*

Preface

The Point-to-Point Protocol is a flexible and extensible communications protocol for use with many types of point-to-point connections. PPP is unquestionably the most widely used technology for connecting home computer users to the Internet. But it's not limited to connecting remote users with telephone lines. PPP is also suitable for connections that are part of the core infrastructure of the Internet and for private networks. PPP also supports different and mixed types of data networks, not just those that use Internet technologies.

For the majority of the PPP end-user population, most major online service providers and Internet service providers (ISPs) supply sign-on software for personal computers. This software automatically sets up and configures dial-out PPP on behalf of users. Thus, users can achieve the Internet online experience and still choose to remain completely oblivious to PPP technology.

But what about the network administrator? What if you're responsible for designing and implementating PPP communications? PPP is complex and depends on other serial communications and networking technologies to be useful. To set up PPP, you may have to sift through numerous reference materials about modems, serial interfaces, "how to" documents, frequently asked questions (FAQs), and incomplete PPP software manuals that raise more questions than answers. If you're in this situation, this book is for you.

This book collects most of the knowledge areas necessary for using and managing PPP. This is a practical book, with specific examples for configuring PPP with common computer software products, the Internet, and the ubiquitous telephone service. More importantly, the book discusses both the hows and whys. This should give you the insight necessary to implement PPP with equipment and communications technologies that aren't explicitly covered here.

Audience

This book is primarily intended for system and network administrators responsible for implementing and managing PPP communications in their data network infrastructure. We assume you have an understanding of data networks, especially the Internet. We expect you're also familiar with computers and how to use them. Although we describe PPP with Microsoft Windows NT/95/98, the focus is on Linux and Unix for the more complex PPP configurations. Windows 95/98 just doesn't support more complex configurations. Windows NT does support just about any configuration imaginable but doesn't provide enough diagnostics to let you see what's happening "under the hood." Therefore, we used Linux and Unix to demonstrate these features for pedagogical reasons. Once you understand what's happening, you shouldn't have trouble with Windows NT. Thus, general familiarity with Unix system administration is a plus.

The audience includes those PPP power users who access the Internet with Linux and other platforms not common to mass-market users. You're also a power user, like it or not, if you require a nontypical configuration. If you're in this category, consider yourself a system administrator. Chapter 6, *Dial-out PPP Setup*, is perhaps the most useful for you.

This book is not intended for software developers, who should consult Internet standards for PPP implementation specifics.

Organization

There are sixteen chapters and two appendixes in this book. However, groups of chapters have special significance and purpose. These are:

Overview of technologies important to PPP

> Chapters 1 through 4 include an overview of PPP and other critical technologies. In particular, information about the Open Systems Interconnect model, RS-232 serial interfacing, modems, and TCP/IP is included in these chapters.

Setting up PPP

> Guidelines for selecting PPP products and supporting services, and details about setting up both dial-in and dial-out PPP are included in Chapters 5 through 7.

Network architectures, routing, and name resolution

> The PPP setup chapters focus only on the PPP connection in a specific network architecture for common dial-in and dial-out. Chapters 8 through 10 discuss the role of PPP connections as part of a greater network architecture. Network architectures are particularly important when PPP connections are

responsible for network-to-network communications, rather than user-to-network communications.

Customizing PPP and advanced PPP usage

Chapters 11 through 14 describe PPP tuning and advanced ways to use PPP connections. Proxies, network address translation, and virtual private networks are a few examples of how to use PPP for nontraditional purposes.

Troubleshooting

Chapter 15 is for troubleshooting; if your PPP connection is malfunctioning, you can find numerous problem symptoms and solutions. A PPP connection can fail due to serial interface, modem, and TCP/IP problems; this chapter also covers these ancillary troubleshooting areas.

The future of PPP

Many enhancements to PPP are developing. Chapter 16 describes some that are emerging, including multilink PPP, data encryption, extensible authentication, and others.

Conventions

This book uses the following typographical conventions:

Italic

For email addresses, filenames, URLs, and for emphasizing new terms when first introduced.

Constant-width

To show the contents of files or the output from commands and to designate programs and utilities.

Constant-width-bold

In examples to show commands or text that would be typed.

user$, root#

When we demonstrate commands you would give interactively, we use the Bourne or bash shell prompt (user$). Note that this isn't the default prompt; if the command must be executed as root, the superuser prompt (root#) is used.

Throughout this book, most of the IP addresses that appear in network architectures aren't valid for use with the Internet. These are reserved addresses for use with private networks without a direct connection to the Internet. If you want valid Internet IP addresses, you can obtain them from your ISP, a higher-tier ISP, or the InterNIC.

There are numerous references throughout this book to Request for Information (RFC) documents. Some of these documents are the official Internet standards for PPP. You can obtain complete copies of these documents from many Internet sites. Links to these sites are available from:

http://www.rfc-editor.org/

Some RFC repositories are:

ftp://ftp.isi.edu/in-notes/
ftp://nisc.jvnc.net/rfc/
ftp://nis.nfs.net/internet/documents/rfc/

The index file *rfc-index.txt* contains a listing of all existing RFCs.

Some repositories also maintain Internet drafts that are proposals for upcoming networking technology enhancements and changes. These drafts include PPP as a topic.

Acknowledgments

First, a special thanks to Victoria Baldwin for initially asking me questions about PPP that later prompted this book. Well, Victoria, I hope I answered all your questions here. A special thanks also goes to Greg Brenner, for helping me verify some of the less common network architectures with PPP and the less common ways for using PPP. All the contributors to the Usenet group *comp.protocols.ppp* also helped in developing the material for this book.

I must give thanks to my primary editor, Mike Loukides, for reviewing and commenting on the multiple revisions for most of the chapters in the book. Andy Oram, another editor, also looked over and commented on some material. Thanks, Andy.

My book reviewers include Richard Birchall, David N. Blank-Edelman, and Jon Forrest. Thanks for all the wonderful and harsh comments. Jon, you almost beat the book to death, but those critical comments are really what makes for better books.

Cover design credits go to Edie Freedman. I'll forever wonder whether the "turtle" implies PPP is "slow" for many users accessing the Internet.

And finally, thanks to O'Reilly & Associates for giving me the opportunity to author this PPP book and for their patience. Both the book length and time required greatly exceeded our expectations. Much has changed during the two and half years of mostly part-time and weekend time I needed to write about PPP. Well, I need a long vacation now.

In this chapter:
- *Early Remote Access
  and Networking*
- *Serial Line Internet
  Protocol (SLIP)*
- *Point-to-Point
  Protocol (PPP)*
- *Open Systems
  Interconnect Model*
- *What You Need to
  Know*

What Is PPP?

You subscribe to an online service, and you're connected to the Internet. You're visiting Internet sites and retrieving all types of information in the form of text, graphics, audio, and video. You may not even know it, but it's certain that the Point-to-Point Protocol (PPP) is the technology you're using to transfer data over a telephone line.

The explosive growth of the Internet has contributed to a like growth in PPP usage. Also adding to this phenomenon is PPP use by telecommuters dialing into their corporate Intranets. PPP is now perhaps the most widely used technology for dial-up networking. It's a powerful technology; its users become part of the network, not just observers. PPP is an open, extensible standard that promises compatibility with a wide range of computers and online service providers. Best of all, numerous, and inexpensive, PPP software products are widely available.

This book is for the network administrator and others responsible for setting up computers and networks to use PPP. To date, there is little practical information about PPP, all in one place, for administrators. Many of you may have contended with protocol specification documents, incomplete product documentation, or the experiences of your peers, for advice. Here, you can find out how PPP works, how to configure it, how to design networks with it, and how to troubleshoot it. Although the information here is also helpful for Internet and other PPP end users, users can benefit from PPP without knowing much of the technical details.

Early Remote Access and Networking

Point-to-point serial connections existed long before the development of PPP. In its earliest form, a hardwired cable simply connected an input/output device to a computer that resided in a data center down the hall. It was some time later that serial connections enabled two or more computers to communicate with each other.

Data Terminals

During the late 1970s, many computers were bulky, expensive, and resided in environmentally controlled data centers. Networking was unheard of, and many central computers operated standalone. The development of time sharing enabled multiple users to access central computing resources with data terminals. This was perhaps the first major use of serial connections that extended beyond the data center.

Data terminals offered little local intelligence. They were simply printers or displays with a keyboard. Essentially, they were the equivalent of an enhanced electric typewriter. Figure 1-1 illustrates a data terminal communicating with a computer. The physical connection between the two was simply a cable or a telephone line. Early transmission speeds were limited to 110 and 300 bps, about as fast as a data terminal's printer prints characters.

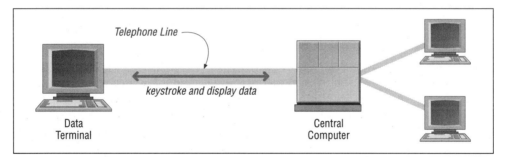

Figure 1-1. Data terminal connection

Even with a data terminal, there existed a point-to-point serial connection for data. The data protocol was quite simple; all the connection carried was keystrokes and characters for the printer or display.

Personal Computers

The general availability of PCs in the early 1980s offered desktop data processing and storage. These capabilities were far beyond those of data terminals. Although early PCs were limited, they could emulate a data terminal and connect to central computers. Once again, serial communications consisted of keystroke and characters for display.

As PCs became available with larger floppy and hard disk drives, they developed file-storage abilities similar to those of larger computers. Since PCs have files they can share with others, rudimentary forms of computer communications at the desktop became possible. This led to the development of protocols and programs for transferring files over a serial connection. Some of the widely available included:

- Kermit (Columbia University)
- Xmodem (Ward Christensen), Ymodem, Zmodem

A connection between two computers still carried interactive traffic, but when users were ready to transfer files, they ran a file transfer program. Multiprocessing wasn't available; while a transfer operation was active, no other activity was possible.

Transferring files between distant computers was a rudimentary form of networking with a serial connection. However, the connection was to one remote computer at a time and supported only one activity at a time.

ARPAnet

The Internet is an outgrowth of the Defense Advanced Research Project Agency (DARPA) research and experimentation with the Advanced Research Project Agency Network (ARPAnet). This network developed in the 1970s and early 1980s, and connected the large computer systems of the military, research, and educational institutions.

As a communications backbone, the ARPAnet was an experimental packet-switching network. With this network technology, computers submitted packets of data to the network infrastructure. Every packet carried information about its destination, and the ARPAnet individually routed them accordingly. The ARPAnet consisted of expensive leased lines, packet-switching nodes (PSN), and specialized PSN ports. Computers connecting to it required custom PSN hardware and software, none of which became industry standards. Transferring data across the ARPAnet required its members to use an obscure protocol known as "1822." Computers with packets to send had to forward them to specific destination ports on a specific PSNs. In later developments, PSN ports supported the industry standard X.25 protocol.

The ARPAnet disregarded the data format inside the packets it delivered. It was up to the communicating computers to agree on a data convention they sent or received on their PSN ports. Around 1980, the TCP/IP protocols were developing as this standard data convention. TCP/IP had its own addressing scheme, and these addresses were mapped into those understood by the underlying packet switching network. By 1983, DARPA required all computers connected to the ARPAnet to use TCP/IP.

Also at this time, the ARPAnet was split into a newer, smaller ARPAnet and MIL-net. The two were collectively known as the Internet, which marked the beginning of the Internet as we know it today.

The Internet operated as a true computer network, in contrast to the limited file transfer capabilities between two personal computers at the time. Each of the computers in the Internet can communicate with any other network member, at any time.

Serial Line Internet Protocol (SLIP)

The Serial Line Internet Protocol (SLIP) was defined in the early 1980s as a method for extending TCP/IP networking with dedicated and dial-up serial connections. The availability of the Unix workstation, with its TCP/IP capability, motivated SLIP's development. In 1984 Rick Adams implemented SLIP for 4.2 Berkeley and Sun Microsystems Unix platforms. It quickly became a popular method for connecting TCP/IP capable computers to networks, including the Internet.

SLIP migrated to personal computers later, when the PC evolved to support TCP/IP. With a SLIP connection, a PC communicated with native Internet protocols and became a true Internet host. No longer was the PC user insulated behind an expensive, Internet-connected central host. All the Internet services that users previously ran on a central computer were now available directly on their PCs. Figure 1-2 illustrates an Internet SLIP connection.

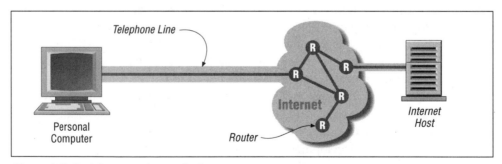

Figure 1-2. Serial connection to the Internet

A PC uses a telephone line to connect with an Internet router with SLIP support. These routers relay TCP/IP protocols. In practice, an Internet router may, in fact, be an Internet host with routing functions; thus, SLIP users may still dial-up and physically connect to a central computer. Once SLIP starts, that computer functions as part of the Internet infrastructure; users can then access other Internet hosts transparently.

The SLIP standards document, RFC-1055 by J. Romkey, described itself as a "non-standard." SLIP was a simple protocol that was relatively easy to implement. But its design overlooked several important deficiencies. SLIP supported only the TCP/IP protocol family and was therefore limited to the Internet and other networks that use TCP/IP. It didn't support negotiations of communication parameters, error detection, error correction, and compression. Even the SLIP document noted that working groups were actively developing its successor, which would resolve many of these deficiencies.

Although SLIP and its variant, Compressed SLIP* (CSLIP), are still in use, they are obsolete. The successor to SLIP is PPP, which has developed into a formal Internet standard for use with point-to-point serial connections. Today, ISPs may still offer dial-in compatibility with older SLIP implementations. If you're responsible for new networks and new dial-in remote access service, select PPP; you should support SLIP only for backward compatibility, if necessary.

Point-to-Point Protocol (PPP)

The Point-to-Point Protocol working group of the Internet Engineering Task Force (IETF) published RFC-1134 as a proposal for PPP in November 1989. Drew Perkins of Carnegie Mellon University wrote the RFC and also wrote a PPP implementation for Unix.

PPP developed due to a need for an Internet standard for encapsulating and sending datagrams over point-to-point serial connections. A *datagram* is a block of data, much like a packet in a packet-switching network. TCP/IP, for example, depends on the delivery of IP datagrams. Datagrams are independent from the physical networks that carry them. In other words, you won't find packet-switching node numbers and PSN destination ports inside a datagram.

Prior to PPP, there existed many nonstandard methods for carrying datagrams through serial connections, including SLIP. The standards that did exist supported only datagram encapsulation for popular local area networks, not serial connections.

---

* CSLIP is identical to SLIP, but compresses communications overhead using Van Jacobson (VJ) compression (see Chapter 4, *TCP/IP*).

PPP is now a mature, full-featured protocol suitable for use with numerous point-to-point serial communication media and point-to-point services. It supports the following, which were absent in the original SLIP design:

Multiplexing of network protocols
> PPP isn't limited to the Internet and other TCP/IP networks. It can accommodate numerous other network technologies requiring other datagram types. Many of these alternative network technologies developed in parallel with TCP/IP.

Link configuration
> PPP includes a negotiation mechanism for establishing communication parameters between two PPP peers.

Error detection
> PPP detects datagram corruption upon reception and discards such corrupted data.

Value-added communication features
> PPP supports negotiating data compression and encryption.

Establishing network addresses
> PPP sets network addresses necessary for the routing of datagrams.

Authentication
> PPP peers may authenticate to each other before useful communications begin.

Furthermore, PPP is extensible, yet maintains backward compatibility. Many older PPP implementations still function with newer ones, since PPP includes an "I don't understand" error capability. PPP is still evolving, and the IETF working groups continue to add new capabilities to it.

A PPP configuration for Internet access is physically identical to the earlier SLIP configuration (Figure 1-2). As before, like any other Internet host, a user with a PPP connection becomes an active Internet member.

Open Systems Interconnect Model

To better understand the role of PPP in data communications, you need to understand the Open Systems Interconnect (OSI) reference model. This model shows how PPP depends on a serial connection and how network layer datagrams depend on PPP.

The OSI reference model, defined by the International Standards Organization (ISO), divides protocol suites into a structure consisting of seven layers. Each layer defines a set of functions common to networking environments transferring data from one place to another. Many protocol choices are frequently available for each layer, and some overlap in functionality with several layers. The OSI layers are traditionally shown from the top, application layer 7, to the bottom, physical layer 1, as Figure 1-3 illustrates. These layers are largely conceptual. Networks utilizing TCP/IP, for example, define some OSI layers but combine several others. Other networks may omit, combine, or add to the layers in this model.

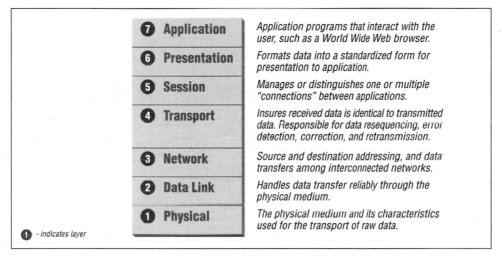

Figure 1-3. Open Systems Interconnect (OSI) reference model

A protocol at a given layer communicates with its equivalent on a remote system. Each layer passes its own data structures for use by its peer. It doesn't interpret any of the data for the layers above and below. On a given computer, data passes from users to their application software. Data then passes down the stack, layer by layer, until the physical layer sends it into the network. At the receiving end, this data passes up the stack to the receiving application. In other words, a layer in the OSI model provides service to the layer immediately above and relies on the layers below for transferring its data. This modularity enables network designers to select different protocols for each layer to accommodate varying networking situations. The IP datagram at layer 3, for example, may traverse serial connections, Ethernet, FDDI, token ring, or satellite by selecting different data link and physical layer protocols.

Since PPP is responsible for data transfer through serial connections, it belongs to the Data Link layer. Thus, PPP is analogous to IEEE 802.3, which is responsible for data transfer over Ethernet. Figure 1-4 illustrates PPP in the OSI reference model.

PPP provides a service for application programs and software that frequently use TCP/IP at layers 3 and above. However, it can also simultaneously multiplex other network protocols including Novell IPX, Appletalk, DECnet, and many others. The PPP layer flags datagrams in a manner enabling its peer to deliver it to the appropriate protocol stack upon reception. Our focus here is the TCP/IP protocol stack.

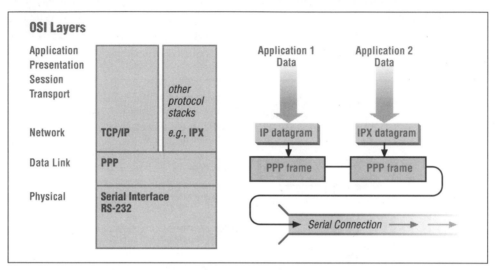

Figure 1-4. PPP in the Open Systems Interconnect reference model

PPP encapsulates a datagram inside a PPP frame and calls upon the physical layer to deliver this frame (right half of Figure 1-4). This means the PPP layer receives an IP datagram, an IPX datagram, and others, from the layers above and adds its own control information in the form of PPP headers placed in front of each datagram. PPP adds a trailer as well. At the receiving end, the peer layer interprets the PPP header and trailer, strips it, and passes the remaining datagram to the appropriate upper layers. Upper layers remain unaware of activities internal to the PPP layer. Thus, any data transformations PPP uses to successfully deliver data to a remote endpoint is invisible to the layers above.

What You Need to Know

As you can see from the OSI reference model, PPP is only a small piece of a large data-communications puzzle. By itself, PPP is useless. It depends on a physical infrastructure capable of sending and receiving data in serial form. PPP provides service not directly to users, but to network and application software. In summary, PPP is one of many dependent hardware and software layers in a data-communications system.

If you're designing with PPP, you should have broad knowledge extending well beyond PPP. Expertise areas required to successfully configure PPP for useful purposes include:

- Serial interfaces, serial connections, and modem technology

- PPP itself

- Networking protocols, including addressing and routing

Most administrators rarely have a background this broad. Thus, I include material for each of the non-PPP topics in the preceding list. Unfortunately, dozens of combinations of serial connections and networking protocols are suitable with PPP, and it's impossible to discuss them all.

In PPP environments, the most common serial connection is a RS-232 serial interface that connects to a standard telephone line. Although I cover this in detail, general information is also included about other serial-communications technologies.

Likewise, many network protocols are in use today, and each one is a topic of its own book. The common one PPP supports is TCP/IP. Adding PPP into the Internet or another TCP/IP network requires significant knowledge about IP addressing and routing. After all, a network must know when to send data to a PPP connection. Thus, we'll discuss IP addressing and routing details, as they pertain to PPP

If you plan to work with other serial communication technologies or network protocols, you may need to consult additional references. However, much of the information here about how PPP functions applies to these other situations.

2

Serial Interfaces
and Modems

Computers frequently have a serial interface for long-distance communications. Additional combinations of hardware, wiring, and telecommunication services form the physical connection between two distant serial interfaces. At the high end, dedicated fiber optics are part of this connection. However, most PPP users build connections with some low-cost equipment and plain old telephone service.

A serial interface is a demarcation point where a computer presents electrical signals representing the data it wishes to send and receive. The most common serial interface standard is the Electronic Industry Association (EIA) and Telecommunications Industry Association (TIA) EIA/TIA-232-E. This standard is also referred to as RS-232 and describes the signals and signal formats necessary for serial binary data interchange. The term *serial* refers to one-bit-at-a-time data transmission, over a wired circuit. By their nature, serial interfaces and their long-distance connections are point to point. The bits a computer sends through a point-to-point connection must exit at the other end.

In this chapter, you will see how serial interfaces work, how to wire them, the requirements PPP imposes, and how you as an administrator should configure them. I also cover modems, since they are quite common for transmitting digital signals through telephone service.

Serial Interfacing

In its history, RS-232 developed more as a guideline and was general enough to cover interfaces that already existed. As a consequence, RS-232 serial interfaces vary in many ways, including the connector types and gender. It's possible that one RS-232 interface won't be able to interoperate with another without modification, though this problem is rare with modern equipment.

The Physical Connection

Almost all modern desktop computers are equipped with one or more RS-232 serial interfaces, also known as communication ports. Low-cost serial interface expansion boards are available for older PCs that may not have enough of them.

Serial interface connectors are usually of two types, designated as DB-25 or DB-9. Figure 2-1 illustrates these and identifies the signals present at each pin. The numbering shown applies when one views a male connector that actually has pins. A matching female connector has sockets. Although the DB connectors are most common, others do exist. Apple Macintoshes, Sun IPX stations, NeXTstations, and some Silicon Graphics equipment use a circular DIN connector. There are no pin-out standards for these. Thus, unless the pin-outs are the same, a Macintosh DIN serial cable doesn't work on other equipment brands with the same serial interface connector.

Serial interface connectors may have a label indicating "modem." Alternatively, some labels have obscure symbols like 10101-1 and 10101-2, representing a serial binary bit stream. I must caution that DB connectors aren't exclusive to serial interfaces. DB-25 is also popular for parallel ports on PCs, which are unrelated to a serial interface. Incorrectly attaching wrong components can cause serious and expensive hardware damage. Thus, it's important to check the connector's label before using it.

Connecting serial devices requires an RS-232 cable. Such cables vary considerably in configuration and quality. A cable should have at least nine wires and connect all available signal pins. It's important to avoid the very low-cost three-wire cables that connect only RD, TD, and GND signals. Although this is the minimum for bidirectional serial communications, the omission of signals for flow control and interface hardware status can cause PPP performance impairments and disconnect detection failures.

Cables may be the *straight-through* type or the *null modem* type. A straight-through cable connects two serial devices of unlike classifications, namely DTE to DCE. In contrast, a null modem cable has several wires crossed and connects serial devices of identical classification. Any mixup here prevents communication. I describe serial device classifications later in this chapter.

A variety of null modem adapters and gender changers accommodate various RS-232 interfacing situations. It's best to find a straight-through cable and a null modem adapter, if necessary, that exactly matches the need. A female DB-9 to male DB-25 cable is common for PCs connecting to modems.

PCs with internal modems don't require an RS-232 cable. However, an internal RS-232 interface still exists between the computer and the modem. Thus, all the

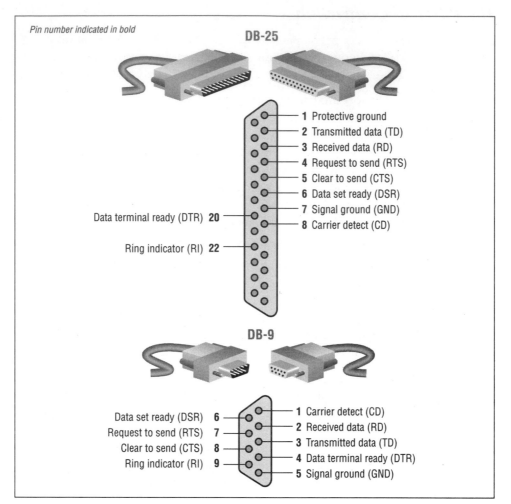

Figure 2-1. RS-232 serial interface pin-outs

RS-232 signals described are still applicable. When installing internal modems, its serial interface may conflict with another one in the PC. Internal modems are usually assigned to COM2:. You may need to change this assignment or disable other COM2: interfaces, which requires altering jumpers on the modem card or PC motherboard, using the PC BIOS setup screens or a system utility program.

Classifying Serial Devices

A device with an RS-232 serial interface is classified either as data terminal equipment (DTE) or data communications equipment (DCE). A computer or a display terminal are typically DTE. All RS-232 signal names are based on a DTE's viewpoint. A DTE electrically generates a signal at the TD pin of its RS-232 interface, for example. In other words, TD is an output signal for transmitting data. On the other hand, modems typically have a DCE classification. On a DCE RS-232 interface, TD is actually an input that electrically receives a signal. Thus, "transmitted data" (TD) is somewhat misleading. Similar inversions apply to all the other RS-232 signals also, on the DCE.

Connecting a DTE to a DCE is a simple matter of connecting all equivalent signal pins (Figure 2-2). However, connecting two computers or a computer and a display terminal is a DTE-to-DTE connection. A straight-through cable doesn't work in this case. Such cables connect a TD output to another TD output, an RD input to an RD input, and so forth, resulting in electrical signal contention. A null modem cable or adapter solves this problem. This adapter causes one DTE to perceive its DTE peer as a DCE. Figure 2-3 illustrates a connection between two DTEs with DB-25 connectors. The reasons for this wiring configuration will be easier to understand after I discuss the purpose of the individual RS-232 signals.

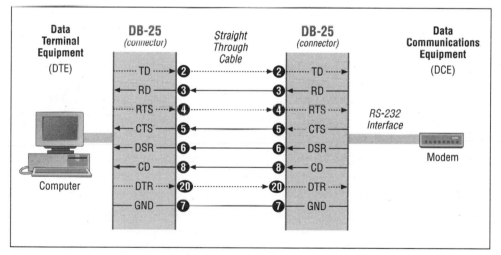

Figure 2-2. DTE to DCE connection

One common difficulty is determining whether a null modem is required. Unfortunately, there isn't a fixed set of rules that determine what devices are DTE and what are DCE. Sometimes what you expect as DTE may in fact be a DCE. Serial devices rarely identify their classification, and this information is sometimes difficult to find, even in documentation. An RS-232 line tester or a *breakout box,* available in electronic shops, can determine the device classification by identifying its active RS-232 interface signals. An indicator of a DTE is an active TD output signal on an unconnected serial interface. For a DCE, the RD signal is active instead. Input signals on unconnected interfaces usually, but not always, appear dead on a line tester.

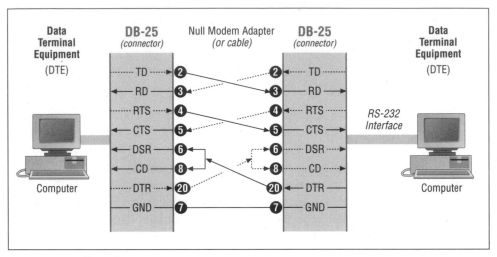

Figure 2-3. Null modem connection

Line Formats

The transmitted data, TD, and the received data, RD, signals are the two that actually carry data. A ground reference, GND, yields the minimum three wires necessary for serial communications. The two separate lines, TD and RD, enable connected devices to simultaneously send and receive data. In other words, this enables devices to communicate "full duplex," if they choose to.

Serial interface settings define the transmission line format that sends data from one device to another. Figure 2-4 illustrates an active TD signal and shows the transmission of a single character "a" (ASCII code 97, binary 1100001) from a computer to a modem. All bits that constitute a single character are sent as a burst. The logic level* of the line, at a designated bit time interval, determines the bit's value—0 or 1. A start bit marks the beginning of a character. Actual data bits follow in sequence with the least significant bits sent first. Each character ends with an optional parity bit and one or more stop bits. When no information is available for transmission, the line remains idle at a continuous "1" state. New characters appear with arbitrary intercharacter idle times. Thus, devices with RS-232 interfaces communicate asynchronously.

The data transmission line format and bit timings have the following characteristics:

Start bit

A flag indicating to a receiver that a character is arriving. All characters must have a leading logic 0 start bit.

---

* The RS-232 standards specify that a logical "1" is –3 to –12 volts. A logical "0" is +3 to +12 volts.

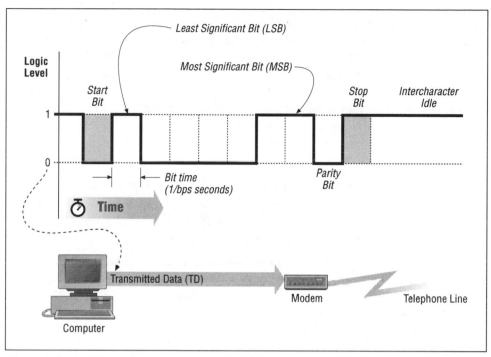

Figure 2-4. RS-232 line format

Speed

This determines how quickly to send bits through the serial interface. Speed, in bits per second,* defines the duration of the bit time in Figure 2-4. Common standard values are 110; 300; 1200; 2400; 4800; 9600; 19,200; 38,400; 57,600; and 115,200. For PPP, higher rates are more desirable and enable more data throughput per unit of time. Users should select the highest rate possible, subject to limitations of their hardware and modem.

Data bits

The number of data bits sent between start and stop bits may be 5, 6, 7, or 8. For PPP use, the number of data bits must be set to 8. Interfaces with different settings, such as 7, aren't suitable for PPP, even though they may be suitable for readable text. PPP carries binary data, which is oriented as multiple units of 8 bits.

---

* "Baud" is misused as a synonym for bits per second. The correct meaning for baud is symbols per second. This term is more applicable to high-speed modems operating at 2400 baud. Since each symbol a modem sends is the equivalent of multiple data bits, the high Kbps modem speeds can be achieved.

Parity

> Parity may be set to none, mark, space, even, or odd. None means the parity
> bit is simply absent. Mark and space signify the parity bit is a fixed value of
> "1" and "0", respectively. Parity is meaningful only with even or odd settings.
> In these cases, the sum of the data bits, including the parity bit, are always
> even or odd. This enables receivers to detect errors. PPP and modern modems
> already include other error detection methods and don't require a serial inter-
> face to produce parity bits. Therefore, the parity setting for PPP should be
> none. Other settings just add needless communications overhead.

Stop bits

> Stop bits mark the end of a character and provide a separator before the start
> bit of the next character. The number of stop bits is usually configurable as 1,
> 1.5, or 2. One stop bit is all that's necessary. Only vintage equipment some-
> times needs additional stop bits to increase intercharacter delay.

Serial interface settings are frequently abbreviated as a speed and a three-character sequence. PPP requires "8N1" meaning 8 data bits, no parity, and 1 stop bit. In
total, the "8N1" format transmits 10 bits per character—1 start, 8 data, 1 stop. At
57,600 bps, 5760 characters per second would be the maximum data-transfer
throughput.

The speed, data bits, parity, and stop bits settings are usually set consistently for
both sending and receiving functions of one serial device. The settings must match
those of a peer serial device. Mismatch symptoms between two devices include
character loss or garbled characters. When connecting two computers, you must
explicitly configure serial interfaces, one by one, with consistent settings. However, when a computer connects to a modem, most modems automatically match
their serial interface setting to those of the host computer. Once established, serial
interface settings may not be changed without interrupting communications.

Flow Control

At various times, computers or modems are busy and temporarily can't accept new
data arriving on their serial interfaces. Any data that does arrive at that time is lost.
Furthermore, the resulting loss can trigger retransmissions that further compound
the data loss problem.

The purpose of *flow control* is to suppress data transmission when the receiving
device isn't ready. A receiving device notifies its sending peer that it's busy with a
flow-control signal. At this point, the sender must suspend data transmission until
the receiver's busy condition clears. Three flow-control signaling options are available with RS-232. They are:

*   Hardware (RTS/CTS)

- Software (XON/XOFF)

- None

Hardware flow control utilizes the RS-232 RTS and CTS control signals. These are busy indicators for each serial device. For a computer, DTE, that is connected to a modem, DCE, the computer is ready to receive data when it sets Ready To Send, RTS, to ON.* This is also known as *input hardware flow control.* Conversely, with *output hardware flow control*, the modem is ready to receive data when it sets Clear To Send, CTS, to ON. Notice that "ready to send" is misleading from the DTE perspective since it's really ready to receive. The current RTS interpretation differs from the historic past. Some vintage serial devices supported only output hardware flow control, and RTS literally meant that the DTE was ready to send.

In data-relaying situations, intermediate serial devices are responsible for relaying hardware flow control indications too. For example, if a modem observes the RTS OFF condition, it must notify its peer modem to turn OFF its CTS. Any two interconnected serial devices must have hardware flow control enabled for it to be effective.

Software flow control uses XON (Ctrl-Q, ASCII code 17) and XOFF (Ctrl-S, ASCII code 19) characters inserted into the serial data stream. Serial devices, such as a computer, with software flow control enabled must intercept and interpret these special characters. A device must suspend its output whenever it receives an XOFF and resume output whenever it receives an XON. If data is arriving too fast, a device must send an XOFF to its peer. Software flow control may be implemented in software but may also be a feature embedded into the serial-interface hardware. Two connected serial devices must both have software flow control enabled for it to be effective.

Due to the special role of Ctrl-S and Ctrl-Q characters, software flow control may present problems. These can no longer be sent as ordinary data and therefore can cause complications with PPP. PPP features asyncmaps (see Chapter 3, *How PPP Works*) and can recode flow control characters if they should appear as ordinary data. Thus, as long as you take this special precaution, PPP works with software flow controlled links. Without it, Ctrl-S and Ctrl-Q in PPP data results in data corruption and can cause serial-interface flow-control deadlocks.

The last flow control option is none. Disabling flow control is useful for checking communications since a serial device then unconditionally sends any data it has. If some data transfers succeed without flow control, but fail with flow control enabled, a flow control problem exists.

---

* The function is ON when the electrical signal level is between +3 to +12 volts. OFF is an electrical signal level between −3 to −12 volts.

Modem Control Signals

RS-232 includes several signals, DTR, DSR, RI, and CD, used for serial connection status and control. The meaning for these names is apparent when a computer communicates with a modem. Hence the term *modem control signals*. Nevertheless, these signals can also control that state of a serial connection between any two serial devices.

The DTR signal is the one under the control of a DTE. The DCE manages all other control signals. They function as follows:

Data Terminal Ready (DTR)

When DTR is ON, a computer is notifying a modem to maintain an existing telephone connection, if any. A modem also accepts or initiates a new telephone connection in this state, if none already exists. When DTR is OFF, an active modem disconnects. It remains disabled in this state and doesn't accept control commands or answer incoming telephone calls. *Cycling DTR* means this signal transitions from ON to OFF to ON. This causes a modem to disconnect, but then makes it ready for a new telephone connection. A DTR ON signal doesn't necessarily mean data transfer occurs; this still depends on the state of flow control.

Data Set Ready (DSR)

A modem sets DSR ON, indicating to a computer that it's ready to operate. By default, modems usually maintain DSR ON at all times. For those configured to manage the DSR signal, it's ON when it's simply sending a carrier signal (audible tones that carry data), or receiving one on a telephone connection. Many communications programs don't use the DSR signal for any meaningful purpose.

Carrier Detect (CD)

Carrier detect is also known as the *received line signal detector*. CD is ON when a modem has established a two-way carrier handshake with a peer. This is also an indication that a remote modem peer is active and can send or receive data. When CD transitions to OFF, a computer can immediately assume a serial connection has terminated.

Ring Indicator (RI)

An incoming call normally causes a telephone to ring first. A modem can indicate this to a computer with the RI signal. RI cycles between ON and OFF, consistent with the cycling of a telephone ringing. A modem answers the call only if it's configured to do so and only if the DTR signal is ON. Many communications programs don't take advantage of the RI indicator.

Computers with modem control support can directly detect the state of a serial connection. Without it, a computer may continue to send data until it discovers, through alternate means, that the serial connection is dead. Dial-in servers accepting incoming calls must use modem control signals as a security measure. These servers need to reliably detect the beginning of a new data call. More importantly, it must detect a modem disconnect and reset, in order to prevent a new call from resuming a previous session.

Whenever possible, you should configure your computers to take advantage of modem control signals. Software for PCs usually includes hardware reset, carrier detect, online status detection, or equivalent names in configuration menus. These names all refer to DTR and CD signals. Sometimes, modem control isn't available or is not obvious. In these cases, it may be either enabled or disabled. PPP can still operate, as long as a computer sets DTR to ON and ignores the other control signals.

Universal Asynchronous Receiver/Transmitter (UART)

A universal asynchronous receiver/transmitter (UART) is an integrated circuit that produces and receives the electrical bit stream present at an RS-232 serial interface. It converts data between a bit stream format and a parallel format for a computer's CPU. A UART assembles 8-bit characters, as they arrive, into a receiver first in first out (FIFO) buffer. Buffers can hold from 1 to as many as 64 characters at a time, depending on the UART model.

You don't need to be concerned about UARTs for most modern equipment. This wasn't so with earlier PCs. Many old PCs use 8250 or 16450 UART chips that have unfortunate limitations when operating at the speeds of modern modems. The early chips have only a single character transmit and receive buffer. This doesn't give a CPU enough time to perform overhead functions between character arrivals. Therefore, incoming data can cause frequent buffer overruns, resulting in data loss. Flow control can't solve this problem because there isn't sufficient time to assert or detect it before data loss. More recent UARTs in PCs and modem cards are 16550A. The 16550A has a 16-character buffer, if enabled. These larger buffer sizes give CPUs additional precious time for other functions, before they must read and empty the UART receiver buffers.

Windows 98 users can determine the UART type in their PCs by invoking modem diagnostics. Figure 2-5 shows how to initiate modem diagnostics and the result.

If the UART: entry shows one of the earlier chips, consider the following options:

- Upgrade the UART itself, if possible
- Install an expansion card with more modern serial interface hardware; disable the older onboard serial interfaces
- Use an internal modem that is equipped with a more recent UART chip

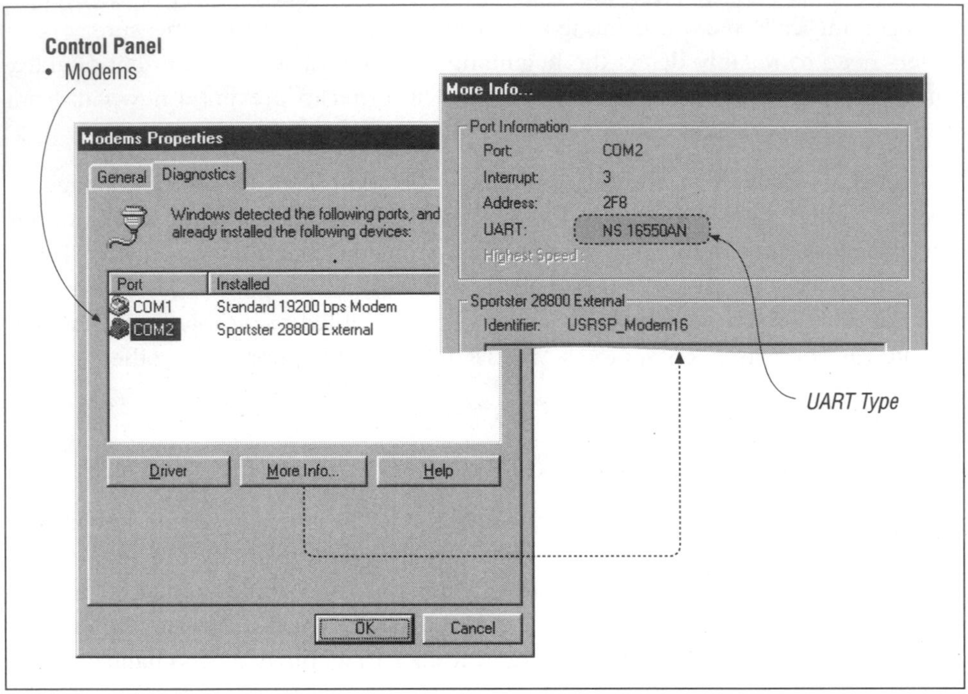

Figure 2-5. Windows 98 UART identification

These options are essential for PPP at speeds consistent with current modem speeds. Without an up-to-date UART chip, PPP performance suffers substantially, due to error recovery by retransmission.

Unix Serial Device Driver Settings

Unix represents serial interfaces as device files with names such as */dev/ttyS0* or */dev/term/a*. Programs accessing these files interact with the Unix serial device drivers to read and write serial data. These files also permit changing serial I/O settings. It's normally the responsibility of Unix programs, such as PPP, to configure serial I/O appropriately before using the serial device. Some programs may require you to specify settings using the vocabulary of the Unix general terminal interface, `termio`. Unfortunately, other programs may not change serial I/O settings at all and may require you to configure serial I/O through manual means.

One Unix utility that can set serial I/O options is `stty`. Depending on the version, `stty` sets modes for the device attached to either its standard input or output. An example of its use is:

```
root# stty 38400 cs8 < /dev/term/b
```

Serial I/O options are numerous because Unix serial device drivers have many built-in special functions. These options belong in the category of control modes, local modes, input modes, and output modes. Input and output refer to the handling of characters a serial interface receives and sends, respectively. `stty` mode arguments are similar to `termio` option names. Table 2-1 shows some important `stty` modes. These modes may vary by name and interpretation among different Unix versions.

Table 2-1. Unix STTY Modes (Partial List)

Mode Name	Mode Category	Function
19200, 38400, etc.	Control	Set serial interface speed to the indicated bps
cs8, cs7, cs6, cs5	Control	Set character size, 8, 7, 6, or 5 bits
parenb, -parenb,	Control	Enable parity, disable parity
parodd, -parodd	Control	Set odd parity, set even parity
cstopb, -cstopb	Control	2 stop bits, 1 stop bit
crtscts,	Control	Enable output hardware flow control with CTS
crtsxoff	Control	Enable input hardware flow control with RTS
clocal, -clocal,	Control	Assume modem control, ignore modem control
hupcl	Control	Hangup signal upon CD loss
ixon,	Input	Enable output software flow control
ixany,	Input	Allow any character to represent XON
ixoff	Input	Enable input software flow control
-istrip	Input	Don't strip input characters to 7 bits
-opost	Output	Don't post process output

During PPP communications, a Unix serial device driver must operate raw; that is, you or your PPP software must disable all output mode features with `-opost`. Many input modes, such as character remapping and parity checking, must be disabled. Also important is disabling local mode features including character echoing, canonical input, and signals. Canonical input, for example, is a serial device driver function responsible for command-line editing on behalf of line input-oriented Unix applications. It's oriented for use with Unix shells, not PPP binary data streams.

Additional details about serial I/O settings appear in the `stty` and `termio` manual pages.

Modems

Modem is a word derived from the communication terms *modulation* and *demodulation*. Its primary function is the conversion of digital signals into an analog form suitable for transmission over ordinary telephone lines. The digital-to-analog conversion process requires modulation. A digital signal creates fluctuations in carrier tones sent to a remote modem. These tone fluctuations are what actually carries information. A remote modem that receives the carrier must recover the original digital signal using the reverse process of demodulation.

A vintage modem functions only as its name describes. However, modems have become increasingly sophisticated with data-processing capabilities that now rival earlier computer systems. The functions modern modems currently perform include:

- Automatic detection and negotiation of different carrier rates and modulation methods; maximum carrier rates are currently asymmetrical at 56 and 33.6 Kbps

- Error detection and correction

- Data compression

For PPP, I suggest using modems capable of all the preceding functions, at communication speeds exceeding 14.4 Kbps. Older, slower modems with fewer functions become a real inconvenience. Many applications that use PPP can take full advantage of data speeds much higher than what state-of-the-art modem technology provides today.

In the following sections, I describe how to set up modems. I also describe the common modem standards for modulation, error detection/correction, and compression.

Connecting and Configuring Modems

Modem installation for external models requires two connections: the RS-232 serial interface and the telephone line. The RS-232 interface connects to the computer. Be sure the line jack, not the telephone jack, connects to the telephone line. The telephone jack is for an optional telephone set.

Now, before you can use it, you need to configure the modem.

Speed

Modems can perform speed conversion between the RS-232 interface and the telephone connection. The *DTE rate* for the RS-232 interface should be set to a high fixed value, such as 57.6 Kbps for 28.8-Kbps modem. This is the speed between a computer and its modem. In contrast, the *carrier rate* is the communications speed between two modems. This rate depends on the modem's modulation method. It's dynamic and, due to changes in line quality, may change during a single dial-up session. A modem uncompressing data at a carrier rate can produce a DTE rate two to three times higher. This explains how 28.8-Kbps modems can sometimes appear to transfer data faster than its rated speed. Figure 2-6 shows DTE and carrier rates.

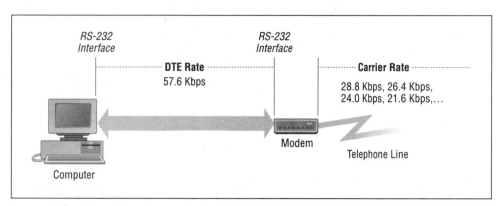

Figure 2-6. DTE and carrier rates

A fixed DTE rate avoids the need for computers to perform messy rate detection procedures. "Autobaud" features, if available, should be disabled. This gives the modem responsibility for selecting optimal carrier rates, under differing conditions, without any special attention from a computer. However, DTE and carrier rate differences mean hardware or software flow control is absolutely essential to prevent data loss.

Modem commands

Configuring a modem requires sending it command strings through the same serial interface that conveys actual data. Many modems adopt the de facto Hayes-compatible command set. These commands include the distinguishing **AT** attention prefix, followed with various characters. Modems recognize commands only when they are offline or in command mode. Usually they are in data mode and transparently pass characters from the serial interface to the telephone line.

A computer's communication software is responsible for generating commands that initialize and cause the modem to dial out. Many PPP software products allow you to select the modem model during configuration. Otherwise, you must manually interact with a modem using a terminal program, to determine the necessary command strings. `cu` or `minicom` are terminal programs for Linux. Microsoft Windows NT/98 offers Hyperterminal.

```
user$ cu -s 57600 -l /dev/ttyS0
Connected.
at
OK
at i4
USRobotics Sportster 33600 Fax Settings...
```

```
B0   E1   F1   M1   Q0   V1   X4   Y0
BAUD=9600   PARITY=N   WORDLEN=8
DIAL=HUNT   ON HOOK

&A3   &B1   &C1   &D2   &G0   &H1   &I0   &K1   &M4   &N0
&P0   &R2   &S0   &T5   &U0   &Y1

S00=000   S01=000   S02=043   S03=013   S04=010   S05=008   S06=002
S07=060   S08=002   S09=006   S10=014   S11=070   S12=050   S13=000
S15=000   S16=000   S18=000   S19=000   S21=010   S22=017   S23=019
S25=005   S27=000   S28=008   S29=020   S30=000   S31=128   S32=002
S33=000   S34=000   S36=014   S38=000

LAST DIALED #:

OK
```

An OK response following an empty **at** command is an indication that the computer to modem physical connection is working. Otherwise, the modem may be set not to respond, or a problem exists with the RS-232 interface (see Chapter 15, *Troubleshooting*).

For this modem, **at i4** reports its current configuration. Each setting has a one- (B, E, F, etc.), two- (&A, &B, etc.), or three-character (S00, S01, etc.) name, with an associated value. These affect nearly all aspects of the modem, including its behavior in command mode, use of RS-232 signals, telephone line control, minimum carrier rates, maximum carrier rates, modulation, compression, and error correction. The meaning of some typical modem commands and settings appears in Table 2-2.

Table 2-2. Typical Modem Commands

Command String	Action
at dt 17005554545	Dial, using touch tones, the specified telephone number and connect
at dp 17005554545	Dial, using pulses (rotary phone service), the specified telephone number and connect
pause, +++, pause	Escape to command mode from data mode; this enables issuing commands to a modem that's already connected
at h	Hang up
at o	Switches from command mode to data mode if the modem already has an active telephone connection; in other words, resume online mode
a/	Reexecute last command
at e0	Command mode local echo off; modem doesn't display your keyboard commands
at e1	Command mode local echo on

Table 2-2. Typical Modem Commands (continued)

Command String	Action
at q0	Display result codes
at q1	Suppress result codes and strings, such as "OK" and "CON-NECT"; useful in answer modes when result codes may be mistaken as remote user's input by the host computer
at s00=0	Modem doesn't answer telephone calls
at s00=2	Set modem to answer telephone calls in two rings
at s2=43	Set data mode to command mode escape character to "+" (ASCII code 43)
at s2=128	Disable escape character; cycling the DTR signal, or power cycling the modem, is the only means to force modem disconnect and hang-up
at s7=60	Maximum waiting time for remote modem carrier, in seconds
at m0	Modem speaker off
at m1	Modem speaker on until carrier detect
at &f1	Set defaults for RS-232 hardware flow control configuration (US Robotics)
at &f2	Set defaults for RS-232 software flow control configuration (US Robotics).
at i4	Display modem configuration settings (model-dependent)
at &v	

The good news is commands that initiate basic actions, such as dialing telephone numbers, are the same across multiple modem brands. In general, the available settings and their names are modem model-dependent. Users need to consult their modem manual for further details. It's best to initially configure modems with default settings. Usually, default profiles are available for hardware and software flow control situations.

Modulation

Modems modulate an analog signal with digital data. Many modulation standards have emerged over time as modem technology evolved. A frequent goal for new standards is pushing data transmission speeds to new levels. Vendors sometimes have to develop proprietary techniques for the latest emerging technologies. Unfortunately, this means modems from different vendors are incompatible until international standards become available. The International Telecommunications Union (ITU), formerly CCITT, develops standards on behalf of, and in conjunction with, governments and vendors of telecommunications equipment.

Currently, modems that comply with the latest ITU V.90 standard can communicate at a maximum raw speed of 56 Kbps in one direction and 33.6 Kbps in the other. Speed fall back and fall forward ability is part of many high-speed modem standards. Compatibility is still important with older equipment that uses earlier international and proprietary standards. Thus, late-model modems can detect or negotiate numerous modulation standards. Part of this process occurs when an answering modem generates different carrier tones until it elicits a response from the originating modem that recognizes a carrier. Table 2-3 shows some of the modulation standards that have developed, ordered by data transmission speed.

Table 2-3. Modem Modulation Standards (Partial List)

Standard	Carrier Rate (bits per second)	Comments
V.90	Up to 56K downlink; up to 33.6K uplink	Standard for 56-Kbps modems
K56Flex USR X2	Up to 56K downlink; up to 33.6K uplink	Proprietary and competing technologies from Rockwell and US Robotics, respectively; predecessor of V.90
V.34	2400 to 28.8/33.6K	Standard for 28.8-Kbps modems; extended to 33.6 Kbps
V.FC	16.8K to 28.8K	Rockwell proprietary standard; popular with early 28.8-Kbps modems before the availability of V.34; V.FC is now considered obsolete
V.32bis	4800 to 14.4K	Standard for 14.4-Kbps modems
V.32	4800 to 9600	
V.22bis	2400	
V.22 Bell 212A	1200	
V.21 Bell 103	300	

When a modem successfully connects, it usually reports the speed and protocols it establishes, following a CONNECT message:

```
CONNECT 28800/ARQ/V34/LAPM/V42BIS
```

This indicates a carrier rate of 28.8 Kbps using the V.34 modulation standard. The other strings are error-correction and data-compression protocols. Messages of this type vary considerably. Some modems report DTE rates, rather than carrier rates; others omit error correction and compression information, or provide it on multiple lines. The information included in a CONNECT message is usually configurable, to accommodate software that expects specific response styles.

Modem connections may not always succeed. This may be a failure to find a compatible modulation or error-correction method. One possible solution is to force use of lower carrier speeds. You may control a modem's modulation protocol by configuring it not to exceed a given speed. Unfortunately, a 9.6-Kbps selection may still result in a 9.6-Kbps V.34 connection, rather than V.32. Alternatively, you can try to lower the DTE speed. If a computer communicates at 9.6 Kbps, a 28.8-

Kbps modem may prefer V.32. Experimentation and trial and error may be the only way to successfully establish a connection. Modem documents tend to avoid specifics regarding modulation selection and compatibility issues.

Error Detection and Correction

Data transmission over telephone lines has always been prone to errors. This is especially true at faster speeds, when data integrity is more sensitive to noise and other telephone service anomalies. Modem error detection and correction should be enabled when transmitting data at speeds exceeding 2400 bps.

The current generation of high-speed modems includes several error detection and correction protocols. Modems performing this function encode data in blocks and include additional information the receiving modem uses to validate data integrity. All blocks sent require the receiver's acknowledgment. A receiver requests retransmission for errored blocks. All this occurs transparently to the computers sending and receiving data.

Table 2-4 shows the common modem error detection and correction standards. Use of these standards is available for connections operating above 1200 bps. There also exist older MNP standards for error correction, not shown in Table 2-4, that are no longer in common use.

Table 2-4. Modem Error Detection and Correction Standards (Partial List)

Standard	Comment
V.42 LAPM	Uses high level data link control (HDLC) frames with 16- or 32-bit cyclic redundancy check (CRC); V.42 includes link access procedure for modems (LAPM)
MNP4	Microcom proprietary error correction; still in wide use; also supported in V.42

The preferred choice is ITU V.42/LAPM. Modems usually attempt this first by default before trying MNP. A modem successfully establishing an error-correction connection may report **ARQ**, meaning "automatic request for repeat/retransmission" is in effect. More specific messages include **LAPM** or **MNP**.

Another source of connect problems may be the result of:

- Mandatory error control, depending on modem configuration
- A remote modem without MNP capability misinterpreting MNP requests

For the first problem, users should verify that their modem supports error-control negotiation and selects V.42/LAPM, MNP, or none. A solution for the second problem is to disable all attempts to negotiate MNP.

Data Compression

Modem data compression attempts to reduce the quantity of data, without loss, that actually must traverse the telephone line. This process analyzes the data, detects redundancy, and recodes data into fewer bits. Compression is frequently advantageous for modems, since telephone service is still a primary bottleneck in most data-communication scenarios. Depending on the nature of the data, compression may reduce data by factors as much as two to three. This means that a 57.6-Kbps data stream from a computer may be recoded to require only 28.8 Kbps through a telephone line.

Modems today include the ability to compress and expand data transparently, offloading this responsibility from communicating computers. Modem compression isn't available unless a modem can negotiate one of the two error control protocols discussed earlier. Also, the computer's DTE rate must exceed the modem's carrier rate. Not all data streams are compressible at any given time.

Common modem compression standards appear in Table 2-5. The preferred choice is V.42bis. Modems negotiate compression based on the error-correction protocol in use. However, data compression is optional and may be disabled, even in the presence of error correction.

Table 2-5. Modem Data Compression Standards (Partial List)

Standard	Comments
V.42bis	Compresses with algorithms similar to Lempel-Ziv coding; V.42/LAPM is a prerequisite.
MNP5	Microcom proprietary data compression standard—still in wide use. MNP5 uses techniques such as run length encoding and adaptive frequency encoding. MNP4 error correction is a prerequisite.

V.42bis compresses data only if there is a benefit. Otherwise, V.42bis transparently passes data. In contrast, MNP5 attempts to compress all data, including incompressible data. MNP5 shouldn't be used when sending already compressed data. This includes *zip* files, Unix *Z* files, *jpg* files, and others. In fact, MNP5 increases the size of already compressed data, resulting in a throughput penalty worse than a modem without data compression. Users communicating with incompressible data should disable all use of MNP5.

PPP also supports *compressed datagram,* where the computer is responsible for compressing data before forwarding the data to a modem. Whether the modem, computer, or both, should compress data depends on performance and convenience issues. For highly compressible data, the computer DTE rate becomes a communications bottleneck; so it's better to have the computer perform the compression. When a modem performs compression, it's available to all computer-communication programs, including those without data-compression features.

In this chapter:
- *PPP Frame Format*
- *PPP Connection States*
- *Link Control Protocol*
- *Authentication in PPP*
- *Network Control Protocol*
- *Internet Protocol Control Protocol*
- *Compressed Datagram*
- *What PPP Doesn't Provide*

3

How PPP Works

PPP is basically responsible for encapsulating and carrying network layer datagrams across two endpoints of a serial connection. PPP communication starts after a physical serial connection is up. However, before PPP can start carrying data, numerous negotiations take place between peers to configure, establish, and monitor the connection. PPP is a symmetric, peer-to-peer protocol. Each endpoint interacts with its peer in an identical manner. Strictly speaking, there is no "client" or "server." However, these designations are still useful for distinguishing the endpoint that initiates, or answers, the telephone call. Once a physical serial connection is up, PPP doesn't care who established it or how it got there.

In this chapter, I describe how PPP works. This includes how PPP formats data into frames prior to transmission. I also describe PPP overhead and transaction messages necessary for managing PPP communications. If you understand all this, you'll have an easier time troubleshooting. Many problems are made evident by examining PPP traces that PPP software produces in log files. These traces are often cryptic, and interpreting them requires an understanding of PPP messages, how they are used, and what should be expected.

The real details about PPP are in the RFC documents. Readers seeking complete information have many documents to consult, beginning with RFC-1661 and RFC-1662. This overview summarizes portions of these two documents, in addition to many other RFCs. What I present here is designed to outline the basics; if you wish to implement PPP software, consult the original RFCs.

PPP Frame Format

The PPP frame consists of a header and a data block. All information in a frame is composed of multiple 8-bit octets. These 8-bit units are also known as words, 8-bit characters, or bytes. Eight is a special number, since serial connections, networks, and computers, are 8-bit character-oriented. The PPP frame structure (Figure 3-1) is similar to the frames defined by the high level data link control (HDLC) standards. Octets in the PPP frame are transmitted in order from left to right. The default lengths for both the Protocol and the Frame Check Sequence (FCS) field are 16 bits. This frame structure represents a "full" PPP frame. Later, the Link Control Protocol (LCP) can negotiate abbreviated field lengths and eliminate fields unnecessary for many serial connections. However, PPP communications must still begin using the full frame.

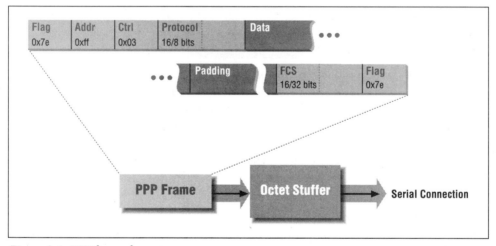

Figure 3-1. PPP frame format

Some important fields in a frame include a flag, a protocol field, encapsulated data/padding primarily from network layer protocols, and a FCS. The description of these are:

Flag, value 0x7e, bit pattern 01111110
　　The flags identify the starting and ending boundaries of a PPP frame. Frames sent back to back may be separated by one flag, rather than two.

Protocol field
　　This field identifies the type of information in the data/padding fields of this PPP frame. The default field length is 16 bits.

Data/Padding field

This field is variable in length with a maximum defined by a Maximum Receive Unit (MRU) setting. The default MRU is 1500 octets. The data/padding field usually contains data for upper-layer protocols. However, this field may also contain PPP control packets, as determined by the protocol field.

Frame check sequence (FCS)

FCS helps verify the data integrity of the PPP frame. It's a value computed using all the bits in the address, control, protocol, and data/padding fields. The receiver discards the PPP frame if the computed FCS value doesn't match the received value. The default field length is 16 bits. RFC-1662 contains further information about the FCS computational algorithm.

Although each frame contains an address and control field, both are usually fixed values. The address 0xff corresponds to the "all stations address," and the control value 0x03 corresponds to "unnumbered information." No other values for either field are valid in PPP frames, unless PPP peers previously negotiate the nondefault "numbered modes." If unexpected values appear, PPP implementations must discard the frame.

The protocol field is the most interesting since it identifies what is in the data/padding fields. Standard protocol values exist for TCP/IP, Novell IPX, Appletalk, and many other network layer protocol families. This feature enables multiple network protocols to share the communication resources of a single serial connection. Protocol values also identify frames containing PPP control protocols. These are for PPP connection management and are invisible to network layer protocol stacks. Table 3-1 shows some protocol field values that can appear when PPP encapsulates TCP/IP. The Internet Assigned Numbers Authority (IANA) maintains a complete, and changing, list of protocol field values (see Appendix A, *PPP Assigned Numbers*). This list evolves with further data communications developments.

Table 3-1. PPP Frame Protocol Field Values (Partial Listing)

Value	Protocol	Type
0x0021	Internet Protocol (IP)	Network layer
0x002d	Van Jacobson Compressed TCP/IP	Network layer
0x002f	Van Jacobson Uncompressed TCP/IP	Network layer
0x00fd	Compressed Datagram	
0x8021	Internet Protocol Control Protocol (IPCP)	NCP
0x80fd	Compression Control Protocol	
0xc021	Link Control Protocol	
0xc023	Password Authentication Protocol (PAP)	Authentication

Table 3-1. PPP Frame Protocol Field Values (Partial Listing) (continued)

Value	Protocol	Type
0xc025	Link Quality Report	Authentication
0xc223	Challenge Handshake Authentication Protocol (CHAP)	

Octet Stuffing, Asyncmap

Octet stuffing is controlled by the asynchronous control character map (ACCM), commonly called the "asyncmap." If you monitor PPP traffic passing through an asynchronous serial interface, you will see that the data stream isn't an exact replica of the PPP frame structure in Figure 3-1. PPP includes the provision for escaping certain octets into a two octet sequence. The term *octet stuffing* refers to the extra octets inserted into the data stream prior to transmission.

Octet stuffing is independent for each direction of the connection. It provides data transparency over communication paths that may have a habit of intercepting special characters—frequently XON and XOFF. Stuffing is also essential for data that would otherwise have special meaning as part of a PPP frame. Such values include the PPP frame flag, 0x7e, and the "control escape" value, 0x7d, used with the octet stuffing procedure itself.

Transmitter

Octet stuffing applies to the octets between, but not including, the two PPP frame flags. All occurrences of the flag, 0x7d and any other values marked in the transmitter async control character map (ACCM) are replaced with a two-octet sequence. This sequence consists of the control escape character, 0x7d, followed by the original octet exclusive ORed with 0x20. Figure 3-2 illustrates this with the input octet, 0x11, resulting in two output octets, 0x7d and 0x31. The XOR function flips the third most significant bit of the input octet. This alters its value actually transmitted through the serial connection, hopefully to a value that passes unmolested to the receiver. Notice the eighth bit in the octet is never affected. Thus, this algorithm is inadequate for PPP with 7-bit serial connections.

What determines which octets need to be escaped?

The octet stuffer accepts as input 256 bits of configuration information. Each bit indicates whether to escape a specific octet value during transmission. The least significant bit 0 represents octet 0x00 and bit 255 represents 0xff. The default transmitting ACCM (0x0...0ffffffff) for asynchronous connections specifies all octets less than 0x1f must be escaped. With synchronous serial connections typical of leased lines, the default ACCM is 0x0...000000000. It's important to realize that the PPP peer negotiates changes only to the first 32 bits of a local transmitter's ACCM

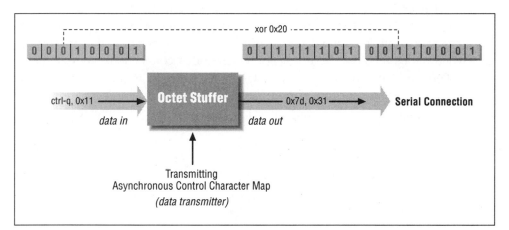

Figure 3-2. Octet stuffing

number. You must locally configure any octet values above 0x1f that require escaping. PPP has no provisions to negotiate this between peers.

Escaping 0xff, for example, is typical for serial connections that include rlogin sessions (see Chapter 14, *Virtual Private Networking and Tunneling*). However, if you set escape for octets less than 0x20 you override portions of the local transmitter ACCM the remote PPP peer can negotiate and change. This is useful in cases where we have known communication limitations, in our transmit direction, that the PPP peer is unaware of.

The constraints regarding the transmitter ACCM are as follows:

- Data octets 0x7e and 0x7d must be escaped to prevent misinterpretation by the receiver as the flag and escape characters, respectively. A transmitter must send these octets as 0x7d, 0x5e, and 0x7d, 0x5d, respectively. This is done by default.

- Value 0x5e can't be escaped since that would transform it, via XOR 0x20, to the flag value 0x7e.

- The transformed value of an escaped octet can't be a value that must also be escaped. For example, configuring escape for both 0x13 and 0x33 is a conflict.

Receiver

In order to recover the original PPP frame, a computer that receives PPP must reverse the octet stuffing procedure. This process is straightforward; all occurrences of 0x7d indicate the receiver must decode the next octet in the data stream, by XOR 0x20. The receiver must remove the control escape octet itself upon reception.

A PPP receiver maintains a receive ACCM parameter. Unlike the transmitting ACCM, this is a 32-bit number indicating the octet values between 0x00 and 0x1f the receiver expects in escaped format (Figure 3-3). The default value is 0xffffffff for asynchronous serial connections. For synchronous connections, the default is 0x00000000. An astute reader may wonder why a receiver requires an ACCM; it determines the extraneous characters that must be removed from the incoming data streams. These extra characters may have been inserted by intervening communications equipment.

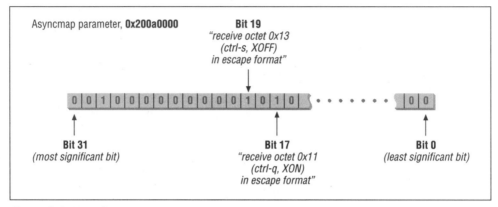

Figure 3-3. Asynchronous map

PPP can accommodate serial connections that may insert octet values 0x00 to 0x1f into the data stream. This situation occurs, for example, in equipment that translates a carriage-return character to a carriage return and line feed sequence. When the receiver has an ACCM 0x00000400 with octet 0x0a flagged, it deletes any occurrence of 0x0a in the incoming data stream. An actual 0x0a octet arrives as 0x7d 0x2a. Since the receiver ACCM is only 32 bits, PPP can't accommodate serial connections that may insert other octets greater than 0x1f into the data stream.

You establish a local receiver's ACCM indirectly with the PPP *asyncmap* setting. PPP negotiates this asyncmap with the remote peer. Based on the negotiation outcome, the final receiver ACCM value that is actually active may be different from the original asyncmap value you request. By loading a 32-bit portion of the remote transmitter ACCM, the asyncmap setting affects only how a PPP endpoint receives data. Note that the remote PPP peer also has an independent asyncmap setting, which affects our local transmitter's ACCM, after PPP negotiations.

To minimize the communications overhead necessary when receiving PPP data, asyncmaps should be set with as many zero bits as possible.

Autodetecting PPP

Dial-in servers sometimes feature the ability to autodetect whether a dial-in session is PPP, SLIP, interactive, or something else. Autodetection is based on character patterns the dial-in server initially receives. If the first few characters are carriage returns, it's likely that an interactive user wants a command line interpreter. However, if the initial characters appear as a PPP frame, this indicates to the server that it should initialize PPP software.

With PPP, the first frames carry LCP packets. Based on the formats of frames discussed previously, and considering the defaults for octet stuffing, the first characters in any PPP session are reasonably well defined. For synchronous serial connections using an ACCM value of zero, initial transmitted data is as follows:

```
0x7e 0xff 0x03 0xc0 0x21 . . .
```

This sequence is consistent with Figure 3-1. In the case of asynchronous communications with RS-232 serial interfaces, octet stuffing can create several variations of the initial PPP frame:

```
0x7e 0xff 0x7d 0x23 0xc0 0x21 . . .
0x7e 0x7d 0xdf 0x7d 0x23 0xc0 0x21 . . .
```

This sequence creates telltale PPP strings on ASCII display terminals:

```
~}#@!}!}*}}8}!}$}%\}"}&} } } } }%}&T|}>M}'}"}(}"7z~
```

What appears as the garbled message is an indication that a user or dial-in server wishes to communicate with PPP.

PPP Connection States

Establishing PPP communications requires transitioning a connection through several states. A connection is ready for user data when it achieves the network state (Figure 3-4, from RFC-1661). In reality, PPP implementations may not strictly follow the transitions shown in this state diagram. Several authentication attempts may be permitted, for example, before declaring an authentication failure. It's also possible to transition into the "establish" state and renegotiate a PPP session from other states besides "dead."

Each state defines a set of additional states, control packets, and procedures necessary for a connection. All control packets fit into PPP frames in Figure 3-1. What distinguishes control packets from user data is the value of a PPP frame's protocol field. Some control packets apply to certain states, and some control packets may be sent and received at any time during a PPP session.

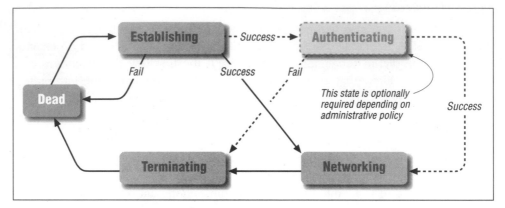

Figure 3-4. PPP connection state diagram

The sequence of events that prepares a connection for user data transfer follows:

1. *Establishing state*

   Two endpoints exchange Link Control Protocol (LCP) messages. These messages negotiate PPP parameters for the duration of this connection.

2. *Authenticating state*

   If the PPP peers successfully negotiate to use authentication, they exchange authentication messages using an agreed-upon authentication protocol.

3. *Networking state*

   The PPP endpoints exchange Network Control Protocol (NCP) packets for one or more network layer protocols. There is a set of NCP messages that establishes parameters specific to each network layer protocol. Once the network layer is up, PPP carries network layer datagrams with user data.

   A PPP connection terminates as a result of a user request, idle time-out, a lost connection, poor link quality, or some other anomaly. In this case the PPP connection transitions to the "terminating" state.

4. *Terminating state*

   Endpoints may exchange LCP terminate messages to shutdown the PPP connection. This message can be sent at any time during an active session.

When PPP terminates, software normally disconnects the physical serial connection. Typically, this means a modem hangs up the telephone line.

Link Control Protocol

The Link Control Protocol (LCP) carries packets for establishing, maintaining, and ending PPP. Establishing PPP requires negotiating operating parameters. LCP manages PPP options that are independent of the network layer protocols PPP encapsulates. In other words, the same LCP packets, with the same PPP options, apply to connections carrying TCP/IP, IPX, or another network protocols.

The first LCP packets that PPP endpoints send negotiate configurable options at the beginning of a PPP connection. Both endpoints must reach an agreement regarding these options; otherwise, the connection terminates. The negotiation process is discussed in following sections. If a connection succeeds, other LCP packets are available for monitoring.

Overall, there are three classes for LCP packets:

Link configuration
Configure-request, configure-ack (acknowledge), configure-nak (negative acknowledge), and configure-reject

Link termination
Terminate-request and terminate-ack (acknowledge)

Link monitoring and troubleshooting
Code-reject, protocol-reject, echo-request, echo-reply, and discard-request

All LCP packets must conform to the standard PPP frame format (Figure 3-1). What identifies LCP from other packets is the value 0xc021 in the protocol field. The information in the data area of the PPP frame is the LCP packet. Figure 3-5 shows a PPP frame containing an LCP packet. This frame, like others, is subject to octet-stuffing procedures. However, all frames with LCP packets are always sent and received on the assumption that all negotiable parameters are at their defaults, including the asyncmap. This guarantees that frames with LCP are always recognizable, even if previous LCP packets specify changes to the PPP frame format.

The single octet code field identifies the LCP message. Common values for this field are in Table 3-2. The IANA maintains the complete list of codes for LCP packets. The ID field is a single octet that matches LCP requests with responses. When a PPP endpoint receives a request and replies, the reply includes the ID number of the request. A Length field counts the number of octets in this LCP packet. The count includes the code, ID, length, and LCP data fields. Finally, the LCP data field contains supplemental information for some LCP messages that need it.

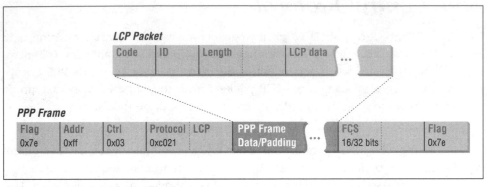

Figure 3-5. PPP LCP packet format

Table 3-2. LCP Codes (Partial List)

Code Value	LCP Packet Type
0x01	Configure-request
0x02	Configure-ack (acknowledge)
0x03	Configure-nak (negative acknowledge)
0x04	Configure-reject
0x05	Terminate-request
0x06	Terminate-ack (acknowledge)
0x07	Code-reject
0x08	Protocol-reject
0x09	Echo-request
0x0a	Echo-reply
0x0b	Discard-request

LCP Configure

PPP starts with LCP configure packets (see Table 3-2) that negotiate option settings, acknowledgments, and rejects. PPP negotiation is an iterative process. One endpoint proposes to a peer the list of PPP options it wants the peer to use. If the peer rejects the proposal, this endpoint must send a revised one. This continues until an agreement is reached. Figure 3-6 illustrates the PPP negotiation sequence and the LCP packets involved. Link options are independent for each direction of a point-to-point connection. Each endpoint actively negotiates options for its receiving direction. Thus, both Host A and Host B begin by sending a configure-request packet. It doesn't matter who initiated the call, since PPP operates peer to peer. Although the diagram shows negotiations separately in time for each direction, in practice, these events are intertwined.

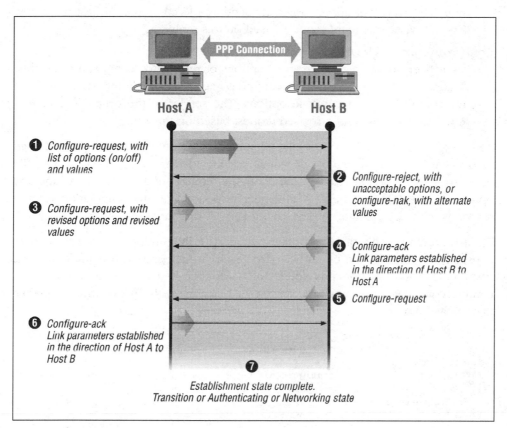

Figure 3-6. PPP negotiation

The LCP configure packets are:

Configure-Request (code=1)

The PPP endpoint sending the configure-request places the list of all options (zero or more) it wishes to negotiate into the LCP data field. All configurable options must be negotiated simultaneously.

Configure-Ack (Acknowledge) (code=2)

If all the options listed in the configure-request are recognizable and acceptable to the peer, the peer replies with a configure-ack. The acknowledgment includes the options as requested in the original configure-request message.

Configure-Nak (Negative Acknowledge) (code=3)

If the peer recognizes all options, but some options have unacceptable values, the peer responds with a configure-nak. This response contains the offending option and hints regarding acceptable values. A peer can also reply with configure-nak if it requires an option omitted in the original configure-request. The PPP endpoint originally sending the configure-request must now send a revised configure-request based on this reply.

Configure-Reject (code=4)

If the peer doesn't recognize some options or refuses to accept some "do this" options, the peer replies with a configure-reject. This reply includes the list of unrecognized or unacceptable options. The sender of the original configure-request must now send a revised request based on this reply.

A configure-request LCP packet embeds multiple PPP options. Only those that need to be changed from their default values are included in this packet. When PPP operates with all default settings, the configure-request sender doesn't include any options in the LCP data field. A PPP peer responding to a configuration request responds with LCP configure-reject, configure-nak, or configure-ack.

The maximum number of LCP configure-requests a PPP endpoint sends to its peer is usually 10. This should be sufficient to reach an agreement. In many cases, the first configure-request contains options all acceptable to a peer, which results in a configure-ack response. But in a successful worst case, the negotiation sequence may be as follows:

```
configure-request --->
                    <--- configure-reject
configure-request --->
                    <--- configure-nak
. . .
configure-request --->
                    <--- configure-nak
configure-request --->
                    <--- configure-ack
```

If there is never an agreement, the configure-request sender never receives a configure-ack reply. The session terminates, and you must then troubleshoot.

To better understand how one endpoint negotiates with a peer, let's examine a real example with PPP-2.3 on Linux. PPP-2.3 features extensive trace capability that shows LCP packets during connection establishment. Any problems with negotiations appear in the trace log.

For a Host A connected to Host B, we start dial-out PPP on Host A as follows:

```
user$ /usr/sbin/pppd debug /dev/ttyS0 38400 defaultroute escape 0d,ff \
nopcomp connect "/usr/sbin/chat -v -f ./.pppchat" user myname remotename \
hostb 172.16.0.69:172.16.0.193
```

The important command-line options in this example are nopcomp, which indicate Host A doesn't negotiate and doesn't accept PPP protocol field compression. The escape 0d,ff are the octets Host A must escape at its transmitter, despite any asyncmap option Host B may request.

This is what happens when **Host** B sends an LCP configure-request to **Host** A. Host B is negotiating PPP options for the A to B direction of the PPP connection. This activity corresponds with transaction 5 in Figure 3-6:

```
Aug  3 11:26:46 hosta pppd[881]: rcvd [LCP ConfReq id=0x1f <mru 1500>
<asyncmap 0x0> <auth upap> <magic 0x2f5990a6> <pcomp> <accomp>]
Aug  3 11:26:46 hosta pppd[881]: fsm_rconfreq(LCP): Rcvd id 31.
```

A examines each of B's requested options and determines whether each is acceptable:

```
Aug  3 11:26:46 hosta pppd[881]: lcp_reqci: rcvd MRU
Aug  3 11:26:46 hosta pppd[881]: (1500)
Aug  3 11:26:46 hosta pppd[881]:  (ACK)
Aug  3 11:26:46 hosta pppd[881]: lcp_reqci: rcvd ASYNCMAP
Aug  3 11:26:46 hosta pppd[881]: (0)
Aug  3 11:26:46 hosta pppd[881]:  (NAK)
Aug  3 11:26:46 hosta pppd[881]: lcp_reqci: rcvd AUTHTYPE
Aug  3 11:26:46 hosta pppd[881]: (c023)
Aug  3 11:26:46 hosta pppd[881]:  (ACK)
Aug  3 11:26:46 hosta pppd[881]: lcp_reqci: rcvd MAGICNUMBER
Aug  3 11:26:46 hosta pppd[881]: (2f5990a6)
Aug  3 11:26:46 hosta pppd[881]:  (ACK)
Aug  3 11:26:46 hosta pppd[881]: lcp_reqci: rcvd PCOMPRESSION
Aug  3 11:26:46 hosta pppd[881]: (REJ)
Aug  3 11:26:46 hosta pppd[881]: lcp_reqci: rcvd ACCOMPRESSION
Aug  3 11:26:46 hosta pppd[881]:  (ACK)
```

Many of the options are acceptable. However, the request for PPP protocol field compression, **pcomp** and **PCOMPRESSION**, is not. Since this is a "do this" option, the correct reply by **Host** A is a configure-reject:

```
Aug  3 11:26:46 hosta pppd[881]: lcp_reqci: returning CONFREJ.
Aug  3 11:26:46 hosta pppd[881]: sent [LCP ConfRej id=0x1f <pcomp>]
```

Now B must revise its configure-request message and omit its request for protocol field compression. The new configure-request must have a new ID number:

```
Aug  3 11:26:46 hosta pppd[881]: rcvd [LCP ConfReq id=0x20 <mru 1500>
<asyncmap 0x0> <auth upap> <magic 0x2f5990a6> <accomp>]
Aug  3 11:26:46 hosta pppd[881]: fsm_rconfreq(LCP): Rcvd id 32.
```

A again examines the options in B's revised configure-request:

```
Aug  3 11:26:46 hosta pppd[881]: lcp_reqci: rcvd MRU
Aug  3 11:26:46 hosta pppd[881]: (1500)
Aug  3 11:26:46 hosta pppd[881]:  (ACK)
Aug  3 11:26:46 hosta pppd[881]: lcp_reqci: rcvd ASYNCMAP
Aug  3 11:26:46 hosta pppd[881]: (0)
Aug  3 11:26:46 hosta pppd[881]:  (NAK)
Aug  3 11:26:46 hosta pppd[881]: lcp_reqci: rcvd AUTHTYPE
Aug  3 11:26:46 hosta pppd[881]: (c023)
Aug  3 11:26:46 hosta pppd[881]:  (ACK)
Aug  3 11:26:46 hosta pppd[881]: lcp_reqci: rcvd MAGICNUMBER
```

```
Aug  3 11:26:46 hosta pppd[881]: (2f5990a6)
Aug  3 11:26:46 hosta pppd[881]:  (ACK)
Aug  3 11:26:46 hosta pppd[881]: lcp_reqci: rcvd ACCOMPRESSION
Aug  3 11:26:46 hosta pppd[881]:  (ACK)
```

A recognizes all the requested options. However, the asyncmap value conflicts with the **escape 0d** setting the user specifies as a **pppd** command-line option. Host A must reject this value, but another value is acceptable. Therefore, this requires A to reply with configure-nak. The reply indicates to B that it can't request asyncmap 0x0 but it can request asyncmap 0x2000:

```
Aug  3 11:26:46 hosta pppd[881]: lcp_reqci: returning CONFNAK.
Aug  3 11:26:46 hosta pppd[881]: sent [LCP ConfNak id=0x20 <asyncmap 0x2000>]
```

The next configure-request from B is:

```
Aug  3 11:26:46 hosta pppd[881]: rcvd [LCP ConfReq id=0x21 <mru 1500> <auth
upap> <magic 0x2f5990a6> <accomp>]
Aug  3 11:26:46 hosta pppd[881]: fsm_rconfreq(LCP): Rcvd id 33.
```

This time B didn't request a nondefault asyncmap setting. Rather than revising asyncmap to an acceptable value, B simply omitted it. This means B decided not to further negotiate this option but to accept the PPP asyncmap default of 0xffffffff. At this point, all options are acceptable to A, and A replies with a configure-ack:

```
Aug  3 11:26:46 hosta pppd[881]: lcp_reqci: returning CONFACK.
Aug  3 11:26:46 hosta pppd[881]: sent [LCP ConfAck id=0x21 <mru 1500> <auth
upap> <magic 0x2f5990a6> <accomp>]
```

While the preceding sequence is in progress, Host A is also negotiating with Host B to establish PPP communications options in the B to A direction of the PPP connection. These correspond to events 1 to 4 in Figure 3-6. These events are also interspersed in the same PPP log file, which begins and ends as follows:

```
Aug  3 11:26:46 hosta pppd[881]: sent [LCP ConfReq id=0x1 <mru 1500>
<asyncmap 0x0> <magic 0x6105a109> <accomp>]
Aug  3 11:26:46 hosta pppd[881]: rcvd [LCP ConfAck id=0x1 <mru 1500>
<asyncmap 0x0> <magic 0x6105a109> <accomp>]
```

B accepted all the options in A's initial configure-request.

At the conclusion of all the negotiations above, the next PPP connection state is authentication. During negotiation, Host A agrees to authenticate to B using the password authentication protocol. It must now send a PPP username and password to B for validation. Since A doesn't impose authentication for B, B doesn't need to prove its identity.

PPP options

LCP packets can carry many PPP options. The format of one option inside the LCP packet appears in Figure 3-7. An 8-bit type field identifies the option. For those with associated values, or other data, the option's data area contains this information. The 8-bit length field counts the number of octets that include the type, length, and option data fields. LCP packets carrying multiple options concatenate all the options into the LCP packet data field.

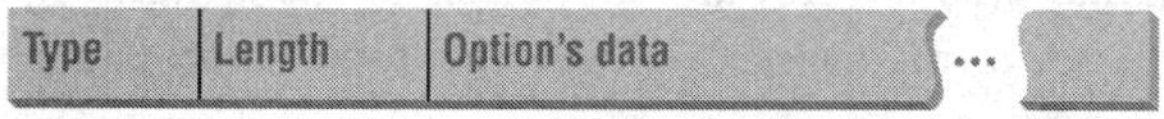

Type	Length	
Type	Length	
0x01	4	Maximum Receive Unit
0x02	6	Async Control Character Map
0x03	>=4	Authentication Protocol
0x04	>=4	Quality Protocol
0x05	6	Magic Number
0x07	2	Protocol Field Compression
0x08	2	Address and Control Field Compression
0x09		FCS Alternative
...		

Figure 3-7. PPP configuration options format

A partial listing of PPP options appears in Figure 3-7. This list is extensible, and PPP now defines many additional new ones (Appendix A). Most options, unless otherwise noted, apply to the receiving direction of the PPP connection, from the viewpoint of the configure-request sender. This is important to understand when configuring PPP.

Some of the fundamental PPP options, their defaults, and what they mean are detailed in the list that follows. Negotiated options don't affect PPP frames with LCP packets. They become effective for other PPP frames sent and received outside the establishment state of a connection.

Maximum Receive Unit (MRU), default 1500

This option informs the peer that we are capable of receiving PPP frame sizes larger than the default. We can also inform the peer to use smaller frame sizes. The MRU option includes a 16-bit number that specifies the maximum size in octets, omitting octet stuffing, for the PPP frame's data and padding area. The total option length is 4.

Async Control Character Map (ACCM), default 0xffffffff

ACCM, also known as the asyncmap option, specifies a set of data octets values. These are the octets in the PPP data stream we must then receive from the peer in escaped format. The previous section "Octet Stuffing, Asyncmap" describes the effect of this option in more detail. The ACCM option carries a 32-bit number that defines its desired value. The total option length is 6.

Authentication Protocol, default "no protocol"

This informs the peer that it must prove its identity with some form of name and password. Embedded in the option is a 16-bit number, which specifies the authentication protocol to use. Some acceptable values are 0xc023 and 0xc223 (see Table 3-1). If we don't request this PPP option, no authentication occurs. This option may include additional octets, as determined by the needs of a specific authentication protocol. Thus, the total option length is 4 octets, or more.

Quality Protocol, default "no protocol"

Link quality monitoring helps determine the quality of a PPP connection by measuring data loss and other quantities. The quality protocol option, if present, informs the peer that we wish to receive monitoring information. Embedded in the option is a 16-bit number identifying the quality protocol to use. One value is 0xc025 for "Link quality report" (Table 3-1). If the peer acknowledges this option, it must send monitoring information packets regularly throughout the duration of the PPP session. This option may include additional octets for quality protocol specific information. The total option length is 4 octets or more.

Magic Number, default 0 "no number"

The magic number option informs our peer about a 32-bit random number we select for use during this PPP session. If acknowledged by the peer, we send our magic number in discard-requests, in PPP echo-replies, and in link quality monitoring packets. Magic numbers are for detecting looped back serial connections. Both endpoints must agree to use different magic numbers. If we receive PPP frames with magic numbers matching our own, we can conclude[*] that the serial connection is looped back. The magic number option length is 6 octets. If we don't negotiate magic numbers at all, we insert zero in places where magic numbers would otherwise be sent.

Protocol Field Compression, default "off"

The standard PPP frame has a 16-bit protocol field. If we request protocol field compression, we request from our peer modified PPP frames with an 8-bit protocol field. An 8-bit field expresses protocol values in the range of 0x00 to 0xff. Common network layer protocols use values in this range. Even with protocol field compression in effect, we still receive values over 0xff as two octets. Legal protocol values must have an even first octet and an odd second octet. Thus, PPP can always determine whether a protocol value arrived as 1

---

[*] It's possible for our peer to select a magic number in its configure-request message that's identical to our own. In nonloop-back cases, this number collision resolves itself by configure-nak, which contains a random alternative number the peer can use. If the line is really looped back, an endless configure-request/configure-nak cycle results. See RFC-1662 for more details.

or 2 octets. Protocol field compression is disabled by default. If present, this is a length 2 option.

Address and Control Field Compression, default "off"

A PPP frame has an address and control field with fixed values, 0xff and 0x03, respectively. The address and control field option informs our peer that these fields may be omitted in the frames we receive. By default, this option is absent. This is a length 2 option.

FCS Alternative, default is 16-bit FCS

This option informs our peer that we wish to receive PPP frames with a non-default frame check sequence field. An 8-bit value indicates the alternative to the standard FCS format. The alternatives are none (value 1), 16-bit FCS (2), and 32-bit FCS (4). Multiple FCS formats may be negotiated by adding any combination of these values. By default, this option is absent, and the standard 16-bit FCS applies. RFC-1570 describes FCS alternative as "additional LCP configuration options." Support for this option may be limited among PPP implementations.

Chapter 11, *Customizing and Tuning PPP*, describes how to set some of these options in a number of software products. There are now many more advanced options appearing in the PPP specification, all of which can't be described here. Chapter 16, *What's New for PPP?*, presents examples of some newer PPP options from recent PPP developments.

New options shouldn't affect compatibility between older and newer software. Any time PPP fails to recognize an option, it responds with a configure-reject. Although configure-reject includes the bad option, the sender doesn't need to know what the option really means. The peer must then assume the rejected option doesn't exist and continue negotiations.

Link Termination Packets

LCP link termination packets ends active PPP connections. When an endpoint wishes to disconnect gracefully, it firsts sends an LCP terminate-request. Assuming the connection is still intact, the peer must acknowledge with a terminate-ack. Terminate-requests can't be denied; a peer that doesn't respond is disconnected after several terminate-request retransmissions.

Link termination can occur at any time after LCP negotiations succeed. Some reasons for expected and unexpected disconnects are:

*   The user has requested to disconnect.

*   An idle timer expired due to lack of traffic over the connection. Idle timers may be set at either or both ends of the connection.

- A required option, such as authentication, was rejected by the peer.

- Authentication problems. The obvious is an authentication failure. However, problems also include attempts to transition a PPP connection to the network state when the authentication state is still required.

- A serial connection loopback is detected. Magic numbers can detect loopbacks using LCP echo requests.

- Link quality is unacceptably poor as measured by a link quality report protocol or lost replies to echo-request messages.

There are also ungraceful causes of PPP termination. These include physical connection loss and other problems PPP software can't anticipate.

The PPP LCP packet format for link termination appears in Figure 3-5. The values of the code field are 5 for terminate-request and 6 for terminate-ack. ID fields for the acknowledgment must match the corresponding request. The data field is available for arbitrary text messages for both terminate packets.

Here is a termination transaction for PPP-2.3 software follows. In this case, the peer's idle timer expired, causing it to request a disconnect:

```
. . .
Aug  3 12:26:47 hosta pppd[881]: rcvd [LCP TermReq id=0x24]
Aug  3 12:26:47 hosta pppd[881]: fsm_rtermreq(LCP): Rcvd id 36.
Aug  3 12:26:47 hosta pppd[881]: LCP terminated at peer's request
. . .
Aug  3 12:26:47 hosta pppd[881]: sent [LCP TermAck id=0x24]
Aug  3 12:26:47 hosta pppd[881]: fsm_sdata(LCP): Sent code 6, id 36.
Aug  3 12:26:47 hosta pppd[881]: Hangup (SIGHUP)
```

Network protocol layers may not receive notification about a terminated PPP connection. Some applications, such as Telnet or FTP, may discover a lost connection only after long time-out periods. Sometimes users can restore an interrupted PPP connection quickly, before a file transfer application has time to fail, for example. A PPP connection restore can succeed without application interruption, as long as network addresses doesn't change.

Link Monitoring and Debugging Packets

A third type of PPP LCP packets are those supporting PPP debugging and monitoring. These are LCP error and echo testing packets, respectively.

Errors

LCP includes two error packets, *code-reject* and *protocol-reject*. These errors are designed to accommodate PPP extensibility. The set of LCP packet types (Table 3-2), and the number of network protocols PPP can carry is growing. Frequently, a new PPP implementation interacts with an older one with fewer capabilities. The less capable software can respond to its more capable peer with LCP error packets indicating "I don't understand that LCP packet" or "I can't support the requested network protocol."

The code-reject error occurs if our endpoint receives an LCP packet with an unrecognized code field. Although the value in the code field may be valid, our PPP implementation may not recognize its meaning. We then send an LCP code-reject packet to our peer. This LCP packet has a code field of 0x07. The ID field is a new number for every code-reject packet we send, and we place a copy of our peer's offending PPP frame into the LCP data field. The copy of the PPP frame we reject includes only the data/padding field, and we may truncate it to prevent exceeding MRU limits in the code-reject packet. As an example, we may receive an LCP identification (LCP code 0x0c) packet for a peer. This packet includes local software name, version, and license serial number strings. If we don't know how to handle this message, we respond with code-reject.

A protocol-reject occurs when we receive a PPP frame with an unrecognizable protocol field value. The protocol-reject error is an LCP packet, code 0x08. The ID field is a new number for every protocol-reject packet we send, and the LCP data field contains the 16-bit protocol number we reject. We insert a copy of the rejected PPP frame data/padding field into the LCP data field, as in the code-reject case. Protocol rejects frequently occur when a peer is attempting to use PPP for a new network layer protocol. Here's what happens when Solaris PPP receives a request for Novell SPX/IP:

```
16:20:52 000185 ipdptp1 RECEIVE PPP ASYNC 23 Octets IPX_NCP
16:20:52 000186 ipdptp1 SEND PPP ASYNC 29 Octets LCP Proto-REJ  ID=37 LEN-24
Rej_proto=104 Rej_info: 01 04 00 12 02 08 02 6f 6f 84 64 80 03 06 00 02 03 00
16:20:58 process_ipd_msg: interface ipdptp1 has disconnected
16:20:58 disconnect: disconnected connection from  ipdptp1
16:20:58 000187 ipdptp1 RECEIVE PPP ASYNC 9 Octets LCP Term-REQ  ID=01 LEN=4
16:20:58 000188 ipdptp1 SEND PPP ASYNC 9 Octets LCP Term-ACK  ID=01 LEN=4
16:20:58 000189 ipdptp1 PPP ASYNC DEVICE HANGUP
16:20:58 000190 ipdptp1 PPP DIAG CLOSE
```

Solaris PPP is receiving and recognizing the Novell IPX Control Protocol (IPX_NCP) protocol 0x802b. Since this PPP implementation doesn't support IPX, it responds with an LCP protocol-reject. The Rej_info is a copy of the data/padding field from the PPP frame that initially carried the IPX_NCP request. These rejects aren't acceptable to the peer, which later requests PPP termination. Note the preceding output should show Rej_proto=802b but doesn't due to a software bug.

Echo back

LCP includes echo request and response packets. These may be sent at any time to check whether a PPP connection is functioning in both directions. PPP echo operations are invisible to network layer protocols. They don't interfere with PPP communications, as perceived by users.

Echo request and response are PPP LCP packets (Figure 3-5) with 0x09 and 0x0a, respectively, in the code field. Each request includes a different ID number used for matching replies. The LCP packet data field includes a 32-bit magic number and may include additional arbitrary data, if any. Each PPP endpoint uses its own magic number in all echo request and reply packets it sends.

Echo works in a straightforward manner. PPP endpoints receiving an echo request must send an echo reply. The conditions for sending requests are implementation dependent. They may be sent on-demand by users or periodically by PPP software. A PPP endpoint that sends periodic echo requests every 20 seconds would show the following in its logs:

```
Aug  7 22:29:06 hosta pppd[1065]: sent [LCP ConfReq id=0x1 <mru 1500>
<asyncmap0x0> <magic 0x610e589a> <accomp>]
. . .
Aug  7 22:29:07 hosta pppd[1065]: rcvd [LCP ConfReq id=0x26 <mru 1500>
<asyncmap 0x0> <auth upap> <magic 0xe116be83> <pcomp> <accomp>]
. . .
Aug  7 22:29:47 hosta pppd[1065]: sent [LCP EchoReq id=0x2 61 0e 58 9a]
Aug  7 22:29:47 hosta pppd[1065]: rcvd [LCP EchoRep id=0x2 e1 16 be 83]
. . .
Aug  7 22:30:07 hosta pppd[1065]: sent [LCP EchoReq id=0x3 61 0e 58 9a]
Aug  7 22:30:07 hosta pppd[1065]: rcvd [LCP EchoRep id=0x3 e1 16 be 83]
. . .
```

In the example, this PPP endpoint establishes a magic number as 0x610e589a and includes it in its echo-request. The peer replies with its magic number, 0xe116be83.

Discard

Another LCP packet is discard-request. This packet is identical to an echo-request packet except the code field value is 0x0b. PPP endpoints receiving discard-request packets simply ignore them. Discard-requests are useful for detecting looped-back conditions.

Authentication in PPP

PPP can support authentication operations at the beginning of a connection. In some cases, reauthentication is also possible during a session. Endpoints negotiate authentication in the same manner as other options. Authentication is peer to peer, again without distinction between calling and called parties. This allows either, or both, endpoints to request authentication credentials from each other. In fact, the protocol for passing credentials may be different for each endpoint. The default is "no authentication required." However, you can configure your PPP software to require it.

The authenticating state of a PPP connection follows the establishing state if either endpoint agrees to use an authentication protocol. Otherwise, the connection transitions immediately to the network state, skipping authentication steps altogether. The two common authentication protocols are:

- The Password Authentication Protocol (PAP)

- The Challenge Handshake Authentication Protocol (CHAP)

The reference for PAP and CHAP are RFC-1334 and RFC-1994, respectively. These protocols have assigned numbers (Table 3-1) and are arguments to the authentication protocol option PPP endpoints include in LCP configure packets. As usual, if one PPP endpoint requests its peer to authenticate itself with a protocol the peer doesn't understand, the peer rejects it in an LCP configure-nak response. This endpoint may propose another protocol its peer understands, or terminate the connection.

Each authentication protocol has well-defined procedures regarding the messages that endpoints must send and receive during the authenticating state. Besides PAP and CHAP, there are other extensible authentication protocols in development. And there exists several proprietary protocols as well (see Appendix A).

Password Authentication Protocol

PAP implements the traditional username and password-authentication method. At the request from an authenticator, the client responds with both a PAP name and password in a single transaction. The authenticator validates this information and replies with a positive or negative acknowledgment. This acknowledgment can include readable text, such as "Permission granted" or "Access denied." Figure 3-8 illustrates the relevant PAP packets.

PAP is the simplest of the PPP authentication protocols available. User credentials are transmitted in plain text and only at the beginning of a PPP session. All the advantages and disadvantages of PAP are identical to other dial-up services secured with reusable usernames and passwords.

The PAP packet format inside a PPP frame appears in Figure 3-9. The PPP frame protocol field is 0xc023 when it carries a PAP packet in its data/padding field. Any LCP negotiated changes to the PPP frame format apply to frames that carry PAP. The PAP packet code field identifies the PAP message. The authentication-request

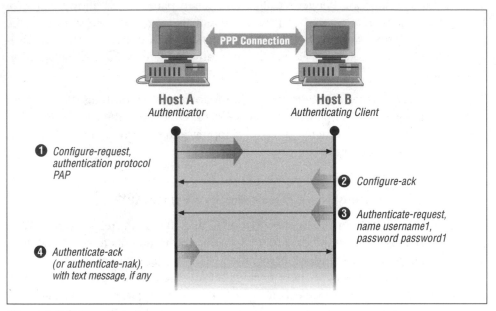

Figure 3-8. PAP transaction

(code 0x01) packet includes fields allocated for a username and password. Packets for authentication-ack and authentication-nak are to authentication success and failure notifications. These packets have code values 0x02 and 0x03, respectively, and include an explanatory text message area PPP software can use.

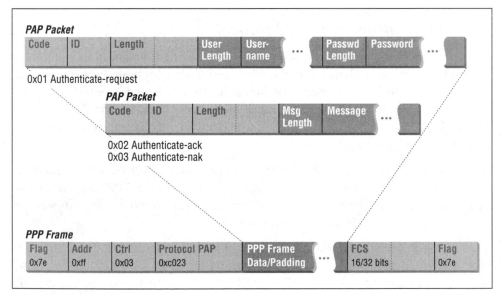

Figure 3-9. PAP packet

PPP traces in a log file can show PAP authentication transactions taking place. The following log entries shows this for the situation consistent with Figure 3-8:

```
Jul  7 00:03:18 hosta pppd[9343]: sent [LCP ConfReq id=0x1 <mru 1500>
<asyncmap 0x0> <auth upap> <magic 0x62de5c8c> <pcomp> <accomp>]
. . .
Jul  7 00:03:18 hosta pppd[9343]: rcvd [LCP ConfAck id=0x1 <mru 1500>
<asyncmap 0x0> <auth upap> <magic 0x62de5c8c> <pcomp> <accomp>]
. . .
Jul  7 00:03:18 hosta pppd[9343]: rcvd [PAP AuthReq id=0x1 user="username1"
password="password1"]
Jul  7 00:03:18 hosta pppd[9343]: sent [PAP AuthAck id=0x1 msg="Login ok"]
. . .
```

Challenge Handshake Authentication Protocol

CHAP, as its name implies, implements a form of authentication that requires a challenge and a response. A CHAP authenticator challenges its client peer with its CHAP name and a random string. The client must transform this random string with a computation algorithm and a CHAP secret key. It then returns the result with its own name. The challenger evaluates the reply with its own copy of the secret key. Then, it forwards a success or failure acknowledgment. Figure 3-10 illustrates CHAP packets when **Host A** is the authenticator. In summary, CHAP is a three-way handshake consisting of a challenge, a response, and an acknowledgment.

The challenge, response, and response computation are all built-in to PPP software. Users need to supply only a CHAP name and a secret key, known by both endpoints of the PPP connection. As long as both endpoints use the same keys, a CHAP reply matches what the CHAP challenger expects. The important security characteristic of CHAP is that PPP endpoints never send keys in plain text through the PPP connection.

CHAP can extend the list of cryptographical one-way functions used for computing CHAP responses. When PPP endpoints negotiate CHAP authentication, an LCP configure-request packet carries the authentication protocol 0xc223 option (Figure 3-7). This option must include an extra octet for specifying the CHAP algorithm. The standard algorithm number available is 0x05, representing Message Digest 5 (MD5). As with any other PPP option, a peer that doesn't understand a request for CHAP, or MD5 CHAP, can reject it with an LCP configure-nak.

After PPP endpoints agree to use CHAP authentication, the CHAP packets to exchange appear as in Figure 3-11. CHAP packets include four different messages, as distinguished by different codes. Challenge (code 0x01) and response (code 0x02) packets both carry an identifying CHAP name, representing the packet sender and a string necessary for the authentication process. The authenticator

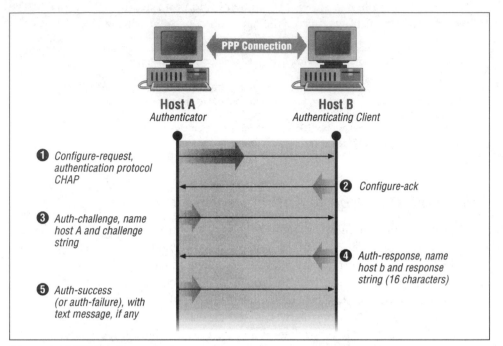

Figure 3-10. CHAP transaction

sends success (code 0x03) and failure (code 0x04) packets at the end of the process. Like PAP, these final acknowledgment packets include fields for explanatory text, if any.

Here's a trace that shows CHAP activity for the configuration in Figure 3-10:

```
Jul  9 22:24:51 hosta pppd[9665]: sent [LCP ConfReq id=0x1 <mru 1500>
<asyncmap 0x0> <auth chap 05> <magic 0x62efd5c6> <pcomp> <accomp>]
. . .
Jul  9 22:24:52 hosta pppd[9665]: rcvd [LCP ConfAck id=0x1 <mru 1500>
<asyncmap 0x0> <auth chap 05> <magic 0x62efd5c6> <pcomp> <accomp>]
. . .
Jul  9 22:24:52 hosta pppd[9665]: sent [CHAP Challenge id=0x1
<163b18ece5e51c511e94eeb8ecbcb86d85e29cf1f12b3500a384a1b0b13506a03830c661d0b5
5c4d574f9bc97b11185167091d36>, name = "hosta"]
Jul  9 22:24:52 hosta pppd[9665]: rcvd [CHAP Response id=0x1
<690acfe5fbad06ed92d51a8cb07adb0f>, name = "hostb"]
Jul  9 22:24:52 hosta pppd[9665]: sent [CHAP Success id=0x1 "Welcome to
hosta."]
. . .
```

This shows Host A issuing a challenge with the CHAP name, hosta, and a 52-character challenge string. Host A accepts its peer's response by acknowledging with CHAP success and a Welcome to hosta. text message.

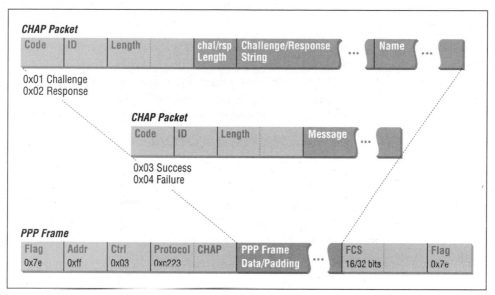

Figure 3-11. CHAP packet

If Authentication Fails

When authentication fails, the connection terminates. The obvious problem case is invalid authentication credentials. PPP LCP terminate-request and terminate-ack messages exchanges occur, and PPP disconnects. However, failures also occur if PPP endpoints can't agree on an authentication protocol to use.

After a disconnect, users must usually reestablish PPP for another authentication attempt. Some PPP implementations can enter the establishing or authenticating states again for several authentication failures. This enables users to retry authentication several times, avoiding the time-consuming disconnect and reconnect cycle.

Network Control Protocol

The network state for a PPP connection follows either the authenticating state or the establishing state, depending on authentication requirements. At this point, LCP has already established all the PPP options. The connection is up and almost ready to begin carrying user data.

The Network Control Protocol (NCP) configures the network layer protocols a PPP connection carries. There exists a separate NCP for every network layer protocol PPP supports. If any network protocol specific settings are necessary, an NCP must now negotiate these. After specific NCPs complete their work, the connection remains in the network state and may begin passing network layer datagrams. NCP can also dynamically establish and remove network layer protocols while the connection is active.

Some examples of specific NCPs are the Internet Protocol Control Protocol for TCP/IP, Appletalk Control Protocol for Appletalk, Internetwork Packet Exchange Control Protocol for Novell IPX/SPX, and others (see Appendix A). Due to its widespread use and its importance for the Internet, we'll cover only IPCP here.

Internet Protocol Control Protocol

The Internet Protocol Control Protocol (see RFC-1332) establishes, configures, and terminates the TCP/IP network protocol layer in a PPP connection. The IPCP packet format inside a PPP frame appears in Figure 3-12. PPP frames with IPCP packets are subject to PPP frame structure modifications negotiated during the PPP connection-establishing stage. IPCP fields, including ID, length, and IPCP data, are all similar to the corresponding LCP fields.

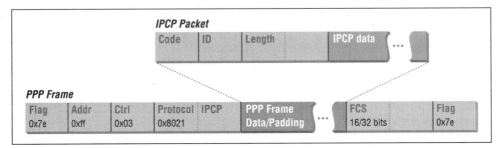

Figure 3-12. IPCP packet

IPCP packets include an 8-bit code to distinguish among different IPCP messages. Table 3-3 lists the legal values for the code field and their meanings. These codes are analogous to the ones used by LCP. But don't be misled by the similarity. Although IPCP appears similar to LCP, it has nothing to do with LCP responsibilities. IPCP is only for establishing TCP/IP network layer-specific options.

Table 3-3. IPCP Codes

Code Value	IPCP Packet Type
0x01	Configure-request
0x02	Configure-ack
0x03	Configure-nak
0x04	Configure-reject
0x05	Terminate-request
0x06	Terminate-ack
0x07	Code-reject

A PPP endpoint can send the first IPCP configure-request packet after a PPP connection reaches the network state. If a peer responds with an LCP protocol-reject, TCP/IP transport isn't available. Otherwise negotiations continue in a manner similar to LCP, and IPCP may or may not succeed in configuring TCP/IP. PPP endpoints can also continue to negotiate other networking protocols, regardless of the status of TCP/IP.

IPCP packets may be categorized into three types, again like LCP. These are configuration, termination, and errors. There is only one error: code-reject. An IPCP code-reject references an earlier IPCP configure-request message, but otherwise operates identically to the LCP code-reject conditions. The following sections describe the remaining IPCP types.

IPCP Configure

A PPP endpoint sends an IPCP configure-request packet with the desired TCP/IP options to its peer and awaits a reply. If the reply is an IPCP configure-reject or configure-nak, this PPP endpoint must send another configure-request message with option modifications. This IPCP iterative procedure is identical to Figure 3-6. Both PPP endpoints must send an IPCP configure-request to its peer, since TCP/IP options are independent for each direction of a PPP connection.

IPCP packets carry their own distinct set of TCP/IP options in the IPCP packet data field (Figure 3-13). The IPCP configure packets all carry these options. Options encoding uses the same format as LCP packets. IPCP negotiates all TCP/IP options simultaneously. Currently, the only standard TCP/IP options are for setting IP addresses and IP compression.

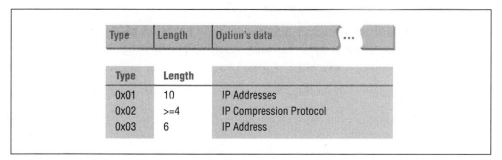

Figure 3-13. IPCP configuration options format

When a IPCP configure-request sender includes the IP Compression Protocol option, the sender is requesting to receive TCP/IP packets in compressed form. However, the IP Address option is the desired local address of the configure-request sender. We discuss IP addresses in Chapter 4, *TCP/IP*. For now, you can just consider IP addresses as a 32-bit number for a PPP connection endpoint, analogous to a telephone number. There are actually two options that set IP addresses for both endpoints in a PPP connection. IP Address is preferred; the IP Addresses is obsolete. Here are the option descriptions:

IP Address, default none

> This option carries the desired local IP address for the IPCP configure-request sender. The desired address is a 32-bit number in the option's data field, giving this option a total length of 6. If this address is zero, the sender is requesting its peer establish the local IP address. The peer can suggest the address in a configure-nak reply.

IP Addresses, default none

> This is an IPCP option where the configure-request sender specifies both its desired local and remote IP address for a PPP connection. The option's data area carries a 32-bit local and a 32-bit remote address. Any address set to zero indicates the peer should suggest an address in a IPCP configure-nak. This option is obsolete due to historical difficulties that can prevent successful IP address agreement between PPP endpoints. It should be used only for backward compatibility with PPP implementations that don't understand the newer IP address option (see RFC-1332 and RFC-1172).

IP Compression Protocol, default none

> The sender of this option indicates to a peer that it wants to receive IP datagrams compressed in a specified manner. The requested compression protocol is the first 16-bit number inside the option's data area. Additional octets may specify parameters specific to this compression protocol. This option's length is 4 octets or more. Only the Van Jacobson Compressed TCP/IP compression protocol (number 0x002d) is currently valid. VJ compression requires two parameters: max slot ID and comp slot id.

The best method to understand IPCP is to examine its actual behavior. Consider a Host A that begins a PPP connection with Host B. The IP addresses for the PPP endpoints are 172.16.0.69 and 172.16.0.193, respectively. We arrange A to learn its address from B. The initial IPCP packet A sends is as follows:

```
Aug 18 11:04:50 hosta pppd[1483]: sent [IPCP ConfReq id=0x1 <addr 0.0.0.0>
<compress VJ 0f 01>]
```

This IPCP configure-request includes the IP address option with a zero argument. Also included is the request that A wishes to receive VJ compressed TCP/IP packets. The VJ parameters for compression are 15 for max-slot-id and 1 for comp-slot-id. The response from Host B is:

```
Aug 18 11:04:50 hosta pppd[1483]: rcvd [IPCP ConfNak id=0x1 <addr
172.16.0.69>]
```

Host B recognizes that all the IPCP options. However, the requested IP address of 0.0.0.0 prompts B to respond with an IPCP configure-nak containing an alternative address. This is how B establishes the IP address for A. A can now send a new IPCP configure-request and receive an acknowledgment for all requested TCP/IP options:

```
Aug 18 11:04:50 hosta pppd[1483]: sent [IPCP ConfReq id=0x2 <addr
172.16.0.69> <compress VJ 0f 01>]
Aug 18 11:04:50 hosta pppd[1483]: rcvd [IPCP ConfAck id=0x2 <addr
172.16.0.69> <compress VJ 0f 01>]
```

While Host A was negotiating with Host B, the converse was also in progress:

```
Aug 18 11:04:50 hosta pppd[1483]: rcvd [IPCP ConfReq id=0x41 <compress VJ 0f
01> <addr 172.16.0.193>]
Aug 18 11:04:50 hosta pppd[1483]: sent [IPCP ConfAck id=0x41 <compress VJ 0f
01> <addr 172.16.0.193>]
```

This shows Host A receiving an IPCP configure-request. Host B is requesting to use address 172.16.0.193 and is requesting that TCP/IP packets A sends to B to be VJ-compressed. All this is acceptable to A, which sends an IPCP configure-ack. Notice in this transaction, A is now aware of the IP address for the far end of its PPP connection.

IPCP Termination

IPCP, like LCP, includes termination-request and termination-ack packets. Unlike LCP, these packets don't terminate the PPP connection. Instead, IPCP terminate-request notifies the peer that TCP/IP transport shall cease. Communications for other network layer protocols, if any, continue unaffected. At a later time, IPCP may again reestablish and renegotiate parameters for TCP/IP transport again.

Although IPCP terminate-requests aren't necessary when really disconnecting PPP, PPP endpoints may send them anyway. Some PPP software shuts down each layer in the protocol stack when shutting down the physical serial connection. In this case, terminate-requests first occur for each active network layer protocol. LCP terminate-requests then follow:

```
Aug 18 16:54:20 hosta pppd[1557]: rcvd [IPCP TermReq id=0x53]
Aug 18 16:54:20 hosta pppd[1557]: IPCP terminated at peer's request
Aug 18 16:54:20 hosta pppd[1557]: ipcp: down
. . .
Aug 18 16:54:20 hosta pppd[1557]: sent [IPCP TermAck id=0x53]
. . .
Aug 18 16:54:20 hosta pppd[1557]: rcvd [LCP TermReq id=0x54]
Aug 18 16:54:20 hosta pppd[1557]: LCP terminated at peer's request
. . .
Aug 18 16:54:20 hosta pppd[1557]: sent [LCP TermAck id=0x54]
. . .
Aug 18 16:54:20 hosta pppd[1557]: Hangup (SIGHUP)
```

Applications, such as Telnet, FTP, and web browsers, may or may not receive notification of these termination events.

Compressed Datagram

PPP supports the Compress Datagram protocol as an option. This protocol is a
general feature that can offer data compression for any network layer datagram
PPP supports. The compressed datagram feature operates by compressing entire
PPP frames that contain a network layer datagram. Another normal PPP frame,
with protocol field 0x00fd, encapsulates the compressed one. This is the frame the
PPP endpoint sends to its peer. This PPP frame compression method operates
independently from address/control field compression, protocol field compression, and others.

Before PPP endpoints can exchange compressed PPP frames, they must first agree
to a compression algorithm and establish any relevant compression parameters.
The Compression Control Protocol (CCP) manages this in the network state of a
PPP connection. CCP operates much like the LCP and includes similar configure-
request messages, in addition to other control messages. PPP frames carrying CCP
use the protocol field 0x80fd. Implementations that don't recognize CCP at all
respond with an LCP protocol-reject. Sample CCP negotiations appear as follows:

```
Jul 23 01:00:11 hosta pppd[203]: rcvd [CCP ConfReq id=0x1 <deflate 15> <bsd
v1 15>]
Jul 23 01:00:11 hosta pppd[203]: sent [CCP ConfReq id=0x1 <deflate 15>]
. . .
Jul 23 01:00:12 hosta pppd[203]: rcvd [CCP ConfReq id=0x3 <bsd v1 15>]
Jul 23 01:00:12 hosta pppd[203]: sent [CCP ConfAck id=0x3 <bsd v1 15>]
. . .
Jul 23 01:00:12 hosta pppd[203]: BSD-Compress (15) compression enabled
. . .
```

Here we see Host A receiving a request to compress outgoing PPP frames with
either deflate 15 or bsd v1 15. Although Host A recognizes CCP, it does not
recognize the deflate 15 compression algorithm. As negotiations proceed,
Host A recognizes bsd v1 15, and this becomes the active data compression
algorithm.

The PPP compressed datagram feature is active only after successful CCP negotiations; no PPP frame compression occurs otherwise. Thus, CCP errors don't affect
the integrity of a PPP connection. CCP disagreements are frequent when two PPP
endpoints each have different PPP implementations; in this case, each endpoint
often fails to recognize the compression algorithms its peer understands. This is
usually not a great loss, since modems also perform data compression.

Chapter 16 presents additional information about PPP frame compression and its relationship to PPP frame encryption. In the meantime, the various PPP implementations you encounter later recognize Deflate, BSD, MPPC, and Stac compression algorithms.

What PPP Doesn't Provide

Much of this chapter discusses how PPP works for the capabilities PPP provides. However, it's also helpful for you to understand the functions PPP doesn't provide. Some of these are:

Flow control
> Any PPP frames sent that overflow a receiver's buffer are lost. It's the responsibility of the network layer protocols to detect and recover from this situation. A retransmission is necessary to recover the lost PPP frame. Serial interfaces and serial connections must provide flow-control functions essential for eliminating retransmissions as a result of missing flow control.

Error correction
> PPP includes only a Frame Check Sequence to validate the PPP frame's integrity. A receiver simply discards frames with errors. It's the responsibility of the network layer protocols to detect and recover from this situation.

Resequencing
> PPP assumes all frames sent and received retain their original, intended order. This assumption is true for many physical serial connections.

4

In this chapter:
* *The Internet Protocol*
* *Van Jacobson Compression*
* *IP Addresses*
* *Media Access Control Addresses*
* *Routing*

TCP/IP

An active PPP connection doesn't do anything useful by itself. Its surrounding network infrastructure must recognize the presence of the connection and is responsible for routing network layer datagrams through it. Thus, you as the administrator must understand more than just PPP. You must also understand the relationship between PPP and the infrastructure around it that handles network layer datagrams.

There are many network layer protocols a PPP connection can carry, the most common being the protocols of the TCP/IP suite. This is the language of the Internet and many private networks. An *IP datagram* is the network layer datagram that a TCP/IP network ultimately delivers to a user's computer and application program. It's the unit of information that completely traverses through the network. In contrast, PPP frames carry IP packets only between two intermediate nodes inside the network.

The relationships between TCP/IP and PPP include:

* PPP features compression capabilities specifically designed for IP datagrams

* PPP connections require a network address assignment at both ends; for connections inside TCP/IP networks, this is the IP address assignment

* TCP/IP network routing must reference the IP address of a PPP connection, in some manner

This chapter introduces TCP/IP concepts and describes their relationship to a PPP connection. I also describe the relationship between TCP/IP and shared medium local area networks, since communications equipment with PPP network interfaces frequently have a LAN network interface too.

The Internet Protocol

When a computer sends a file, a web page, or keystrokes, it breaks down this data into small units that fit into IP datagrams (Figure 4-1). The computer then sends these datagrams through a network infrastructure to the recipient. The final recipient computer is the one responsible for reassembling the datagrams and recovering the data in its original form. A PPP connection is part of this network infrastructure. For dial-up users, PPP carries IP datagrams between them and an Internet dial-in PPP server. The dial-in server extracts IP datagrams from PPP frames and forwards them along towards their destination. Numerous technologies, including other PPP connections, can carry IP datagrams around the Internet.

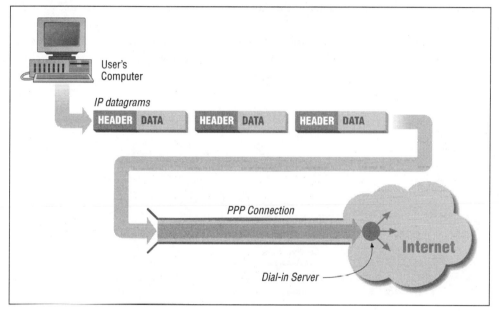

Figure 4-1. Sending IP datagrams to the Internet

An IP datagram is a self-contained unit with a *header* and *payload data*. The network infrastructure routes datagrams, individually, based on the information in the header. Since the network doesn't maintain any relationships among IP datagrams, each may traverse different physical routes. A series of datagrams may arrive at its final destination out of sequence, and some may even be lost in transit. It's the datagram originator and recipient that are responsible for recovering from these conditions. Notice that PPP, the dial-in server, and the Internet itself, doesn't guarantee reliable IP datagram delivery. However, the Internet appears reliable to users because TCP/IP software stacks hide these communication abnormalities from users, as well as their application programs.

Since datagrams are self-contained, TCP/IP allows traffic *multiplexing*. A PPP user can interact with numerous Internet sites simultaneously. A computer's TCP/IP stack mixes datagrams with different destinations on to a single PPP connection. IP datagrams also contain information regarding their originating source. Conversely, computers can also receive incoming datagrams arriving from many Internet sites and demultiplex the traffic based on each datagram's originating source information.

IP Datagram Format

The format and content of an IP datagram appears in Figure 4-2. The upper portion of the figure shows the header fields that corresponds to the Internet Protocol (IP) layer in TCP/IP. This is the layer the network infrastructure uses for IP datagram routing and delivery. The IP headers also have *options* extensions. Options, if present, include information that further determines how the network handles this datagram. All the other fields are really just payload data, from the point of view of the IP datagram. In Figure 4-2, an IP datagram is shown that's carrying a TCP segment.

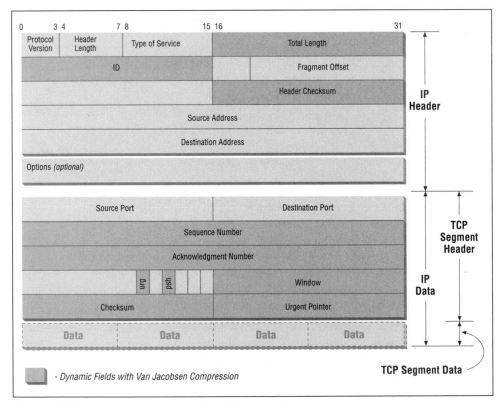

Figure 4-2. IP datagram format, with a TCP segment

TCP/IP is itself a layered protocol. Thus, the IP datagram can encapsulate a TCP segment, UDP packet, and other types of TCP/IP packets inside its data area. These packets are for interpretation by two communicating computers and represent the higher layers in the TCP/IP family.

Overall IP datagrams are of variable length, up to about 64K octets. The total length field indicates its actual length. In practice, datagrams are limited to sizes that fit within the *maximum transmission unit* (MTU) as communications media dictate. For PPP connections, the MTU is 1500 by default. Too-large datagrams must be broken into multiple "fragments" for transmission.

The *destination address* is for datagram routing. This is a 32-bit number that identifies the datagram's intended recipient. The network uses this address (assuming no options) to route the datagram. If a problem occurs, the network may return errors to the originating *source address*. This source address is also crucial as a return address for normal communications. In other words, a replying computer produces datagrams destined for the originating sender's address.

It's not essential when working with PPP for you to understand all the other fields in IP datagrams. Further information about TCP/IP headers are available in references such as Craig Hunt's *TCP/IP Network Administration*, also published by O'Reilly & Associates.

TCP/IP Family of Protocols

The lowest layer protocol belonging to the TCP/IP family is IP. The TCP/IP family also features many higher layer protocols, which IP datagrams must carry. We already show the TCP segment as an example of what may appear inside a datagram. In general, the value of the protocol field in an IP datagram header identifies a TCP/IP protocol the datagram is carrying.

The most common TCP/IP family protocol members are:

- User Datagram Protocol (UDP): IP protocol number 1
- Transmission Control Protocol (TCP): IP protocol number 6
- Internet Control Message Protocol (ICMP): IP protocol number 17

There are also General Routing Encapsulation (GRE), GGP, EGP, PUP, and other protocols, but they are far less common than these three.

UDP

UDP provides connectionless service. It's a service that behaves much like the delivery of a single IP datagram. There is no acknowledgment in UDP that can verify delivery of a message. Thus, UDP is also known as an unreliable protocol.

UDP is well-suited to application programs that don't need to, or want to, process a continuous data stream. A query and response service, such as the Domain Name System (DNS), fits this characteristic. To use DNS, an application forms a query that fits into one UDP packet. The application sends the query and awaits a response. If the network loses the query or response, then the application can just send another query.

TCP

In contrast, TCP provides connection-oriented service for applications wishing to send a stream of data reliably to the recipient. A file transfer operation with FTP, or a browser retrieving web pages, are examples of applications that use TCP. TCP implements its service over a connectionless-oriented IP datagram networking infrastructure. TCP segment headers contain sequence numbers, acknowledgment numbers, window, and other information necessary to assist computers in assembling data streams, detecting losses, and sorting out of sequence data. TCP software, not the network, must retain outgoing data for possible retransmission and request retransmissions from its peer as needed. This overhead activity is invisible to users and their application programs.

ICMP

ICMP carries messages that aid diagnostics and indicate network errors. It also supports network information requests such as the time of day and IP address masks. A common utility that produces ICMP messages is *ping*. *ping* sends an echo request message that should elicit an echo response from a desired address. Another source of ICMP messages is the equipment in the network itself. It can respond to users with errors if it can't deliver IP datagrams to the requested destination. The usual messages users may see as a result of ICMP are "network unreachable" and "host unreachable."

Port Numbers

A TCP segment fits within an IP datagram and includes source port and destination port fields (Figure 4-2). UDP packet headers in an IP datagram also contain these field names. Both port numbers are 16 bits, frequently expressed in decimal notation from 0 to 65535. Ports identify the application process on a computer that is sending or receiving data. Whereas IP address fields help distinguish datagrams for an individual computer, port numbers help to further distinguish datagrams for different applications running on that computer. In other words, a computer can have multiple simultaneous conversations with a single Internet site. The port number identifies the datagrams belonging to each conversation.

There exists a standard list of port numbers, known as Well Known Ports and Registered Ports. The Internet Assigned Numbers Authority (IANA) maintains these port assignments. A partial listing of these appears frequently in a *services* file. On Unix, this file is in the */etc* or */etc/inet* directory. On Windows NT/98, this file is in the operating system's root directory, usually *c:\winnt* and *c:\windows*, respectively. These ports numbers are the contact ports for various network services an Internet site may offer. Note that the same network service name, such as HTTP, may have identical TCP and UDP port number assignments. However, each are distinctly separate services.

When users cause an application to initiate a TCP connection, their computer dynamically assigns itself a unique source port number, usually 1024 and above, for that connection's duration. A web browser contacts the well-known port for HTTP (port 80). The Internet site must reverse port numbers in its reply, since it's now the source, and the user's computer is the destination (Figure 4-3). The combination of the TCP/IP protocol (TCP or UDP), source IP, source port, destination IP, and destination port, clearly identify the datagrams belonging to a single conversation between two Internet endpoints. If a second HTTP connection is simultaneously active in Figure 4-3, the second connection must transfer datagrams with a port number different than 1025.

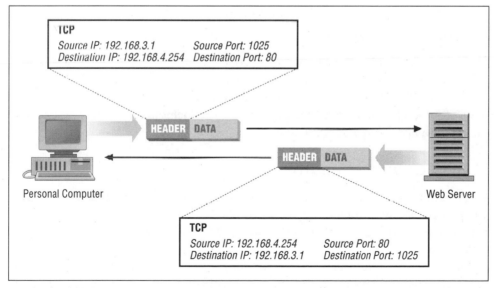

Figure 4-3. TCP ports

Computer users don't need to remember port numbers. Many application programs are already coded to contact any server with their standard port assignment.

Van Jacobson Compression

Van Jacobson compression is especially beneficial for interactive applications that communicate through a low-speed PPP connection. For each keystroke, the application normally sends an IP datagram with more than 40 octets. This poor PPP connection utilization efficiency (40 to 1) can cause unacceptable performance for users waiting for interactive characters to echo back to their display. Most of the header in IP datagrams that carry keystroke data is regularly repeated and redundant.

Van Jacobson compressed TCP/IP (RFC-1144), named after its developer, describes a method to compress header fields in certain IP datagrams. It can reduce a 40-octet datagram overhead into a few octets for transmission. The receiver can then recover the original header on reception. PPP can carry IP datagrams with VJ compression applied; however, once the compressed datagram leaves PPP, the PPP endpoint must recover the IP datagram in its original form.

The PPP frame protocol field identifies whether the frame is carrying VJ compressed IP datagrams. Not all IP datagrams that are candidates for VJ compression actually become compressed. Therefore, this results in several values for the PPP protocol field:

- 0x002d, Van Jacobson compressed TCP/IP
- 0x002f, Van Jacobson uncompressed TCP/IP

VJ compression affects only how PPP encodes IP datagram headers inside a PPP frame. It doesn't affect user data in any way. However, VJ compression is independent of the PPP *Compressed Datagram* feature. Compressed Datagram can compress all of a VJ compressed IP datagram, thereby including both header and user data in a compression algorithm.

How VJ Compression Works

A PPP connection may carry VJ compressed IP datagrams only after its two endpoints successfully negotiate to use VJ with IPCP. Once VJ compression is active, it affects only IP datagrams that belong to a TCP connection. These are IP datagrams that carry TCP segments. To understand how VJ compression works, it's important to understand the IP datagram format for TCP connections (Figure 4-2). User data, such as keystrokes, belong in the TCP segment data area at the bottom of the datagram.

For IP datagrams that belong to a TCP connection, VJ compression takes advantage of the fact that little header information changes between consecutive datagrams (shaded fields in Figure 4-2). The fields that do change are frequently limited to increments within 65535. PPP endpoints each maintain identical local copies of the original, uncompressed, IP and TCP segment headers for each active TCP connection. When sending an IP datagram, the sender strips the header and replaces it with a VJ compression header. This new header includes instructions for the receiver to reconstruct the IP datagram based on the receiver's stored copy of the original IP and TCP segment header. This is the basic principle for VJ compression.

VJ compression header

Figure 4-4 shows the VJ compression header, which substitutes for all the header fields appearing in Figure 4-2.

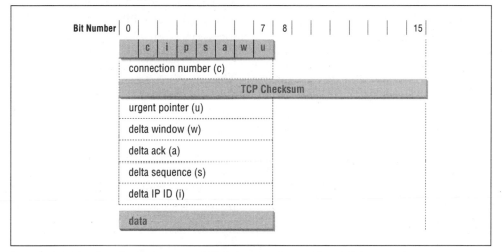

Figure 4-4. Van Jacobson compressed IP datagram format for a TCP connection

The first octet in the VJ compression header is a bit mask that specifies which original, uncompressed header fields are changing. However, the "p" bit is simply a copy of the "push" bit in the normal TCP segment header. Some bit mask combinations in the VJ compression header aren't possible. The impossible ones are reserved for several special case conditions that aren't covered here.

A receiver may maintain uncompressed header copies for many TCP connections. The *connection number* identifies which one. The fields that follow exist only if their bit is "true" in the first octet bit mask. These field values are increments, for those field names with the word "delta" (delta window, delta ack, etc.). Otherwise, the value is a replacement for an uncompressed header field the receiver saved. Increments are encoded as 1 octet (shown), for values from 1 to 255 and 3 octets for values from 256 to 65535. The 3 octet representation always has a leading zero. Multiple increment values may appear in a compressed header according to the order shown. The bit mask determines how many numeric fields exist in the header and what they correspond to. Thus, the compressed header is variable in length.

The data field in the VJ compressed IP datagram is the same as the data field appearing in the original, uncompressed IP datagram. Thus, for IP datagrams that carry a single keystroke character, the 40-octet header in uncompressed datagrams may be reduced to as little as 3 to 5 octets.

VJ compressor procedure

Now that we've seen the basic principle of VJ compression, the procedure that the packet compressor (sender) and decompressor (receiver) follows should be easier to understand. Normally, IP datagrams flow unaltered over a PPP connection using PPP frame protocol field 0x0021. If VJ compression is enabled, the packet compressor looks for any IP datagrams for a TCP connection. When it encounters one:

1. The compressor allocates a new connection number, the *slot-id*, for the TCP connection and copies the header information into this slot. Each TCP connection has a unique set of values for the source IP address, destination IP address, source port number, and destination port number.

2. The compressor sends the first IP datagram for a new TCP connection essentially in its original form using PPP frame protocol field, 0x002f. This is VJ uncompressed TCP/IP. However, the compressor replaces the IP datagram header protocol field with the slot-id. This notifies the receiver to save the IP and TCP segment header of this datagram and associate this slot-id number with it.

3. As additional datagrams arrive for this TCP connection, the compressor determines the datagram header changes since the previous datagram. The compressor then replaces the original header with its VJ compressed form. It then sends the datagram with PPP frame protocol field 0x002d. This is now VJ compressed TCP/IP. Normally, the connection number (slot-id) is embedded in the VJ compressed datagram to aid original header recovery by the receiver.

This procedure is simplified. In practice, VJ compression includes a set of rules that determine when to send datagrams as VJ uncompressed versus compressed. One key consideration is potential for inconsistencies and data corruption that can result when PPP frames are lost. A compressor can send a VJ uncompressed packet to reset the receiver's notion of the saved header, even for an already active TCP connection.

VJ compression parameters

PPP IPCP establishes VJ compression. The following are the VJ compression parameters embedded in IPCP packets carrying the VJ compression option:

Max-Slot-ID

When we request this option, we indicate to a VJ compressing peer that we can save max-slot-id plus one TCP connection headers for decompression purposes. Each saved header has a connection number identifier ranging from zero to max-slot-id. The standard value, 0x0f, indicates we can maintain compression state for 16 simultaneous TCP connections. This limits the number of TCP connections that our peer may send IP datagrams in VJ compressed form. Our peer determines which TCP connections get compressed. IP datagrams for additional TCP connections must remain uncompressed.

Comp-Slot-ID

This is an 8-bit option, but valid values are either zero (false) or one (true). If we request this option as false, all VJ compressed headers we receive must include the 8-bit connection number field. If the option is true, the connection number field may be omitted from consecutive VJ compressed IP datagrams for the same TCP connection. We, the receiver, must remember the last TCP connection number referenced for compressed datagrams that arrive without this field.

What VJ Doesn't Compress

The Van Jacobson compression method is limited to IP datagrams belonging to a TCP connection. In other words, it applies to only IP datagrams that carry TCP segments.

VJ compression never affects IP datagrams containing UDP packets, ICMP, and other protocols belonging in the TCP/IP family. These IP datagrams appear inside PPP frames with the protocol field value 0x0021. This value is for PPP frames that carry plain IP datagrams. For these non-TCP connection IP datagrams, they travel through PPP connections as if PPP never negotiated to use VJ compression.

IP Addresses

All Internet hosts communicating with TCP/IP must have an *IP address* that uniquely identifies them on the network. Since the Internet routes IP datagrams from one network interface to the next, most equipment internal to the Internet also require one or more IP addresses. This requirement extends to the endpoints of PPP connections. If a computer has multiple network interfaces, an IP address is usually required for each.

An IP address is a 32-bit number frequently written in *dotted decimal notation*. This notation consists of four period-separated decimal numbers, representing each set of 8 bits in the 32-bit address, for example, 172.1.0.66. The bits making up an IP address aren't arbitrary. In fact, there is a sort of structure and hierarchy built into the address in order for the Internet to efficiently route IP datagrams.

The Internet is broken into a collection of various size networks (Figure 4-5). IP addresses are divided into three network classes, A, B, and C. Each class devotes 8, 16, and 24 bits, respectively, in the address for the network ID and the remaining bits for the host ID. This separation of network/host bits forms a two-level hierarchy.

By convention, a network number is written using the same notation as a host address, but with the host ID bits set to zero. For example, the last network number suitable for use on the Internet is 223.255.254.0, considering that 223.255.255.0 is reserved. Notice the first few bits in an IP address determine the network class, which in turn determines the network number. Generally, each Internet network with a number must be physically contiguous.* In other words, one network doesn't split up another. Each network has a single edge and appears as a monolithic entity from the outside. As IP datagrams arrive into the network number of its destination, the host ID bits determine more specific routing to reach a specific device.

The InterNIC is responsible for the coordination and allocation of IP network numbers on the Internet. Large numbers of networks may be assigned to various ISPs, who are then responsible for reassigning them for their customers to use.

Subnets

Each of the class A, B, and C network numbers include 2^{24}, 2^{16}, and 2^8 available IP addresses, respectively, including reserved addresses. If you're responsible for a network number, you may assign these addresses to PPP endpoints, computers, routers, and other TCP/IP-compatible equipment. Unfortunately, it's impractical in many network designs to randomly distribute a large block of IP addresses (2^{24} for class A) into numerous physical local area networks. An additional third-level hierarchical interpretation of IP addresses becomes necessary.

Thus, TCP/IP includes provisions for *subnetting*, which allows breaking up one network number into multiple subnets. Each subnet is a smaller, contiguous portion of the network number's IP address space. Subnetting requires designating some host ID bits for subnet identification. The minimum subnet field width is

---

* Since the introduction of Classless Interdomain Routing (CIDR), this rule is relaxed. Also, CIDR can consider contiguous blocks of network numbers as a single "supernet," for routing purposes.

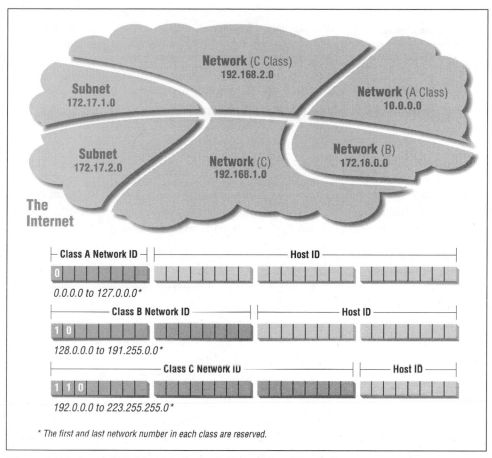

Figure 4-5. Internet IP addresses, network ID, and host ID numbers

2 bits. Also, at least 2 bits must also remain for the host ID. Figure 4-6 illustrates subnetting for the class A network number 10.0.0.0. In this example, we reallocate 10 host ID bits for the subnet field. Class B and class C network numbers may also be subnetted in a similar manner. Only the most significant host ID bits should be reallocated for the subnet field. Many TCP/IP implementations assume this is the case.

The subnet mask describes which IP address bits represent the network and subnet fields. Each "one" bit in the mask corresponds to a bit in the IP address that is a sub/network bit. This notation appears in two forms:

```
10.1.1.64, 255.255.255.192
10.1.1.64/26
```

Both IP addresses represent subnet numbers since all host ID bits are zero. In the second form, 26 is the total number of one bits in the subnet mask. Notice the

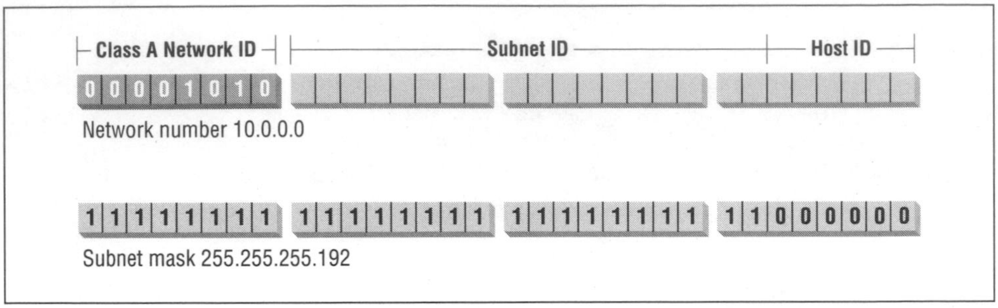

Figure 4-6. Subnetting the class A network 10.0.0.0

subnet mask prevents misinterpreting this address as an actual IP address of a device. For this subnet, valid IP addresses for devices range from 10.1.1.65 to 10.1.1.126. All ones and all zeros in the host ID field are reserved.

Subnetting is a concept local to a network number. The Internet still considers a network number as one entity, even if it's internally subnetted. It's your responsibility to establish the size of the subnet field for network numbers you manage. In many TCP/IP network designs, subnet masks must be unique for each network number. Only recent TCP/IP implementations support variable length subnet masks (VLSM), where subnet masks may vary inside a network number. With VLSM, IP addresses may not overlap among subnets.

Subnets and Local Area Networks

You frequently choose subnet sizes to correspond with the size of a physical local area network. For example, subnets with 64 IP addresses are suitable for Ethernet. A dial-in PPP server with a LAN connection can communicate directly with any IP addresses that are members of the same subnet. The subnet mask setting for the server's LAN network interface defines what IP addresses share this LAN:

```
user$ /sbin/ifconfig eth0
eth0      Link encap:Ethernet  HWaddr 00:60:B0:A1:3D:13
          inet addr:172.16.0.68  Bcast:172.16.0.127  Mask:255.255.255.192
          UP BROADCAST RUNNING MULTICAST  MTU:1500  Metric:1
   . . .
```

This server has an `eth0` network interface with IP address 172.16.0.68. The `Mask` indicates that IP addresses from 172.16.0.64 to 172.16.0.127 belong to this LAN. If this dial-in PPP server has IP datagrams to send to foreign subnet destinations, or to foreign network numbers, this server must forward these datagram to a router. In typical network designs, the router also resides on this LAN and has its own IP address.

Subnets and PPP Connections

A PPP connection is point to point, with an IP address at each end. Generally, you can use PPP to connect different Internet network numbers. Therefore, there is no special relationship between the two IP addresses at each end of a PPP connection.

On a computer with a PPP connection, its PPP network interface may have a configuration that resembles the following:

```
user$ /sbin/ifconfig ppp0
ppp0      Link encap:Point-to-Point Protocol
          inet addr:192.168.1.35  P-t-P:192.169.1.1  Mask:255.255.255.0
          UP POINTOPOINT RUNNING NOARP MULTICAST  MTU:1500  Metric:1
  . . .
```

This PPP connection has an IP address 192.168.1.35 at its local end and an IP address of 192.169.1.1 at its remote end. Each address belongs to a different class C network number.

Many TCP/IP implementations include a subnet mask for PPP. And each implementation interprets this mask in different ways. Since a PPP interface may have two unrelated IP addresses, the subnet mask is irrelevant and really shouldn't exist. If a PPP subnet mask does exist, the correct behavior is to ignore it. Many Unix platforms tend to behave this way. Thus, you can leave this subnet mask setting at its default. On Unix, this default is either the class A, B, or C mask of inet addr (as shown for ppp0 above), or the prevailing subnet mask for the network number of inet addr. Non-Unix platforms may require masks of 0.0.0.0 or 255.255.255.255.

Unfortunately, some network devices annoyingly consider a PPP network interface much like a shared-medium LAN network interface. These devices require you to assign whole IP subnets to a PPP connection, even though at most, two IP addresses can ever be used. In this case, try to assign the smallest possible subnet for PPP. The smallest IP subnet has four IP addresses with two reserved. The PPP subnet mask would be 255.255.255.252.

If both PPP connections and LANs must share IP subnets from a single network number, all the subnets may have a fixed size that matches LAN size requirements. A large IP subnet for each PPP connection significantly wastes IP address space. Most IP addresses in a subnet become unusable, resulting in quick IP address depletion. Some workarounds are:

- Try to split one large IP subnet into smaller ones using variable length subnet mask (VLSM) techniques. (However, your network may not support VLSM.)

- Try to obtain small IP subnets from a different network number, for use with PPP connections.

The second option may not be suitable for connecting two LANs that belong to one network number. Remember the Internet wants to consider each network number as one entity, with a single network boundary. This becomes untrue, from the perspective of a PPP connection, if each of its endpoints routes to two different IP subnets that belong to one foreign network number.

As you can see, there are numerous network design complications that can result when network devices require IP subnets for PPP connections. My best advice is to avoid this issue. If you need further information, however, Chapter 8, *Network Architectures Incorporating PPP*, discusses IP subnets and PPP in greater detail.

Special-Purpose Addresses

TCP/IP reserves special-purpose IP addresses for broadcasts and computers that don't know their own network identity. A typical case is a booting computer that needs to acquire its IP address from another server. In order to find a server willing to reply, it can send a broadcast to a special destination IP address. Since the computer doesn't have its own IP address yet, it must also use a special source IP address in the IP datagrams it sends.

When allocating IP subnets to LANs and IP addresses to computers, you must be aware of reserved IP addresses and the constraints they impose. Reserved IP addresses have all zeros or all ones for the network ID, subnet ID, or host ID fields. When a field contains all ones, it's generally interpreted to mean "all", as in "all hosts" or "all subnets." This is common for broadcasting situations. The interpretation for all zeros is "this" network, "this" subnet, or "this" host.

Consider a host with an IP address of 172.16.0.67 that is a member of the IP subnet 172.16.0.64/26. This host may broadcast IP datagrams by including a reserved IP address in the datagram's destination address field. Some examples of these broadcast IP addresses are:

255.255.255.255
> Broadcast address to all hosts on this local IP subnet only. Routers must not forward this broadcast. This is a special case interpretation of "all", since, fortunately, it doesn't send a broadcast to every Internet host.

172.16.255.255
> Directed broadcast address to all hosts on all subnets of the indicated class B network number. Here, the subnet ID and host ID fields are all ones.

172.16.0.127
> Directed broadcast address to all hosts on the indicated network and subnet number. Here, only the host ID field is all ones.

In practice, there are still many TCP/IP implementations that use all-zero subnet ID and host ID fields in IP addresses for broadcasting IP datagrams.

If the host at 172.16.0.67 doesn't yet know its IP subnet or its entire IP address, this host may still send IP datagrams with reserved addresses inside the datagram's source IP address field. Some examples of reserved source addresses are:

0.0.0.0
> An unknown host on this network

0.0.0.67
> A host with this host ID on this network

172.16.0.0
> An unknown host on the indicated network

Another special address is 127.0.0.1, which is the *loopback* address. All IP datagrams sent to this address must loop back within a computer and never appear on the Internet. The entire class A network number 127.0.0.0 is reserved for this function.

An important implication regarding these conventions is that computers may not have IP addresses where the host ID field is all ones or all zeros. This imposes a 2-bit minimum length host ID field when subnetting network numbers. Similar rules apply to the IP address subnet field. The minimum subnet field size is also 2 bits and the all-zeros and all-ones IP subnets are technically disallowed. This rule avoids IP address ambiguities with 172.16.255.255, for example. If an all ones subnet actually exists, this address is ambiguous and could be either a network or subnet directed broadcast.

The introduction of *classless interdomain routing* (CIDR) relaxes restrictions pertaining to the use of the all zero and all ones subnet. Many network devices now allow use of these subnet numbers. However, you should use them with caution.

Media Access Control Addresses

Ethernet, token ring, FDDI, and other related technologies, are shared-media LANs. As "shared media" implies, many devices are physically connected to one medium, and they all contend for a common communication resource. LANs don't understand or interpret IP datagrams. This independence enables them to carry other network layer protocols without contention. Each LAN technology has its own methods of physical addressing, generally unrelated to IP addresses. These are *media access control* (MAC) addresses.

Dial-in PPP servers receiving IP datagrams from PPP users must forward them to routers or other network equipment. These routers typically reside on a LAN. Sending IP datagrams through a LAN requires a PPP server to encapsulate the datagram into the appropriate link layer protocol frame, such as an Ethernet frame (Figure 4-7). This procedure is analogous to encapsulating IP datagrams into PPP frames for transmission over serial connections. Because there are many devices that share an Ethernet LAN, the Ethernet frame must include an Ethernet MAC address, which indicates the LAN device that should receive this frame.

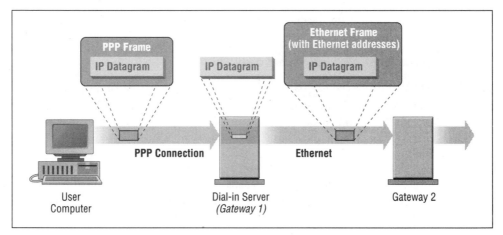

Figure 4-7. PPP and Ethernet link layer IP datagram forwarding

Thus, MAC addressing becomes important for you to understand.

Ethernet Addresses

On an Ethernet, each device has a 48-bit MAC address. This address is expressed in hexadecimal form, where every 8 bits are colon-delimited. For example, 8:0:20:9:3d:a9. The first three numbers represent the vendor responsible for manufacturing this Ethernet device. An 8:0:20, for example, represents Sun Microsystems. The remaining numbers are unique identifiers, analogous to serial numbers. The vendor is responsible for permanently establishing a MAC address for every Ethernet device they produce. The combination of the vendor code and the unique serial number ID insures that no Ethernet device in existence has the same MAC address.

On Unix platforms, the `ifconfig` utility reports MAC addresses for all the LAN network interfaces a computer has:

```
root# ifconfig le0
le0: flags=863<UP,BROADCAST,NOTRAILERS,RUNNING,MULTICAST> mtu 1500
```

```
          inet 172.16.0.66 netmask ffffffc0 broadcast 172.16.0.127
          ether 8:0:20:9:3d:a9
root#
```

MAC addresses don't apply to PPP connections, since there is no need for them. However, some platforms show these addresses for PPP anyway. Their MAC address is frequently zero.

Address Resolution Protocol

When a dial-in PPP server has data to send to another Ethernet device, it must somehow construct an Ethernet frame with a MAC address of the destination Ethernet device. If the Ethernet frame is carrying an IP datagram, there exists a dependency between the IP address in this datagram and the MAC address in the Ethernet frame. After all, we don't want to send the IP datagram to the wrong Ethernet device.

A question that arises is how to resolve the dependency between IP addresses and Ethernet MAC addresses. This is the purpose of the Address Resolution Protocol (ARP). ARP maps IP addresses into Ethernet addresses. It's a broadcast protocol and not part of the TCP/IP family. When the PPP server wishes to send data to another device on the same LAN, it first broadcasts an ARP request using the broadcast Ethernet address `ff:ff:ff:ff:ff:ff`. The request includes an IP address this server is seeking information for. It's the responsibility of the device with the matching IP address to respond, thus revealing its Ethernet address.

The ARP table

Dial-in servers and most other LAN devices cache the replies they receive from their ARP queries. Some even cache ARP replies solicited by other devices sharing the same LAN. Caching IP and Ethernet address mappings prevents needless ARP broadcasts as two devices communicate. On many operating systems, the ARP commnd shows the contents of an ARP cache:

```
user$ arp -a
Net to Media Table
Device   IP Address              Mask            Flags   Phys Addr
------   -------------------     --------------- -----   ---------------
le0      172.16.0.65             255.255.255.255         08:00:20:09:3a:e2
le0      172.16.0.67             255.255.255.255         00:80:5f:02:2d:b1
le0      172.16.0.66             255.255.255.255 SP      08:00:20:09:3d:a9
le0      224.0.0.0               240.0.0.0       SM      01:00:5e:00:00:00
user$
```

Each IP to Ethernet address mapping remains in the cache until a timer expires them. Unused entries that expire require another ARP query, as needed, at a later time.

Forwarding IP datagrams through routers

When a dial-in PPP server has IP datagrams addressed to destinations on its own LAN, the datagram's destination IP address determines the MAC address to include in the Ethernet frame that carries the datagram.

But what happens if a server has IP datagrams addressed to far-away places? In this case, a TCP/IP routing table determines the IP address of a router that can accept this IP datagram. This server now performs an ARP request for the router's IP address and obtains the router's Ethernet MAC address. The Ethernet frame that carries this datagram has an Ethernet MAC address for the router. Notice that there is no relationship now between the destination IP address in the IP datagram and the MAC address in the Ethernet frame. In fact, there is no reference at all to the router's IP address in the Ethernet frame and the IP datagram it carries.

Mapping multiple IP addresses to a single MAC address

It's also possible for ARP to map multiple IP addresses to the same Ethernet address. The result is a single Ethernet device that receives IP datagrams intended for several different IP addresses. Proxy ARP takes advantage of this arrangement (described later in Chapter 8). Proxy ARP is useful for dial-in PPP servers that accept IP datagrams on behalf of many PPP users, each using a different IP address.

Routing

Dial-in PPP servers that receive IP datagrams must first determine whether these datagrams are for itself. If the datagram has a destination IP address representing someone else, the PPP server must *route* it.

All TCP/IP-capable devices consult a routing table when forwarding IP datagrams. The routing table is equivalent to a list of all possible destination IP addresses. Every destination includes a neighboring router that can handle IP datagrams for it. TCP/IP routing tables don't show the structure of the entire Internet. Instead, they show only neighboring routers, PPP connections, and LANs.

Routing on the Internet operates one way. In other words, Internet routers determine where to send IP datagrams based solely on the datagram's destination IP address.* Even though the network may successfully route IP datagrams from point A to point B, the converse may not be true. For two-way communications, independent routes between two IP addresses must exist for each direction. These routes don't necessarily follow the same physical paths through the network.

---

* IP datagrams may include *loose source route* or *strict source route* options that specify how they should be routed.

Classless Interdomain Routing Table

A classless interdomain routing (CIDR) table maps one or more destination IP addresses to an IP address of a neighboring router. Each table entry references destinations as an individual IP address, an IP subnet, network number, supernet, or "default." Since network number routes encompass large numbers of individual IP addresses, this keeps routing tables small and efficient.

A key characteristic of a CIDR routing table is the inclusion of a netmask for every route entry. This netmask determines the number of individual IP addresses each route represents. Routing netmasks are also essential for network designs that take advantage of VLSM. With VLSM, IP subnets vary in size. Thus, routes for an IP subnet must include a netmask that specifies the subnet size.

A CIDR routing table for a dial-in PPP server with an active Ethernet and PPP network interface may resemble the following:

```
user$ /sbin/route -n
Kernel IP routing table
Destination     Gateway         Genmask         Flags Metric Ref    Use Iface
204.146.252.97  0.0.0.0         255.255.255.255 UH    0      0        0 ppp0
172.16.0.64     0.0.0.0         255.255.255.192 U     0      0        4 eth0
172.16.0.0      172.16.0.69     255.255.0.0     UG    0      0        1 eth0
127.0.0.0       0.0.0.0         255.0.0.0       U     0      0        2 lo
0.0.0.0         204.146.252.97  0.0.0.0         UG    0      0        0 ppp0
user$
```

The IP address for this server's eth0 network interface is 172.16.0.67. The local IP address for ppp0 is 166.72.92.219. Both interface IP addresses don't appear in this routing table.

To route an IP datagram, the datagram's destination IP address must match one of the rows in the routing table. A match occurs if the Genmask specifies bits in the Destination number that match the corresponding bits in the datagram's destination address. (The Genmask is equivalent to a route's netmask.) Consider an IP datagram with 172.16.0.68 as its destination:

```
IP datagram
destination:     172.16.0.68      10101100 00010000 00000000 01000100

Destination:     172.16.0.64      10101100 00010000 00000000 01000000
Genmask:         255.255.255.192  11111111 11111111 11111111 11000000
```

The bit pattern for 172.16.0.68 matches the first 26 bits of the routing table entry for 172.16.0.64. Therefore, this server routes datagrams for 172.16.0.68 to the Gateway 0.0.0.0. In this case, this is a special gateway number that represents this server's own Ethernet network interface. Therefore, this server delivers the datagram directly onto the Ethernet LAN. Notice this route matches all destination IP addresses in the range 172.16.0.65 to 172.16.0.126; these are all the IP addresses corresponding to this LAN's IP subnet.

It's possible for one route to include the destinations associated with another route. This is the case for entry 172.16.0.0 in the preceding routing table, which overlaps IP addresses with the entry 172.16.0.64. Servers must select routes based on the *longest match* algorithm. Routes with more one bits in their netmask describe a smaller set of IP address destinations than another route with fewer ones. The former is a more specific route. A server must select the more specific route for any given IP address it wishes to send datagrams to. In the preceding table, routing datagram to 172.16.0.68 would match the 172.16.0.64 table entry with a 26-bit netmask. However, there is also a matching 172.16.0.0 entry in the table with a 16-bit netmask. According to the longest match algorithm, the 172.16.0.64 entry applies.

Another entry of interest is 0.0.0.0 with a netmask that results in a match for any destination IP address. This is the least specific route in the table and applies if a destination address matches no other table entry. This is the default route, used as a last resort for any destination IP addresses for which more-specific routes don't exist.

If it becomes necessary for you to adjust the routing table, many operating systems provide the equivalent of a **route** utility. For route additions, this utility must accept a routing destination, a netmask, a gateway, and various other arguments. Adding a route for IP subnet 172.16.1.0/24 requires a command resembling the following:

```
root# route add -net 172.16.1.0 netmask 255.255.255.0 gw 172.16.0.70
```

This new entry affects IP datagrams with destination IP addresses ranging from 172.16.1.0 to 172.16.1.255. This server forwards these datagrams to a router with IP address 172.16.0.70.

Classful Routing Table

A *classful* routing table is one that primarily maintains class A, B, and C network numbers as routing destinations, hence the name. This type of table predates the introduction of CIDR, and many current TCP/IP implementations still use it.

Netmasks for each routing entry don't appear in a classful routing table. Nevertheless, there still exists an implied netmask that determines all the IP addresses that pertain to a route. It's not possible to break up the IP address space of a network number and establish different routes for each piece. A route for 10.0.0.0, for example, affects all IP datagrams with destination IP addresses ranging from 10.0.0.0 to 10.255.255.255. These are all the addresses belonging to a class A network.

Classful routing tables can also maintain routes for specific IP addresses. Under special circumstances, the table can also maintain routes for some IP subnet numbers.

A sample routing table for a Unix server, with PPP and LAN network interfaces, appears as follows:

```
user$ netstat -rn
Routing Table:
   Destination          Gateway              Flags  Ref  Use     Interface
   -------------------- -------------------- -----  ----- ------  ---------
   127.0.0.1            127.0.0.1            UH     0    13   lo0
   204.146.252.97       166.72.92.184        UH     2    0    ipdptp0
   172.16.0.128         172.16.0.126         UG     0    0
   172.16.0.192         172.16.0.126         UG     0    0
   192.168.1.0          172.16.0.126         UG     0    0
   172.16.0.64          172.16.0.66          U      3    308  le0
   224.0.0.0            172.16.0.66          U      3    0    le0
   default              204.146.252.97       UG     0    0
user$
```

This server has a primary IP address of 172.16.0.66 for its LAN network interface. The IP addresses in use on the LAN is an IP subnet with a 26-bit netmask. The PPP connection address is 166.72.92.184 at the local end and 204.146.252.97 at the remote end.

Each routing table entry may be one of the following:

Host-specific destination IP address
> This route includes an H flag and applies only to IP datagrams with this specific IP address as the destination.

Subnet destination
> Let's assume this server has a connection to an IP subnet, which is a member of a network number. Routes to other destinations in this network number must be IP subnet routes.

Network destination
> Class A, B, or C network numbers are destinations in the routing table, as long as this server has no direct connections to them.

Default destination
> This is the wildcard entry if no other routes match a desired IP address.

The previous routing table is for a server with a direct connection to the subnetted class B network number, 172.16.0.0. This server assumes all IP subnets for network 172.16.0.0 have the same netmask, fffffc0 (255.255.255.192). The netmask is part of the configuration settings for the LAN network interface:

```
user$ ifconfig le0
le0: flags=863<UP,BROADCAST,NOTRAILERS,RUNNING,MULTICAST> mtu 1500
        inet 172.16.0.66 netmask fffffc0 broadcast 172.16.0.127
user$
```

Thus, 172.16.0.128 in the table is a route to an IP subnet. This route applies for individual IP addresses from 172.16.0.128 to 172.16.0.191. The entry for 192.168.1.0 is a route to a class C network number. Network 192.168.1.0 may in fact include subnets, but since this server has no direct connection to it, there is no netmask knowledge available. Therefore, this route must remain as a network number.

All the `Gateway` IP addresses must be directly accessible through any connected LANs or PPP connections. The G flag indicates that IP datagrams to the destination require forwarding to the `Gateway`. In the absence of this flag, this server forwards IP datagrams to the `Interface`, using ARP as necessary. A U flag denotes the route is up.

You can use the Unix `route` command to manually add or delete entries in the routing table. `route` accepts as arguments such as `add`, `delete`, `net`, `host`, a destination address, a gateway address, and a metric. Sample commands that create the entries in the table above, are:

```
root# route add net 172.16.0.128 172.16.0.126 1
add net 172.16.0.128: gateway 172.16.0.126
root# route add net 192.168.1.0 172.16.0.126 1
add net 192.168.1.0: gateway 172.16.0.126
root#
```

A 1 metric sets the gateway route G flag. On Unix, this metric is usually unimportant, as long as it's greater than zero. A zero indicates the destination is sharing the same LAN as this server, which isn't correct in this case. Metrics measure the desirability of a route entry. However, TCP/IP routing programs, not the server's routing table, maintain metrics. That is why specific metric numbers are unimportant for this case.

The keyword `net` causes the destination address to be interpreted as a network or IP subnet number. In contrast, using `host` defines a route for a specific IP address and sets the host H flag.

Routing Protocols

One question that arises is how one maintains routing tables for every device in a complex network. Depending on its location inside the network, devices may have different neighboring routers, each of which serve different subsets of Internet destinations.

TCP/IP routing protocols can dynamically distribute routing information among routers and other network devices. Many routing protocols are available. These include Routing Information Protocol (RIP) version 1, RIP version 2, IGRP, OSPF, EGRP, BGP, and others. Dynamic routing is frequently essential for multihomed devices (multiple network interfaces) and devices that must selectively forward IP datagrams to one of many neighboring routers. It's senseless for you to manually edit routes when there can be hundreds of destinations and gateway IP addresses in a complex network.

Dial-in PPP servers based on router platforms usually include extensive software that supports multiple TCP/IP routing protocols. Many Unix and lower-end PPP servers include only RIP-1. And PPP software for end users normally omits routing protocols altogether.

When working with PPP at the edges of a network you can avoid using routing protocols. This situation is frequent for dial-in PPP servers. However, for PPP connections that connect networks, rather than individual users, use of routing protocols is almost unavoidable.

5

In this chapter:
- *Selecting Serial Connections*
- *PPP Hardware*
- *PPP Software*

Selecting Hardware, Software, and Services

Network administrators have many choices for hardware, software, and telecommunication services. In this chapter, I describe products in each of these three categories and some features to look for. Choosing products depends strongly on what you wish to use PPP for. It's useful for setting up dial-up remote access service, network interconnection, and virtual private networks. Ultimately, you must integrate your product choices into a working PPP solution.

On the other hand, users typically already own the computer. The additional items they may need are data communications equipment, such as a modem and PPP software. Users select computers on the basis of the applications they wish to run, rather than PPP requirements. This is important to realize. If you're arranging PPP for a user population, it's best to minimize assumptions regarding their equipment. Therefore, try to select only PPP products that meet industry standards and use only widely supported PPP features. Avoiding vendor-proprietary PPP solutions achieves the best compatibility with a general user population.

I suggest considering product categories in order representing each layer in the OSI model, from the bottom up. Thus, I describe telecommunication services first, which provide physical point-to-point serial connections. PPP hardware and software sections follow.

Selecting Serial Connections

The serial connection is what physically carries PPP frames from one point to another. For very short distances inside a room, RS-232 interfaces and connecting cables are all that's necessary. However, for longer distances, you frequently must select services from telecommunications vendors.

Telecommunications vendors provide point-to-point serial connections, whenever the distance between the endpoints exceeds the distance of a single building. Services suitable for data usually fall into the following categories:

Leased line service

A permanent service with two fixed endpoints. The communications speed, in bits per second, is fixed for a given service.

Dial-up and switched services

These establish a point-to-point connection after you place a call to a telephone number. Once the connection is up, it behaves much like a leased line. However, you can disconnect and reconnect to alternate endpoints on demand.

Packet switching service

This service is oriented to the transmission of small units of data, known as *packets*. Note these aren't IP datagrams. Packets contain information about its recipient. Depending on the service, the packet network may behave like a leased line, like a switched service, or like the Internet itself. Packet services may also feature multipoint capability, variable bandwidth, multiple logical channels, and traffic priorities.

Many networks that support PPP tend to use them with dial-up services. Predominantly, this is regular telephone service, which is the most readily available to general PPP users. However, PPP with digital dial-up services, such as ISDN, is becoming more popular.

If you're responsible for PPP in network interconnect arrangements, you can select from a myriad array of communication services. These are likely to be leased line, but switched and packet services are also valid choices. Serial-connection capacity is critical since it affects performance, as perceived by all users sharing this resource. Other factors that may influence your choice of data service are its availability, economics, and communication usage patterns.

Packet services including frame relay, X.25, and ATM, require their own protocols. Nevertheless, they can behave as point-to-point connectors and carry PPP as a data stream. I won't say much about packet services, since PPP isn't commonly used with them.

Leased Lines

Leased lines are useful for connecting networks. They are for high volume data communications.

Leased-line services are also known by names like private line and Digital Data Service (DDS). These services offer minimal functionality and simply transport a bit stream from one point to another. Some telecommunication vendors offer reliability enhancements, such as protection switching (automatic fail over to alternate leased lines), or performance monitoring options.

The important characteristics of leased-line services are:

Permanent communication channel between two fixed endpoints
> The channel is available whether or not data transmission actually occurs

Leased lines are available for analog or digital data
> Digital lines are the preferred choice for data; however, some networks may still use analog lines with modems for data

Standard communication bandwidths available
> Bandwidths for digital lines range from fractions of 64 Kbps to hundreds of megabits per second

Leased lines are billed at flat rates

The bandwidths available with leased lines frequently extend well beyond those available with dial-up services. Table 5-1 illustrates the leased-line services available. Not all services are available from all vendors. Also, availability may be limited in some geographical areas. SONET, in particular, is relatively new. In the table, the term "T1" represents the service or technology, while "DS1" is a rate. The networking industry tends to use both terms interchangeably.

Table 5-1. Leased Line Services

Service	Data Communications Bandwidth (Approximate)
56-Kbps Circuit	56 Kbps
Fractional T1 (Fractional DS1)	Nx64 Kbps where N = 1 to 24
T1 (DS1)	1.5 Mbps
T3 (DS3)	45 Mbps
SONET OC-1	50 Mbps
SONET OC-3	150 Mbps

PPP configuration notes

An established leased line is permanently connected to the other end. This simplifies PPP configuration since the overhead for initiating and terminating calls is entirely unnecessary. Authentication between PPP endpoints is also unnecessary. Leased lines, by their nature, involve two known endpoints. Presumably, only your equipment, and perhaps an ISP's equipment, is responsible for terminating a leased line.

Dial-up Lines

Dial-up and switched services economically favor situations where data transmission is infrequent. This is the usual case for dial-in PPP. Sometimes, this is also true for small remote networks that temporarily connect to a larger one.

Dial-up services establish connections on-demand to physical destinations a telephone number specifies. After establishing a call, the line behaves much like a leased line. It transports bit streams from one end to the other.

Dial-up services share the following characteristics:

* One endpoint calls another to establish communications; the endpoints may be changed at any time, simply by disconnecting and placing another call

* Dial-up services are available for analog or digital data transmission

* Bandwidth availability for digital dial-up services usually range from 56 Kbps to 45 Mbps

* Dial-up services usually have usage sensitive billing; there is a fixed recurring cost, plus costs that are a function of connect time and distance

Examples of dial-up services available appear in Table 5-2. The most common one is Plain Old Telephone Service (POTS). This is the most ubiquitous, easiest to obtain, and the lowest cost service available. Most PPP users only have POTS due to economic or service availability constraints. ISDN-BRI promises a low-cost alternative. In fact, it's compatible with the same wiring as POTS. ISDN offers independent 64-Kbps lines. These behave as multiple telephone lines, and each may carry separate voice or data calls. Although PPP itself is oriented for use with a single line, the emerging Multilink PPP can combine resources of several lines, increasing data bit rates. Multilink PPP is useful for achieving 128 Kbps with ISDN-BRI. Chapter 16, *What's New for PPP?*, provides more information about ISDN and Multilink PPP.

Table 5-2. Dial-Up and Switched Services

Service	Data Communications Bandwidth (Approximate)
Plain Old Telephone Service (POTS)	Asymmetrical 56 Kbps and 33.6 Kbps; varies with modem technology
Switched 56	56 Kbps
Integrated Services Digital Network Basic Rate Interface (ISDN-BRI)	64 Kbps or 128 Kbps (may require Multilink PPP)
Integrated Services Digital Network Primary Rate Interface (ISDN-PRI)	Nx64 Kbps where N=1 to 23 (may require multilink PPP)

Table 5-2. Dial-Up and Switched Services (continued)

Service	Data Communications Bandwidth (Approximate)
Switched T1 (switched DS1)	1.5 Mbps
Switched T3 (switched DS3)	45 Mbps

PPP configuration notes

All dial-up services allow calls to almost anywhere at any time. Consequently, this requires you to configure PPP software to place or accept calls and disconnect afterwards.

Another special concern with dial-up service is security. Many services are public. This means anyone could attempt unauthorized access to a network via PPP. To deter intrusion, PPP software that accepts data calls must verify the caller's identity. This procedure can include ascertaining the telephone number placing the call (using caller ID) or challenging callers to authenticate themselves.

Economics

The fixed charges for dial-up services are much lower than the equivalent leased-line rate. We expect this, since the telecommunications vendor dynamically assigns communications resources for your use only when a connection is up. Time- and distance-sensitive charges account for added resource use while a connection is up.

At usage levels beyond a threshold, the cost for dial-up service exceeds the fixed cost of a leased line. This is the basic characteristic of the dial-up versus leased line economic model. If a dial-up service is going to be constantly active and "nailed up" to a single destination, a lease line service is usually more economical.

Using regular telephone service for cross-town communications may be an exception to this economic model. This happens because flat-rate telephone service is generally available within a local calling area.

PPP Hardware

Hardware that supports PPP ranges from low-end PCs, mid-range Unix and PC servers, and high-end communication servers and routers. Any of this hardware also requires standard or optional PPP software.

What hardware platform is the correct choice? The answer again depends on how you plan to use PPP. When selecting hardware, the technical items to consider are functionality, performance, reliability, and capacity. Nontechnical items to consider include your budget and favored vendors. Table 5-3 highlights some advantages and disadvantages for several different PPP hardware platforms.

Table 5-3. PPP Hardware Platforms

PPP Hardware Platform	Advantages	Disadvantages
Communications servers	High performance, line capacity, and reliability	Proprietary hardware and software
Routers	High performance and reliability	Proprietary hardware and software, number of PPP connections may be limited
Unix servers	Customizable software, user and application services on same platform	
General-purpose PCs	Flexibility, with many hardware and software options available, low cost	Difficult hardware and software integration, reliability and uptime is frequently low

I suggest routers for network-to-network interconnects that require permanent point-to-point connections. With mission-critical or high-volume dial-in PPP, the best hardware to choose is the communication server. Unix and PC equipment are useful for more modest requirements. These are more open platforms, which offer much configuration flexibility.

The trade-offs for lower-cost hardware solutions includes less capability, less reliability, and more maintenance overhead. This may not be a concern, if you're using PPP for temporary purposes or you're just a single user dialing in with PPP.

Communications Servers

Communication servers, also known as terminal servers and remote access servers, are hardware products specifically designed for dial-up service. The hardware and software design is vendor-proprietary. Vendors optimize their communications servers for a single primary purpose; to support large numbers of serial connections and large volumes of data. You can expect these products to offer full feature communications software, management software, and extensive networking support.

Network equipment vendors, rather than computer vendors, offer communication server products. Some examples include Ascend Communications' MAX family, Bay Network's Remote Annex, Cisco Systems' Series 2500 Access Server, 3Com's Access Builder, and Livingston's Portmaster. Line capacities vary and range from as few as four ports to hundreds. Some servers include modems built into the unit. Here are some of the unique features of communication servers:

- Each dial-up port can independently support PPP, SLIP, command-line, and other protocols; if permitted, users can select these on demand

- The PPP software supports multiple network layer protocols, besides TCP/IP

- Includes software for supporting multiple network routing protocols

Some of these features are difficult to obtain with alternative PPP hardware. Not all these features may be available on all communication server products.

Installing communication servers can be an extensive process. Many models require an adjunct PC or Unix host for maintenance, monitoring, and user authentication. You must install these additional computers as part of the communication server setup process. There are no standards pertaining to communication server configuration and maintenance. If you're unfamiliar with a product, you need to learn its command set and its supporting software.

Routers

Many vendors that offer communication server products also offer routers.

Routers interconnect multiple networks. They offer physical network interfaces of various types, including serial interfaces of various types (not limited to RS-232). Routers typically support PPP, as well as alternative protocols, on its serial interfaces.

Routers aren't substantially different from communication servers. Their interface configuration is different, and they don't offer as many serial interfaces for modem pools.

Unix Servers

Unix servers are available from Sun Microsystems, Inc., Hewlett-Packard Co., Digital Equipment Corp., etc. These servers can support PPP connections and also run numerous network application programs, which minimizes a PPP user's need to access resources elsewhere in a network. The Unix operating system is already multiuser, multitasking, and includes most software necessary for TCP/IP networking. Many Unix computers also include two onboard serial interfaces for PPP. Additional products available from hardware vendors can add additional serial interfaces.

PPP, TCP/IP, and related software for Unix are available on the Internet as C source code. This is a real advantage for Unix. If the bundled software doesn't meet your PPP requirements, you could conceivably install and modify additional software as necessary to overcome deficiencies. Unix is among the best for customization and programming.

The difficult areas you may encounter for PPP and networking are as follows:

- Unix tends to support only TCP/IP networking with PPP. Few Unix solutions go beyond this limit. But some do support Novell IPX/SPX.

- There may be artificial limits in the number of active PPP sessions that can be active. This limit may be difficult to change and may not be consistent with the number of available serial interfaces.

- Routing software supplied with Unix systems is inadequate for PPP connections between networks.

Sites that select Unix for PPP tend to use them for low-volume dial-in and dial-out. The number of lines is usually on the order of ten or less.

Personal Computers

Due to the general popularity of PCs and supporting hardware, they are likely to be the lowest in cost. PCs usually have two serial interfaces usable for PPP. Many hardware options are available for adding additional interfaces in multiples of four, eight, or more.

PCs are extremely flexible because a myriad array of hardware and software options are available from hundreds of manufacturers. This flexibility and the historical development of the PC can create unusual hardware and software incompatibilities for all but the most common configurations. Remember the original IBM-compatible PC design never included networking ability. Successfully integrating PC hardware and software piece parts into a functioning router or dial-up server may be a difficult challenge for you.

Here are some issues pertaining to PC operating systems you should beware of:

- MS-DOS 6.22 and Windows 3.11 aren't true multitasking environments, essential for simultaneously serving multiple PPP connections. These operating systems are inadequate for networking without significant additional software and device drivers.

- Windows 95/98 networking support is intended only for a single PPP end user. Its authentication and management features are limited. Windows 95/98 doesn't support routing protocols. Its stability as a multiuser network device is questionable.

- Multitasking Unix and Windows NT are available. Not all PCs' hardware are certified for use by these operating systems. For those that are, there may be missing pieces, such as multiport serial interface device drivers.

Of the operating-system choices, the best are Unix and Windows NT. With some configuration work, either can function as a router or dial-in PPP server. These are the high-end PC operating systems. The lower-end operating systems are really for use only with individual PPP end users.

A common problem with PC hardware is resource conflicts, especially for less popular peripheral products. Interrupt request (IRQ) and direct memory access (DMA) resources frequently must remain unique among multiple peripheral devices. Sometimes, this may be impossible to achieve. With persistence, you can find a PC hardware configuration suitable for PPP. The right combination of hardware and software can match the functionality available with Unix servers.

Capacity and Performance

When selecting PPP hardware, consider both current capacity needs and future growth. PPP connections must offer acceptable service availability and performance for remote networks and users. Frequent busy signals for a dial-in PPP pool is usually unacceptable. Similarly, network congestion that reduces communications performance is also undesirable.

Administrators installing PPP connections should consider user-to-modem ratio for dial-in pools. This ratio determines how frequently modem pools may be busy. Bandwidth to user ratios gauge how frequently network congestion may occur. This ratio is important for both dial-in and network to network PPP connections.

User-to-modem ratio

The busy signal has become a subject of competitive advertising among ISPs. It's now a metric for assessing the quality of dial-up PPP. Busy signals deny users access to a network, simply because there isn't an available modem that can answer the call. If the shortage is severe, users may be unable to dial-in for hours.

The solution to an insufficient number of dial-up lines is straightforward: either limit the user population or install additional dial-up lines. The user-to-modem ratio measures the average number of users that must share one modem in your pool. The smaller the ratio, the less chance of busy signals.

For ISPs with dial-in PPP, some suggested ratios are:

- Ten users per modem: acceptable, but probably poor
- Eight users per modem: good
- Six users per modem or better: excellent

The acceptable ratio for a dial-in service depends on the behavior and usage pattern of users. Generally, a modem pool that serves users with unlimited connect time requires better ratios. Smaller modem pools should also maintain better ratios since user behavior variance is much higher.

Bandwidth-to-user ratio

The bandwidth-to-user ratio estimates the communications speed a network has available to an average user. A higher bandwidth per user represents better service. If this ratio is too low, performance suffers. To users, poor performance means low overall communication throughput, and delays become intolerable. The place to measure the bandwidth-to-user ratio is at that point in your network that is the first to become a congestion bottleneck.

The ideal bottleneck point for dial-in PPP is the modem itself. Each user connected to a 56-Kbps modem can transfer at most 56 Kbps of data. Unfortunately, the first place for congestion is usually not the modem, but a LAN or a leased line that all users must share. For example, if you aggregate Internet traffic for 100 modems into a T1 leased line, the bandwidth per user is 15.4 Kbps. This is well below the maximum 56-Kbps speed of one modem.

When PPP connects two networks, the first bottleneck is usually the PPP connection itself. Again, the number of users sharing this connection determines the bandwidth available to each. If 100 users on one network wish to communicate to another network via PPP on a T1 leased line, the bandwidth per user is 15.4 Kbps.

What is an acceptable bandwidth-to-user ratio? This is a very difficult question. The answer depends widely on the usage pattern of your users. Users rarely demand maximum network resources all the time, and not all users are active at any one time. Therefore, network performance monitoring is the only practical means to determine if you need to detect and resolve a network congestion situation that's related to your PPP connections.

Bandwidth versus throughput

The physical characteristics of data communication media determine their bandwidth. Thus, a modem that connects at 56 Kbps offers 56 Kbps of bandwidth. This doesn't mean that the connection can always carry 56 Kbps of continuous data. Over time, a network may slow down communications, resulting in an average throughput much less than rated bandwidths. This is the essential difference between bandwidth and throughput. In the absence of data compression, throughput can never exceed bandwidth.

Besides the network infrastructure, the processing capacity of a communications server or a computer terminating a PPP connection can limit throughput. If more data arrives at a server than it can process, it asserts flow control to temporarily stop data flow. With PCs and Unix servers, throughput performance depends on many factors difficult to analyze and predict. These include the load of the primary CPU, the processing responsibilities of the serial controllers, Ethernet controllers, and other peripheral hardware. Communication server vendors rarely quote throughput specifications for their products. Thus, conducting a performance evaluation is the only practical means to determine if a product performs acceptably for PPP. Product reviews, published from time to time, may report performance test results.

PPP Software

Numerous PPP software products are currently available. Your initial PPP selection criteria is to choose among products that are compatible with your hardware, operating system and the serial connection you wish to use for PPP.

The hardware vendor for communication servers and routers provides PPP software. If the features are inadequate, you must select different hardware. The PPP software choices for Unix and PC platforms are numerous; you can select PPP software based on the features you require.

PPP software is available from many places, including the following:

- PPP may be integrated, or included, with an operating system

- Commercial vendors offer PPP software for sale

- Several PPP software packages are free and available for download on the Internet; downloadable software may also be shareware or evaluation products

- For PPP end users, an ISP or network administrator may provide them PPP software

The Windows NT/95/98, Solaris, and Linux operating systems include PPP; Windows 3.1 doesn't. If the features of bundled software are inadequate, consider third-party alternatives. Commercial vendors including Netmanage, FTP Software, and Trumpet (shareware) offer products for PCs. Progressive Systems supports Unix platforms, including Unix on PCs. Some products also include applications, such as FTP, Telnet, and web browsers, for computers that didn't initially have them. Vendors' web sites are sources for additional information about their products.

When cost is of concern, PPP and its related utilities are available at various Internet sites for download. There are also numerous sites that collect and centrally archive Internet distributable software. Some of these are:

> *http://www.shareware.com*
> *http://www.simtel.net/simtel.net*
> *ftp://ftp.uu.net*

The first two are sites oriented to PCs and available on the Web. The third site is an FTP service, which web browsers can also access.

Table 5-4 shows specific examples of some PPP software that's available for various PC, Linux, and Unix operating systems.

Table 5-4. PPP Downloadable Software

Title	File	Internet Site
PPP 2.3 Linux and Unix	*ppp-2.3.5.tar.gz*	*ftp://cs.anu.edu.au*
Trumpet Winsock Windows 3.1 Windows 95	*twsk30d.exe* (base PPP) *twsk30w6.doc* (documentation) *winap21f.zip* (application programs)	*ftp://ftp.trumpet.com.au*
FreePPP 2.6 Macintosh	*freeppp262.sit.hqx*	*http://www.rockstar.com*
Slirp 1.0c Unix	*slirp.tar.gz*	*http://blitzen.canberra.edu.au/slirp/*

Connection Management

PPP communications commences only after a serial connection is available. However, it's typically the responsibility of PPP software to initiate and accept dial-up connections. PPP products vary widely in these capabilities. Connection management frequently distinguishes otherwise similar products from each other.

When selecting PPP software, some connection management features you may consider are:

Dial-in only, dial-out only, or both
> Dial-in PPP software listens for incoming serial connections. For services with telephone lines, this software is responsible for answering modem calls. Similarly, dial-out PPP software must cause a modem to initiate a call to a telephone number.

Number of simultaneous PPP connections
> Consider limits in the simultaneous PPP sessions a product supports. Dial-in pools many require a large number. Those PPP implementations limited to a single connection are unsuited for this task.

Inactivity time-out and session time-out
> Inactivity time-out disconnects idle calls after a configurable duration. Session time-out limits the total PPP session time. Both are useful in limiting connect time and charges for telecommunication services.

Connection management is unrelated to PPP as a protocol. Remember that PPP is a peer-to-peer protocol. Once a connection is up, PPP operates without distinguishing between calling and answering parties. As a useful consequence, two

PPP products that can only dial out may still communicate as long as they both believe they initiated a call to the same physical communications media.

I admit that it's inelegant to arrange communications between two PPP software products capable of dial-out only. However, it can be a quick and dirty solution when interconnecting two PCs with a serial null modem cable.

Dial-in features

Internet or private network access is typical for modem pools set to accept dial-in calls. Some dial-in features to look for in PPP software are:

Port monitoring and management
Allows ascertaining dial-in port status, locally or remotely. The ability to selectively disable a dial-in port is important if a modem or telephone line has gone bad.

Automatic serial line protocol detection or command-line interface (CLI)
Dial-in ports may serve both PPP and non-PPP users. A CLI lets users select how they wish to use their connection. Automatic protocol detection automates this selection by adapting to the data users transmit first.

Interactive authentication
If PPP authentication methods are inadequate, a dial-in server can interactively prompt users for their authentication credentials, before PPP communications begins.

Call back
After user authentication, the dial-in PPP server disconnects and then initiates a dial-out connection back to the user. This feature is mainly for security, but is also useful for reversing telecommunication charges.

Many of these features aren't necessary for all dial-in PPP installations. Administrators need to select among these according to their dial-in PPP requirements.

Dial-out features

For online users accessing the Internet or private networks, dial-out PPP is a priority. Some dial-out features to look for include:

Chat script language, its capability, and its documentation
A script that automates procedures necessary to initiate a serial connection. This activity includes configuring serial interfaces, modems, dialing telephone numbers, and informing the remote server to start PPP.

Terminal windows for connection setup
This is for users who want to initiate a serial connection manually.

On-demand connect

> This automatically initiates a dial-out PPP connection whenever an application program, such as a web browser, wishes to access remote resources via PPP. Idle time-out can disconnect PPP when the application completes its communications.

Automatic redial and automatic restart

> If an initial dial-out PPP connection fails, automatic redial tries to initiate the PPP connection again. Automatic restart initiates a new PPP connection if an existing connection terminates due to a communications fault.

Chat script languages enable PPP software to automatically issue command strings necessary for modems and other devices, during connection establishment. Chat scripts send strings through the same serial interface that supports PPP. A simple language is a list of strings to send to the interface and strings to expect in response (send/expect). More complex languages feature looping and conditional programming. In other words, scripts could retry multiple phone numbers several times to connect. Whatever script language is available, good documentation is essential to effectively use its full capabilities. Chat scripts frequently require use of text editors to create and modify.

If the procedure to initiate a PPP connection is unknown or must not appear in a stored program for security reasons, a terminal window is indispensable. This enables users to interact directly through their serial interface. They manually type strings to initiate a modem connection, reply to remote password prompts, and perform other operations necessary to prepare the serial connection for PPP. A terminal window is also a useful aid to help create automatic connect scripts.

PPP Tuning

When PPP communications begin, peer-to-peer negotiations establish PPP options for the duration of a connection. Some PPP implementations hardcode numerous settings and don't offer configurability. This is unfortunate, because the ability of administrators to set options is an important PPP software feature.

Some PPP options workaround serial connection limitations. Other options help communications efficiency, as long as PPP endpoints agree and correctly use them. Counters and timers control the PPP negotiation process, and each of these may sometimes require adjustments.

The configurable options PPP software may offer are:

- Maximum transmission unit (MTU) and maximum receive unit (MRU)
- Asyncmap
- On/off options and other PPP valued parameters
- PPP negotiation counters and timers

The most desirable adjustments to have are MTU, MRU, and asyncmap. MTU and MRU set the maximum PPP frame size and affects PPP performance. Asyncmap accommodates serial connections that filter or translate control characters in data. This happens with connections that have numerous intervening hardware and software components. Chapter 11, *Customizing and Tuning PPP*, provides further information about PPP options and how to set them.

The defaults for most other PPP settings are fine for all but the most unusual situations. Sometimes, it's necessary to specifically disable a PPP option if there is an incompatibility between the PPP endpoints. This may happen with different vintages of PPP or with PPP software bugs. PPP counters and timers rarely require adjustment from standard values. However, peers that are especially slow in responding may require higher delays or retries.

Authentication Options

PPP supports optional authentication as part of its protocol. Either or both PPP endpoints can demand its peer to authenticate. In practice, PPP software products may not support all authentication situations.

The authentication features PPP software can offer are:

Authenticator only
> An authenticator is a server that demands authentication credentials from its peer

Authenticating client only
> An authenticating client, or authenticatee, supplies credentials to a server, in order to prove its identity to the server

PPP authentication protocols
> The standard PPP authentication protocols are none, Password Authentication Protocol (PAP), and Challenge Handshake Authentication Protocol (CHAP); proprietary protocols also exist

Choice of PPP authentication methods on-demand

Authentication database
> When multiple sets of authentication credentials exist, the PPP software must look up or validate credentials in a database

PPP allows either peer or both peers to optionally challenge the other to authenticate. Who initiated the connection is immaterial. However, it's common for the PPP endpoint answering an incoming call to request calling party authentication. Many dial-out PPP products function only as an authenticating client and omit authenticator capabilities. More advanced products support two-way authentication and can demand an answering party to authenticate.

The standard PPP authentication methods are PAP and CHAP, and Chapter 12, *Authentication*, shows you how to set these up. It's crucial that you and your users select PPP software with compatible authentication. Incompatibilities result in authentication failures and service denial. For this reason, stay away from proprietary authentication methods, unless you have an unusual security policy that requires a proprietary solution. If you're an ISP, stick with standard PPP authentication.

Network Protocols

PPP can simultaneously carry different network layer protocol families. In practice, a PPP software product may support only one or maybe a few network layer protocols. For every network layer protocol a PPP software supports, it must support the corresponding PPP Network Control Protocol (NCP).

Here are some PPP software features to look for in the network protocols category:

- Simultaneous multiplexing of network protocols
- TCP/IP and IPCP
- Novell IPX/SPX and IPXCP
- Other network layer protocols and PPP NCPs

Due to its popularity and ubiquity, many PPP implementations support only TCP/IP. This is adequate for the Internet, but insufficient if you plan to use PPP with PC networks, for example. A single physical network infrastructure can support multiple network layers. Thus, with the right PPP software, you can extend all these protocols simultaneously across a PPP connection.

The NCP for each network layer protocol often establishes network addresses and other network layer specific options. This is another area where PPP software feature vary. Consider IPCP for TCP/IP. The following are available methods for setting IP addresses:

- Acquiring IP addresses from a peer
- Configuring either or both local and remote IP addresses

In dial-in arrangements, you must set user IP addresses to be compatible with the TCP/IP network infrastructure. This requires you to configure your dial-in server to negotiate and set both local and remote IP addresses for all PPP connections. In this scenario, PPP users must use software capable of acquiring IP addresses from a peer. If PPP serves a network-to-network connection, both PPP endpoints can set their own IP address and notify their peers about their setting.

There are additional PPP software features specific to TCP/IP, but I'll defer these to Chapter 11.

Virtual Private Networking, Tunneling

In virtual private networking, you arrange a private network with the help of Internet communication resources. Normally, PPP operates over leased lines or telephone lines. In contrast, VPN requires PPP to operate over a tunnel connection through the Internet. This requires PPP software to communicate, not through a serial interface, but through an existing Internet network connection.

PPP software with VPN capabilities may establish PPP connections through one or more Internet tunneling protocols. Some tunneling protocols are:

*   Point-to-Point Tunneling Protocol (PPTP), Layer 2 Forwarding (L2F) Protocol, and Layer 2 Tunneling Protocol (L2TP)

*   A raw TCP connection

*   An ad hoc tunneling protocol, such as rlogin and Telnet

All these tunneling protocols are the equivalent of a serial connection for PPP. Chapter 14, *Virtual Private Networking and Tunneling*, further describes how to set up VPNs with these protocols.

Miscellaneous

New capabilities in the PPP specification appear rather frequently. PPP connections may be designed to take advantage of these, either on a mandatory or optional basis. Obviously, if you're looking for new features you must obtain PPP software that recognizes and implements them.

Some examples of recent, or less known, PPP additions are:

*   Compression and encryption control protocol

*   Callback control protocol

*   Multilink

*   Vendor proprietary PPP extensions

Some new PPP features encompass numerous subfeatures. One example is data encryption. There are numerous encryption algorithms each PPP implementation may choose to support. However, both PPP endpoints must understand the same algorithm for encryption to be effective.

Chapter 16 provides more information about some of the newer features and related technology developments with PPP.

Comparing PPP Software

One way to select PPP software is to compare its features with your PPP requirements. Next, compare several candidate products with each other in a matrix. It may be difficult to find PPP software that meets all your needs, but there probably exists a product that can meet your most essential requirements. Table 5-5 compares some basic features for several popular PPP software products.

Table 5-5. Comparing PPP Software Features

	PPP-2.3	Solaris 2.6 PPP	Trumpet Winsock 3	Win 98 DUN	Windows NT 4.0
Connection management:					
Dial-in, dial-out	Both	Both	Dial-out	Both	Both
Simultaneous sessions	> 1	> 1	1	> 1	> 1
Inactivity time-out	Yes	Yes	Yes	Yes	Yes
Dial-in features:					
Command-line interface	Yes	Yes			
Interactive authenticate	Yes	Yes			
Call back					Yes
Dial-out features:					
Scripting language	Expect/ Send	Expect/ Send	Program	Program	Program
Terminal window			Yes	Yes	Yes
On-demand connection	Yes	Yes	Yes	Yes[a]	Yes[a]
Auto reconnect	Yes				Yes
PPP configurability:					
MRU and MTU	Yes	Yes	Yes	Some	
Asyncmap	Yes	Yes			
Other	Yes	Yes			Yes
Authentication:					
Authenticator or client	Both	Both	Client	Both[b]	Both[b]
Standard protocols	PAP, CHAP	PAP, CHAP	PAP, CHAP	PAP, CHAP[c]	PAP, CHAP[d]
Authenticate database	Yes				Yes
Network protocols	TCP/IP IPX[e]	TCP/IP	TCP/IP	TCP/IP, IPX, NetBEUI	TCP/IP, IPX, NetBEUI
VPN tunneling				PPTP	PPTP

[a] Triggers for all network access on the basis of name resolution or dial-out history rather than IP route settings

[b] Authenticator only for dial-in service; authenticating client only for dial-out service

[c] No CHAP for dial-in; supports additional nonstandard protocols for dial-out

[d] CHAP for dial-in available in service pack; supports additional nonstandard protocols for dial-out

[e] Available with the Linux operating system

This matrix is likely to change frequently, because PPP software changes with each new release. The idea here is to show you how to compare products with each other. It's difficult to state with certainty whether a product offers a particular feature. For this reason, we omit "No" in Table 5-5. Optional software additions or patches can add features unavailable in the base PPP product installation. For example, the `ppptcp` package available on the Internet adds VPN tunneling with raw TCP connections to PPP-2.3. Additional PPP configurability may exist for the Windows PPP products, but these settings are obscure or undocumented.

In this chapter:
- *PPP Sign-on Procedures*
- *General PPP Setup Steps*
- *Linux PPP-2.3*
- *Solaris PPP*
- *Windows 3.1*
- *Windows 98 (and 95)*
- *Windows NT 4.0 Workstation*

6

Dial-out PPP Setup

Computer users most commonly use PPP to dial out and connect to either the Internet or a corporate private network. The relationship between users and the network they're accessing appears in Figure 6-1. From their point of view, PPP is present only on the physical serial link that connects them to a greater network. Typical dial-out PPP arrangements support standalone PCs only. In other words, we assume users don't have networks of their own that share a PPP connection.

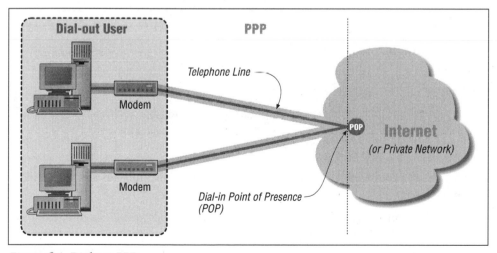

Figure 6-1. Dial-out PPP

As a network administrator or ISP, you must supply instructions for dial-out users to successfully configure their PPP software for network access. One method is to supply users with software that automatically sets up their PPP. This doesn't avoid dial-out PPP configuration tasks, but merely shifts this responsibility from users to you. Major ISPs frequently prepare and distribute free sign-up software for popular computer equipment (e.g., IBM PC-compatible) and operating system (e.g., Microsoft) combinations.

Unfortunately, PPP setup software isn't always available or appropriate for all users. As long as you offer service with PPP, authorized users with equipment that supports PPP can successfully connect. However, users who can't use some sort of automated setup software must manually configure their own PPP software. Although PPP is well standardized, its many implementations vary widely. Thus, the purpose of this chapter is to describe to you and your users how to manually configure dial-out PPP with several popular, but diverse, PPP implementations.

This chapter limits its discussion to standalone computers dialing out. PPP also supports entire networks that wish to dial-out. But this requires additional configuration work with network layer forwarding and routing, which later chapters expand on.

PPP Sign-on Procedures

Dialing out and signing-on with PPP requires users to have basic service information. Users can then arrange their computers to issue interactive command strings through its serial port, which controls and prepares communications equipment (e.g., modem, remote communication server, etc.) for PPP.

Gathering Service Information

For Internet access or other TCP/IP network access, it's the responsibility of network administrators to provide the following:

- Access telephone numbers; users should select a number in their local dialing area, if possible

- Username and password

- Interactive procedure, if any, to select PPP communications mode, after dialing in

- Authentication methods and procedures; some services require authentication before PPP begin; others request authentication within PPP

- The method for assigning IP addresses at both the user and service provider endpoints of a PPP connection

- The IP addresses of DNS servers, necessary for users to resolve hostname to IP addresses

The answers to these questions can determine the PPP software choices available to dial-out users. One common constraint is PPP authentication. Those PPP software products limited to PAP (see Chapter 12, *Authentication*), for example, are incompatible with services requiring CHAP. It's unfortunate that some Internet providers configure their PPP service to require proprietary PPP features. This is a disservice to users, since it severely limits the computers and software combinations they can choose for dial-out. Some users may switch to other ISPs as a result.

Another problem with some Internet providers are network administrators who are unable to provide the information users need to configure their software. This situation usually arises when the ISP depends too much on some automated setup software and doesn't understand the issues faced by users of different packages. Although it's a great inconvenience, sophisticated users can still install the setup software on a computer they don't wish to use, register, locate the files containing the configuration data, and use the data in those files to do their own configuration. Needless to say, a user who goes through this process doesn't end up feeling that his ISP is helpful, or even competent.

Dial-out Commands to Initiate PPP

When PPP software dials out via a telephone line, the commands it issues and the responses it receives typically look like Figure 6-2.

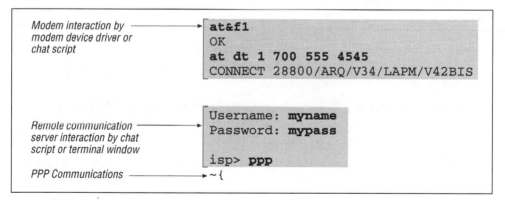

Figure 6-2. Initiating a PPP session

In Figure 6-2, we assume that you have set up a dial-in modem pool with a communication server. This server prompts for the user's name, password, and a **ppp** command.

After PPP starts, we assume the following:

- Users must authenticate themselves again with a PPP authentication method
- The communications server assigns the IP addresses for both endpoints of the connection

This configuration encompasses the cases most dial-out PPP users encounter. Thus, the software configuration examples in this chapter assume that you're trying to establish a configuration like this one.

In practice, users should need to authenticate only once. If a communications server already asked for a password, there's no reason for it to require authentication again after beginning PPP communications. Many ISPs can also automatically detect PPP traffic from users. This eliminates the need for the remote communication server interaction phase shown in Figure 6-2.

General PPP Setup Steps

Dial-out PPP setup generally begins with computer hardware, PPP software, and other related software (e.g., operating system components) installation on a user's computer.

After obtaining all software components, you should configure communications layer by layer, from the bottom up:

1. Configure serial interfaces.
2. Establish modem settings and determine modem commands. If a user's computer doesn't have its modem's profile, users must determine the cryptic strings to set and control the modem.
3. Develop chat scripts, if necessary. Chat scripts may first converse with a modem to dial-out, then converse with a remote server to initiate PPP. This conversation may include user authentication, if required.
4. Configure PPP. This step may also include arranging authentication within PPP.
5. Configure TCP/IP. This includes IP addresses and routing.
6. Establish, test, and use the connection.

These steps may all be rolled into the setup procedure for a single PPP software product, depending on its implementation. However, it's more likely that users must set up several interdependent software items. As an example, TCP/IP, serial communications, and PPP may all be separate items.

Linux PPP-2.3

PPP-2.3 is available on the Internet (*ftp://cs.anu.edu.au/* and others) in the form of C source code for a variety of Unix systems. At this writing, Paul Mackerras at Australian National University currently maintains this software distribution.

PPP-2.3 is very thorough in features, configuration flexibility, and the number of adjustable options. In addition, its frame-logging ability provides extensive information useful for debugging. The software is compatible with numerous Unix platforms, including Linux, Solaris, NetBSD, FreeBSD, NeXTStep, and others. PPP-2.3 for Linux, in particular, also features IPX/SPX networking, in addition to the usual TCP/IP networking support.

Here, we install PPP-2.3 on Slackware 3.4 Linux and configure it according to the assumptions in the previous section, "PPP Sign-on Procedures." We configure PPP-2.3 manually, which requires users to edit several text files.

PPP-2.3 setup frequently challenges new Linux users. As a result, Linux developers are creating graphical user interface and menu-driven PPP management utilities to assist such users. The following utilities may help with software installation and automate PPP-2.3 configuration:

- EzPPP (Jay Painter)
- PPPSETUP (Kent Robotti)
- TkNet (Charlie Kempson)
- X-ISP (Dimitrios Bouras)
- XPPP (Peter Hofmann)

Additional information about these utilities are available at numerous Linux Internet sites, under the heading "Linux Applications and Utilities." Downloads are available from Linux distribution sites, such as *sunsite.unc.edu*. Beware that installing the source code version of these utilities could be as complex as manually configuring PPP-2.3.

Installation

The PPP-2.3 distribution is a GNU gzipped tar file, such as *ppp-2.3.5.tar.gz*. Since PPP-2.3 requires Linux kernel support, users must also install the Linux kernel source code, typically in */usr/src/linux*, in order to build a revised kernel.

The first step is unpacking the PPP-2.3 distribution into a directory. The Linux source directory, such as */usr/src*, is one suggested destination to place these files:

```
root# pwd
/usr/src
```

```
root# gunzip -c ppp-2.3.5.tar.gz | tar xf -
root# cd ppp-2.3.5
root# ls -F
FAQ                README.osf       configure*      osf1/
NeXT/              README.sol2      etc.ppp/        pppd/
README             README.sunos4    freebsd-2.0/    pppstats/
README.MSCHAP80    README.svr4      include/        scripts/
README.NeXT        README.ultrix    linux/          sunos4/
README.bsd         SETUP            modules/        svr4/
README.cbcp        chat/            netbsd-1.1/     ultrix/
README.linux       common/          netbsd-1.2/
root#
```

Be sure to review the *README* files since they contain information useful for the installation process.

The `configure` utility identifies the Unix platform type and sets up the necessary links to compile PPP-2.3. Here is the result:

```
root# ./configure
Creating links to Makefiles.
  Makefile -> linux/Makefile.top
  pppd/Makefile -> Makefile.linux
  pppstats/Makefile -> Makefile.linux
  chat/Makefile -> Makefile.linux
root#
```

Before compiling PPP-2.3, we'll first install PPP support into the Linux kernel.

Building a Linux kernel with PPP

PPP-2.3 must install or update various C header and source files into the Linux kernel source tree. Typing `make kernel` in the PPP-2.3 directory performs this task:

```
root# pwd
/usr/src/ppp-2.3.5
root# make kernel
cd linux; ./kinstall.sh
. . .
Installing into kernel version 2.0.30 in /usr/src/linux
. . .
Kernel driver files installation done.
root#
```

To configure, compile, and install a new Linux kernel, Linux users must have a full understanding of the computer hardware. For Linux kernels with PPP, you should include at least the following kernel configuration options:

Loadable module support
    Also include the autoloading of kernel modules (kerneld) support.

TCP/IP networking

PPP

> May be built-in to the kernel, or may be a loadable module. PPP datagram compression capabilities are all loadable modules.

Standard/generic serial support

> These are the RS-232 interface drivers necessary for PPP. Multiport serial controllers, if available, can substitute for generic serial support.

Obviously, these options are in addition to many others required for the Linux computer's hardware.

Here are the commands necessary to create and install a new kernel in Slackware Linux:[*]

```
root# cd /usr/src/linux
root# make menuconfig
root# make install
root# make modules
root# make modules_install
```

More detailed instructions about building kernels appear in the *README* file in directory */usr/src/linux*. The Linux kernel *HOWTO* guide is another useful reference.

After installing a new kernel, you must reboot. The startup file */etc/rc.d/rc.modules* includes */sbin/modprobe ppp*, which loads the PPP module. The following kernel messages should appear, either onscreen or in system logs, confirming PPP support:

```
PPP: version 2.3.5 (demand dialing)
PPP line discipline registered.
```

Compiling PPP-2.3

Compiling PPP-2.3 requires executing **make** at the top of its software distribution directory:

```
root# pwd
/usr/src/ppp-2.3.5
root# make
cd chat; make  all
make[1]: Entering directory '/usr/src/ppp-2.3.5/chat'
cc -c -O2 -pipe -DTERMIOS -DSIGTYPE=void -UNO_SLEEP -DFNDELAY=O_NDELAY -o
chat.o chat.c
 . . .
```

---

[*] The installation procedure for ppp-2.3.5 and later versions of the Linux 2.0 series kernels may result in compilation errors for *ppp.c*. This requires you to forcefully copy ppp.c from the ppp-2.3.5 distribution to the kernel source tree. Furthermore, Linux version-checking statements in *ppp.c* pertaining to FREE_SKB may also require repair.

```
cc -O -D_linux_ -I../include -o pppstats pppstats.c
make[1]: Leaving directory '/usr/src/ppp-2.3.5/pppstats'
root#
```

Now we can install the software. As the root user, execute `make install`:

```
root# make install
cd chat; make BINDIR=/usr/sbin MANDIR=/usr/man  install
. . .
install -o 0 -g daemon -c -m 600 etc.ppp/chap-secrets /etc/ppp/chap-secrets
root#
```

The standard Slackware Linux installation directories for PPP-2.3 are */usr/sbin*, */usr/man*, and */etc/ppp*, for PPP binaries, manual pages, and other files, respectively. These directories vary for PPP-2.3 installations on other Unix platforms. The important executable files in */usr/sbin* are *pppd*, *chat*, and *pppstats*.

Linux Operating System Configuration

Before setting up Linux PPP-2.3, you should complete some preliminary Linux operating system configuration tasks in the areas of basic networking, serial interfaces, and syslog.

Linux base network configuration

Linux with TCP/IP capability requires a primary network interface. If Linux has a permanent network connection, a LAN interface (such as Ethernet `eth0`) is usually primary. However, many users have a network connection only when PPP is active. At other times, their computer is standalone, with no networking and no IP address. Standalone computers should set their loop-back interface as primary; if an unconnected Ethernet or an inactive PPP interface is primary, system hangs could result.

The menu-driven utility for configuring networks with Slackware Linux is `netconfig`. One question it asks is:

```
If you only plan to use TCP/IP through loopback, then your
IP address will be 127.0.0.1 and we can skip a lot of the
following questions.

Do you plan to ONLY use loopback?
```

Answering `yes` arranges the standalone network configuration. The resulting */etc/hosts* file resembles the following code:

```
root# cat /etc/hosts
127.0.0.1       localhost
127.0.0.1       myhost.mydomain.org myhost
root#
```

Much of the networking initialization code appearing in */etc/rc.d/rc.inet/* is disabled.

Here's a base networking configuration for Linux. Linux creates PPP interfaces ppp0, ppp1, etc. dynamically, whenever a PPP connection becomes active. However, no PPP interfaces should be active yet.

```
root# /sbin/ifconfig
lo          Link encap:Local Loopback
            inet addr:127.0.0.1  Bcast:127.255.255.255  Mask:255.0.0.0
            UP BROADCAST LOOPBACK RUNNING  MTU:3584  Metric:1
            RX packets:68 errors:0 dropped:0 overruns:0 frame:0
            TX packets:68 errors:0 dropped:0 overruns:0 carrier:0 coll:0
root#
```

Serial interfaces

Linux designates RS-232 serial interface devices as Table 6-1 shows. These are the standard devices for PCs with onboard serial interface hardware.

Table 6-1. Linux Serial Interface Devices for PCs

Linux Device File	DOS Equivalent	IRQ	I/O Address Base
/dev/ttyS0	COM1:	4	0x3f8
/dev/ttyS1	COM2:	3	0x2f8
/dev/ttyS2	COM3:	4	0x3e8
/dev/ttyS3	COM4:	3	0x2e8

Sharing IRQs can prevent the conflicting serial interfaces from functioning properly. To use *ttyS0* or *ttyS2*, for example, users must reconfigure their hardware physically to use nonconflicting IRQs or disable one of the devices. Then Linux requires serial device driver configuration to match its hardware settings. Users can use the setserial utility for this purpose.

It is absolutely essential to make sure IRQ and I/O address base assignment for a serial interface is conflict free and is consistent with what Linux believes. Users must not ignore this, even if they believe the serial interface is functioning. Hardware resource conflicts or inconsistencies can later manifest themselves as PPP problems and make troubleshooting extremely frustrating.

Syslog

Syslog is a Linux system resource responsible for recording messages pertaining to application and system activities. By default, the directory */var/log* maintains the message files. Syslog categorizes messages by facility name and priority. The configuration file, */etc/syslog.conf,* determines where and what the `syslogd` process does with incoming messages.

PPP-2.3 sends PPP debugging traces, conversational activity with remote systems, and other information, to Linux syslog. To view these messages, users must arrange `syslogd` to record them. The `pppd` and `chat` programs produce facility `daemon` and facility `local2` messages, respectively, at various priorities. Capturing these require the following lines in */etc/syslog.conf*:

```
daemon.debug                                /var/log/daemon
local2.debug                                /var/log/local2
```

A `kill -1` to the `syslogd` process is necessary for */etc/syslog.conf* changes to become effective.

Recording PPP-2.3 syslog messages is highly recommended, particularly for troubleshooting and for monitoring PPP activity.

Configuring chat

PPP-2.3 includes `chat`, a program that sends text strings to a serial interface, which is necessary for dialing out. It also interacts with any login and other prompts produced by a modem and a remote system. The desired result, after `chat` succeeds, is a connection to a remote system that is ready for PPP.

`chat` is not invoked directly. The main PPP program, `pppd`, is responsible for invoking `chat`, as follows, when it needs to set up a dial-out connection:

```
/usr/sbin/chat -v -f $HOME/.pppchat
```

This command is part of the startup options for `pppd`. `chat` converses with the serial interface `pppd` attaches to. When the `-v` option is present, syslog receives messages about this conversation. Option `-f` indicates a chat script appears in the named file. Alternatively, the script may be included as command-line arguments to `chat`, but this results in a lengthy and confusing line.

A `chat` script generally consists of strings to expect from and strings to send to a serial interface. Expect/send string pairs have spaces separating each string. `chat` also interprets certain pairs as command directives for `chat` itself. A typical *.pppchat* file is:

```
ABORT BUSY
ABORT "NO CARRIER"
"" "at&f1"
OK "at dt 1 700 555 4545"
CONNECT "\c"
name: myname
word: mypass
"isp>" "ppp\r\d\c"
```

This chat script implements the dialog shown in Figure 6-2. The first two lines abort the script immediately if chat receives the word BUSY or NO CARRIER. A modem that fails to connect responds with one of these. The first expect/send pair is "expect nothing" and "send at&f1," which resets the modem. All other string pairs follow this pattern. Strings following the CONNECT line are dial-in service-specific.

chat supports a collection of special characters and sequences that may be embedded in its strings. The use of double or single quotes groups contiguous strings and prevents chat from misinterpreting them as multiple expect/send pairs. By default, chat sends a carriage return after a send string, unless it ends with \c. The reply following a CONNECT is truly nothing at all. The command that starts PPP remotely is specifically ppp, carriage return (\r), delay one second (\d), suppress final carriage return (\c). Other special sequences appear in the chat manual page.

When developing a script, look for partial strings, such as name:, instead of User-name:. Sometimes, the initial characters remote servers send may become corrupt or lost in transit. The user's computer could miss the User part of the string it expects immediately after the modem connects. A one-second delay after sending ppp gives time for the remote PPP to start before the user sends the first PPP frame.

Since pppd invokes */usr/sbin/chat*, users should configure pppd and execute it to test and verify a chat script.

Configuring pppd

pppd requires information about its serial interface, PPP Link Control Protocol (LCP), IP Control Protocol (IPCP), authentication, and other options. We use the Linux standard RS-232 serial interface, */dev/ttyS0* (COM1:), with an attached modem as the dial-out device.

On Linux, the full path to pppd is */usr/sbin/pppd*. It collects configuration options from the global file */etc/ppp/options*, the file *.ppprc* in the user's home directory, and the command line. Since there are many options, users can place them all into their *.ppprc* file. To prevent potential confusion and pppd options conflicts, users should start with an empty */etc/ppp/options* file:

```
root# cd /etc/ppp
root# mv options options.orig
root# cp /dev/null options
root# ls -l options*
-rw-r--r--  1 root            0 Feb  3 03:18 options
-rw-r--r--  1 root            5 Feb  3 03:17 options.orig
root#
```

Now create a *.ppprc* file as required for the PPP sign-on procedures (earlier section):

```
# Log PPP control frames to syslog
debug
# Serial interface options
/dev/ttyS0 19200
lock
modem
crtscts
# Chat script
connect "/usr/sbin/chat -v -f $HOME/.pppchat"
# Link Control Protocol (LCP) options
asyncmap 00000000
# User name for PPP authentication
user myname
remotename isp
# IP Control Protocol (IPCP) options
noipdefault
# Use PPP peer as default gateway in system routing table
defaultroute
```

All options may be strung together into a single line, but we show them on separate lines for readability. The manual page, */usr/man/man8/pppd.8*, describes other option keywords that may be included in this file.

Unless otherwise specified, **pppd** requests address/control field compression, protocol field compression, MRU 1500, VJ compression, magic numbers, and several others. In the preceding *.ppprc*, a user is dialing out via the serial interface, */dev/ttyS0*, set at 19,200 bps. Hardware flow control, **crtscts**, and modem control, **modem**, apply. The program **chat** and its script file described previously arranges PPP startup at the remote end. As **noipdefault** indicates, the peer assigns both local and remote IP addresses. **defaultroute** arranges the PPP connection's far end to be the default gateway for all outgoing network traffic.

With PPP-2.3, PPP authentication as client requires the **user** and **remotename** options. The **user** option defines the authentication name. However, the **remotename** is only a local option to locate the correct password to use in the */etc/ppp/pap-secrets* file. Here's how *pap-secrets* looks:

```
root# cat /etc/ppp/pap-secrets
# Secrets for authentication using PAP
# client        server  secret          IP addresses
myname          isp     mypass          *
root#
```

The name and password to send is **myname** and **mypass**, respectively, whenever **pppd** connects to **isp** as the **remotename**. The * indicates any IP address is acceptable for this PPP connection.

Establishing the PPP Connection

Users execute **pppd** to initiate a PPP connection. Since configuration files reside in the user's home directory, it's important to execute **pppd** as that user:

    user$ **/usr/sbin/pppd**

If an error message appears, it indicates an immediate fatal problem. Other problems are evident only in log files. With the **debug** option enabled, **pppd** generates extended messages for Linux syslog that appear in */var/log/daemon*, in our sample configuration. **chat** messages appear in */var/log/local2*.

chat first controls the dial-up process. Successfully sending the string **ppp** at end of the script completes this process. Next is PPP LCP negotiations, which concludes with the exchange of LCP Config-ACK. PPP authentication follows; then IPCP negotiation establishes both IP addresses and VJ compression. The log excerpts showing this activity are:

```
user$ cat /var/log/local2
Apr  7 22:59:20 myhost chat[188]: abort on (BUSY)
. . .
Apr  7 22:59:20 myhost chat[188]: send (ppp^M\d)

user$ cat /var/log/daemon
Apr  7 22:59:16 myhost pppd[187]: pppd 2.3.5 started by user, uid 2001
Apr  7 22:59:23 myhost pppd[187]: Connect: ppp0 <--> /dev/ttyS0
. . .
Apr  7 22:59:23 myhost pppd[187]: rcvd [LCP ConfAck id=0x1 <asyncmap 0x0>
<magic 0xfc86d8b7> <pcomp> <accomp>]
Apr  7 22:59:24 myhost pppd[187]: sent [LCP ConfAck id=0x1c <mru 1500> <auth
pap> <magic 0xa358edcc> <pcomp> <accomp>]
. . .
Apr  7 22:59:24 myhost pppd[187]: sent [PAP AuthReq id=0x1 user="myname"
password="mypass"]
Apr  7 22:59:24 myhost pppd[187]: rcvd [PAP AuthAck id=0x1 ""]
. . .
Apr  7 22:59:24 myhost pppd[187]: sent [IPCP ConfAck id=0x1d <compress VJ 0f
01> <addr 192.168.1.34>]
Apr  7 22:59:24 myhost pppd[187]: rcvd [IPCP ConfAck id=0x2 <addr
192.168.1.35> <compress VJ 0f 01>]
. . .
Apr  7 22:59:24 myhost pppd[187]: local  IP address 192.168.1.35
Apr  7 22:59:24 myhost pppd[187]: remote IP address 192.168.1.34
. . .
```

After **pppd** reports its local and remote IP address, the PPP connection is up and ready for use.

An active PPP connection is a Linux systemwide resource. All users on the Linux computer can access this connection, even though a particular **user** initiated it.

Only the user who started pppd or root is allowed to shut down pppd and its corresponding connection.

When PPP is active, it alters the Linux computer's network configuration. The changes now include an additional active network interface, ppp0:

```
user$ /sbin/ifconfig -a
lo          Link encap:Local Loopback
. . .
ppp0        Link encap:Point-to-Point Protocol
            inet addr:192.168.1.35  P-t-P:192.168.1.34  Mask:255.255.255.0
            UP POINTOPOINT RUNNING NOARP MULTICAST  MTU:1500  Metric:1
            RX packets:19 errors:1 dropped:0 overruns:0 frame:0
            TX packets:20 errors:0 dropped:0 overruns:0 carrier:0 coll:0
. . .
```

Another item to check is a new default route, essential for reaching any Internet IP address destination. pppd automatically installs this route:

```
user$ netstat -rn
Kernel IP routing table
Destination     Gateway         Genmask         Flags  MSS Window  irtt Iface
192.168.1.34    0.0.0.0         255.255.255.255 UH     1500 0         0 ppp0
127.0.0.0       0.0.0.0         255.0.0.0       U      3584 0         0 lo
0.0.0.0         192.168.1.34 0.0.0.0            UG     1500 0         0 ppp0
user$
```

Now, any network activity via the PPP connection produces statistics visible with pppstat:

```
user$ /usr/sbin/pppstats
      IN  PACK VJCOMP  VJUNC  VJERR  |     OUT  PACK VJCOMP  VJUNC NON-VJ
     520    19     8      1      0  |     670    20    10      1      9
user$
```

This utility, as well as ifconfig, can detect errors at the serial interface communications layer.

Domain Name System

Networking applications, particularly the World Wide Web, refer to Internet sites by DNS name. Linux must resolve these names into IP addresses.

On Linux, DNS settings control the behavior of its name resolution libraries; these settings are entirely separate from PPP-2.3. DNS configuration requires an */etc/resolv.conf* file, listing DNS servers by IP address. An */etc/host.conf* file establishes when Linux uses DNS to resolve names. The netconfig utility can help users set up these files. DNS with PPP is covered more fully in Chapter 10, *Domain Name System*.

Shutting Down

PPP-2.3 normally remains active until the local user or the remote peer disconnects. If a user configures it to do so with an `idle` option in *.ppprc,* PPP-2.3 also disconnects automatically after a period of inactivity. Otherwise, the user that initiated the PPP connection can manually disconnect it when he and other users have completed their session with the Internet. This requires sending a kill signal to `pppd`:

```
user$ ps -auxww | grep ppp
user       236  0.0   0.4    936    316  p0 S   23:44   0:00 grep ppp
root       187  0.0   0.6    948    448  S0 S   22:59   0:00 /usr/sbin/pppd
user$ kill 187
user$ tail /var/log/daemon
. . .
Apr  7 23:46:29 myhost pppd[187]: Connection terminated.
Apr  7 23:46:30 myhost pppd[187]: Hangup (SIGHUP)
Apr  7 23:46:30 myhost pppd[187]: Exit.
user$
```

Before `pppd` terminates, it records disconnect messages in syslog. `pppd` also undoes other Linux system changes it made, if any. For example, it deletes the default route it previously created and removes the `ppp0` network interface.

Solaris PPP

Sun Microsystems Solaris features PPP software in its distribution. Solaris is available for both SPARC workstation platforms and IBM-compatible PCs. PPP configuration is similar for both, since the software is essentially the same.

Solaris PPP supports TCP/IP networking only. It has many configurable PPP options and multiple debug levels useful for tracing chat scripts, PPP frames, and IP datagrams. One feature of Solaris PPP is its on-demand connection capability. Users establish a connection by sending traffic that requires a PPP connection. If a connection is idle, Solaris automatically disconnects after a specified time.

In the next section, PPP is configured for Solaris 2.6 on a Sun Microsystem workstation. Most aspects of Solaris PPP configuration remain unchanged since Solaris 2.5.

Installation

PPP software components are included as part of the initial "Entire Distribution plus OEM support" or "Entire Distribution" Solaris installation. To check if PPP is present, use `pkginfo`. The following is the list of essential Solaris PPP packages:

```
user$ pkginfo
. . .
```

```
system         SUNWapppr       PPP/IP Asynchronous PPP daemon configuration files
system         SUNWapppu       PPP/IP Asynchronous PPP daemon and PPP login
service
system         SUNWbnur        Networking UUCP Utilities, (Root)
system         SUNWbnuu        Networking UUCP Utilities, (Usr)
 . . .
system         SUNWpppk        PPP/IP and IPdialup Device Drivers
 . . .
```

Dial-out PPP also requires the Networking UUCP Utilities packages. If there are questions concerning the installation integrity of existing packages, use the package check utility:

> user$ **pkgchk SUNWapppr SUNWapppu SUNWbnur SUNWbnuu SUNWpppk**

If any were omitted in the initial Solaris installation, there are several methods to incrementally install PPP components. The graphical **swmtool** can add Point-to-Point Protocol (**SUNWCppp**) and Basic Networking (**SUNWCnet**) software clusters. Together, these clusters include all the packages listed previously. Alternatively, the **pkgadd** utility individually installs each of the five packages listed. More detailed instructions about Solaris software management are available in the Solaris administrator guides and the manual pages. After installation, be sure to perform a reconfiguration boot. If they didn't already exist, this may be necessary to install PPP device files, including */dev/ipd, /dev/ipdptp,* and */dev/ipdcm.*

The main Solaris PPP program is */usr/sbin/aspppd.* This is the background PPP connections manager process. The main configuration file is */etc/asppp.cf,* but chat scripts belong in the UUCP directory, */etc/uucp.* **aspppd** logs its activities in */var/adm/log/asppp.log.* There are other files including kernel modules, device files, and startup files (in */etc/rc0.d* and */etc/rc2.d*), but you don't need to know these to use PPP. For reference, the important manual pages are **aspppd** and **ppp**.

Solaris Operating System Configuration

Some Solaris operating system configuration may be required to prepare Solaris for PPP. The tasks at hand are establishing a base TCP/IP networking configuration and setting up serial interfaces for dial-out. Users may also need to reconfigure any inbound login services, if they're active.

Base network configuration

A Solaris workstation requires a primary network interface. If the workstation is a permanent member of a LAN, it has a static name and IP address. The LAN interface (e.g., **le0**) is its primary network interface, and a PPP connection becomes an additional network interface.

For many dial-out users, the workstation has a network connection only when PPP is active. The loopback interface should be primary in this case. Although it's possible to arrange a PPP network interface as primary, I don't recommend this since the workstation could spontaneously initiate a connection, for reasons that aren't obvious.

To establish the loopback interface as primary, the Solaris workstation must have */etc/inet/hosts* and */etc/hostname.xx0* files, as follows:

```
root# cat /etc/inet/hosts
127.0.0.1       myhost localhost loghost
root# cat /etc/hostname.xx0
myhost
root#
```

There may also exist similar files such as *hostname.le0*, *hostname.hme0*, *hostname.be0*, etc., that set permanent IP addresses for the network interface device matching the file suffix. If these files are for unused or nonexistent network interfaces, they should be removed.

After rebooting with this network configuration, but before configuring PPP, the resulting network configuration is:

```
root# ifconfig -a
lo0: flags=849<UP,LOOPBACK,RUNNING,MULTICAST> mtu 8232
        inet 127.0.0.1 netmask ff000000
root#
```

Solaris may start TCP/IP routing protocol daemons *in.routed* and *in.rdisc* at boot time. These aren't needed nor desirable for the dial-out PPP arrangement assumed here. Leaving them active can trigger unnecessary PPP connections and may cause TCP/IP routing complications. You can edit the file */etc/rc2.d/S69inet* and disable *in.routed* and *in.rdisc*. Alternatively, renaming the executable files also prevents them from starting at boot time. Another daemon that can trigger unnecessary PPP activity is the name services cache daemon, nscd. Unnecessary PPP activity occurs if nscd requires the Internet to cache DNS lookup results, for example. You may wish to disable this daemon as well.

Serial interfaces

On Solaris workstations, serial interface device files have names like */dev/term/a* and */dev/term/b*. Solaris for PCs include */dev/tty00* (COM1:) and */dev/tty01* (COM2:). The */dev/tty01* name may be missing on some PCs equipped with a second serial interface. In this case, users can edit */platform/i86pc/kernel/drv/asy.conf* and enable the following lines:

```
name="asy" class="sysbus" interrupts=12,3 reg=0x2f8,0,0
ioaddr=0x2f8;
```

Then perform a reconfiguration reboot or execute both `drvconfig` and `dev-links` utilities.

The device files with */dev/tty* prefixes are for dial-in. If there are any inbound login services active (e.g., `ttymon` processes) and bound to these device files, they should be disabled for now. Inbound login can interfere with dial-out connections, depending on how it's set up. The dial-out PPP devices are */dev/cua/a* and */dev/cua/b*, which should already exist. Improper permissions settings for them can also interfere with dial-out PPP. For now, dial-out device ownership and permissions may be set as follows:

```
root# chown uucp:uucp /dev/cua/a; chmod 666 /dev/cua/a
root# chown uucp:uucp /dev/cua/b; chmod 666 /dev/cua/b
```

Dial-in and dial-out devices enable one to lock out the other when a serial interface is used for both services. The dial-out device is special since it may be opened without a carrier detect signal, which is important for controlling modems that are still "on-hook."

UUCP Chat

Solaris PPP shares the same chat facilities as UUCP for initializing communications through a serial interface. UUCP chat scripts are responsible for issuing command strings and responses that prepare a serial connection for PPP (or even UUCP).

Setting up chat scripts requires editing several files residing in `/etc/uucp`. These files are the repository for many chat scripts that establish communications with many different remote systems:

```
user$ cd /etc/uucp
user$ ls
Config          Dialcodes       Limits          Sysfiles
Devconfig       Dialers         Permissions     Systems
Devices         Grades          Poll            remote.unknown
user$
```

Various portions of a single UUCP chat script reside in several different files. After a modem connects, the information necessary for interacting with a specific remote system appears in the *Systems* file. Modem initialization and dialing strings for many different modems are in the *Dialers* file. And, *Devices* associates a specific modem to a specific serial interface device file. All three files are essential for dial-out PPP.

Systems, Devices, and Dialers files appear in Figure 6-3 for use with the assumptions in the previous section "Dial-out Commands to Initiate PPP." By carefully examining this example, you should be able to develop your own UUCP chat script.

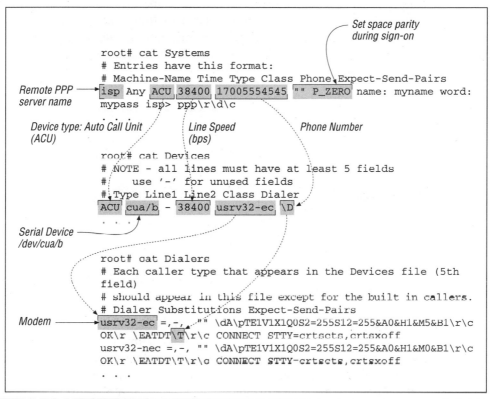

```
                                                          ┌── Set space parity
                                                          │   during sign-on
                    root# cat Systems
                    # Entries have this format:
                    # Machine-Name Time Type Class Phone Expect-Send-Pairs
Remote PPP ──────▶ isp Any ACU 38400 17005554545 "" P_ZERO name: myname word:
server name         mypass isp> ppp\r\d\c

   Device type: Auto Call Unit        Line Speed            Phone Number
   (ACU)                              (bps)

                    root# cat Devices
                    # NOTE - all lines must have at least 5 fields
                    #   use '-' for unused fields
                    # Type Line1 Line2 Class Dialer
                    ACU cua/b - 38400 usrv32-ec \D

Serial Device ──────
/dev/cua/b

                    root# cat Dialers
                    # Each caller type that appears in the Devices file (5th
                    field)
                    # should appear in this file except for the built in callers.
                    # Dialer Substitutions Expect-Send-Pairs
Modem ───────────▶ usrv32-ec =,-, "" \dA\pTE1V1X1Q0S2=255S12=255&A0&H1&M5&B1\r\c
                    OK\r \EATDT\T\r\c CONNECT STTY=crtscts,crtsxoff
                    usrv32-nec =,-, "" \dA\pTE1V1X1Q0S2=255S12=255&A0&H1&M0&B1\r\c
                    OK\r \EATDT\T\r\c CONNECT STTY-crtscts,crtsxoff
                    . . .
```

Figure 6-3. UUCP chat, System, Devices, and Dialer files

Solaris PPP requests a connection to a remote system by name. If this name is `isp`, then UUCP chat must find `isp` as an entry in the *Systems* file. This entry begins with a telephone number, the dial-out device type, and the line speed the user wishes to use to make the serial connection.

The dial-out device type and line speed must match one or more entries appearing in the *Devices* file. The match shown in the figure indicates that dial-out PPP to `isp` occurs through serial interface */dev/cua/b*. This interface has attached error correcting, U. S. Robotics V.32 modem, named `usrv32-ec`. Chat interacts with this modem according to instructions for `usrv32-ec` appearing in *Dialers*.

If the modem successfully connects, chat returns to the *Systems* file and interacts directly with remote system `isp` according to the script information, if any, following the telephone number. At the successful conclusion of this script, PPP communications may begin.

UUCP chat file entries contain sections with strings to expect from a serial interface and strings to send to a serial interface. Each of these expect/send strings pairs can include escape character sequences for substituting telephone numbers, inserting special characters, or invoking special functions. Table 6-2 shows the ones appearing in Figure 6-3.

Table 6-2. UUCP Escape Character Sequences (Partial)

Sequence	Meaning
\d	Delay two seconds
\p	Pause, 1/4 to 1/2 second
\r	Carriage return (CR)
\n	Line feed (LF)
\s	Space character
\c	Suppress carriage return at end of string
\D	Substitute telephone number string
\T	Substitute telephone number after translating it using the *Dialcodes* file
\E	Turn on echo checking

With Solaris PPP, UUCP chat can also set serial interface parameters. Special keywords that appear as send strings perform this function. In the *Systems* file, we include an "expect nothing" and "send P_ZERO." Chat doesn't send this string; instead, it sets the serial interface to 8 bits and zero parity. The `usrv32-ec` entry in the *Dialers* file has a `STTY=rtscts,crtsxoff` directive as a send string. These are serial interface parameters that enable hardware flow control. In UUCP chat script files, any parameter the Solaris `stty` utility supports can follow `STTY=`.

Now that we have a chat script configured for PPP, the next step is testing it. The `cu` command is useful for this purpose:

```
user$ cu -d -L isp
```

After it executes chat scripts residing in */etc/uucp* to set up a serial connection, `cu` functions as a terminal emulator. Here, we request `cu` to connect with `isp` in the *Systems* file. A `-d` enables debugging and shows chat activity. By default, `cu` executes only chat script portions in the *Devices* and *Dialers* files. A `-L` (login) causes it to also execute the portion in *Systems* that interacts with the remote system. The debug output helps isolate chat problems, if any.

For further details regarding UUCP, consult such books as *Using and Managing UUCP* by Ed Ravin, Tim O'Reilly, Dale Dougherty, and Grace Todino, also published by O'Reilly & Associates. The Solaris *Answerbook* includes more specific instructions and a list of escape characters that can be included in the UUCP files.

Configuring asppp

Solaris requires an active */usr/sbin/aspppd* for PPP to function. A single configuration file, */etc/asppp.cf*, defines the characteristics for all PPP connections available to this workstation. As long as this configuration file is valid, Solaris automatically starts asppppd at boot time.

The file */etc/asppp.cf* consists of two parts. At the top are one or more ifconfig commands that establish PPP network interfaces. These interfaces may have names ranging from ipdptp0 to ipdptp63, and many can exist simultaneously. Each ifconfig statement at minimum must include plumb, a local IP address for the PPP connection, a remote IP address, and up. Additional options to ifconfig appear in its manual page. The second part of the configuration file are path sections. Each path section describes options for a PPP connection to a remote system.

For the configuration assumptions in the previous section, "PPP Sign-on Procedures," we need to define a PPP network interface with dummy IP addresses and one set of PPP options for the remote system named isp. Here is a suitable */etc/asppp.cf* file:

```
root# cat /etc/asppp.cf

ifconfig ipdptp0 plumb 1.2.3.4 1.2.3.5 up

path
# PPP network interface
        interface ipdptp0
# Name of remote system, the PPP peer, as defined in /etc/uucp/Systems
        peer_system_name isp
# LCP options
        ipcp_async_map 00000000
# PPP authentication with PAP
        will_do_authentication pap
        pap_id myname
        pap_password mypass
# IPCP, permit our peer to establish our local IP address
        negotiate_address on
# TCP/IP, use PPP peer as default gateway
        default_route
# Miscellaneous
        inactivity_timeout 600
        debug_level 8
root#
```

A path section consists of the word path followed by option keywords and values. These words are strung together with whitespace (blanks, tabs, newlines). For readability, we include one option and its value, if any, per line. Each path requires the interface and peer_system_name keywords. The values of these associate the PPP network interface ipdptp0 to the remote system isp in the UUCP *Systems* file.

The remaining lines in the path section define PPP, TCP/IP, and other miscellaneous settings. A complete list of the available option keywords are in the manual page for aspppd. Unless otherwise specified, aspppd automatically negotiates with its peer for PPP magic numbers, protocol field compression, address/control field compression, and MRU 1500.

default_route is included explicitly. When PPP is up, Solaris PPP arranges the IP address of the remote system, isp, to become the default gateway for this workstation's outgoing traffic. This IP address is not known until after the PPP connection is active, and it may also change for every new PPP connection. Thus, the default_route option creates and destroys the default route entry in the routing table for each PPP connect and disconnect cycle. If the remote system isp requires our PPP authentication credentials, will_do_authentication pap indicates this workstation has a name and password it can respond with. Debugging is set at a level high enough to trace PPP frames. The connection inactivity time-out is 10 minutes (default is 2 minutes). This can be set to 0 for no time-out. We are assuming the PPP peer, isp, assigns the IP addresses for both endpoints of the PPP connection. Solaris PPP disallows IP address changes at the local end of ipdptp0 (shown initially as 1.2.3.4) unless the negotiate_address on option appears. This permits ipdptp0 to inherit a new local IP address the dial-in server assigns at PPP connect time.

If the process */usr/sbin/aspppd* isn't already active, you must either reboot the workstation or execute the following command, with the start argument (you can use stop to stop PPP):

```
root# /etc/init.d/asppp start
```

This executes all the ifconfig commands in */etc/asppp.cf* and starts aspppd. If aspppd is already active, you must issue a kill -1 to aspppd, causing it to reload any path section changes in its configuration file:

```
root# ps -e | grep aspppd
   697 pts/0    0:05 aspppd
root# kill -1 697
root# tail /var/adm/log/asppp.log
16:48:14 catch_sighup: HUP caught
16:48:14 parse_config_file: Successful configuration
root#
```

Establishing the PPP Connection

Solaris PPP remains idle until a user routes outgoing IP datagrams to the workstation's PPP network interface. aspppd initiates the PPP connection, as necessary when this happens. At this point in our Solaris PPP configuration, accessing a random Internet IP address won't initiate a PPP connection. The problem is that this Solaris workstation doesn't know that IP datagrams for an Internet IP address requires use of the PPP network interface, ipdptp0. In other words, there is no TCP/IP route to the Internet.

To initiate PPP, users must first inspect the current settings for ipdptp0. The ifconfig utility serves this purpose:

```
user$ ifconfig ipdptp0
ipdptp0: flags=8d1<UP,POINTOPOINT,RUNNING,NOARP,MULTICAST> mtu 8232
        inet 1.2.3.4 --> 1.2.3.5 netmask ff000000
user$
```

Notice ipdptp0 is already UP even though its modem isn't yet active. To actually initiate PPP, we can route IP datagrams through ipdptp0 with a ping to the dummy IP address, 1.2.3.5. This is the current, remote (far end) IP address for ipdptp0, even though PPP is not yet active.

```
user$ ping 1.2.3.5
```

The ping triggers a series of events that appear in the log file */var/adm/log/asppp.log*. The events include UUCP chat, PPP LCP, authentication, and NCP transactions. Any errors aspppd encounters are also recorded to aid debugging. Here are some log excerpts for a successful connection:

```
user$ cd /var/adm/log
user$ cat asppp.log
16:23:33 process_ipd_msg: ipdptp0 needs connection
conn(isp)
Trying entry from '/etc/uucp/Systems' - device type ACU.
. . .
expect: (CONNECT)
^M^JCONNECTgot it
STTY crtscts,crtsxoff
. . .
16:24:01 000138 ipdptp0 PPP DIAG OPEN
16:24:01 000139 ipdptp0 SEND PPP ASYNC 23 Octets LCP Config-Req  ID=1f LEN=18
MRU=1500 MAG#=ffab974e ProtFCOMP AddrCCOMP
16:24:02 000140 ipdptp0 RECEIVE PPP ASYNC 23 Octets LCP Config-ACK  ID=1f
LEN=18 MRU=1500 MAG#=ffab974e ProtFCOMP AddrCCOMP
. . .
16:24:04 000150 ipdptp0 RECEIVE PPP ASYNC 21 Octets IP_NCP Config-ACK  ID=21
LEN=16 VJCOMP MAXSID=15 Sid-comp-OK IPADDR=166.72.92.184
16:24:04 start_ip: IP up on interface ipdptp0, timeout set for 600 seconds
. . .
```

Examining the PPP network interface ipdptp0 confirms that the peer (remote server, isp) has indeed negotiated changes to all the initial dummy IP addresses:

```
user$ ifconfig ipdptp0
ipdptp0: flags=8d1<UP,POINTOPOINT,RUNNING,NOARP,MULTICAST> mtu 1500
```

```
        inet 166.72.92.184 --> 204.146.252.97 netmask ff000000
user$
```

The **asppp.cf** configuration instructs **aspppd** to install a default route. As we expected, this route references the remote IP address for **ipdptp0**:

```
user$ netstat -rn
Routing Table:
  Destination          Gateway              Flags  Ref   Use   Interface
  -------------------- -------------------- -----  ----- ------ ---------
  127.0.0.1            127.0.0.1            UH     0     13    lo0
  204.146.252.97       166.72.92.184       UH     2     0     ipdptp0
  default              204.146.252.97      UG     0     0
user$
```

This Solaris workstation now has an active PPP connection and the TCP/IP routes necessary for users to communicate with the Internet. If an idle time-out occurs after 10 minutes, **aspppd** removes the default route and closes the connection.

Reinstating the same PPP connection requires routing another IP datagram to the current **ipdptp0** far-end IP address. Users may obtain this information again with the **ifconfig** utility. Notice this IP address has changed since the last successful PPP connection. Now, it's necessary to initiate PPP with a **ping 204.146.252.97**.

On-demand PPP connections

On-demand PPP means that the workstation automatically establishes PPP whenever users access any Internet IP address. For this to work, **aspppd** must detect outbound Internet IP datagrams at a PPP network interface, even if the PPP connection is down.

A permanent default route can send all Internet traffic to a PPP network interface. This eliminates the need for a dynamic route. Thus, users must remove all **default_route** options in the */etc/asppp.cf* configuration file. The permanent route can be the same as the one the **default_route** option creates:

```
root# route add default 204.146.252.97 1
```

This permanent route functions correctly only as long as the remote IP address for the PPP network interface remains static. Alternatively, users can also install a default route as follows:

```
root# ifconfig ipdptp0
ipdptp0: flags=8d1<UP,POINTOPOINT,RUNNING,NOARP,MULTICAST> mtu 1500
        inet 166.72.92.184 --> 204.146.252.97 netmask ff000000
root# route add default 166.72.92.184 0
```

It's important to create this route with a zero metric and with the current local IP address of **ipdptp0**. This insures the default route always points to the PPP interface, **ipdptp0**, even if its local IP address changes later.

If the workstation user creates the file */etc/defaultrouter* with an IP address as its contents, Solaris can install a permanent default route at boot time. The route must refer to `ipdptp0` local IP address at boot time. In this case, `1.2.3.4` is the address to include in this file:

```
root# echo "1.2.3.4" > /etc/defaultrouter
```

It's also necessary to edit the startup file */etc/rc2.d/S69inet*. The `route add default` statements appearing in this file need zero metric arguments. The usual metric is one, which is the normal case for default routes to gateways residing on LANs. This won't work for this PPP example, since we want the default route to point to the workstation's own PPP network interface.

With on-demand PPP, users must beware that if the PPP connection is down, it can take as much as one minute to connect. This may cause application programs accessing the Internet to time out and fail. Once PPP is up, users can try their application again, which should now behave normally.

Domain Name System

A Solaris PPP connection isn't too useful if user applications (Telnet, web) can't resolve names of Internet sites to their IP addresses.

Solaris DNS name resolution requires a */etc/resolv.conf* file containing IP addresses for DNS servers. Once users create this file, Solaris must know when to perform DNS lookups when resolving names. This requires the keyword `dns` in the name services switch file, */etc/nsswitch.conf*. Chapter 10 presents more details about DNS and Solaris.

Shutting Down

Solaris PPP maintains an inactivity timer and automatically shuts down a PPP connection that has remained inactive for a preconfigured time. The `inactivity_timeout` option in the *asppp.cf* file sets this time.

To manually terminate PPP connections before inactivity timers expire, users can send a hang-up signal to `aspppd`, causing it to reset:

```
root# ps -e | grep aspppd
  699 ?        0:07 aspppd
root# kill -HUP 699
```

However, this disconnect is temporary because `aspppd` can still reestablish PPP connections on demand. Permanently disabling all PPP service requires permanently terminating the `aspppd` process itself:

```
root# /etc/init.d/asppp stop
```

Windows 3.1

Microsoft Windows 3.1 doesn't include built-in networking. Therefore, Windows 3.1 PPP products add significant "plumbing." These include software components that implement a TCP/IP protocol stack, drivers for networking hardware and libraries that present the Winsock applications programming interface (API).

The Winsock API enables third-party programmers to develop user applications software (Telnet, FTP, etc.) that are compatible with a PPP product. In other words, Netscape Navigator is compatible with any number of Windows 3.1 PPP products that include Chameleon (Netmanage), PC-NFSpro (SunSoft), PC/TCP OnNet (FTP Software), Trumpet Winsock (Trumpet Software International), and others. PPP networking products must provide *winsock.dll*. This dynamically loadable library presents the Winsock API for applications accessing network services.

Windows 3.1 is dated, and many of its users have either migrated to Windows 95, Windows 98, or Windows NT. The later-generation Windows maintain the Winsock API model and, in fact, include the necessary Winsock libraries. Thus, many network applications that ran under Windows 3.1 should continue to operate under Windows NT/95.

Windows 98 (and 95)

Microsoft Windows 98 includes dial-up networking (DUN) as an integral component of the operating system. DUN supports PPP access to TCP/IP networks, in addition to Novell IPX/SPX networks and those using NetBEUI. In fact, users can use all three simultaneously with a single PPP connection, if the PPP peer and its remote network supports all these protocols. Note the DUN instructions presented here focus only on TCP/IP.

Microsoft Windows 98 DUN is not significantly different from Windows 95 DUN. Much of the description for Windows 98 also applies to Windows 95.

The latest, and perhaps the last, DUN software for all Windows 95 releases is DUN upgrade 1.3. This upgrade is available for download as *msdun13.exe*, free of charge, from the Microsoft web site. DUN 1.3 patches bugs and provides enhancements to the DUN in the original Windows 95 retail release. I suggest all dial-out PPP users obtain this upgrade before proceeding.

Installation

Windows 98 consists of many optional operating-system components users may select (or deselect) at installation time. Users can verify whether DUN components are installed by selecting `Control Panel` → `Add/Remove Programs` →

Windows Setup → Communications. The following should appear with a check in their checkboxes:

- Dial-Up Networking
- Phone Dialer

If any of these items are missing, users can add them by clicking the corresponding checkbox and then "OK" the changes. Windows 98 then prompts for its CD-ROM installation media and installs the files for the missing items.

Dial-out PPP also requires Windows 98 networking components. In turn, networking requires one or more network adapters and drivers. The current setup status for Windows 98 networking appears by selecting Control Panel → Network → Configuration. Items necessary for PPP are:

- Client for Microsoft Networks
- Dial-Up Adapter
- TCP/IP

A Dial-Up Adapter is a network adapter that operates over a serial interface with an attached modem. If this adapter is missing, users should select Add → Adapter. Dial-Up Adapter appears under the manufacturer Microsoft. Select it to install.

Each Windows 98 network adapter may have one or more network layer protocols bound to it. Dial-out PPP to the Internet requires TCP/IP. If TCP/IP is missing, then select Add → Protocol. TCP/IP also appears under manufacturer Microsoft. Users must select this and any others as necessary. After installation, these protocols appear in the main Network setup window.

Client for Microsoft Networks provides access to network disk drives, printer, and others services available on remote Microsoft Windows NT/98 servers. It's not essential to have this, since basic Internet connectivity doesn't require it. I recommend installing it to obtain the password caching feature for DUN. This enables Windows 98 to remember sign-on names and passwords users need for dial-out PPP.

Serial Interface and Modem Setup

The first resource users should set up on their PC is a serial interface and modem. The Windows 98 control panel shows a Modems icon. This invokes the main Modems Properties window that appears in Figure 6-4. Modems Properties manage default settings for all serial interfaces and modems attached to the PC.

Users can install a new modem by selecting Add in Modem Properties. Windows 98 can either try to detect the modem model or let the user specify this

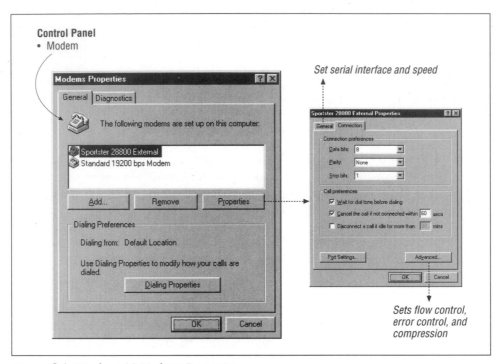

Figure 6-4. Windows 98 Modems Properties

manually. It's important to correctly identify the modem, since Windows 98 needs to know how to control it. Furthermore, the modem model establishes the initial settings for its serial interface.

Modems Properties also includes a **Dialing Properties** button. This establishes dialing procedures for the user's telephone service. Another **Properties** button is available for each installed modem. This controls serial interface and related modem settings. There are a total of four properties per modem definition. These are:

General tab

Establishes which serial interface the user connected her modem to. This tab also sets the serial interface bits per second (shown as **Maximum Speed**) for PC to modem communications. Set this to 57600 or 115200 for 28.8-Kbps data compressing modems.

Connection tab

Data bits, parity, and stop bits settings for the serial interface are here. For PPP, these should be 8 bits, no parity, and 1 stop bit. Dialing time-outs also appear in this window. Users who check **Cancel the call if not connected within** should make sure the delay is at least a minute.

Port Settings button

> This manages the buffers available on the 16550 UART chip (see Chapter 2, *Serial Interfaces and Modems*). The default settings are appropriate for most dial-out PPP configurations.

Advanced button

> Configures the modem to use error control (e.g., V.42) and data compression (e.g., V.42bis). Users should enable these for modems that support these features. Use flow control should be (RTS/CTS) whenever possible. In Windows 95, there is also a checkbox to Record a log file. If enabled, a *modemlog.txt* file (usually *c:\windows\modemlog.txt*) in the Windows 95 root directory records a history of modem strings Windows 95 sends and responses it receives.

> Windows 98 always records a history of modem strings it sends and responses it receives in a modem log file residing in the Windows 98 root directory. The name of this file corresponds to the modem description with a *.log* extension. This log is particularly useful for troubleshooting modem interaction problems. The checkbox, Append to Log, controls whether Windows 98 overwrites or appends the log file for each new PPP call.

Users should beware that Modems Properties mostly set defaults only. A dial-out PPP configuration users define for a specific remote server can override many of the settings that appear in Modems Properties.

Dial-up Adapter Setup

The dial-up network adapter and the TCP/IP protocol that's bound to it, has numerous settings users can access with the Network icon in the Windows 98 control panel. Figure 6-5 illustrates some of these configuration windows.

Nearly all the settings that appear in Dial-Up Adapters Properties should remain at their defaults. The only exception is the setting for recording PPP frame traces, useful for debugging. The Dial-Up Adapter Properties settings are as follows:

Driver Type tab

> These are Windows 98 system-specific settings. Be sure to set to Enhanced mode (32 bit and 16 bit) NDIS driver.

Bindings tab

> On this list are the network protocols available for the dial-up adapter. At minimum, TCP/IP should appear with a check in the checkbox. Other network protocols may be enabled too, for users accessing remote networks that require them.

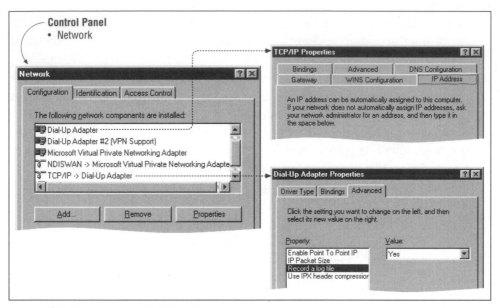

Figure 6-5. Windows 95, Dial-Up Adapter Properties

Advanced tab

> This tab includes the property `Record a log file`. Setting this to yes causes Windows 98 to create the file *ppplog.txt* (usually *c:\windows\ppplog.txt*) in the Windows 98 root directory. This file records PPP negotiation activities with a peer, useful for troubleshooting PPP problems.

Another collection of network control panel settings for the dial-up adapter appear under `TCP/IP Properties` (Figure 6-5). There are six tabs for items including `IP Address`, `WINS`, and others. The presence of these `TCP/IP Properties` is a confusing and annoying feature of Windows 98. Equivalent and duplicate settings appear later when users configure a dial-out PPP connection. It's critically important for users to leave all dial-up adapter `TCP/IP Properties` settings here untouched (leave as defaults) in the `Network` control panel. If users inadvertently change something here, they interfere with DUN's ability to dynamically configure these items during dial-out PPP. To prevent difficult to troubleshoot problems later, the `TCP/IP Properties` here should show the following:

- `IP Address` tab must show `Obtain an IP address automatically`.

- `WINS Configuration` tab must show `Disable WINS Resolution`.

- `Gateway` tab must show blank entries.

- `Bindings` tab may show Windows 98 network client services associations to the TCP/IP protocol. Leave these as is.

- **Advanced** tab doesn't have any settings. However, a checkbox enabled for **Set this protocol to be the default protocol** may appear.

- **DNS Configuration** tab must show **Disable DNS**.

Configuring Dial-out PPP Connections

Users manage PPP connections through the Windows 98 **Dial-Up Networking** folder. The default locations to access this folder are the **My Computer** icon on the desktop, and the **Start** menu (**Programs → Accessories → Dial-Up Networking**). Figure 6-6 shows this folder.

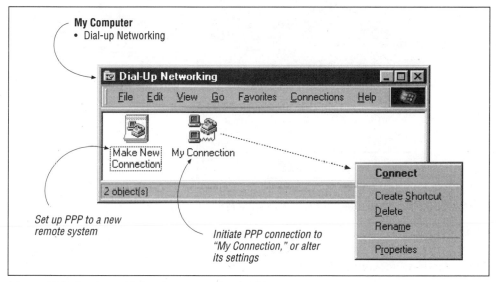

Figure 6-6. Windows 95, Dial-Up Networking folder

Inside this folder is the icon **Make New Connection**. Users double-click this icon if they wish to configure dial-out PPP to a new remote system. Windows 98 asks for the modem, the name of the remote system, and its telephone number. This procedure creates a new icon in the name of the remote system, such as **My Connection**, that retains all the settings necessary to initiate a PPP connection to it.

Right-clicking **My Connection** shows a menu that includes **Properties**. This invokes the windows (Figure 6-7) necessary to configure dial-out PPP. The **General** tab lists all the general information Windows 98 prompted for, when it initially created the **My Connection** icon.

One button appears in this tab: **Configure**. This presents modem properties similar to the ones from the Windows 98 control panel (Figure 6-4). Although these

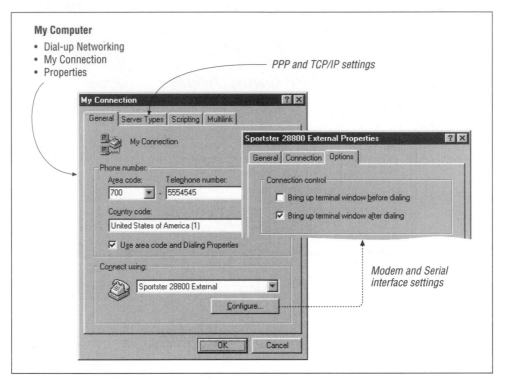

Figure 6-7. Windows 98 dial-out PPP connection properties

serial interface modem settings appear identical to those in the control panel, these settings are really separate. They override the control panel settings whenever the user initiates a PPP connection to **My Connection**.

An additional **Options** tab can enable a terminal window during the PPP connect process. This lets users interactively enter login and other commands necessary to start PPP on the remote system. The previous section "Dial-out Commands to Initiate PPP" shows the interactive steps. Later, Windows 98 dial-up scripts can automate these steps. For dial-in services that can automatically detect PPP communications, dial-out PPP users should not enable terminal windows.

PPP settings

The **Server Types** tab (Figure 6-8) configures PPP and other network layer protocols users may choose. The first item is the dial-up server type Windows 98 is connecting to. Obviously, the correct choice is PPP. The other server types appearing in the pull-down list are for obsolete and proprietary serial line protocols.

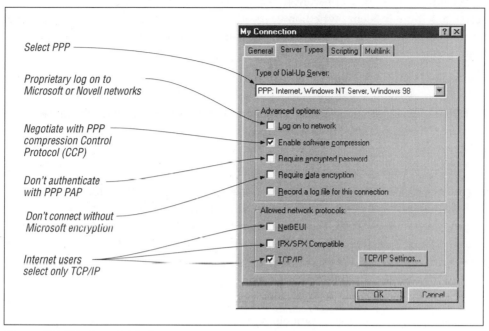

Figure 6-8. Windows 95 dial-out PPP settings

One of the advanced options is **Enable software compression**. This tells Windows 98 to negotiate the PPP compression control protocol (CCP) with its peer. Data compression is active only if both endpoints understand and agree to:

* STAC option 4
* Microsoft Point-to-Point Compression Protocol (MPPC)

PPP compression methods are independent of modem compression. **Enable software compression** may be enabled, even if Windows 98 fails to negotiate it with its peer. However, if it causes fatal PPP negotiation failures due to peer incompatibilities and bugs, you should disable this option.

The forms of PPP authentication (see Chapter 12, *Authentication*) Windows 98 supports are:

* PAP
* CHAP
* Microsoft CHAP (MS-CHAP)
* Shiva PAP (SPAP)

With **Require encrypted password**, Windows 98 agrees to authenticate with any method, except PAP. If a remote system requests PAP, Windows 98 refuses. This is a precaution designed to prevent transmission of passwords in clear text through a serial link and modem. Whether users can enable this feature depends on the remote system. **Require encrypted password** is incompatible with dial-up peers that absolutely require PAP for access.

Windows 98 also supports data encryption over PPP connections using a Microsoft encryption algorithm. The **Require data encryption** option is a security feature that guarantees that communication occurs only if both endpoints can understand and use Microsoft encryption. This option is only compatible with Microsoft PPP implementations. Enabling this feature can cause failures when users wish to communicate with PPP peers that don't use Microsoft software.

The **Record a log file for this connection** enables PPP trace logging. The PPP trace logs are almost identical to those users can obtain by enabling **Record a log file** in the **Dial-Up Adapter Properties** (Figure 6-5). The difference is that this setting enables logging for a PPP connection to this specific remote server. In contrast, **Dial-Up Adapter Properties** are global settings that affect all Windows 98 dial-out PPP connections.

The last group of settings in Figure 6-8 is **Allowed network protocols**. Windows 98 supports all the protocols shown with PPP, assuming the appropriate drivers have been installed. Users should select only the ones applicable to the remote system they're dialing into. Internet users should only select TCP/IP and disable the others. Sometimes, PPP connections can fail if Windows 98 requests the use of network protocols unrecognized by the remote system.

TCP/IP settings

The **Server types** tab includes a **TCP/IP Settings** button. This accesses TCP/IP settings (Figure 6-9) that are active when dialing out to **My Connection**. Users must adjust these settings to fit requirements of the remote system they're dialing into.

At the top are the settings concerned with how Windows 98 acquires its IP address for PPP. With the assumptions in the section "Dial-out Commands to Initiate PPP," the proper setting is **Server assigned IP address**. The PC's local IP address is likely to change with each new dial-out connection. If the PC should have a static IP address, you can enter this in the **Specify an IP address** setting.

The second group of settings determines IP addresses of DNS servers. DNS resolves Internet site names to their IP address. Usually, users must configure DNS servers explicitly as shown, with DNS IP addresses of their ISP. WINS also provides name resolution, but it's proprietary and specific to Microsoft networks. There is a setting that allows the dial-in PPP server to assign DNS and WINS name server addresses. However, this functions only with remote systems that imple-

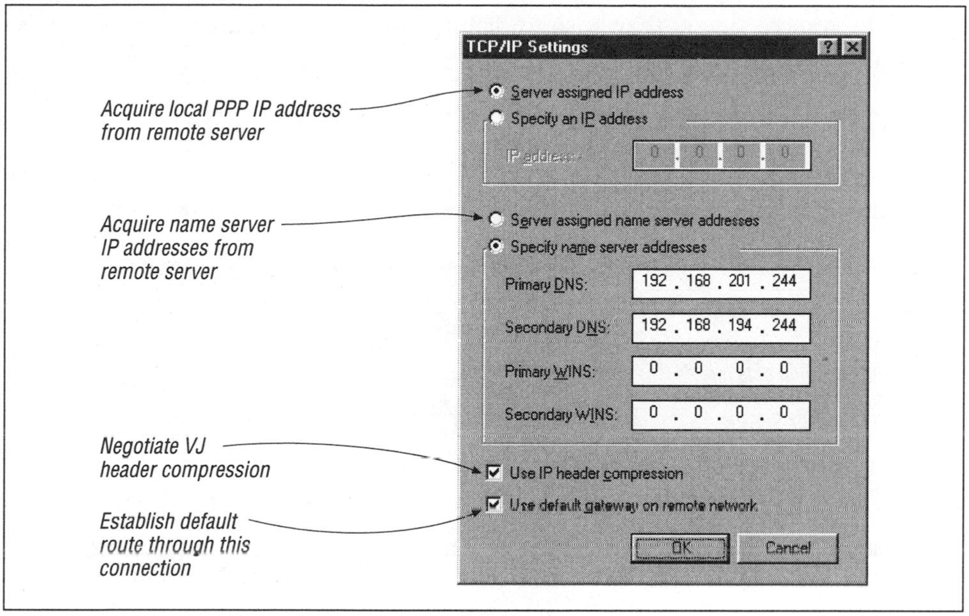

Figure 6-9. *Windows 95 TCP/IP settings for dial-out PPP*

ment Microsoft's PPP extensions for DNS. Chapter 10 describes this extension in further detail. `Server assigned name server addresses` won't function with strictly standards-compliant PPP peers and others that don't support Microsoft features.

An additional option is `Use IP header compression`. IP header compression is another name for negotiating VJ compression in PPP. This compresses IP datagram headers only. Unlike the PPP CCP setting, it doesn't manipulate user data in any way. It's desirable to enable `Use IP header compression` often, since it reduces TCP/IP overhead. Users should disable this if their dial-up peer has a faulty VJ compression implementation or if there are PPP problems connecting.

`Use default gateway on remote network` arranges the default route for outbound IP datagrams to be this PPP connection. Users who have only a single network adapter (the dial-up adapter) must route all outgoing traffic through it. The circumstance requiring users to disable this default route occurs when users have additional network adapters (e.g., Ethernet) that connect them to the Internet or other TCP/IP networks.

Establishing a Connection

Windows 98 dial-up networking normally requires users to initiate a PPP connection first, before they can access Internet resources. Users must first access the

`Dial-Up Networking` folder (Figure 6-6). They then double-click the icon representing the remote system they wish to dial-in. This causes a `Connect To` window to appear, as Figure 6-10 shows.

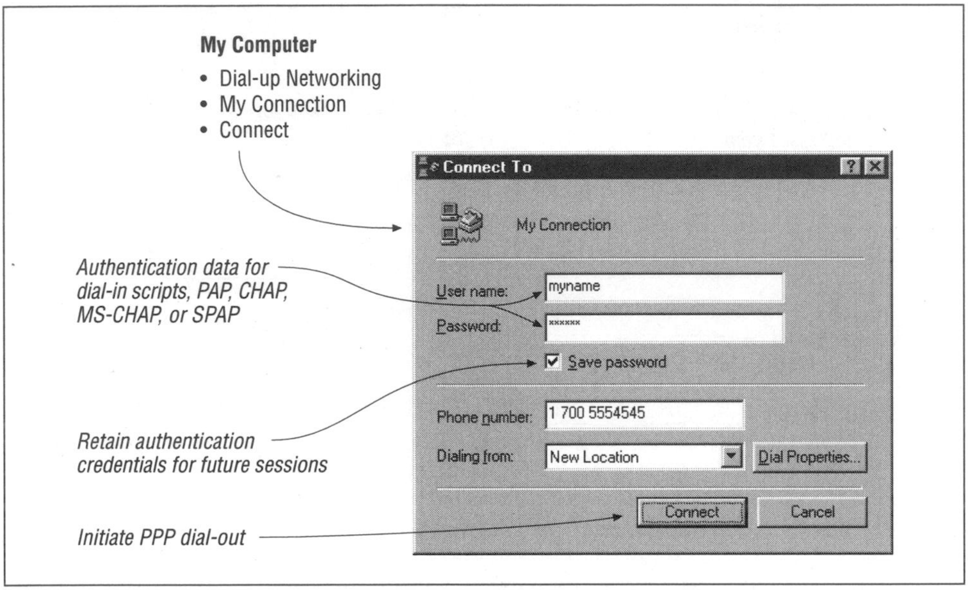

Figure 6-10. Windows 95 initiating a PPP connection

`Connect To` includes fields for users to fill in their authentication credentials. DUN uses the `User name:` and `Password:` information for any one or more of the following:

- As part of a dial-up script that requires this authentication data

- As the name and password for authenticating with PPP password authentication methods (either PAP or SPAP)

- As the name and key for authenticating with PPP challenge handshake authentication methods (either CHAP or MS-CHAP)

`Save password` stores user credentials for future dial-in sessions. The `Phone number` enables temporarily telephone number changes for this dial-out connection. Once all the information that appears in the `Connect To` is satisfactory to the user, he selects `Connect` to initiate dial-out PPP to `My Connection`.

DUN initializes a serial interface, issues modem commands, and receives modem responses for dialing out. DUN hides this process from users. If the modem successfully connects, a terminal window appears (Figure 6-11). Remember the preceding dial-out PPP connection properties include `Bring up terminal window after dialing`. The user must now use the keyboard to log in to the remote system and start PPP there. After PPP has started, the window may display PPP frames that appear as garbage, or nothing at all. Once PPP starts at the remote system, users select `Continue`. Windows 98 DUN then negotiates PPP and TCP/IP options, completing the connection.

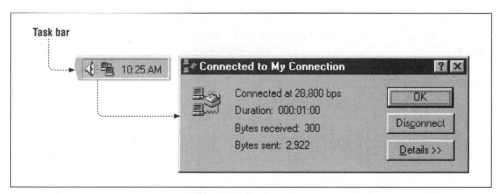

Figure 6-11. Windows 95 Post-Dial Terminal Screen

An icon in the Windows 98 task bar indicates that a dial-out PPP connection is active. Connection status is available by clicking this icon, as shown in Figure 6-12. At this point, the dial-out user is online and can access Internet sites. The `Disconnect` button terminates the connection.

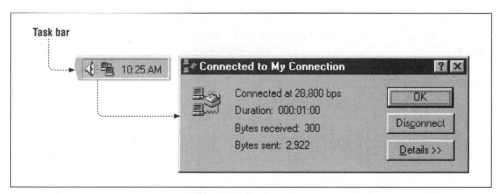

Figure 6-12. Windows 95 dial-out PPP connected

If dial-out connections fail, DUN includes features to help users diagnose the problem. Users can enable modem logs to record modem commands and responses. If the problem is PPP, DUN records PPP negotiations if dial-up adapter logging (see the previous section, "Dial-up Adapter Setup") is enabled. This log file is *ppplog.txt*

in the Windows root directory. If the connection is successful, it should look like
this:

```
C:\WINDOWS>type ppplog.txt
09-10-1998 17:34:26.82 - Microsoft Dial Up Adapter log opened.
09-10-1998 17:34:26.82 - Server type is  PPP (Point to Point Protocol).
09-10-1998 17:34:26.82 - FSA : Adding Control Protocol 80fd (CCP) to
control protocol chain.
09-10-1998 17:34:26.82 - FSA : Protocol not bound - skipping control
protocol 803f (NBFCP).
09-10-1998 17:34:26.82 - FSA : Adding Control Protocol 8021 (IPCP) to
control protocol chain.
. . .
09-10-1998 21:53:45.47 - LCP : Layer started.
09-10-1998 21:53:45.47 - PPP : Transmitting Control Packet of length: 25
09-10-1998 21:53:45.47 - Data 0000: c0 21 01 01 00 17 02 06 | .!...?..
09-10-1998 21:53:45.47 - Data 0008: 00 0a 00 00 05 06 00 c1 | ........

09-10-1998 21:53:47.89 - PPP : Received Control Packet of length: 18
09-10-1998 21:53:47.89 - Data 0000: 80 21 01 01 00 10 03 06 | .!......
09-10-1998 21:53:47.89 - Data 0008: c0 a8 01 01 02 06 00 2d | .......-
09-10-1998 21:53:47.89 - Data 0010: 0f 01 00 00 00 00 00 00 | ........
09-10-1998 21:53:47.89 - IPCP : Received and accepted IP address of c0a80101.
09-10-1998 21:53:47.89 - IPCP : Received and accepted compression protocol
request f 1.
. . . .
```

Negotiation problems should be evident in this log. Once a PPP session terminates, serial interface error and traffic statistics appear at the end of this file.

Another useful Windows 98 utility is **winipcfg**, which shows active IP addresses,
DNS server addresses, and default gateways. **Route print** and **tracert** (see
Chapter 15, *Troubleshooting*) are available via the MS-DOS prompt. These print the
TCP/IP routing table and trace routes to an IP address, respectively. The status of
connections at the TCP/IP layer is available with **netstat -a**.

On-demand PPP connections

DUN includes provisions for on-demand PPP. The settings for on-demand PPP
appear when you select the Internet icon in the Windows 98 control panel. This
shows the **Internet Properties** window. The **Connect to the Internet
using a modem** option (in the **Connection** tab) arranges on-demand PPP. Users
of Windows 95 may not find the Internet icon. In this case, they can obtain the
icon and the **Internet Properties** window after installing Microsoft Internet
Explorer.

On-demand PPP enables a web browser accessing an Internet site to automatically trigger a dial-out connection. A connection can also terminate after a configurable idle time-out.

Dial-up Scripting

Windows 98 includes dial-up scripting capability for automatically sending text strings to remote system. Dial-up scripts (which is a Windows 98 term, equivalent to chat scripts) respond to prompts from the remote system and issue all commands needed to start PPP. A functioning script bypasses the need for users to **Bring up terminal window after dialing** during the PPP connect process.

Establishing a Windows 98 DUN script consists of creating a script file for a PPP connection icon (such as **My Connection**), which appears in the **Dial-Up Networking** folder. The properties for the PPP connection includes a **Scripting** tab, with buttons to managing a script file (Figure 6-13). Users can create a script by filling in a filename and selecting **Edit**. This invokes **notepad** as the text editor for the script.

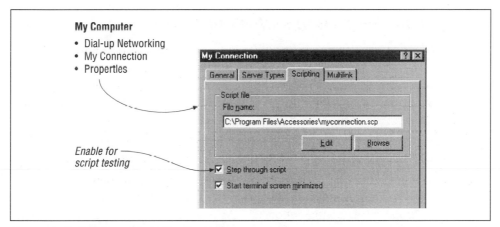

Figure 6-13. Windows 98 dial-up scripting

DUN scripting resembles a programming language with variables, loops, and conditional statements. Its programming statements are available in the file *script.doc* (Microsoft Word format) DUN installs in the Windows 98 root directory (usually *c:\windows*). For the dial-out procedures appearing in the section "Dial-out Commands to Initiate PPP," a suitable script is:

```
proc main
    waitfor "name:"
    transmit $USERID
    transmit "<cr>"
    waitfor "word:"
    transmit $PASSWORD
    transmit "<cr>"
    waitfor "isp>"
    transmit "ppp<cr>"
endproc
```

Windows 98 replaces the predefined $USERID and $PASSWORD variables with their respective values in the **Connect To** window (Figure 6-10). Certain character sequences in strings have special meanings, such as "<cr>" for carriage return. Other sequences appear in the scripting language documentation. After saving the script file, be sure to check **Step through script**. This enables users to observe script execution line by line and is essential for detecting programming errors.

A dial-up script eliminates the need for a terminal window. Thus, users should disable the terminal window for **My Connection** (see Figure 6-7). The user then initiates the connect process. A script-testing window should appear that allows step-by-step script execution. If all is correct, users can complete the script installation by returning to the dial-up script settings (Figure 6-13) and disabling **Step through script**. Initiating a PPP connection now requires no further manual intervention.

Null Modem Connection with Windows 98

Windows 98 has a direct cable connection feature for connecting two PCs with a null modem at a fixed 19,200-bps speed. In fact, it's a PPP connection with fixed settings, but requires a special handshake procedure at the beginning of the PPP session. This handshake is similar to the null modem behavior described later with Windows NT 4.0. As a result, direct cable connection is generally compatible only when both PCs have Microsoft Windows NT, 98, or 95 installed.

To establish a generic null modem connection for PPP, it's necessary to include a null modem type in **Modems Properties**. Windows 98 dial-up networking must then access this modem. Unfortunately, a null modem is not valid in the Windows 98 **Modems Properties** configuration tab. As a result, when Windows 98 DUN initiates a PPP connection, it insists on interacting with a modem before PPP communications begin. Two solutions exist:

- Install a modem information file (*.inf* file), which includes a definition for a null modem

- Arrange the PPP peer to behave as a modem would, to satisfy Windows 98's need to interact with a modem

nullmodem.inf

This file is similar to the device files that manufacturers provide for real modems. It's available under the name *nullmodem.inf* at various Internet sites.

The procedure to install a null modem is identical to the procedure to install a real one (use **Modems Properties**). To Windows 98, a null modem is like any other. However, it has empty setup and dial-out command strings and empty responses. When initiating a PPP connection, Windows 98 progresses through an empty dialog, resulting in a physical serial connection that existed all along with its peer. PPP can then commence.

False modem

Another method to start Windows 98 PPP through a null modem is arranging the PPP peer to masquerade as a modem. Once Windows 98 believes it has a modem connection, albeit a false one, PPP communications may begin.

The modem a peer masquerades as should be a simple one. These are similar to `Standard 19200 bps Modem` in `Modem Properties`. Users must install the modem description that matches the serial interface speed for the null modem cable connection.

Windows 98 can open a `Pre-dial terminal screen` when `Bring up terminal window before dialing` is enabled for this PPP connection. A user can then interact directly with the peer system and start its modem masquerading software. Here is a program for a Unix peer:

```
user$ cat modem.sh
#!/bin/sh
# read "AT"
read line; echo "OK"
# read "ATE0V1"
read line; echo "OK"
# read "AT"
read line; echo "OK"
# read "ATDT17005554545"
read line; echo "CONNECT"
sleep 1
user$
```

At the end of the `Pre-dial terminal screen`, Windows 98 issues the dialing commands to the preceding program. This program generates the responses Windows 98 expects. After the dialing phase completes, Windows 98 can display a `Post-dial terminal screen`, which lets the user continue to interact with the peer as needed to start its PPP. At the conclusion of this terminal screen, Windows 98 starts PPP, completing the connection.

It's not always possible to arrange a Windows 98 PPP peer to masquerade as a modem. In these cases, *nullmodem.inf* is the only other solution.

Windows NT 4.0 Workstation

Microsoft Windows NT 4.0 Workstation features the remote access service (RAS). RAS enables its user to establish a dial-out PPP connection and access remote networks that support any combination of TCP/IP, Novell IPX/SPX, and NetBEUI. We consider only TCP/IP here.

The dial-out features available with Windows NT 4.0 RAS are nearly identical to those available with Windows 98.

Installation

Dial-out PPP requires Windows NT 4.0 Workstation to have networking services installed. Users can install it by selecting the **Network** icon in the Windows NT control panel. If network services are missing, the following message appears:

```
Windows NT Networking is not installed. Do you want to install it now?
```

Answering **Yes** starts the **Network Setup Wizard**, where users can select the option **Remote access to network**. The prompts and procedures that follow install and configure nearly all aspects of RAS, including dial-out networking protocols, serial interfaces, and modems. When Window NT asks, be sure to include TCP/IP* as a network protocol for RAS. Afterwards, users can define PPP connections in the dial-up networking Phonebook.

In cases where some form of networking already exists on Windows NT Workstation 4.0, users arranging dial-out PPP must verify the software components for RAS dial-up networking. They must then install and configure any missing RAS components. The section "Windows NT 4.0 Server" in Chapter 7, *Dial-in PPP Setup*, describes RAS installation for dial-in PPP. Most of the procedure is identical for dial-out PPP. A summary of items to check are:

Network protocols and network services
> Users can add networking protocols for dial-out PPP by selecting **Control Panel → Network → Protocols**. Access to the Internet requires TCP/IP.

Serial interfaces and modems
> Selecting **Control Panel → Modems** accesses **Modems Properties**. Each modem definition includes settings for a serial interface. Configuring modems in Windows NT is almost identical to Windows 98. Some additional details for Windows NT also appear in Chapter 7.

Remote access service
> If **Remote Access Service** doesn't appear in **Control Panel → Network → Services**, then the instructions to install it is in Chapter 7.

A key difference in the RAS configuration for dial-in PPP, versus dial-out PPP, are the settings that appear in **Remote Access Setup**, as Figure 6-14 shows. Users must press the **Configure** button to mark a modem and serial interface pair for dial-out use. The **Network** button defines the networking protocols *available* for

---

* When Windows NT asks, Do you wish to use DHCP? for TCP/IP, select No.

this modem. It's a good idea to select all available protocols in case unused ones are necessary later. The Phonebook (see the next section) sets the networking protocols to use for any given PPP connection.

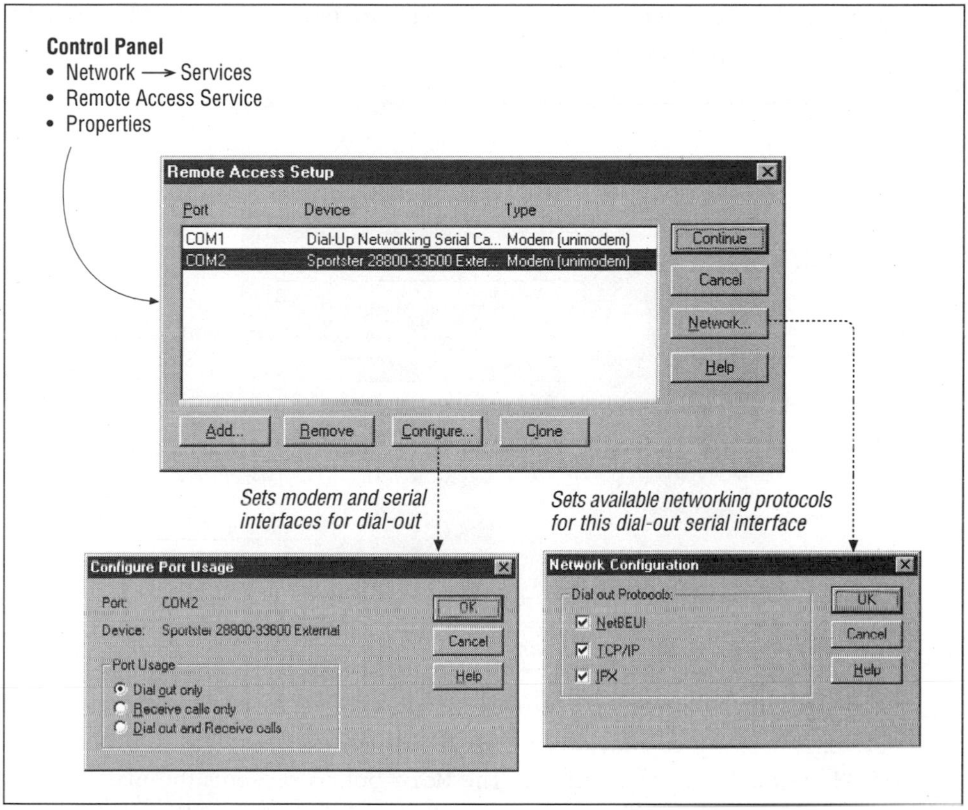

Control Panel
- Network —→ Services
- Remote Access Service
- Properties

Figure 6-14. Windows NT Remote Access Setup

Annoyingly, any changes to `Remote Access Setup` require rebooting Windows NT. Therefore, I suggest that you anticipate and configure as many RAS resources as you plan to use for dial-up networking.

A reboot starts several RAS background processes that manage PPP connections. These RAS processes appear in `Control Panel → Services`. The active ones are:

- Remote Access Autodial Manager

- Remote Access Connection Manager

Another process is `Remote Access Server`, but this serves only dial-in PPP.

Managing the Dial-up Networking Phonebook

`Dial-Up Networking` is the main Windows NT 4.0 Workstation window for managing dial-out PPP connections. Users can access `Dial-Up Networking` by selecting its icon in `My Computer`. This window (Figure 6-15) manages Phonebook entries and dial-up connections.

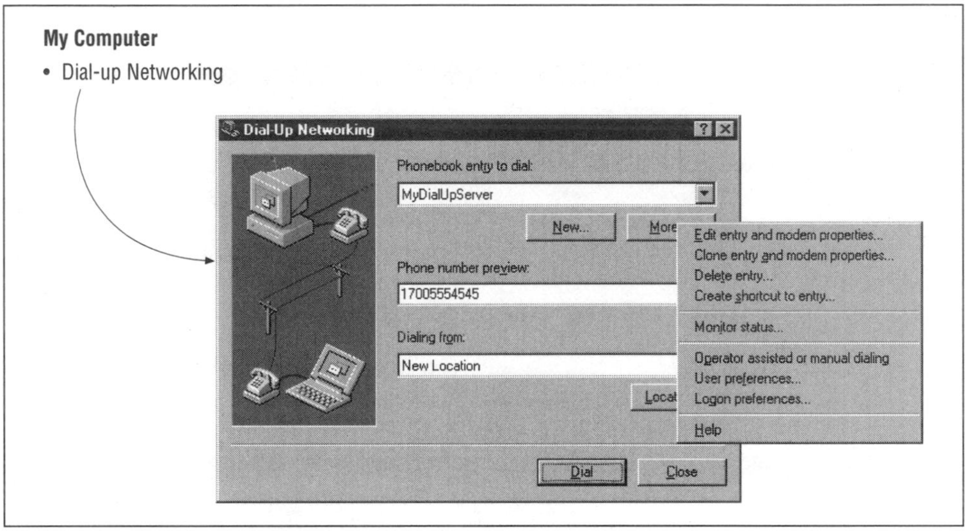

Figure 6-15. Windows NT Dial-Up Networking

A named Phonebook entry is a collection of settings necessary to dial-out to a remote system. A listing of previously configured entries appears as a pull-down list below `Phonebook entry to dial:`. The `More` button presents the main menu of items for managing Phonebook entries.

Users must first create and name a new entry for a dial-in remote system they wish to access. The `New...` button invokes the `New Phonebook Entry Wizard`, which prompts for a minimal number of settings necessary to connect with a remote system. New entries frequently require further editing, even after the wizard creates them.

PPP connection settings belong in the categories `Basic`, `Server`, `Script`, `Security`, and `X.25`. These settings appear when users select `Edit entry and modem properties...` under the `More` menu in the `Dial-Up Networking` main window. Online help is available by selecting `Help` in the `More` menu. The help information is also available in file *c:\winnt\system32\rasphone.hlp*, which the *winhlp32* utility can read.

Our configuration example arranges the settings for a dial-out PPP connection, named `MyDialUpServer`.

Basic tab

The basic information for a dial-out PPP connection is a telephone number, and a modem and serial interface pair to use. These settings are in the `Edit Phonebook Entry Basic` tab that Figure 6-16 shows. All the values correspond to the assumptions in the previous section "Dial-out Commands to Initiate PPP."

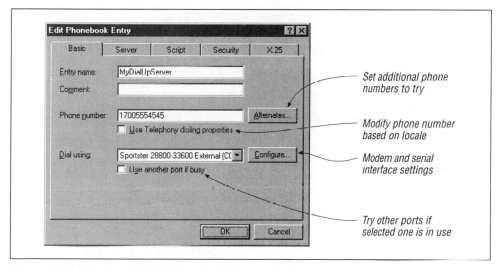

Figure 6-16. Windows NT Edit Phonebook Entry

`Dial using:` assigns a modem and serial interface pair for this connection. All pairs that appear here are listed as dial-out resources in the `Remote Access Setup`. In addition, the `Dial using:` field may include a special `Multiple Lines` selection, which enables Windows NT multilink PPP (see Chapter 16, *What's New for PPP?*).

In more usual dial-out arrangements with one modem/interface pair, the `Configure` button sets the initial serial interface speed, hardware flow control, and some modem properties. These are settings that apply to this PPP connection, they take precedence over any settings that may appear in the control panel `Modem Properties`.

Server tab

The `Dial-up server type:` in the `Server` tab (see Figure 6-17) determines the serial line protocol Windows NT uses after its modem successfully connects. Obviously, users must select `PPP`, for dial-out PPP. The other choices in this pull-down menu are proprietary or obsolete serial line protocols.

Windows NT PPP can support all the `Network protocols` listed, as long as the remote system also supports them. Selecting a protocol causes Windows NT only

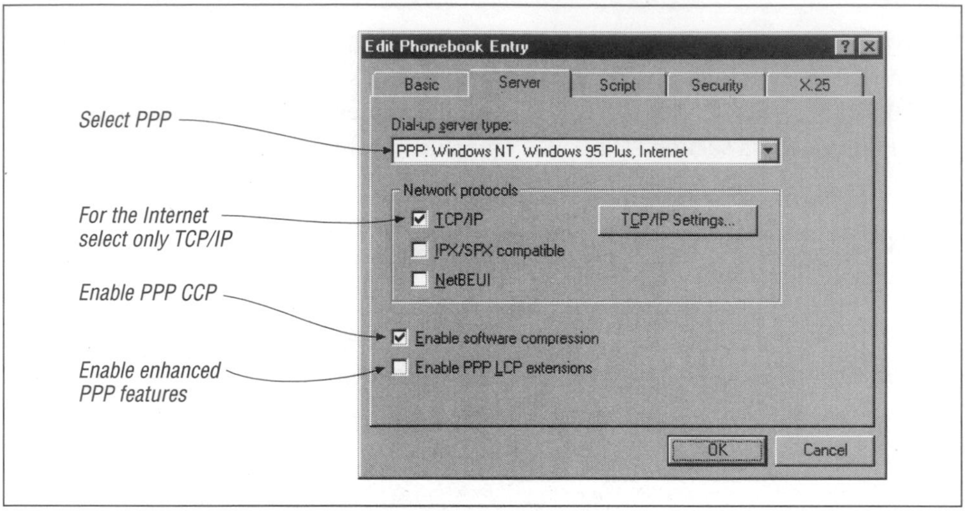

Figure 6-17. Windows NT Edit Phonebook Entry, Server

to request it, with the dial-out peer. A protocol becomes active only if the peer agrees. I suggest that you select only the network protocols you need. In particular, TCP/IP is an Internet requirement. If Windows NT attempts negotiation for unusable and unneeded protocols, it takes time and can cause communication failures with some remote systems. The `TCP/IP Settings...` button presents TCP/IP settings for this PPP connection. What appears is identical to Figure 6-9 for Windows 98. The explanations are also identical to Windows 98.

If a check appears with `Enable software compression`, Windows NT tries to negotiate the use of PPP data compression (via the compression control protocol) with the remote system. User data compression is effective only if both PPP endpoints understand and agree to use this Windows NT–compatible compression method, Microsoft Point-to-Point Compression Protocol (MPPC).

`Enable PPP LCP extensions` causes Windows NT to try to negotiate several enhanced PPP options. Some of these are:

- Request LCP "Call Back" configuration option.

- Send LCP identification with string `MSRASV4.00` to peer. Also send an LCP identification string with the Windows NT hostname.

- Request various multilink PPP options. This happens on Windows NT without service pack patches.

Users can enable either or both of these two checkboxes if they wish to use these enhancements with dial-out peers that support them. Otherwise, it's wise to disable these. If Windows NT negotiates for PPP enhancements a remote system doesn't understand, it's possible for the connection to fail.

Script

After a modem completes its connection, the `Script` tab determines what the dial-out user, or Windows NT, must do to start PPP on a remote server. Further information about script settings is provided in the previous section "Dial-up Scripting."

The scenario I described earlier in the section "Dial-out Commands to Initiate PPP" requires sending text strings and commands to the remote system in order to start PPP there. This requires the `Pop up a terminal window` setting (Figure 6-20), which causes Windows NT to pause and display a terminal window after dialing. You can then perform interactive steps with the keyboard to start PPP at the remote system.

The `None` setting is suitable for remote systems that don't require any interaction to start PPP communications.

Security

The Phonebook maintains a `Security` tab (Figure 6-18) for each dial-out connection. This controls how Windows NT authenticates itself to a remote system. These settings apply only to PPP authentication methods and don't affect terminal window authentication prompts that may exist before a remote system grants access.

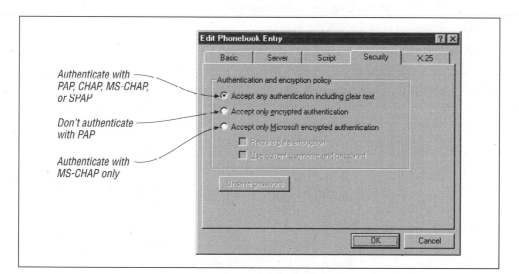

Figure 6-18. Windows NT Edit Phonebook Entry, Security

Windows NT can authenticate with PAP, CHAP, Shiva PAP, or Microsoft CHAP. Users must supply authentication credentials at PPP connect time. If `Accept only`

`Microsoft encrypted authentication` is checked, Windows NT authenticates only with Microsoft CHAP and refuses all the others. `Accept only encrypted authentication` allows methods that don't transmit passwords in clear text. Finally, `Accept any authentication including clear text` allows Windows NT to authenticate with any method it recognizes. For simple username and password authentication, `Accept any` is the only suitable setting. Be aware that if Windows NT refuses all the PPP authentication methods its dial-up peer wants, the connection fails.

The Microsoft-only setting also features `Require data encryption` and `Use current username and password`. The latter feature passes Windows NT login credentials for authentication. Unfortunately, both features are Microsoft-specific and require PPP endpoints with Microsoft-compatible software.

Other settings

The `User preferences` menu item in `Dial-Up Networking` (Figure 6-15) has additional settings that affect dial-out PPP. Some preference items users can adjust are:

- `Dialing` counters and timers determine redialing behavior, when PPP connection attempts fail. Arrangements for on-demand PPP and PPP idle time-out also appear here.

- `Callback`. Windows NT supports remote systems that impose PPP callback security. After establishing and terminating an initial PPP connection, these settings arrange a wait for callback.

- `Appearance` controls cosmetic aspects of dial-up networking.

- `Phonebook` defines where to seek Phonebook entries. An arbitrary file may be set as the Phonebook.

Establishing a Connection

Selecting a Phonebook entry in `Dial-Up Networking` (Figure 6-15) and pressing the `Dial` button initiates a dial-out PPP connection. Windows NT usually displays PPP connection progress on-screen; users can suppress these messages in `User preferences`.

A Windows NT onscreen prompt that appears before the dial-out begins is an authentication window (Figure 6-19). Users must fill in credentials, if any, required by the remote system. `Domain:` is a Microsoft-specific feature for representing a Windows NT domain. If the `User name:` and `Domain:` are `myname` and `mydomain`, respectively, the name for PPP authentication purposes is `mydomain\myname`. `Save password` retains user authentication credentials for reuse and

suppresses this on-screen prompt for future PPP connections to MyDialUp-
Server. To undo a previously saved password, users can return to the Edit
Phonebook Entry Security tab (Figure 6-18) and select Unsave password.

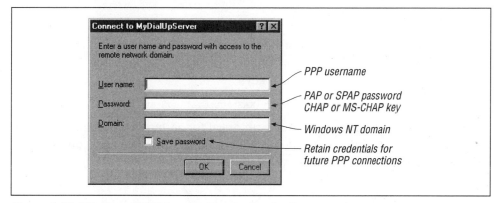

Figure 6-19. Windows NT PPP connection authentication request

After the dial-out process completes and the modem successfully connects, a terminal window appears. This window is similar to the one for Windows 98
(Figure 6-11), and the instructions for its use are identical. Users must respond to
remote system prompts with their keyboard and start PPP at the remote end of the
connection.

Windows NT then negotiates PPP options and completes the connection. Errors, if
any, appear onscreen. The Dial-Up Monitor in the Windows NT control panel
shows the status of active connections. Another indicator is the telephone icon that
appears next to the clock in the task bar. Both the Dial-Up Monitor and the
Dial-Up Networking window have the controls necessary for terminating connections.

In case of problems, Windows NT offers PPP and modem trace facilities. PPP
traces are available by changing the PPP logging registry value. Modems Properties includes settings to obtain modem traces. More details for enabling logging
and the files they reside in are in the Windows NT Server RAS discussion in
Chapter 7.

On-demand PPP

Windows NT features a limited form of on-demand PPP, which can automatically
initiate PPP dial-out to selected Internet sites. The Enable auto-dial by location setting in the Dialing category of User preferences (see Figure 6-15)
enables this feature. Another related Appearance setting, Always prompt before
auto-dialing, determines whether Windows NT prompts users for permission
to dial.

Auto-dial functions only for names and IP addresses users have visited during previous PPP connections. In other words, Windows NT remembers all the sites its applications access via PPP connection. The following command displays the auto-dial list:

```
rasautou -s
```

If a site doesn't appear, users must bring the connection up manually and then connect to it to add it to the auto-dial list. To remove entries from this list, use the `regedt32` utility and edit the following key:

```
HKEY_CURRENT_USER\Software\Microsoft\RAS Autodial\Addresses
```

There's no convenient means to arrange auto-dial for all Internet destinations. This is a strange characteristic of Windows NT auto-dial, which differs considerably from the on-demand PPP available with Linux and Unix.

Dial-up Scripting

Dial-up scripting replaces procedures that normally require a terminal window. Scripts automatically respond to remote system prompts, typically for authentication and PPP start commands. A script completes when a remote system is ready with PPP. If Run this script is enabled in the Script tab settings for a PPP connection (Figure 6-20), Windows NT executes a script file.

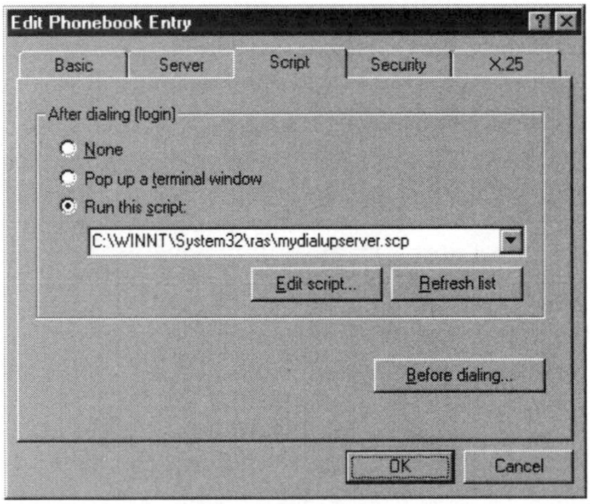

Figure 6-20. Windows NT Edit Phonebook Entry, Script

The DUN script-programming language is identical to Windows 98. Sample scripts are in the *c:\winnt\system32\ras* directory with the *.scp* extension. Users may create new ones in the same directory. Further information about this language is available in the Microsoft Word file, *c:\winnt\system32\ras\script.doc.* A major flaw with dial-up scripts is Windows NT doesn't appear to offer any way to trace and debug the script programs.

Dial-up networking also offers an alternative script language. If `Run this script` includes a simple name, that name refers to a code section inside a master script file *c:\winnt\system32\ras\switch.inf.* Multiple scripts appear in this file, each with a named section header. A *switch.inf* script is of the send-and-expect type, without conditionals or looping ability. An example is:

```
; Section header with name
[PPP login]
; Send nothing
    COMMAND=
; Wait for "Username:"
    OK=<match>"name:"
    LOOP=<ignore>
; Send user name from authentication window
    COMMAND=<username><cr>
; Wait for "Password:"
    OK=<match>"assword:"
    LOOP=<ignore>
; Send password from authentication window
    COMMAND=<password><cr>
; Wait for "isp>"
    OK=<match>"isp>"
    LOOP=<ignore>
; Send "ppp"
    COMMAND=ppp<cr>
```

The lines alternate between a `COMMAND=` statement that sends strings to a peer and statements for matching strings in a response. Response processing is especially confusing. First, scripts consider all responses to be a received string terminated with a two-second idle time. Unfortunately, such delay can occur anywhere and can break a large response message into many smaller ones. When the `OK=` statement matches a substring in a response, it's an indication to proceed, apparently to the next `COMMAND=` statement. A `LOOP=` retries the previous statement and is usually set to match anything a previous `OK=` failed to match. This is an awkward workaround that accommodates conditions where string reception delays break up large responses into several smaller ones. A script fails if no statement matches the response strings DUN receives.

Windows NT includes tracing capability for *switch.inf* scripts. The following registry value controls this:

```
HKEY_LOCAL_MACHINE\System\CurrentControlSet\Services\
RasMan\Parameters\Logging
```

Setting this value to 1 and restarting the RAS service (or rebooting) produces the log file *c:\winnt\system32\ras\device.log.* Consult this file if a script doesn't function. This log records activity only with *switch.inf* scripts.

Additional information about *switch.inf* and its script language appears in the online help for `Dial-Up Networking`.

Null Modem Connections with Windows NT

A Windows NT workstation may physically connect to another computer with a null modem cable. This cable can carry PPP, much like a modem does over a telephone line. Since there is no modem, Windows NT doesn't need to issue modem or dial commands when initiating (dial-out) a PPP connection. The `Dial-Up Networking Serial Cable between 2 PCs` in `Modem Properties` establishes this behavior. This defines a serial interface without a modem.

With a null modem connection, Windows NT can immediately start sign-on chat scripts and PPP with its peer. Unfortunately, when Windows NT dials out, it sends the string `CLIENT` several times without a carriage return, while it waits for its peer to respond with `CLIENTSERVER`. Without this response, Windows NT refuses to communicate. This is not the behavior of a true null modem configuration and can be especially frustrating to users trying to connect Windows NT to non-Microsoft platforms.

The previous section, "Null Modem Connection with Windows 98," describes methods that can also circumvent Windows NT null modem annoyances. Either the PPP peer can emulate a modem, or the user can try to locate a *nullmodem.inf* modem driver. Windows NT RAS also supports *c:\winnt\system32\ras\modem.inf* as the source for modem information, which users can edit and perhaps modify an entry into a null modem definition. Arranging RAS to use this file requires changing the registry key:

```
HKEY_LOCAL_MACHINE\Software\Microsoft\RAS\Protocols
```

Add the name `EnableUnimodem` of type `REG_DWORD` and value 0.

In this chapter:
- *Dial-in PPP Architecture for Internet Access*
- *Communication Servers*
- *Linux PPP-2.3*
- *Solaris PPP*
- *Windows NT 4.0 Server*

7

Dial-in PPP Setup

As network administrator or Internet service provider, you must arrange dial-in access to your networks. Accomplishing this requires you to install remote access equipment, which may include modems, routers, telephone lines, and dial-in servers that can answer incoming telephone calls.

The relationship between users, the dial-in servers, and the network they dial into, appears in Figure 7-1. Typical dial-in services assume users dial-out with a stand-alone PC. In other words, the dial-in server believes there is only one device with one network address at the originating end of an incoming telephone connection.

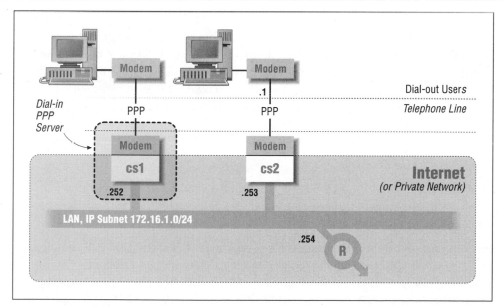

Figure 7-1. Dial-in PPP

In this chapter, you will learn how to set up a dial-in PPP server. I use the term "PPP server" loosely, to mean that it listens for and accepts incoming telephone calls. Remember that PPP is a peer-to-peer protocol and doesn't really distinguish between clients and servers. You can implement a dial-in PPP server with a communications server, a Unix server, or a PC.

Our discussion in this chapter limits its scope to one dial-in PPP network architecture. It's clearly possible to design an architecture where entire networks call each other, but we'll cover this in later chapters.

Dial-in PPP Architecture for Internet Access

It's insufficient to attach a dial-in PPP server somewhere and configure PPP. For starters, one must engineer and define requirements for telephone service, modem pools, the dial-in PPP server platform, how PPP starts up, user authentication, how the dial-in server connects to the network, and IP addressing. In effect, you're defining the dial-in PPP service policies, as well as the service characteristics visible to users.

A typical architecture suitable for Internet access appears in Figure 7-1. This architecture requires a dial-in PPP server with a LAN network interface. This LAN, in turn, has a connection to the rest of the Internet. We'll assume this architecture when discussing how to configure various dial-in PPP servers. Additional assumptions are noted in the following sections.

If you still need to select dial-in PPP server equipment, the dedicated communication server is the best approach for critical dial-in service. Communication server manufacturers are supposed to optimize their equipment for performance, reliability, and scalability, for a single purpose: dial-in. Lower-cost platforms, such as PCs, tend to be less stable and may run into performance and management problems with large numbers of dial-in lines.

Network Addressing

On the Internet, most devices must have a globally unique IP address that is compatible with the Internet addressing structure. Dial-in PPP users and the servers they connect to are no exception.

The simplest IP addressing scheme for a dial-in PPP is the Proxy ARP configuration. I describe this and other more advanced configurations in detail in Chapter 8, *Network Architectures Incorporating PPP*. What you need to know now about Proxy ARP is that PPP users, the PPP server, and a LAN all use IP addresses belonging to single IP subnet. Figure 7-1 shows the subnet 172.16.1.0/24. A PPP server has a single IP address, such as 172.16.1.253, which it uses for its LAN network interface, as well as for all of its PPP network interfaces.

The Proxy ARP configuration also requires the PPP server to perform proxy ARP on its LAN. You may also need to set this up. PPP itself will work without proxy ARP, but users won't be able to communicate with any Internet sites.

Modem and Serial Interface

Dial in PPP servers have a modem pool to connect them to telephone lines. The technologically advanced pools are digital modems that interface directly to the digital infrastructure most telephone carriers have today. Digital modems are required to achieve 56-Kbps service for users. Modems in traditional pools have an analog connection to a telephone line and an RS-232 serial interface connection to the PPP server.

Whether a modem is digital or analog, there exists a logical or a physical RS-232 serial interface. To best accommodate dial-in PPP, we assume serial interfaces at the modem and set the PPP server for 8-bit characters, no parity, hardware flow control, and modem control. Interface speed should be a fixed value, at 57,600 bps or higher, whenever possible.

Modems are usually feature-rich and have numerous settings that control modulation protocols, error correction, data compression, and miscellaneous items. For dial-in PPP, I suggest that you initially configure modems with default settings to enable all modem features. If several default templates exist, select the one with serial interface hardware flow control. Unless noted otherwise, the following additional modem settings are necessary for dial-in PPP:

- Answer telephone after one ring
- Disable response codes and message
- Disable escape characters

Disabling response codes prevents problems when PPP servers misunderstand codes such as user data. Disabling escape characters prevents unexpected modem disconnects that can result if the escape pattern appears in user data.

Dial-in PPP Server, PPP Startup Procedure

An answering PPP server can respond in several ways. Windows NT 4.0 Server must immediately begin PPP communications. However, some communication servers and many Unix servers naturally prompt for "login" and then prompt for the serial line protocol users want. PPP starts later, if the user issues the proper command strings to the server in a terminal window, or chat script. In our configuration examples, all the servers with the exception of Windows NT first prompt for "login."

I'll assume you want to use PPP to request a username and password. There may be a second authentication step, but this time, PPP frames carry authentication credentials.

Following successful authentication, we assume the PPP server assigns IP addresses to both itself and the remote user. Users aren't permitted to establish an IP address of their own choice.

Other Assumptions and Considerations

There is much more you must consider when deploying a dial-in server, besides details about PPP. It may be important, for example, to audit usage and remotely maintain the dial-in server:

Auditing
> You may need to record hours of usage, on a per user basis, for billing purposes.

Simple Network Management Protocol (SNMP)
> A network operations center may want to monitor the condition of dial-in servers installed in geographically disperse locations with SNMP. This requires supporting software on the PPP server.

Setting up these ancillary items is outside the scope of this discussion.

Communication Servers

Communication servers are responsible for managing a modem pool and connecting the pool to a network. These servers are special-purpose computers with their own operating system and utilities. Recent models can simultaneously support dial-in services for dumb terminals, PPP, and other serial line protocols. The same server may also support numerous network layer protocols, besides TCP/IP.

Figure 7-2 shows dial-in PPP with a communication server. Communication servers frequently need to depend on a management station for maintenance, authentication, usage logging, and other functions. This station is nothing more than a general-purpose Unix workstation or PC. One management station can usually support many communication servers from the same vendor.

Vendors sometimes include source code, allowing you to customize the management station as needed. Common tasks include changing the authentication pro-

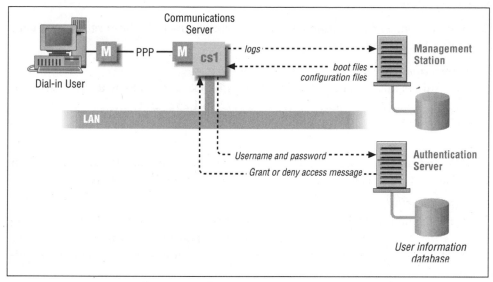

Figure 7-2. Communication server and supporting servers

cess to consult third-party security software (e.g., SecurID) on an authentication server. You need to be familiar with programming to modify software.

System Configuration

A new communication server requires basic configuration, such as its IP address and the whereabouts of its management servers, before it can initialize. Vendors have specific procedures for bootstrapping and configuring a new server. The common methods are:

- Attach a terminal, or a computer with terminal emulation software, to the server's RS-232 console interface

- The communications server may broadcast over its LAN and expect a response from a management station that supplies it with operating software and configuration data

- A combination of the two previous items

What you need depends on the communication server's built-in capabilities. Some models already include onboard operating software, and you can completely configure them with a terminal. Others include only network bootstrap code and require you to establish its management station before they can operate at all.

Once a communication server initializes, there are usually several ways to manage its configuration. Graphical administration tools may be available at the management station, or you may also be able to `telnet` into the communication server itself.

Network settings

Communication servers featuring TCP/IP networking include these settings pertaining to its LAN network interface:

IP address and subnet mask for the LAN interface

The subnet mask defines the IP address block associated with the LAN. For `cs1` in Figure 7-1, its IP address is 172.16.1.252 and the subnet mask is 255.255.255.0.

Routing protocols and gateways

A communication server may need a default route, set to 172.16.1.254 in Figure 7-1. Alternatively, it may run TCP/IP routing protocol software.

Management stations

Some communication servers load their operating software and configuration files from a designated management station. You may also need to configure boot software, such as TFTP, so the communication server can autoload various files by name.

Network settings pertaining to PPP connections are specific to a communication server's dial-in port.

Security settings

Since a communications server for Internet access is usually open to the public telephone network, access security must be established. Common security parameters are:

Local passwords

Communication servers may include locally stored passwords for access to administrative functions. Sometimes, small numbers of special usernames and passwords pairs may reside in the server.

Authentication servers

Authentication for large numbers of users requires a database. The communication server needs to know the authentication server's IP address and the authentication protocol to use. Authentication protocols include Livingston's RADIUS, Cisco's TACACS, or other vendor-proprietary protocols.

Filtering

This feature, if available, may be useful for communication servers with connections to private networks. Filtering screens traffic between users and the LAN. Its rules can deny access for certain network destinations or certain traffic types. Communication servers may support such rules on a serial interface-, user-, or server-wide basis.

Dial-in Port Configuration

Some communication server models have as many as 72 serial interfaces. The term "port" collectively refers to a server's serial interface and its attached modem, PPP settings, and network settings. Parameters for each port are frequently independent. Although this flexibility allows you to group ports for different purposes, large-scale, dial-in installations configure most ports almost identically.

The following example shows the configuration for one port on a Bay Network's (formerly Xylogics) Annex Communications Server with release 9 software. You can expect similarities in the parameters for products of other vendors.

The command to show the configuration of port 16 on an Annex is:

```
admin : show port=16 all
```

This command is available by accessing the **admin** mode after logging in to the server as a privileged user. If any of these parameters need to be changed, use the **set** command. For example:

```
admin: set port=16 speed 57600 data_bits 8 stop_bits 1 parity none
```

The output of the **show** command begins with **Port Generic Parameters**:

```
Port 16:
```

```
                    Port Generic Parameters

           mode: cli                        location: ""
           type: dial_in                    term_var: "unknown"
         prompt: ""                             speed: 57600
      data_bits: 8                          stop_bits: 1
         parity: none              max_session_count: 3
 allow_broadcast: Y            broadcast_direction: port
     imask_7bits: N                       cli_imask7: Y
ps_history_buffer: 0                          banner: Y
   tcp_keepalive: 0             dedicated_address: 0.0.0.0
   dedicated_port: telnet         type_of_modem: "USR28800"
```

All the usual RS-232 serial interface settings are in this group. One parameter of interest is **mode**, which specifies how the server responds to the user after the modem connects. The command-line interface **cli** setting starts a terminal session with the user. Another **mode** setting of interest is **ppp**, which starts this serial line protocol immediately upon modem connection.

The following parameters establish modem control and flow control for an Annex serial interface:

```
          Flow Control and Signal Parameters

   control_lines: both         input_flow_control: eia
 input_start_char: ^Q            input_stop_char: ^S
```

```
output_flow_control: eia          output_start_char: ^Q
    output_stop_char: ^S            input_buffer_size: 1
 bidirectional_modem: Y           ixany_flow_control: N
             need_dsr: N
```

control_lines indicates which of the two controls, if any, apply to this interface. The recommended setting is both and includes both the modem_control and flow_control keywords. The other parameters define what flow control method to use. For hardware flow control with RTS and CTS signals, you must set output_flow_control and input_flow_control to eia.* There are additional parameters that specify software flow control characters, but they're not applicable in this case.

Port timers and counters include parameters that automatically disconnect inactive dial-up users with a modem connection to the Annex. Activity parameters determine how the Annex interprets the meaning of "active." If a user must transmit data to be a considered active, for example, set Input_is_activity, to Y. Notice in this example that inactivity_timer is set to off. This means this Annex server never disconnects an idle user, despite the presence of other related settings.

Port Timers and Counters

```
forwarding_timer: off             forwarding_count: 0
    cli_inactivity: off           inactivity_timer: off
  input_is_activity: Y            output_is_activity: N
 reset_idle_time_on: input              long_break: Y
         short_break: Y
```

The port security parameters here partially determine when the Annex challenges dial-in users for their name and password. Other security parameters appear elsewhere that also determine if users must supply authentication credentials. Here cli_security is Y, indicating users accessing the Annex CLI must authenticate first. Cli_security also affects security for ports set to PPP communications only, despite the cli in its name.

Port Security Parameters

```
         user_name: ""                  cli_security: Y
 connect_security: N            port_server_security: N
    port_password: "<set>"
```

Line editing parameters are for terminal users who interact with the Annex CLI. Users initially connecting to a CLI usually just type the ppp command. These settings therefore have little impact, unless someone mistypes ppp.

CLI Line Editing Parameters

```
       attn_string: ""                           echo: Y
```

---

* Electronic Industry Association

```
      telnet_escape: ^]                          telnet_crlf: N
       map_to_lower: N                          map_to_upper: N
         char_erase: Y                            line_erase: Y
      hardware_tabs: Y                            erase_char: ^?
         erase_word: ^W                           erase_line: ^U
      redisplay_line: ^R                       toggle_output: ^O
    newline_terminal: N
```

`Serial Networking Protocol Parameters` generally refer to TCP/IP parameters applicable to a PPP connection. What's important here are the IP addresses. The `local_address` is the IP address of the Annex server's end of a PPP connection. In this dial-in architecture, you must set the address of all ports to the address of the communications server's LAN interface. To be consistent with Figure 7-1, I've used 172.16.1.252.

Serial Networking Protocol Parameters

```
     local_address: 172.16.1.252         remote_address: 172.16.1.16
   dialup_addresses: N                            metric: 1
   slip_ppp_security: Y                   do_compression: Y
   allow_compression: Y
```

The Annex assigns the `remote_address` to the user. This address must be a member of the subnet 172.16.1.0/24 in our dial-in architecture assumptions. Here, we use 172.16.1.16 as the permanent remote address for port 16, 172.16.1.15 for port 15 and so forth. Because these addresses belong to the IP subnet of the Annex network interface, this server automatically recognizes it must perform proxy ARP functions on its LAN. Thus, proxy ARP configuration details, including ARP table and routing table management, are all automatic.

Users dialing in receive a different IP address whenever they connect to a different port. This is common when all the ports share the same telephone number. By enabling `dialup_addresses`, it's possible to assign static IP addresses to users. The Annex must then consult its authentication server to retrieve the user's IP address assignment. If `dialup_addresses` is active, the IP address parameters appearing in `Serial Networking Protocol Parameters` aren't applicable.

`Allow_compression` and `do_compression` set VJ compression for IP datagrams sent through a PPP connection. Allowing compression means the Annex honors VJ compression requests from users. If `do_compression` is enabled, this server actively negotiates with PPP users to use VJ compression.

If `slip_ppp_security` is enabled, the Annex requires a valid name and password from users before they can use the CLI `ppp` command. This setting is useful only if users can access the CLI anonymously.

SLIP parameters shows one parameter that's crucial to PPP: subnet_mask. All the other parameters pertain to the SLIP serial line protocol and aren't applicable for PPP.

SLIP Parameters

```
        subnet_mask: 0.0.0.0           slip_load_dump_host: 0.0.0.0
    slip_allow_dump: Y                     slip_mtu_size: small
      slip_no_icmp: N                           slip_tos: N
```

The Annex has an unusual interpretation of subnet mask for PPP connections. It applies the mask to the remote_address to determine the IP address space of a remote network. In cases where individual users, rather than a network, are dialing in, the subnet_mask must remain unset, as shown.

PPP Parameters are the adjustable settings available for PPP. ppp_mru defines the PPP maximum receive unit, and ppp_acm defines the PPP asynchronous control mask. The values shown are the recommended starting points.

PPP Parameters

```
            ppp_mru: 1500                        ppp_acm: 0x0
ppp_security_protocol: pap          ppp_username_remote: ""
 ppp_password_remote: "<unset>"                  ppp_ncp: all
```

If your users must authenticate using PPP, you must set ppp_security_protocol to a value besides none. Although this Annex software release supports pap only, more recent updates add chap security. An authentication server, if available, validates PAP credentials. Without an authentication server, the port user_name and port_password under Port Security Parameters define the valid authentication credentials for this port. If users want to use PPP and challenge the communication server for its own credentials, the server can respond with the information in ppp_username_remote and ppp_password_remote.

The remaining port configuration task is initializing dial-in modems. This requires you to send command strings to each modem. The string must establish answer mode and the other necessary modem settings we assume in our dial-in PPP architecture. A US Robotics Sportster, for example, requires the following:

```
at &f1
at s0=1 s2=128
at q1
```

Unfortunately, this Annex software release doesn't store or send modem command strings for dial-in ports. (Bay Networks has since rectified this flaw.) You must configure temporarily the server to allow dial-out access to each modem via the Annex network interface. You can then telnet to each modem and send it the appropriate initialization strings. Be sure to save each modem's configuration settings with at&w before you disconnect.

After configuring one port, you must configure the other ports in a similar manner. The Annex includes management station utilities for copying its port settings into a file. You can then edit these settings and load them to other ports. In this example, nearly all the settings for port 16 apply to the other 15 ports. Only the IP address for PPP differs. Copying Annex port settings doesn't configure the port's modem; you still need to configure each modem, one by one.

Verifying Dial-in PPP

To verify dial-in PPP, you can configure a PC with PPP software and connect to the communication server as any user would. Be sure the PC has the necessary chat scripts that interact with the communications server's CLI, if any. The script must send the ppp command at the end.

A communications server frequently manages many modems that share a single telephone number. When troubleshooting a port, you must use an alternate telephone number that's unique to an individual port. If such numbers are unknown, then busy-out all telephone lines except for the one under test. It's essential to know which port to monitor during testing.

When PPP is active on a communication server's port, the server may feature utilities that can be used to monitor data flow. Other utilities may display the state of modem and flow control signals at the RS-232 serial interface. Serial interface error statistics can also assist in troubleshooting the physical connection.

For network-related problems, TCP/IP utilities including ping and traceroute (see Chapter 15, *Troubleshooting*) should be available. Also important are commands for showing and changing the server's routing tables. To verify Proxy ARP, the commands that show the server's ARP table must show permanently published entries for the IP addresses of active users. There should also be commands for manipulating this table, if necessary.

Linux PPP-2.3

PPP-2.3 also functions on Linux servers responsible for dial-in PPP. Most of the setup procedures for dial-out PPP also apply to dial-in. The key differences for dial-in are establishing Internet connectivity for the server and establishing Linux login service. Sign-on chat scripts are unnecessary.

Users dialing into a Linux server frequently encounter a login prompt. Many other Unix servers behave similarly:

```
Welcome to Linux 2.0.30.

myisp login: myname
Password:
```

```
Linux 2.0.30.
Last login: Tue Mar  4 05:58:33 on ttyS0
user$ exec /usr/sbin/pppd
```

PPP starts after users execute pppd. You can also configure the Linux dial-in server to automatically start PPP after users log in, rather than have them type */usr/sbin/ pppd* into the Linux shell.

The PPP-2.3 configuration here assumes a Linux Slackware 3.4 server, named myisp. Most configuration procedures for PPP-2.3 also apply to other Unix operating systems. However, establishing dial-in Unix login varies the most.

Networking

A dial-in Linux server must communicate with the Internet before it can offer the same capability to dial-in PPP users. Dial-in servers usually have an Internet connection via an Ethernet network interface. Thus, you should install and configure an Ethernet card on their Linux server before setting up PPP.

A Linux server requires a kernel containing Ethernet device drivers, TCP/IP networking, and PPP support. It's also important to include IP forwarding/gatewaying support. Additional information for building a new Linux kernel appears earlier in Chapter 6, *Dial-out PPP Setup*. With the appropriate kernel, the netconfig utility is useful for establishing Linux system files for networking. One important file this utility sets up is */etc/rc.d/rc.inet1*, which initializes network interfaces at boot time. rc.inet1 defines the Linux server's IP address, network number, netmask, default router, and other items. It then configures the Ethernet interface.

```
root# cat /etc/rc.d/rc.inet1
. . .
IPADDR="172.16.1.252"
NETMASK="255.255.255.0"
NETWORK="172.16.1.0"
BROADCAST="172.16.1.255"
GATEWAY="172.16.1.254"

/sbin/ifconfig eth0 ${IPADDR} broadcast ${BROADCAST} netmask ${NETMASK}
. . .
root#
```

Other important files are */etc/HOSTNAME* and */etc/hosts*. These contain the Linux dial-in server name and its IP address:

```
root# cat /etc/HOSTNAME
myisp.isp.net
root# cat /etc/hosts
127.0.0.1        localhost
172.16.1.252     myisp.isp.net loghost
root#
```

Once these files appear complete, you can reboot your server. If Linux has problems initializing its Ethernet hardware, the kernel reports error messages to the console. Likely problems include incorrect drivers that fail to detect the Ethernet card or hardware resource conflicts. If all goes well, Linux reports an active Ethernet network interface, `eth0`, with an UP status. PPP network interfaces should not appear yet, even though all of PPP-2.3 should already be installed.

```
root# ifconfig -a
. . .
eth0      Link encap:Ethernet  HWaddr 00:60:B0:A1:3D:13
          inet addr:172.16.1.252  Bcast:172.16.1.255  Mask:255.255.255.0
          UP BROADCAST RUNNING MULTICAST  MTU:1500  Metric:1
          RX packets:5597 errors:0 dropped:0 overruns:0 frame:0
          TX packets:4271 errors:0 dropped:0 overruns:0 carrier:0 coll:0
          Interrupt:9 Base address:0xfcc0 DMA chan:4
root#
```

This Linux server can now communicate with other peers on its LAN. If the default route is correct, it can communicate with any Internet destination. The preceding `rc.inet1` file includes a GATEWAY line that establishes a static default route. This should appear as destination 0.0.0.0 in the Linux routing table:

```
root# netstat -rn
Kernel IP routing table
Destination   Gateway         Genmask         Flags   MSS Window  irtt Iface
172.16.1.0    0.0.0.0         255.255.255.0   U       1500 0         0 eth0
127.0.0.0     0.0.0.0         255.0.0.0       U       3584 0         0 lo
0.0.0.0       172.16.1.254    0.0.0.0         UG      1500 0         0 eth0
root#
```

Some networks require servers to learn the default route, and other routes, via TCP/IP routing protocols. If this is the case, GATEWAY must remain unset, and you need to configure a TCP/IP routing protocol daemon. Linux includes */usr/sbin/routed*, for the Routing Information Protocol. You must first configure `routed`, then edit the startup file, */etc/rc.d/rc.inet2*, to invoke it.

Another important Linux kernel function to verify is IP forwarding. A dial-in PPP server must relay IP datagrams between users and the server's LAN. IP forwarding may be disabled by default for Linux kernels beyond version 2.0.30. You can set Linux IP forwarding as follows:

```
root# echo "1" > /proc/sys/net/ipv4/ip_forward
```

It may be necessary to include this statement in the Linux startup files.

Linux Dial-in

A Linux dial-in server must first answer incoming calls. Linux, like Unix, is oriented to users dialing in with terminals. Thus, Linux includes all the software necessary for it to answer calls with "login". After a user signs on, he can run any Linux programs: one is PPP.

On Linux, `getty` is responsible for monitoring and responding to incoming modem connections. There are numerous versions of `getty` for Linux, including `getty_ps`, `agetty`, `uugetty`, and `mgetty`. Each has its own unique features. For dial-in PPP, you should consider `mgetty`, by Gert Doering, which can invoke any program for an incoming modem connection, including fax connections. It can also autodetect PPP (see Chapter 11, *Customizing and Tuning PPP*), dispensing with the need for PPP users to interact with login prompts. Linux Slackware 3.4 doesn't include `mgetty` in binary form. Therefore, if you wish to use it, you must compile and install it. Note that file and directory paths for `mgetty` may differ from that shown here. The relationship between `mgetty` and other Linux system programs appears in Figure 7-3.

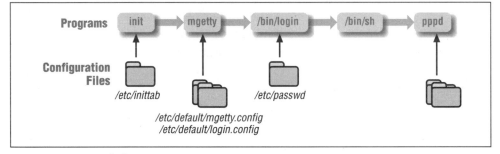

Figure 7-3. Linux dial-in

Linux `init` reads the configuration file */etc/inittab* to invoke the programs that manage dial-in. */sbin/mgetty* must appear in `inittab` for each dial-in serial interface. Further information about the format of `inittab` is available in the Linux manual page. Here are sample entries for the Linux serial interface devices */dev/ttyS0* and */dev/ttyS1*:

```
root# cat /etc/inittab
. . .
# Dialup Lines
# id:runlevels:action:process
d1:12345:respawn:/sbin/mgetty ttyS0
d2:12345:respawn:/sbin/mgetty ttyS1
. . .
Root#
```

The */etc/default/mgetty.config* configuration file includes the modem and serial interface settings `mgetty` uses to initialize dial-in. The important settings necessary for PPP, such as serial interface hardware flow control, are already built-in to `mgetty`. One notable feature is that `mgetty` can directly interact with a modem. It listens for modem `RING` strings and issues modem commands to answer a telephone call. Thus, if you use `mgetty`, you don't need to disable response codes and configure modems for auto-answer mode. `mgetty` uses compiled-in modem commands, but you may need to override some of these in its configuration file:

```
root# cat /etc/default/mgetty.config
# ----- global section -----
port-owner uucp
port-group uucp
port-mode 0664
# ----- port specific section -----
port ttyS0
  speed 57600
  init-chat "" at&f1 OK
  data-only y
  debug 5
root#
```

The `init-chat` is a mini expect/send chat script that resets the modem, a US Robotics Sportster in this case. A similar `answer-chat`, not shown, overrides the default script `mgetty` uses to answer a call. `Data-only` disables this modem for incoming fax. The `mgetty` documentation describes other keywords that can appear in *mgetty.config*.

When `mgetty` detects and answers an incoming call, it prompts for a username. It then consults the configuration file */etc/default/login.config* to determine the Linux program to execute in response. Normally, this program is */bin/login*:

```
root# cat /etc/default/login.config
. . .
# username userid utmp_entry login_program [arguments]
*         -       -         /bin/login @
root#
```

You can now activate `mgetty` by signaling `init`, with `init q`, to reload its configuration file. This Linux server is ready to answer modem calls. If there are problems, you should consult the diagnostic information `mgetty` generates in the file, */tmp/log_mg.ttyS0*.

Dial-in PPP users with Linux accounts can now sign on. You can create accounts with utilities including `useradd`. For now, give all PPP users separate home directories; this provides a place for user-specific PPP configuration files.

Configuring pppd

The PPP-2.3 main program, `pppd`, is identical for both dial-in and dial-out. As before, `pppd` manages one serial interface, negotiates PPP options, and manages the Linux kernel modules that relay IP datagrams through PPP. The configuration information that controls `pppd` behavior includes the global */etc/ppp/options* file, the *.ppprc* file in each user's home directory, and arguments appearing in the pppd command.

What distinguishes between dial-in from dial-out PPP are options passed to pppd. In dial-in arrangements, the options omit the serial device name and line speed. Without these, pppd attaches to the serial interface associated with the current login session. This is normally the same device mgetty has initialized earlier.

Here is an example of a *.ppprc* file for one dial-in user. All the pppd options necessary for dial-in are shown in this *.ppprc*. If you are concerned about server and network security, move security critical options, such as authentication settings, into the global */etc/ppp/options* file, which regular Linux user accounts can't edit. The pppd password file, */etc/ppp/pap-secrets*, or *chap-secrets*, can restrict IP address usage. Additional security details are in the pppd manpage.

```
user$ cd $HOME
user$ cat .ppprc
# Log PPP control frames to syslog
debug
# Serial interface options
modem
crtscts
# Link Control Protocol (LCP) options
asyncmap 00000000
# Require PPP Password Authentication Protocol
auth
require-pap
# Server name for PPP authentication purposes
# Default is  hostname . Only superusers can override this name.
#name myisp
# IP Control Protocol (IPCP) options
# local:remote IP address assignment
172.16.1.252:172.16.1.1
# Establish proxy ARP table entry
proxyarp
user$
```

This configuration specifies IP addresses pppd assigns to each end of the PPP connection. Since the dial-in user's address, 172.16.1.1, belongs to the IP subnet of the dial-in server's LAN, proxyarp is required. proxyarp causes this server to advertise its responsibility for this user's IP address on its LAN.

IP address assignments for active PPP connections must remain unique at all times. Thus, the *.ppprc* file for each dial-in user must have a different remote IP address. It's okay for the local IP address of all PPP connections to remain as 172.16.1.252 for all users. This is the primary IP address of the dial-in server. Another method of assigning addresses for PPP connections is to use a common PPP configuration file but compute IP addresses with shell scripts. This and other IP addressing arrangements are addressed in later chapters.

The `auth` option in *.ppprc* establishes mandatory PPP authentication. Here, the dial-in PPP user must authenticate with the Password Authentication Protocol. Note that this authentication process is unrelated to Linux login authentication. The file */etc/ppp/pap-secrets* maintains PAP authentication credentials acceptable to this dial-in PPP server:

```
root# cat /etc/ppp/pap-secrets
# Secrets for authentication using PAP
# client         server  secret              IP addresses
myname           myisp   mypass              *
myname2          myisp   mypass2             *
. . .
```

Valid usernames and passwords `pppd` accepts are in the client and secrets columns of this file.

Another set of *.ppprc* options are those for the serial interface. I've described the meaning of `modem` and `crtscts` in Chapter 6. Here, `pppd` configures the dial-in serial interface accordingly, despite settings `mgetty` may have previously established. When `pppd` terminates, it restores the serial interface settings to their prior state before `pppd` started.

Many additional PPP options can appear in *.ppprc*, */etc/ppp/options*, and other related configuration files. Chapter 11 presents more of these. The PPP-2.3 documentation is the best source for a complete listing of all the legal options for `pppd`.

Verifying PPPD

With a complete PPP-2.3 configuration, you can use a PC with dial-out PPP software to verify that `pppd` functions correctly. A chat script is necessary to navigate through `login` prompts and start PPP on the server `myisp`. If `pppd` sucessfully starts with debugging enabled, a syslog file, such as */var/log/daemon*, shows PPP activities. Any negotiation, authentication, and other problems are evident in this log.

Several automatic network configuration changes happen on the dial-in server `myisp` when a PPP connection begins. First, PPP network interfaces should appear along with IP address assignments consistent with what we placed in the *.ppprc* files:

```
root# ifconfig -a
. . .
eth0      Link encap:Ethernet  HWaddr 00:60:B0:A1:3D:13
          inet addr:172.16.1.252  Bcast:172.16.1.255  Mask:255.255.255.0
. . .
ppp0      Link encap:Point-to-Point Protocol
          inet addr:172.16.1.252  P-t-P:172.16.1.1  Mask:255.255.255.0
          UP POINTOPOINT RUNNING NOARP MULTICAST  MTU:1500  Metric:1
```

```
    . . .
    root#
```

New routing table entries on `myisp` should appear for each dial-in PPP user. Be sure the default route remains present for the Internet:

```
root# netstat -rn
Kernel IP routing table
Destination  Gateway        Genmask          Flags  MSS Window  irtt Iface
172.16.1.1   0.0.0.0        255.255.255.255  UH     1500 0         0 ppp0
172.16.1.0   0.0.0.0        255.255.255.0    U      1500 0         0 eth0
127.0.0.0    0.0.0.0        255.0.0.0        U      3584 0         0 lo
0.0.0.0      172.16.1.254   0.0.0.0          UG     1500 0         0 eth0
root#
```

Since this dial-in architecture requires Proxy ARP, user IP addresses must appear in the dial-in server's ARP table. These IP addresses also must correspond to the hardware address, 00:60:B0:A1:3D:13, of the server's Ethernet interface:

```
root# /sbin/arp -a
Address            HWtype  HWaddress          Flags Mask       Iface
172.16.1.1         ether   00:60:B0:A1:3D:13  CMP   *          eth0
root#
```

Solaris PPP

The PPP included with Sun's Solaris 2.6 operating system supports both dial-in and dial-out. Chapter 6 covers most of the Solaris PPP installation and setup procedures. In this section, I describe procedural differences and additions for achieving dial-in PPP server capability. These include Internet connectivity, login service, and changing PPP configuration for dial-in. The configuration procedures presented here are for a Sun SPARC server, named `myisp`. Solaris 2.6 for PCs is very similar.

Users connecting to Solaris PPP first encounter a login prompt:

```
ttyb login: myname
Password:
Last login: Sun Apr  6 10:17:54 on term/b
~ }#@!}!}%} }<}!}$}%\}"}&} } } } }#}$@#}%}&hEfr}'}"}{}"
```

Solaris PPP depends on the Unix login name to retrieve user-specific PPP configuration options. PPP can start immediately after a successful login, without requiring responses to shell prompts.

Networking

An Internet network connection on a Solaris dial-in PPP server is necessary to provide Internet access for dial-in PPP users. We assume this connection to be a LAN network interface on the server, which you should configure and test prior to proceeding with PPP software setup.

Solaris 2.6 has numerous system files with references to its IP address, subnet mask, and name. Some of these files are */etc/inet/hosts*, */etc/inet/netmasks*, */etc/ nodename*, and */etc/net/*/hosts*. A Solaris server that designates its Ethernet interface as le0 also has */etc/hostname.le0*, which contains a hostname that determines the interface IP address. It's cumbersome for you to edit all these network configuration files at once. Solaris provides the sys-unconfig utility to assist if you need to reconfigure networking on your PPP server:

```
root# /usr/sbin/sys-unconfig
root# reboot
```

After the server reboots, it prompts for hostname, primary network interface, IP address, subnet mask, and other information. Once you establish these settings, this PPP server should report a network configuration resembling the following:

```
root# ifconfig -a
lo0: flags=849<UP,LOOPBACK,RUNNING,MULTICAST> mtu 8232
        inet 127.0.0.1 netmask ff000000
le0: flags=863<UP,BROADCAST,NOTRAILERS,RUNNING,MULTICAST> mtu 1500
        inet 172.16.1.252 netmask ffffff00 broadcast 172.16.1.255
        ether 8:0:20:9:3d:a9
root#
```

At this point, we've established network connectivity to LAN peers. Now we need a default route to arrange communications between this PPP server and the rest of the Internet. You can define a static default route by creating the file */etc/ defaultrouter* with the IP address of a router. The presence of this file disables TCP/IP dynamic routing protocol software:

```
root# echo "172.16.1.254" > /etc/defaultrouter
```

Solaris can also learn default routes with either RIP or the ICMP router discovery protocol. The in.routed and in.rdisc daemons implement these, respectively. If these protocols are active on the network, you should eliminate */etc/ defaultrouter* and configure the appropriate daemon. The startup file */etc/rc2.d/ S69inet* is the place to invoke routing daemons at boot time. For PPP servers that run in.routed, be sure to include the quiet -q option, which prevents broadcasting undesirable RIP information through PPP connections.

A Solaris PPP server must relay IP datagrams between a PPP connection and the server's LAN connection. To perform this function, place the following command in */etc/rc2.d/S69inet* to enable ip_forwarding in the kernel:

```
ndd -set /dev/ip ip_forwarding 1
```

The ndd utility also verifies the current ip_forwarding setting. Be sure the response is 1 and not 0:

```
root# ndd /dev/ip ip_forwarding
1
root#
```

Solaris Dial-in

Solaris dial-in arranges the PPP server, myisp, to answer incoming modem calls and prompt users with "login". PPP communications may begin after the user successfully signs on.

Solaris includes numerous programs and utilities for monitoring RS-232 serial interfaces and initiating the login process. Figure 7-4 shows the relationships among programs that are necessary to serve a dial-in PPP user. The Service Access Controller (SAC) is a process responsible for maintaining all monitoring services on myisp. One of these is the port monitor for terminal ports, ttymon, that awaits incoming modem connections. A frequent action of ttymon is spawning the login program, */usr/bin/login*.

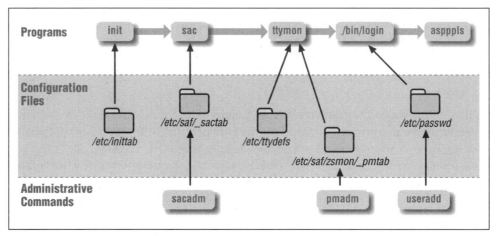

Figure 7-4. Login service, Solaris 2.x Unix

The simple way to configure Solaris login service is to use admintool. This graphical utility includes the Browse pull-down menu. It has an entry, Serial Ports, that is useful for setting up the programs in Figure 7-4 and their configuration files. Just fill in the appropriate forms. This utility requires the X Window System. In situations where admintool isn't usable or is unavailable, you can use the command-line utilities to set up dial-in.

You can use sacadm and arrange the sac process to call ttymon. This command string appears in Figure 7-5, and the resulting configuration is saved in */etc/saf/ _sactab*. Although ttymon is active at this point, you must configure it to respond to modem connections from individual serial interfaces. Each active serial interface has an associated service name, such as ttya and ttyb. pmadm installs the ttymon configuration in file */etc/saf/zsmon/_pmtab* for each service name. This includes serial interface operating modes and parameter settings.

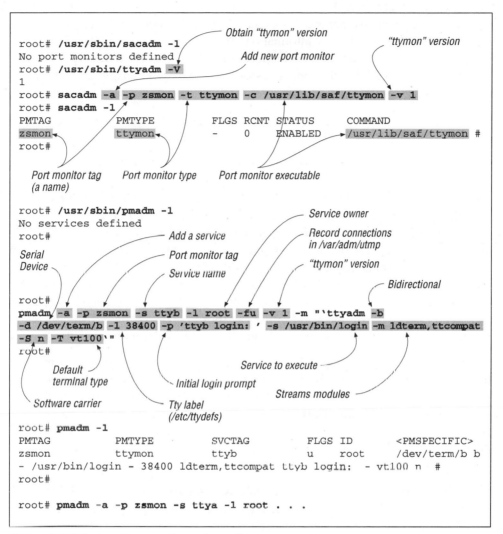

Figure 7-5. Solaris, using sacadm and pmadm

In this example, we set device */dev/term/b* for bidirectional service; both dial-in and dial-out. When `ttymon` detects an incoming connection, it invokes */usr/bin/login*. The streams modules, `-m ldterm,ttcompat`, are essential for most serial devices and should not be changed. Software carrier defines whether Solaris simulates the presence of the carrier detect signal and is unnecessary for peripherals that fully support modem control signals. Other options establish the default terminal type, which sets the `TERM` environment variable and the initial login prompt. The `-l 38400` is a label `ttymon` uses to consult */etc/ttydefs* for serial interface parameters; it's not the line speed.

The */etc/ttydefs* file contains numerous labels, each representing a collection of serial interface settings. Settings associated with the label 38400 include a line speed of 38,400 bps and other information. This is the place to establish 8-bit characters, hardware flow control, and modem control options. Note that 38,400 bps is the maximum speed for the onboard serial interfaces on many of Sun Microsystem's SPARC workstations. Higher speeds require optional serial interface hardware.

```
root# cat /etc/ttydefs
# VERSION=1
38400:38400 hupcl crtscts crtsxoff:38400 hupcl crtscts crtsxoff::38400
. . .
```

The first 38400 is the label. Colon-separated fields that follow are initial-flags, final-flags, autobaud, and next label. Both flag fields specify serial interface settings. Initial-flags applies before ttymon executes */usr/bin/login* and final-flags applies afterwards. If a dial-in user signals with the terminal break key, ttymon sets the serial interface to new settings associated with next label. Here, we've configured output and input hardware flow control with crtscts and crtsxoff, respectively. No parity and 8-bit characters are already the default: -parenb -parodd cs8 -parext. Modem control, -clocal, is also default. See the stty manual page for further information about all possible serial interface settings.

Using the sacadm and pmadm utilities, in addition to editing */etc/ttydefs*, completes the dial-in configuration for this PPP server. Next, make sure the modems attached to */dev/term/a* and */dev/term/b* have the proper serial interface settings and automatically answer incoming calls. Since we've configured the serial interfaces for bidirectional use, tip or cu are available to access and configure the modems as needed. Dial-in service is now active, and users should receive the Solaris login prompt after their modem connects.

Solaris PPP requires a login name for each user. A password is optional since PPP can also perform authentication. You can create user accounts with Solaris admintool. Alternatively, use the useradd utility:

```
root# useradd -u 2001 -g other -c "My Name" -d / -s /usr/sbin/aspppls \
myname
root# passwd myname
. . .
```

This procedure creates the login name, myname. All other options correspond to the fields in the Unix password file, */etc/passwd*. Home directories aren't necessary for Solaris PPP users. Notice the login shell is */usr/sbin/aspppls* rather than */bin/sh*; this causes PPP to start immediately after successful login. It's advisable to start aspppls only in this manner. Although users may invoke aspppls at a shell prompt, aspppd doesn't reset its terminal device to a sane state when it terminates.

Configuring aspppd

The Solaris asynchronous PPP daemon, */usr/sbin/aspppd* and the PPP login service program, */usr/sbin/aspppls* are both necessary for dial-in PPP. aspppls is responsible for connecting the dial-in PPP user's login terminal device to aspppd.

The aspppd configuration file, */etc/asppp.cf*, establishes PPP settings on a per-user basis, rather than on a per-port basis. This is the same file Chapter 6 describes for Solaris PPP dial-out. Each dial-in user requires a unique PPP network interface (ipdptp0 to ipdptp63) and a path section in the */etc/asppp.cf* file. Further details about this file and the available PPP options are in Chapter 6. Here is a sample configuration that defines a dial-in PPP user assigned to ipdptp0:

```
root# cat /etc/asppp.cf

ifconfig ipdptp0 plumb 172.16.1.252 172.16.1.1 up
ifconfig ipdptp1 plumb 172.16.1.252 172.16.1.2 up
. . .

path
# PPP network interface to use
        interface ipdptp0
# Unix login name of remote PPP peer (the PPP user)
        peer system_name myname
# LCP options
        ipcp async_map 00000000
# Authenticate user with PAP
        require_authentication pap
        pap_peer_id myname
        pap_peer_password mypass
# Miscellaneous
        inactivity_timeout 3600
        debug_level 8
path
# PPP network interface to use
        interface ipdptp1
. . .
```

When Solaris PPP initializes, ifconfig installs all the PPP network interfaces, both dial-in and out and marks them as UP. The path sections establish options for each PPP network interface. For dial-in, peer_system_name refers to the login name of the PPP user. Note this is the same statement that refers to entries in the UUCP *Systems* file for the dial-out case. Since Solaris establishes PPP based on login names, dial-in PPP users can receive the same static IP addresses when they connect. In fact, it's actually more difficult to assign PPP options based on the physical dial-in port.

If Solaris login doesn't prompt for passwords, PPP authentication is critical for security. The preceding options configure aspppd to require the PPP name, myname and password, mypass, from the dial-in user. Notice that authentication option names with the `peer` substring refer to information we expect from the dial-in user. In contrast, the dial-out case uses option names without this substring. This is for authentication data we send.

After you create or edit `asppp.cf`, shut down and restart Solaris PPP to make the changes effective:

```
root# /etc/init.d/asppp stop
root# /etc/init.d/asppp start
```

`aspppd` doesn't manage ARP table for user IP addresses. You must configure Proxy ARP for each user IP address that belongs in the IP subnet of the PPP server's LAN network interface. The `arp` utility edits the ARP table:

```
root# arp -s 172.16.1.1 8:0:20:9:3d:a9 pub
root# arp -s 172.16.1.2 8:0:20:9:3d:a9 pub
. . .
```

This links the server's Ethernet address to each user IP address. Rather than perform this step every time the server reboots, you should place these commands in a startup file, such as */etc/rc2.d/S69inet*.

PPP users can now dial-in and establish a connection.

Verifying aspppd

Verify that `aspppd` is configured correctly by configuring a PC with PPP software as a user would and then connecting into the dial-in server.

Solaris considers PPP network interfaces to be active at all times, even if the corresponding connection isn't. Therefore, no network configuration changes are apparent after a PPP connection occurs. In other words, the output of `ifconfig`, `netstat -rn`, or `arp -a`, remains the same.

Solaris PPP records its activity in */var/adm/log/asppp.log*. You can consult this file if any problems are evident. The level of detail appearing in the log is a function of the debugging level set in the `aspppd` configuration file. You can increase the value of the `debug_level` option up to 9 for troubleshooting purposes.

Windows NT 4.0 Server

Microsoft Windows NT 4.0 Server includes Remote Access Service, useful if you wish to implement dial-in PPP. Dial-in RAS users can access networks that use combinations of TCP/IP, IPX/SPX, and NetBEUI. Since we are concerned primarily with Internet access, only TCP/IP is important here. One characteristic of RAS is that users dialing in can't see readable text prompts or command-line interpreters. The only way to communicate is with PPP. Users don't need chat scripts beyond what is necessary to arrange a modem connection. Interactive terminal windows are unusable with RAS.

You must be careful when selecting the base Windows NT 4.0 product. For dial-in arrangements with more than one incoming telephone line, Windows NT 4.0 "Server", rather than "Workstation", is a critical requirement. Although serial interface hardware is a likely constraint, Windows NT 4.0 Server can support about 256 dial-in connections. In contrast, Windows NT 4.0 Workstation limits dial-in to a single user.

When building a dial-in PPP server with RAS, you should first arrange Internet access via LAN connection for the server itself. Next, configure serial interfaces and modems. Finally, install and configure RAS itself.

Networking

Windows NT 4.0 Server requires drivers for each of its network interfaces. In particular, you must first install what Microsoft calls a *network adapter*. This is the equivalent of a LAN card. In addition, drivers are necessary for each network layer protocol. For dial-in PPP users communicating with the Internet, you must install TCP/IP.

After Windows NT boots for the first time, you can begin the networking configuration process by selecting the Network icon in the control panel. Windows NT automatically prompts for the following information:

Wired to the network: or Remote access to the network:
> Since we're setting up a LAN network interface first, select `wired`.

Network adapters
> Select the appropriate driver for the LAN networking hardware on this dial-in server.

Network protocols
> The protocol for the Internet is TCP/IP. However, if this server also connects to PC networks, include IPX/SPX and NetBEUI as necessary.

Network services
> These describe networking applications software to install. For now, just accept the default `RPC Configuration`, `NetBIOS Interface`, `Workstation`, and `Server`.

Windows NT also prompts for information regarding use of the Dynamic Host Configuration Protocol (DHCP), network bindings, the computer's name, and domain. DHCP enables another server to allocate IP addresses. Since you already know the IP addresses to use in the dial-in PPP architecture, select "no" for DHCP. For the other items, you can leave many of them at their defaults for now.

If the initial Windows NT networking configuration is complete, you can reconfigure networking again later by returning to the **Network** icon in the control panel. Figure 7-6 shows how to set important TCP/IP parameters for a LAN network interface. The **IP Address** tab in **Microsoft TCP/IP Properties** defines the dial-in PPP server's primary IP address and its default route. The settings shown are consistent with our earlier dial-in PPP architecture assumptions. Since this dial-in PPP server must relay IP datagrams between PPP and LAN network interfaces, **IP Forwarding** must also be enabled. This is the only setting that appears in the **Routing** tab.

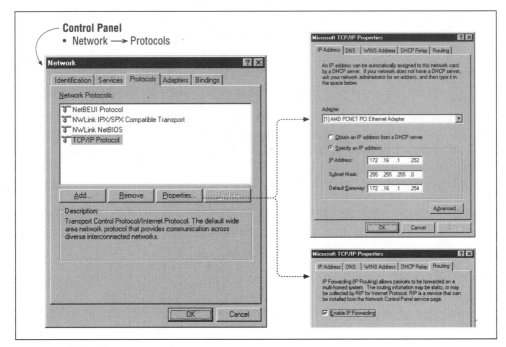

Figure 7-6. Windows NT TCP/IP Properties

Windows NT Server can also learn the default route and other routes using the Routing Information Protocol (RIP). If RIP is active on the LAN, configure the dial-in PPP server to use it by adding this service with the **Services** tab.

This completes the steps for LAN networking. This dial-in server can now communicate with Internet sites by IP address. To use DNS names on the server itself instead of addresses, configure DNS in **TCP/IP Properties**. You can verify Internet connectivity with Microsoft Internet Explorer, **ping**, and other Windows NT utilities.

Serial Interfaces and Modems

Windows NT Server hardware frequently includes two onboard serial interfaces that can support dial-in for remote users. Third-party serial interface cards can expand this number for additional remote users. You should verify that Windows NT device drivers are available for any multiport serial interface card you may want to consider. Since installation procedures vary depending on the hardware, vendor documentation is the best resource for instructions.

Once Windows NT is aware of all its serial interfaces, each may be associated with a modem. The Modem icon in the control panel invokes Modems Properties, much like the one for Windows 98 (see Figure 6-4). This configures both RS-232 serial interface settings and modem settings. The Add button lets Windows NT automatically detect modems or lets you specify the modem model. The modem model defines all command strings Windows NT uses to initialize and control it.

Included in Modems Properties is a Properties button. Again, this invokes configuration windows nearly identical to the ones for Windows 98. The General tab includes the serial interface speed, which we set to 57600 bps. Other settings to use with the Connection tab are no parity, 8 data bits, and 1 stop bit. An Advanced button accesses flow control and modem options. For PPP, enable hardware flow control. You should also enable modem compression.

Once modem and serial interface pairs appear in Modems Properties, you can assign any of them for use with RAS.

Remote Access Service Installation

The Remote Access Service is an optional component of Windows NT Server. A listing of installed network services is available under Network in the Windows NT control panel (Figure 7-7). If Remote Access Service doesn't appear on this list, you can select the Add button to install it. Windows NT prompts for its installation media and guides you through the RAS install process.

The main Remote Access Setup window appears when you select Remote Access Service and then Properties in the network control panel. The Add button in Remote Access Setup adds serial interface and modem pairs that can participate in a dial-in PPP pool. These pairs were defined earlier, during serial interface and modem configuration. As you add each pair, its default usage is Receive calls only. The Configure button changes this usage, if necessary.

The Network button invokes the Network Configuration window (Figure 7-8). This establishes network protocols Windows NT RAS supports for dial-in PPP users. For Internet access, we show TCP/IP. If other protocols are in use on networks connected to this dial-in server, you can enable them here.

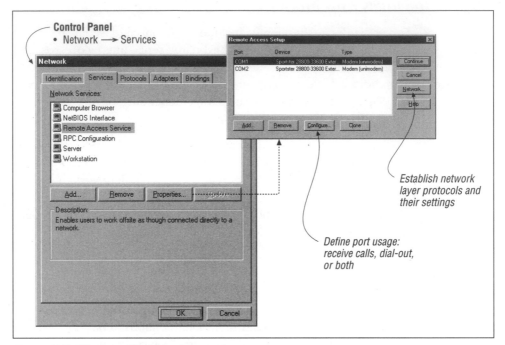

Figure 7-7. Windows NT Remote Access Setup

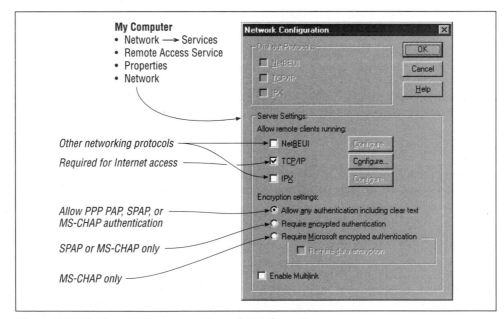

Figure 7-8. Windows NT RAS server Network Configuration

PPP authentication settings also appear in **Network Configuration** and apply to all dial-in ports. **Encryption settings:** define what PPP authentication methods Windows NT imposes on dial-in users. The meaning of the authentication choices, in PPP terminology, are as follows:

Allow any authentication including clear text
> Clear text refers to PPP PAP.

Require encrypted authentication
> This permits dial-in PPP users to authenticate only with MS-CHAP or SPAP. PPP PAP is not acceptable.

Require Microsoft encrypted authentication
> Dial-in PPP users must authenticate using MS-CHAP.

You should be aware that MS-CHAP and SPAP are nonstandard PPP authentication methods. Consider these choices only if you're sure all your users have PPP implementations featuring Microsoft or Shiva authentication compatibility. For Internet access service with RAS, I recommend allowing the standard PPP clear-text authentication. Since the release of Windows NT 4.0 Service Pack 2, Microsoft has added the standard CHAP authentication method. This is beneficial since you can now require password encryption without creating PPP compatibility problems for your users. The Windows registry stores CHAP keys, rather than the Windows NT user authentication facility. Details about setting up CHAP for RAS appear in Chapter 12, *Authentication.*

The last important RAS configuration window is **RAS Server TCP/IP Configuration** (see Figure 7-9). Access this window by selecting the **Configure...** button shown in Figure 7-8. The first item is **Allow remote TCP/IP clients to access:**. Since a dial-in PPP server's sole purpose is to provide dial-in users access to resources elsewhere in a large network, the **Entire network** choice is the most appropriate. The second item manages IP addresses assigned to remote PPP users. DHCP servers, if available, can provide this function. However, the **Use static address pool** approach is simpler and should be more reliable.

Windows NT RAS behaves as follows regarding this pool:

- The static address pool must consist of IP addresses belonging to the IP subnet of the dial-in PPP server's LAN. The pool doesn't need to be contiguous, as evident by the **Excluded ranges** option.

- The dial-in PPP server assigns one address in this pool to itself. This is the address of the local ends of all its PPP connections. All the other addresses are for active dial-in PPP users. In total, the size of the pool must be at least one plus the number of dial-in ports. With two ports, **COM1:** and **COM2:**, a minimum of three addresses, 172.16.1.1, 172.16.1.2, and 172.16.1.3, are required.

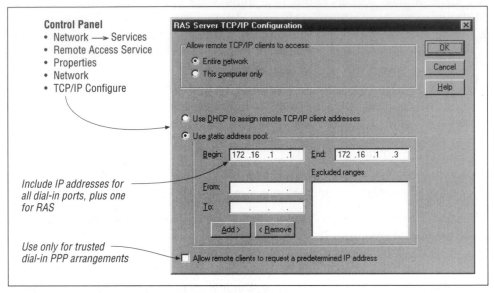

Figure 7-9. Windows NT RAS Server TCP/IP Configuration

- Windows NT RAS performs Proxy ARP on its LAN automatically. However, to prevent conflicts, IP addresses in this pool may not be used elsewhere on the LAN or on other dial-in PPP servers.

The static address pool feature can't reserve particular addresses for an individual dial-in user. Furthermore, it's not possible to assign a fixed address to a port. The `Allow remote clients to request a predetermined IP address` feature does let dial-in users request and retain an IP address they can call their own. Unfortunately, this doesn't prevent them from successfully requesting IP addresses already in use elsewhere. Thus, you should avoid enabling this option for general-purpose dial-in PPP. This option is useful only if you have total control or high trust regarding every dial-in user's PPP configuration.

The remaining configurable Windows NT RAS, PPP, and TCP/IP settings require editing the Windows NT system registry with `regedt32`. Default registry settings are adequate for most common dial-in PPP server arrangements. I therefore defer discussing registry settings until Chapter 11.

This completes the Windows NT RAS configuration. If you made any networking or RAS configuration changes, Windows NT Server annoyingly requires rebooting in most cases. Thus, before proceeding, you must restart Windows NT.

Managing Remote Access Service

There are still administrative tasks to do before Windows NT RAS offers dial-in PPP services for the first time. This includes starting the RAS server process, managing RAS operation, managing Windows NT user accounts, and setting dial-in PPP user permissions.

Since a dial-in server listens for incoming calls, a Windows NT background process performs this task. Start the RAS background process manually or configure Windows NT to start it at server at boot time. Figure 7-10 shows `Services` in the control panel, which lists all Windows NT services, one of which is `Remote Access Server`. If RAS is active, the `Started` flag appears in the `Status` column. If it's not active, select it and press the `Start` button. The `Startup` column indicates if the RAS service is `Automatic` at boot time, `Manual`, requiring your intervention, or `Disabled`. You can change these states, as needed, with the `Startup` button. The `Remote Access Server` operates in conjunction with the `Remote Access Connection Manager`. Enabling RAS also enables the connection manager.

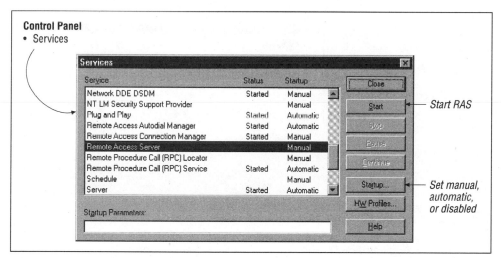

Figure 7-10. Windows NT Services

An active RAS accepts incoming calls only for authorized PPP users. You can create Windows NT user accounts with the `musrmgr` utility. This is equivalent to `User Manager`, which appears under `Administrative Tools (Common)` in the `Start` menu. Users accounts may be local to a server or members of a Windows NT domain, depending on the Windows NT networking environment. The user manager utility can grant users permission to dial-in, among other permissions. Alternatively, the `rasadmin` utility can manage dial-in PPP permissions in its `Users` pull-down menu.

The primary administration utility for Windows NT RAS is `Remote Access Admin` (Figure 7-11). This program also appears in `Administrative Tools (Common)` in the `Start` menu, or as the `rasadmin` utility at a command prompt. `rasadmin` can manage many Windows NT dial-in PPP servers simultaneously. `Select Domain or Server` determines the set of dial-in PPP servers it manages. Management tasks may reference an entire domain with many servers or an individual server, depending on the current administrative scope. As shown, `\\ISP` in the window's title references the name of an individual, local server. A domain name appears without the double backslash prefix.

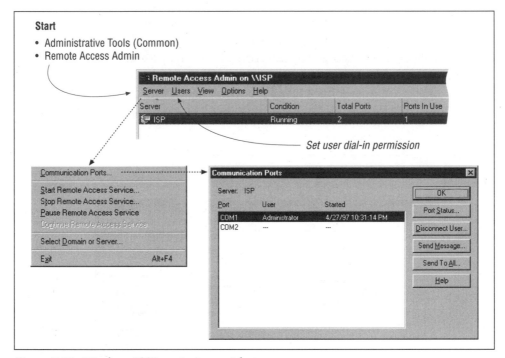

Figure 7-11. Windows NT Remote Access Admin

Once `Remote Access Admin` shows one or more dial-in servers in its list, you can choose to `start`, `stop`, `pause`, or `continue` dial-in PPP. A paused service continues to support PPP communications for active users. However, it doesn't accept new PPP connections. This feature is useful for a scheduled shutdown situation.

When active PPP connections exist, you can get status information by selecting `Communications Ports` in the `Server` pull-down menu. The status window shown in Figure 7-11 has user `Administrator` active on the `COM1` dial-in port. The `Port Status` button provides real-time statistic counters and errors, regarding a dial-in port's activity. More importantly, information about the IP and other addresses the RAS has assigned to the remote user also appears.

Disconnect User obviously terminates an active connection. If you wish to notify users of a pending service shutdown, you can attempt to Send Message to an active user or try to Send To All. Note that PPP doesn't include messaging capability. A TCP/IP application is responsible for sending and receiving these messages. Windows 98 users dialing into a RAS PPP server can use the winpopup utility.

One major flaw with Windows NT RAS is its inability to selectively enable and disable dial-in ports in real time. A condition may arise, such as a bad modem, that requires you to temporarily busy out and remove a dial-in port. This requires reconfiguring RAS with Remote Access Setup (Figure 7-7). Unfortunately, after you modify the active port list, Windows NT requires restarting before the change becomes effective. This terminates all active PPP connections.

Verifying RAS

To verify a Windows NT dial-in server, you should attempt to dial-in with PPP software as a user. Users must authenticate to the RAS server with the server's permitted PPP authentication methods. The authentication name may require the Windows NT domain-name and username format, separated by a backslash:

    usinet\myname

Domains may not be applicable in some dial-in installations. The user's Windows NT login password is either the PAP password or MS-CHAP key.

The dial-in PPP server normally records PPP connections in the event log. You can view this log with the event viewer eventvwr utility. In cases of modem or PPP negotiation problems, you can enable additional debugging logs to help isolate problems.

Modem commands and responses are visible if record a log file is active for a given serial interface and modem pair. First, access Modems Properties in the control panel. Select the serial interface and modem pair, then properties → connection → advanced and check the log recording option. Stopping and restarting RAS creates the log. You can view this log file as follows:

    c:\WINNT>type "ModemLog_Sportster 28800-33600 External.txt"

The log filename varies depending on the model description of the modem.

To enable trace logs, you must edit the following registry value with the regedt32 utility:

    HKEY_LOCAL_MACHINE\System\CurrentControlSet\Services\RasMan\PPP\Logging

Changing this value from 0 to 1 enables you to log PPP negotiation events. Be sure to stop and restart RAS to make this change effective. The location and sample contents of this log file follow:

```
c:\WINNT\system32\ras>type ppp.log
Line up event occurred on port 1
FsmInit called for protocol = c021, port = 1
FsmReset called for protocol = c021, port = 1
FsmThisLayerStarted called for protocol = c021, port = 1
<PPP packet sent at 05/04/1997 01:38:28:325
<Protocol = LCP, Type = Configure-Req, Length = 0x1b, Id = 0x0, Port = 1
<C0 21 01 00 00 19 02 06 00 00 00 00 03 05 C2 23 |.!.............#|
<80 05 06 00 00 25 17 07 02 08 02               |.....%.....    |

>PPP packet received at 05/04/1997 01:38:28:325
>Protocol = LCP, Type = Configure-Req, Length = 0x1a, Id = 0x1, Port = 1
>C0 21 01 01 00 18 01 04 05 DC 02 06 00 00 00 00 |.!.............|
>05 06 6F C8 39 83 07 02 08 02                  |..o.9.....     |
```

. . .

Windows NT Routing Annoyances

Windows NT has several routing idiosyncrasies that occur in network configurations that require forwarding IP datagrams between a PPP connection and a LAN network interface. Clearly, a PPP server that provides Internet access may be affected. These flaws can result in especially frustrating troubleshooting experiences as you try to determine why your PPP users can't communicate with the networks a Windows NT RAS server serves.

Microsoft has released the Routing and Remote Access Upgrade, code name "Steelhead," for Windows NT 4.0 Server. This upgrade is free of charge. Note that it's not available for Windows NT Workstation. I recommend upgrading your Windows NT 4.0 Server with RRAS. This precaution eliminates potential future problems regarding TCP/IP routing with PPP connections.

Alternatively, if you can't or don't wish to install the Routing and Remote Access Upgrade, you may wish to adjust these Windows NT registry values instead:

```
HKEY_LOCAL_MACHINE\System\CurrentControlSet\Services\
    network adapter\Parameters\Tcpip\DontAddDefaultGateway
```

Set the preceding to **REG_DWORD 0x1** on all network interfaces except the one that connects to the Internet. This suppresses multiple default routes that conflict with each other:

```
HKEY_LOCAL_MACHINE\System\CurrentControlSet\Services\
    RasArp\Parameters\DisableOtherSrcPackets
```

Set the preceding to REG_DWORD 0x0. This prevents Windows NT from inappropriately rewriting the source IP address field in IP datagrams when it routes datagrams between its LAN network interface and a PPP connection:

```
HKEY_LOCAL_MACHINE\System\CurrentControlSet\Services\
    RasMan\PPP\IPCP\PriorityBasedOnSubNetwork
```

If a LAN network interface and a dial-out PPP connection belong to different subnets of the same network number and **Use Default Gateway On Remote Network** is enabled for PPP, Windows NT overrides the routes that point to the LAN interface with routes that point to the PPP connection. Setting the preceding registry value to REG_DWORD 0x1 prevents this from happening.

Additional registry adjustments may be necessary to resolve more routing issues. You may wish to consult the latest Microsoft support documents regarding RAS and routing for more instructions.

Null Modem Connections

The Windows NT RAS includes provisions for connecting computers with a null modem cable, rather than with the usual telephone lines and modems. Users with Windows NT and another PPP-capable computer on the same desktop may wish to share data via PPP through a hardwired connection. RAS can wait for incoming PPP connections from a cable, as it does for a modem.

Setting up RAS to answer PPP calls via cable is nearly identical to the procedures for a modem. Windows NT considers a null modem cable as a different modem type. In **Modems Properties**, you can associate a serial interface with this modem:

```
Dial-Up Networking Serial Cable between 2 PCs
```

This item appears in the manufacturer **(Standard Modem Types)**. This null modem profile omits all initialization command strings a real modem normally requires.

When another computer initiates a PPP connection to RAS, it must use a short chat script. RAS listens for the wake-up string **CLIENT** and responds with **CLIENT-SERVER**:

```
Send:   CLIENT
Expect: CLIENTSERVER
. . .PPP. . .
```

This handshake must succeed before Windows NT begins PPP communications. If a peer computer simply initiated a PPP connection by sending a PPP frame, Windows NT RAS ignores everything: it's still waiting for the string **CLIENT**.

In this chapter:
- *Choosing Network Architectures*
- *Proxy ARP*
- *Split Subnet*
- *Unnumbered*
- *PPP in a Subnet*
- *Multipoint PPP in a Subnet*

Network Architectures Incorporating PPP

Incorporating PPP connections into a network, particularly the Internet, can be a difficult challenge. In a TCP/IP network, all computers and most intermediate points inside require specific IP addresses. There exist important relationships between IP addresses, IP subnet numbers, and IP network numbers. This relationship is what determines how and where the network routes IP datagrams to their final destination. Therefore, you must understand the constraints that affect PPP IP address assignment.

In Chapter 7, *Dial-in PPP Setup*, we discussed a proxy ARP network architecture specifically for dial-in PPP. Dial-in users make a connection to the edges of a network infrastructure. But PPP is also useful between routers that connect two or more smaller networks. In other words, a PPP connection can become part of a route between many IP addresses that are unrelated to its own. Thus, the relationship between PPP connections and neighboring network nodes can be much more complex than the dial-in PPP case.

In this chapter, I present several possible network architectures that use PPP for part of the network's infrastructure. The architecture you choose partially depends on how you use your PPP connections and how many you have. We will discuss how to establish the proper relationships between PPP IP addresses and those for the neighboring network infrastructure.

Choosing Network Architectures

TCP/IP network architectures consist of point-to-point connections and shared medium LANs. Computers connecting to a network usually have either a single LAN network interface or a point-to-point network interface. On the other hand, generic network nodes and routers can have a mix of these interfaces. Although point-to-point connections may use different communication technologies, here we assume they are all PPP connections.

When you allocate IP addresses for LANs, you assign them IP subnet numbers. PPP connections can share an IP subnet with a LAN, may have their own unique IP subnets, or may not use IP subnets at all. Figure 8-1 illustrates five network architectures and IP subnet relationships in the vicinity of PPP connections. Where a connection exists between two nodes that serve LANs, degenerate cases also exist where a PPP endpoint is a single node with no other connections. Similarly, any node shown with one connection may have additional interfaces to other networks. Here's a summary of the possibilities:

Proxy ARP

> The IP addresses for PPP connections share the same IP subnet that belongs to a LAN. Proxy ARP is the simplest architecture for dial-in PPP. It eliminates the need to propagate routing information about PPP connections. Products such as Windows NT 4.0 RAS support only the proxy ARP architecture.

Split Subnet

> Split subnet is an extension to the proxy ARP configuration. A LAN becomes split into two or more physical LANs, but they all continue to use the same IP subnet. This architecture is useful if your network constrains you to one IP subnet.

Unnumbered

> Here PPP shares an IP address belonging to another network interface, on the same network node. This other network interface is usually for a LAN. No new IP addresses are necessary for unnumbered PPP network interfaces. This architecture is the simplest when PPP connects two IP subnets. The PPP connection appears invisible as far as the network infrastructure is concerned. This simplifies routing, since an IP subnet doesn't exist for PPP.

PPP in a Subnet

> In this architecture, a single PPP connection belongs to its own unique IP subnet number. Both PPP endpoints have IP addresses belonging to this subnet. This architecture is useful for connecting IP subnets in wide area networks and for dial-in PPP. Also, some PPP network equipment have limitations that require PPP connections to belong exclusively in their own IP subnets.

Multipoint PPP in a Subnet

> Several adjacent PPP connections in a group share a single IP subnet number. This architecture is useful for dial-in PPP where there are large groups of PPP connections. It separates the IP subnet for PPP from IP subnets for other purposes.

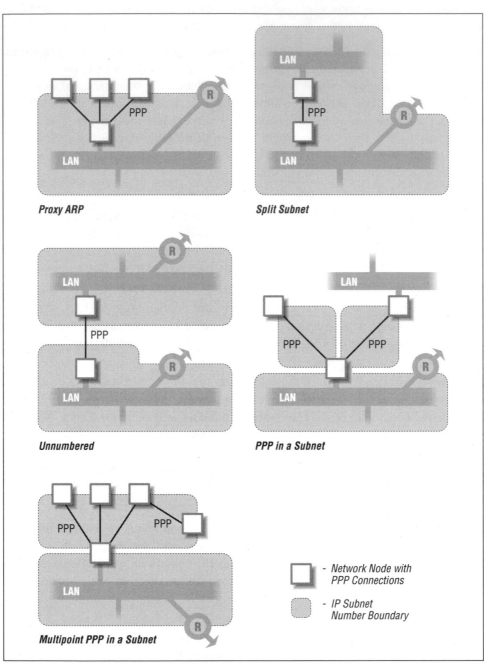

Figure 8-1. Network architectures with PPP connections

This list of architectures is by no means complete. Creative network designers can no doubt develop additional architectures with PPP.

I suggest you choose *Proxy ARP* or *Multipoint PPP in a Subnet* for dial-in PPP. These architectures best accommodate large contiguous groups of PPP connections. If you can obtain large numbers of small IP subnets, consider *PPP in a Subnet* for dial-in. This may be difficult to do in some networks.

When PPP connects IP subnets to form a larger network, the best architectures to choose are *Unnumbered* and *PPP in a Subnet*. For IP address usage efficiency, the connections in the *PPP in a Subnet* architecture should belong to small IP subnets.

I don't recommend *Split Subnets* unless you must use a single IP subnet for multiple LANs. This constraint results if you can't allocate a new IP subnet and disseminate routing information about it into your network infrastructure. Split subnets are generally awkward to maintain, as we'll see later.

Proxy ARP

The Proxy ARP architecture is well suited for large numbers of PPP connections that concentrate their traffic into a common LAN. Dial-in PPP frequently has this characteristic. The use of Proxy ARP causes network nodes with PPP connections to appear on a LAN even though the node doesn't physically reside at the LAN. PPP users use IP addresses that would otherwise belong to LAN nodes. Here are some requirements for using Proxy ARP:

- The IP subnet belonging to a LAN must have enough free IP addresses for PPP users.

- The dial-in PPP server must respond to address resolution protocol queries on behalf of its own IP address and all IP addresses belonging to PPP users. The former is "ARP" while the latter is "Proxy ARP."

Figure 8-2 shows details for a hypothetical Proxy ARP architecture.

Traditionally, a real LAN node responds to ARP broadcast queries with its MAC address whenever such queries reference its IP address. Chapter 4, *TCP/IP*, describes this in greater detail. Proxy ARP modifies this behavior for the dial-in PPP server. The dial-in server must respond to ARP queries for any active IP address of PPP users. Internet IP datagrams destined for PPP users arrive from the router, as usual. Then, Proxy ARP causes the router to forward IP datagrams to the LAN network interface at the dial-in server. In effect, Proxy ARP creates the illusion that a PPP user appears on the LAN.

The PPP user illusion is useful because it eliminates the need for TCP/IP routing changes at the router, Node A, and elsewhere. Routing is the same whether or not PPP connections actually exist. This is a significant advantage for Proxy ARP. Despite this simplicity, there are still important precautions. Be careful to prevent

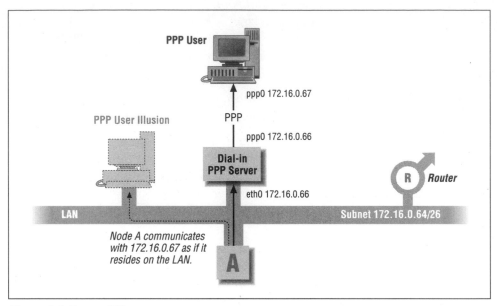

Figure 8-2. Proxy ARP

IP address duplication between LAN nodes and PPP users; should this happen, anything with duplicated addresses can't communicate reliably.

IP Subnet and IP Addresses

In the Proxy ARP architecture of Figure 8-2, IP subnet 172.16.0.64/26 is assigned for the LAN and for PPP connections. After accounting for reserved addresses, the IP addresses available in this subnet are 172.16.0.65 to 172.16.0.126. The dial-in server can assign unused IP addresses to PPP users. The figure shows one PPP user with an active connection. The user receives 172.16.0.67 as her IP address.

The dial-in PPP server has an Ethernet network interface, eth0, and a PPP network interface, ppp0. Additional PPP network interfaces exist, but these aren't in the figure. After several users establish PPP connections, a dial-in PPP server running Linux should show the following network interfaces:

```
user$ /sbin/ifconfig -a
lo        Link encap:Local Loopback
          inet addr:127.0.0.1  Bcast:127.255.255.255  Mask:255.0.0.0
          UP BROADCAST LOOPBACK RUNNING  MTU:3584  Metric:1
. . .
eth0      Link encap:Ethernet  HWaddr 00:60:B0:A1:3D:13
          inet addr:172.16.0.66  Bcast:172.16.0.127  Mask:255.255.255.192
          UP BROADCAST RUNNING MULTICAST  MTU:1500  Metric:1
. . .
```

```
ppp0      Link encap:Point-to-Point Protocol
          inet addr:172.16.0.66  P-t-P:172.16.0.67  Mask:255.255.255.192
          UP POINTOPOINT RUNNING NOARP MULTICAST  MTU:1500  Metric:1
. . .
ppp1      Link encap:Point-to-Point Protocol
          inet addr:172.16.0.66  P-t-P:172.16.0.68  Mask:255.255.255.192
          UP POINTOPOINT RUNNING NOARP MULTICAST  MTU:1500  Metric:1
. . .
ppp2      Link encap:Point-to-Point Protocol
          inet addr:172.16.0.66  P-t-P:172.16.0.69  Mask:255.255.255.192
          UP POINTOPOINT RUNNING NOARP MULTICAST  MTU:1500  Metric:1
. . .
user$
```

It's common practice in the Proxy ARP architecture to set one IP address for all the PPP connections terminating on a dial-in PPP server. This address may even match the IP address for the Ethernet interface. Duplicating an IP address this way is acceptable because this address still unambiguously refers to the same physical equipment. You can still choose to avoid address duplication and assign different IP addresses to every PPP endpoint. This is useful if you need to distinguish the PPP network interfaces from each other.

One question that arises for the Proxy ARP architecture is how to set subnet masks for PPP network interfaces. It's best to set PPP subnet masks to the appropriate value for the IP subnet you're using for this proxy ARP architecture. Since 172.16.0.64/26 has a mask of 26 one bits, the subnet mask is 255.255.255.192. Although the subnet mask is really meaningless for PPP, some Unix versions can misinterpret entries in its routing table, suffer routing table losses, or corrupt the table, if you set PPP subnet masks incorrectly.

Configuring ARP

On Ethernet LANs, ARP translates IP addresses to 48-bit Ethernet addresses. In Proxy ARP, a dial-in PPP server responds to ARP queries in such a way that causes its own Ethernet address to become responsible for all the IP addresses of PPP users.

You may not have to configure Proxy ARP explicitly. Windows NT 4.0 RAS and Annex communication servers automatically perform Proxy ARP whenever a PPP connection uses IP addresses belonging to the IP subnet of a LAN. Other products may require you to configure Proxy ARP explicitly by manipulating ARP tables.

PPP-2.3 can set up Proxy ARP automatically, but only if you include the proxyarp option for pppd:

```
user$ /usr/sbin/pppd proxyarp 172.16.0.66:172.16.0.67 . . .
```

Solaris requires you to manipulate entries in its ARP table. On Solaris, a minimal ARP table appears as follows:

```
root# arp -a
Net to Media Table
Device    IP Address              Mask        Flags   Phys Addr
------ -------------------- --------------- ----- ---------------
le0    myisp                  255.255.255.255 SP     08:00:20:09:3d:a9
le0    224.0.0.0              240.0.0.0       SM     01:00:5e:00:00:00
root#
```

The `le0` on Solaris is the equivalent of `eth0` on Linux.

To Proxy ARP for a PPP user at IP address 172.16.0.67 (Figure 8-2), you must install a permanently published entry in the ARP table:

```
root# arp -s 172.16.0.67 08:00:20:09:3d:a9 pub
root# arp -a
Net to Media Table
Device    IP Address              Mask        Flags   Phys Addr
------ -------------------- --------------- ----- ---------------
le0    myisp                  255.255.255.255 SP     08:00:20:09:3d:a9
le0    172.16.0.67            255.255.255.255 SP     08:00:20:09:3d:a9
le0    224.0.0.0              240.0.0.0       SM     01:00:5e:00:00:00
root#
```

The `P` flag indicates this dial-in PPP server publishes the `phys addr` for ARP queries that match the corresponding `IP address`. This physical address is the Ethernet address for the `le0` network interface. Each IP address for PPP users requires one published entry in the ARP table. You can include as many `arp -s` commands as necessary in the Solaris start up file, */etc/rc2.d/S69inet*, since these entries are critical after booting, whenever PPP is active.

The dial-in PPP server, `myisp`, must reply with its Ethernet address, 08:00:20:09:3d:a9, whenever it receives an ARP request on the LAN for the IP address, 172.16.0.67. You can verify the correct operation of Proxy ARP on Node A, as Figure 8-2 shows. Here is how:

```
user$ ping myisp
myisp is alive
user$ ping 172.16.0.67
no answer from 172.16.0.67
user$ arp -a
myisp (172.16.0.66) at 8:0:20:9:3d:a9
? (172.16.0.67) at 8:0:20:9:3d:a9
user$
```

Although the IP address 172.16.0.67 didn't respond to the `ping`, the `arp -a` output shows Node A correctly learns the Ethernet address for 172.16.0.67. This Ethernet address matches the address of the dial-in PPP server. Whether the PPP user at 172.16.0.67 responds to `ping` is immaterial. We wish only to verify that Proxy ARP is working.

Split Subnet

In the split subnet architecture, one LAN is split into several smaller LANs. The resulting LANs continue to share the IP subnet that once belonged to the original LAN. Each LAN communicates with the others through one or more PPP connections. The nodes on all the LANs continue to behave as if they were connected to one physical LAN. Nodes with PPP connections are the exception, since they are aware of the other LANs that share the same IP subnet.

In the split subnet architecture, PPP's role is to connect two or more distant LANs. The architecture is useful if you have only a single IP subnet to work with and can't break the subnet into smaller ones. We must assume this constraint for networks that aren't CIDR capable and require a fixed subnet mask for subnets in one IP network number. Chapter 4 describes these limitations in further detail.

One key advantage for splitting subnets is that TCP/IP routing remains the same outside the subnet. The rest of the network infrastructure still considers the split subnets as a single subnet entity. Unfortunately, split subnet has significant disadvantages. Problem areas pertain to scalability, table management, and the behavior of reserved IP addresses. We'll discuss these problem areas in the section "Split Subnet Complications."

An example of the split subnet architecture appears in Figure 8-3. This figure illustrates a single logical LAN consisting of three physical LANs. The network nodes with PPP connections, namely A, B, and C, are responsible for proxy ARP. In effect, each of these nodes masquerade for all the other equipment not residing on its own LAN. For regular computers, such as D, E, and F, the network nodes responsible for PPP provide the illusion that far away LAN nodes are all local. A router connects this logical LAN to a greater network infrastructure.

IP Subnets and IP Addresses

The rules for assigning IP addresses among multiple LANs sharing a subnet are no different than the rules for a normal LAN. Every node must have a unique IP addresses in the IP subnet. However, if you allocate a contiguous IP address range for each LAN, you can simplify IP address management. Like the proxy ARP architecture, PPP nodes can use the same IP address for both its PPP and LAN network interfaces.

The IP subnet in Figure 8-3 is 172.20.10.0/24. This subnet accommodates IP addresses from 172.20.10.1 to 172.20.10.254. Node B uses a single IP address for both its Ethernet (eth0) and PPP (ppp0) network interfaces. This and other IP address assignments are:

```
172.20.10.12    node-a  ppp-gateway-1
172.20.10.1     node-b  ppp-gateway-2
```

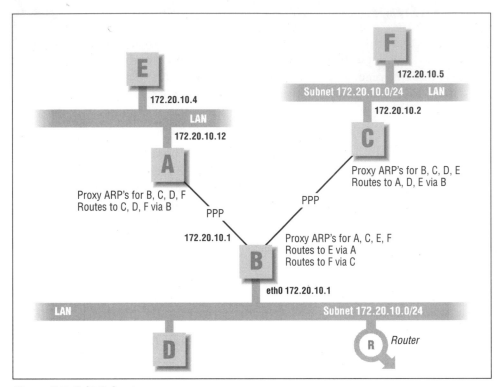

Figure 8-3. Split Subnet

```
172.20.10.2      node-c   ppp-gateway-3
172.20.10.3      node-d
172.20.10.4      node-e
172.20.10.5      node-f
```

Node B's network interface configuration has two PPP connections active, **ppp0** and **ppp1**:

```
user$ /sbin/ifconfig -a
lo        Link encap:Local Loopback
          inet addr:127.0.0.1  Bcast:127.255.255.255  Mask:255.0.0.0
          UP BROADCAST LOOPBACK RUNNING  MTU:3584  Metric:1
. . .
eth0      Link encap:Ethernet  HWaddr 00:60:B0:A1:3D:13
          inet addr:172.20.10.1  Bcast:172.20.10.255  Mask:255.255.255.0
          UP BROADCAST RUNNING MULTICAST  MTU:1500  Metric:1
. . .
ppp0      Link encap:Point-to-Point Protocol
          inet addr:172.20.10.1  P-t-P:172.20.10.12  Mask:255.255.255.0
          UP POINTOPOINT RUNNING NOARP MULTICAST  MTU:1500  Metric:1
. . .
ppp1      Link encap:Point-to-Point Protocol
          inet addr:172.20.10.1  P-t-P:172.20.10.2  Mask:255.255.255.0
```

```
             UP POINTOPOINT RUNNING NOARP MULTICAST  MTU:1500  Metric:1
  . . .
user$
```

Nodes A and C have similar configurations but with different IP addresses. Be careful to assign PPP IP addresses consistently. The equipment on both ends of a PPP connection must have the same notion of the two IP addresses at each end.

The subnet mask for all network interfaces in our configuration is 255.255.255.0. With Linux and Unix, this is set consistently according to the subnet mask that applies to the IP subnet number in use. Non-Unix platforms may require alternate subnet masks for PPP. Further information about this is in Chapter 4.

Configuring ARP

In the split subnet architecture, each node responsible for PPP must relay IP datagrams destined to the IP addresses on far away LANs. To perform this function, the PPP node must first arrange to receive these IP datagrams from other nodes on its own LAN. Arranging proxy ARP achieves this. For example, Node B in Figure 8-3 must masquerade as A, C, E, and F on its own LAN. Whenever an ARP broadcast occurs for any of these destination IP addresses, this node replies with its Ethernet address. The contents of the ARP table controls the Proxy ARP behavior.

Proxy ARP in the split subnet architecture requires masquerading for IP addresses besides those in use with a PPP connection. Therefore, you must manually manipulate the ARP table at each node. It's not sufficient to depend on automatic proxy ARP features in some PPP software. This feature modifies the ARP table for the IP address of PPP endpoints only, which is incomplete for this architecture.

The ARP table configuration procedure on Node B, assuming Linux, is as follows:

```
root# arp -s node-a 00:60:b0:a1:3d:13 pub
root# arp -s node-c 00:60:b0:a1:3d:13 pub
root# arp -s node-e 00:60:b0:a1:3d:13 pub
root# arp -s node-f 00:60:b0:a1:3d:13 pub
root# arp -a
Address          HWtype  HWaddress          Flags Mask       Iface
node-a           ether   00:60:B0:A1:3D:13  CMP   *          eth0
node-c           ether   00:60:B0:A1:3D:13  CMP   *          eth0
node-e           ether   00:60:B0:A1:3D:13  CMP   *          eth0
node-f           ether   00:60:B0:A1:3D:13  CMP   *          eth0
root#
```

As shown, Node B publishes its own Ethernet address, 00:60:B0:A1:3D:13, on behalf of several IP addresses. Although manual entry of arp -s commands is shown, these commands should be part of the start up scripts for Node B, namely */etc/rc.d/rc.inet1* on Linux. This ensures these critical entries are present if this node reboots.

The ARP table setup procedures are similar for the other Nodes A and C. However, the specific IP addresses they masquerade for are different (see Figure 8-3).

Configuring Static Routing

When a PPP node receives IP datagrams for a destination on a distant LAN, it must forward the datagrams through the correct PPP connection; a routing table defines where to send these datagrams. You must configure routing tables separately at each PPP node. The entries in the routing table reflect the location of each IP address within the split subnet architecture.

On Node B, the following unconfigured routing table appears. After all its PPP connections are active, this node already has the routes to all neighboring IP addresses:

```
root# route -n
Kernel IP routing table
Destination    Gateway       Genmask         Flags Metric Ref    Use Iface
172.20.10.12   0.0.0.0       255.255.255.255 UH    0      0        1 ppp0
172.20.10.2    0.0.0.0       255.255.255.255 UH    0      0        1 ppp1
172.20.10.0    0.0.0.0       255.255.255.0   U     0      0       11 eth0
127.0.0.0      0.0.0.0       255.0.0.0       U     0      0        3 lo
root#
```

The H flag indicates host-specific routes that already define paths to destinations corresponding to the far endpoint of each PPP connection. What is missing are routes to IP addresses on the remote LANs. Specifically, the preceding table requires entries for Nodes E and F in the destination column. The next routing hop for Nodes E and F are Nodes A and C, respectively. Here is the procedure for adding these to the routing table:

```
root# route add -host node-e gw node-a
root# route add -host node-f gw node-b
root# route -n
Kernel IP routing table
Destination    Gateway       Genmask         Flags Metric Ref    Use Iface
172.20.10.12   0.0.0.0       255.255.255.255 UH    0      0        1 ppp0
172.20.10.2    0.0.0.0       255.255.255.255 UH    0      0        1 ppp1
172.20.10.4    172.20.10.12  255.255.255.255 UGH   0      0        0 ppp0
172.20.10.5    172.20.10.2   255.255.255.255 UGH   0      0        0 ppp1
172.20.10.0    0.0.0.0       255.255.255.0   U     0      0       12 eth0
127.0.0.0      0.0.0.0       255.0.0.0       U     0      0        4 lo
root#
```

The new entries are gateway routes, as the G flag indicates. The Gateway address is the next node responsible for relaying IP datagrams towards the destination that appears in the Destination column. Thus, this Node B forwards IP datagrams for Node E at 172.20.10.4, to Node A at 172.20.10.12. Since E is on A's LAN, Node A then delivers IP datagrams to E.

Routing tables operate similarly for the other PPP nodes. Node A, for example, requires host-specific routes for IP address destinations corresponding to A, D, and E. The next hop gateway for all of these is Node B at 172.20.10.1.

Split Subnet Complications

There are several important drawbacks for the split subnet architecture.

Split subnets don't scale well for a large subnets. A PPP node ARP table must include the comprehensive listing of all IP addresses that aren't members of its own LAN but are still members of the larger logical LAN. For large lists, ARP tables could overflow. Even if this doesn't happen, the time required to search numerous entries may cause performance and time-out problems. The same may be true for routing tables. Like the ARP table, the routing table requires entries for IP addresses that are outside the node's own LAN. These entries are in addition to other routes that reference destinations outside the split subnet environment. Unusually large routing tables may also cause size and search-time issues.

Ongoing maintenance for a split subnet architecture is difficult. Every PPP node must have consistent information in both its ARP and routing tables regarding the whereabouts of IP addresses on other LANs. Inconsistencies can cause obscure communication problems difficult to troubleshoot. Dynamic routing protocols are frequently not suitable for solving this problem, since they aren't intended for managing ARP tables and frequently don't distribute routes pertaining to IP addresses inside a single IP subnet.

Another consideration is that a split subnet alters the behavior of broadcast IP addresses. Whenever a LAN node sends data to a broadcast address, it expects all members of the subnet to listen. However, this broadcast may fail to propagate to all the LAN members of the larger logical LAN. This behavior can cause some network applications to fail, especially between nodes with intervening PPP connections.

Unnumbered

Unnumbered PPP network interfaces don't have IP addresses of their own. Instead, they inherit their addresses from other network interfaces on the same node. This gives PPP connections an invisible appearance in the network. Consequently, you can avoid most IP addressing and routing issues.

The Unnumbered architecture primarily connects IP subnets (see Figure 8-4). Usually, a PPP node has a PPP network interface that shares the same IP address as its LAN interface. Multiple network interfaces must exist on the node in order to share IP addresses. Otherwise, the Unnumbered architecture doesn't apply. In the

Unnumbered architecture, IP addresses are intentionally duplicated. This is okay because the duplicate address still represents the same physical network node.

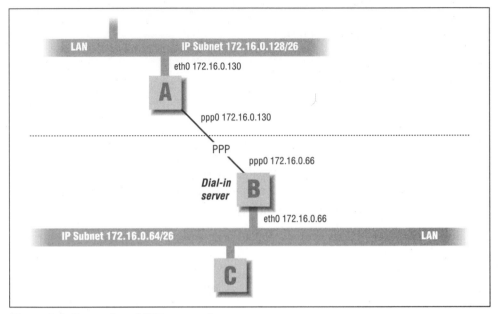

Figure 8-4. Unnumbered PPP connection

The absence of unique IP addresses for PPP is also a drawback. Unnumbered interfaces don't offer a convenient means for TCP/IP utilities to reference them. When many PPP network interfaces share an IP address, the interface an IP address refers to depends on where in the network you make the reference. It's best to consider a shared address to represent the PPP node itself. This characteristic can confuse and complicate troubleshooting procedures.

IP Subnet and IP Addresses

In the Unnumbered architecture, you need to be concerned only with allocating IP subnet numbers to LANs; ignore IP addressing matters for PPP connections.

Figure 8-4 shows a sample Unnumbered architecture that consists of two LANs and two IP subnets belonging to the class B network number 172.16.0.0. Each PPP node possesses a single IP address. When configuring a PPP node, you just set all local PPP endpoint IP addresses to match the one for the LAN network interface. Here is a configuration example for Node B, which is a Linux platform:

```
user$ /sbin/ifconfig -a
lo        Link encap:Local Loopback
          inet addr:127.0.0.1  Bcast:127.255.255.255  Mask:255.0.0.0
```

```
                    UP BROADCAST LOOPBACK RUNNING  MTU:3584  Metric:1
      . . .
      eth0          Link encap:Ethernet  HWaddr 00:60:B0:A1:3D:13
                    inet addr:172.16.0.66  Bcast:172.16.0.127  Mask:255.255.255.192
                    UP BROADCAST RUNNING MULTICAST  MTU:1500  Metric:1
      . . .
      ppp0          Link encap:Point-to-Point Protocol
                    inet addr:172.16.0.66  P-t-P:172.16.0.130  Mask:255.255.255.192
                    UP POINTOPOINT RUNNING NOARP MULTICAST  MTU:1500  Metric:1
      . . .
      ppp1          Link encap:Point-to-Point Protocol
                    inet addr:172.16.0.66  P-t-P:192.168.1.1  Mask:255.255.255.192
                    UP POINTOPOINT RUNNING NOARP MULTICAST  MTU:1500  Metric:1
      . . .
      user$
```

Note that Figure 8-4 omits showing **ppp1**. Nevertheless, **ppp1** connects to a foreign class C network number 192.168.0.0. In general, the IP address for the remote endpoint of each PPP connection may be unrelated to the IP address for the local endpoint. The correct remote IP address settings depend on the network topology. Be careful with subnet adjacency: since this violates adjacency, **ppp1** should not become part of a route path to another subnet of 172.16.0.0.

The subnet mask for all network interfaces at Node B is 255.255.255.192. For PPP network interfaces, Linux and Unix associate the subnet mask with the PPP *local IP address*, 172.16.0.66. Thus, we set the mask consistently with the value that pertains to the IP subnet for address 172.16.0.66. Non-Unix platforms may require alternate PPP subnet masks settings or may associate the mask with the PPP interface remote IP address. Further information about this is in Chapter 4.

Finally, two PPP nodes sharing a PPP connection must have a consistent notion of the IP address assigned to each end. The correct network configuration for Node A resembles the following:

```
      user$ /sbin/ifconfig -a
      lo            Link encap:Local Loopback
                    inet addr:127.0.0.1  Bcast:127.255.255.255  Mask:255.0.0.0
                    UP BROADCAST LOOPBACK RUNNING  MTU:3584  Metric:1
      . . .
      eth0          Link encap:Ethernet  HWaddr 00:60:B0:A1:3D:13
                    inet addr:172.16.0.130  Bcast:172.16.0.191  Mask:255.255.255.192
                    UP BROADCAST RUNNING MULTICAST  MTU:1500  Metric:1
      . . .
      ppp0          Link encap:Point-to-Point Protocol
                    inet addr:172.16.0.130  P-t-P:172.16.0.66  Mask:255.255.255.192
                    UP POINTOPOINT RUNNING NOARP MULTICAST  MTU:1500  Metric:1
      . . .
      user$
```

The local and remote IP addresses for ppp0 at Node A correspond with ppp0 remote and local IP addresses at Node B, respectively.

PPP in a Subnet

In this architecture, every PPP connection belongs to its own unique IP subnet. It's suitable for dial-in PPP, as well as for connecting IP subnets that consists of LANs.

If you're configuring network nodes that require an IP subnet for every network interface, you must use the PPP in a subnet. Such nodes consider PPP network interfaces much like they do LAN network interfaces. Each interface has a single IP address and a subnet mask. The good news is that IP routing is consistent for both PPP and LANs. But, by definition, PPP can connect to only one far-end IP address. Depending on the subnet size, many addresses belonging to the subnet may be wasted.

The PPP in a Subnet architecture appears in Figure 8-5 with two PPP connections. A dial-in PPP server connects three IP subnets. Two of the subnets contain a PPP connection; the third is for a LAN. One PPP connection and one LAN share the same class B network number, 172.16.0.0, although the IP subnet numbers are different.

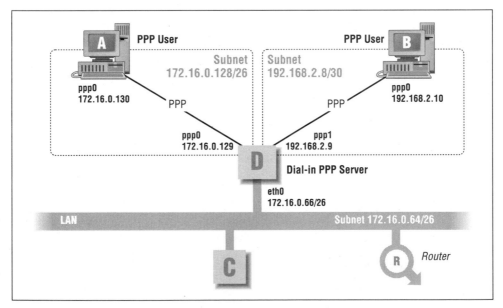

Figure 8-5. PPP in a Subnet

IP Subnet and IP Addresses

To deploy PPP in a Subnet architecture, you must obtain IP subnets for all PPP connections in your network design. Here are several ways to obtain these numbers:

- A new IP network number, such as a class C number, may be broken into multiple IP subnets that are assigned to PPP connections.

- An unused IP subnet of an existing network number may be assigned to a PPP connection.

- An unused IP subnet of an existing network number may be broken down into smaller subnets, each of which is assigned to a PPP connection.

The availability of these choices depends on the networking features of the PPP nodes. The third option is available only if your network nodes understand VLSM (see Chapter 4). VLSM is also related to CIDR.

Using a new network number

The advantage of obtaining a new IP network number for PPP is that its subnet mask hasn't been previously defined. This is particularly important if your network nodes expect fixed subnet masks throughout a specific IP network number.

You can select a subnet mask that is appropriate for PPP. The optimum mask for PPP connections is 30 one bits, or 255.255.255.252. This results in an IP subnet with two usable and two reserved IP addresses. One class C network number can accommodate 62 PPP connections, after excluding the reserved subnets.

An example of a class C network number for PPP connections appears in Figure 8-5. We break the 192.168.2.0 network number into 30-bit subnets. One PPP connection belongs to IP subnet 192.168.2.8/30. Other connections, not in the figure, can share the same dial-in PPP server with different IP subnets that belong to network 192.168.2.0. The network interface configuration on the dial-in server, Node D, resembles:

```
user$ /sbin/ifconfig -a
lo        Link encap:Local Loopback
          inet addr:127.0.0.1  Bcast:127.255.255.255  Mask:255.0.0.0
          UP BROADCAST LOOPBACK RUNNING  MTU:3584  Metric:1
. . .
eth0      Link encap:Ethernet  HWaddr 00:60:B0:A1:3D:13
          inet addr:172.16.0.66  Bcast:172.16.0.127  Mask:255.255.255.192
          UP BROADCAST RUNNING MULTICAST  MTU:1500  Metric:1
. . .
ppp0 . . .
. . .
ppp1      Link encap:Point-to-Point Protocol
          inet addr:192.168.2.9  P-t-P:192.168.2.10  Mask:255.255.255.252
```

```
                UP POINTOPOINT RUNNING NOARP MULTICAST  MTU:1500  Metric:1
        . . .
ppp2        Link encap:Point-to-Point Protocol
            inet addr:192.168.2.5  P-t-P:192.168.2.6  Mask:255.255.255.252
            UP POINTOPOINT RUNNING NOARP MULTICAST  MTU:1500  Metric:1
        . . .
ppp3  . . .
        . . .
user$
```

The two IP addresses for interfaces **ppp1** and **ppp2** are consistent with their respective IP subnet numbers, 192.168.2.8/30 and 192.168.2.4/30. The PPP subnet masks don't have real significance in this example, since each PPP network interface shown maintains a remote IP address. But if this address were absent, the subnet mask defines what IP addresses are valid for use at the far end of the PPP connection.

One important design constraint is that TCP/IP networks that haven't migrated to CIDR impose the rule "all subnets of the same network number must be adjacent." This is because, for routing purposes, the network infrastructure requires a network number to be a single contiguous entity. The distinction among IP subnets occurs only inside a network number.

Thus, connecting two LANs in one network number with a PPP connection in another can violate subnet adjacency. In Figure 8-5, you can't connect Node B to an IP subnet 172.16.1.0/26, for example. The problem is that 192.168.2.8/30 intervenes between 172.16.1.0/26 and 172.16.0.64/26. Another problem case occurs when PPP connections belonging to one network number terminate at two different dial-in PPP servers. A LAN between the servers that belongs to a different network number also violates subnet adjacency. Adding a second dial-in PPP server in Figure 8-5 to serve additional PPP connections in network number 192.168.2.0 causes the LAN to break apart two portions of 192.168.2.0.

Using fixed-size subnets of an existing network number

The second way to get IP subnets for PPP is to obtain them from an already existing network number. This is useful if you can't get a new network number exclusively for PPP.

Figure 8-5 shows a PPP connection in IP subnet 172.16.0.128/26. This subnet belongs to an existing class B network number, 172.16.0.0, that is also active for the LAN. You can assign additional subnets to LANs, as well as PPP connections, as this network grows. We assume the infrastructure inside the class B network requires a fixed 26-bit subnet mask. The configuration of a dial-in PPP server, Node D, can resemble the following:

```
user$ /sbin/ifconfig -a
lo          Link encap:Local Loopback
```

```
               inet addr:127.0.0.1  Bcast:127.255.255.255  Mask:255.0.0.0
               UP BROADCAST LOOPBACK RUNNING  MTU:3584  Metric:1
     . . .
     eth0      Link encap:Ethernet  HWaddr 00:60:B0:A1:3D:13
               inet addr:172.16.0.66  Bcast:172.16.0.127  Mask:255.255.255.192
               UP BROADCAST RUNNING MULTICAST  MTU:1500  Metric:1
     . . .
     ppp0      Link encap:Point-to-Point Protocol
               inet addr:172.16.0.129  P-t-P:172.16.0.130  Mask:255.255.255.192
               UP POINTOPOINT RUNNING NOARP MULTICAST  MTU:1500  Metric:1
     . . .
     ppp1 . . .
     . . .
     ppp2 . . .
     . . .
     ppp3      Link encap:Point-to-Point Protocol
               inet addr:172.16.0.193  P-t-P:172.16.0.194  Mask:255.255.255.192
               UP POINTOPOINT RUNNING NOARP MULTICAST  MTU:1500  Metric:1
     . . .
     user$
```

Figure 8-5 shows ppp0 but omits ppp3. Assuming this node understands only fixed subnet masks, all masks for class B 172.16.0.0 addresses are 255.255.255.192. The addresses for both endpoints of a PPP connection belong within the range for its IP subnet, 172.16.0.128/26 and 172.16.0.192/26, respectively.

With a single network number, by definition, IP subnet adjacency isn't a concern. Referring to the figure, you can easily add additional IP subnets of 172.16.0.0 on either end of a PPP connection.

The biggest concern when PPP has exclusive IP subnet assignments is the waste of IP addresses. For example, with a 26-bit subnet mask, each IP subnet provides 62 usable IP addresses. Although this is fine for shared communication mediums that require many addresses, it's extremely wasteful for PPP. PPP can use only two IP addresses. The other 60 of them are unusable anywhere else. Bigger IP subnets further compound this problem. A class B network with a 24-bit subnet mask can waste over 250 IP addresses per PPP connection. A mere 250 connections would consume almost an entire class B network number, which normally should accommodate 65500+ nodes. Since there are pending shortages of IP addresses, you should be concerned about efficient IP address usage. If you require many PPP connections, avoid assigning them exclusively to subnets intended for LANs.

Breaking up an IP subnet

Rather than assign one large IP subnet to a PPP connection, you can break up a subnet into many smaller ones for use with many PPP connections. In order to break up an IP subnet, your network infrastructure must be able to support variable length subnet masks (VLSM). VLSM requires that different subnet masks be used inside the same network number.

VLSM can offer exclusive IP subnets for PPP and for LANs in the same network number. IP address allocation remains efficient since a subnet for PPP is much smaller than a subnet for a LAN. We also avoid subnet adjacency problems since everything can belong inside one network number.

In a variably subnetted network, different IP subnets may not overlap a common set of IP addresses. This can be confusing to maintain. One suggested management technique is to first assume a network number has a predominate, fixed subnet mask. For example, assume the class B network number 172.18.0.0 predominately uses a 24-bit mask, 255.255.255.0. Each IP subnet then has 254 IP addresses.

One 24-bit IP subnet can accommodate many PPP connections. Assume 172.18.2.0/24 is for PPP. At the same time, change the subnet mask to 30 bits. This change, just for 172.18.2.0/24, creates IP sub-subnets 172.18.2.4/30, 172.18.2.8/30, 172.18.2.12/30, 172.18.2.16/30, and others. Each of these sub-subnets has two available and two reserved IP addresses. Since PPP requires only two addresses, these sub-subnets are perfectly sized for their purpose.

The following output illustrates the network interface configuration for a VLSM-capable dial-in PPP server. This server has Ethernet LAN network interfaces to two IP subnets. PPP connections reside in IP subnets smaller than the ones for the LANs.

```
user$ /sbin/ifconfig -a
lo        Link encap:Local Loopback
          inet addr:127.0.0.1  Bcast:127.255.255.255  Mask:255.0.0.0
          UP BROADCAST LOOPBACK RUNNING  MTU:3584  Metric:1
. . .
eth0      Link encap:Ethernet  HWaddr 00:60:B0:A1:3D:13
          inet addr:172.18.1.1  Bcast:172.18.1.255  Mask:255.255.255.0
          UP BROADCAST RUNNING MULTICAST  MTU:1500  Metric:1
. . .
eth1      Link encap:Ethernet  HWaddr 00:60:B0:A1:3D:14
          inet addr:172.18.3.1  Bcast:172.18.3.255  Mask:255.255.255.0
          UP BROADCAST RUNNING MULTICAST  MTU:1500  Metric:1
. . .
ppp0      Link encap:Point-to-Point Protocol
          inet addr:172.18.2.5  P-t-P:172.18.2.6  Mask:255.255.255.252
          UP POINTOPOINT RUNNING NOARP MULTICAST  MTU:1500  Metric:1
. . .
ppp1      Link encap:Point-to-Point Protocol
          inet addr:172.18.2.9  P-t-P:172.18.2.10  Mask:255.255.255.252
          UP POINTOPOINT RUNNING NOARP MULTICAST  MTU:1500  Metric:1
. . .
ppp2      Link encap:Point-to-Point Protocol
          inet addr:172.18.2.13  P-t-P:172.18.2.14  Mask:255.255.255.252
          UP POINTOPOINT RUNNING NOARP MULTICAST  MTU:1500  Metric:1
. . .
user$
```

The IP subnet numbers for `eth0`, `eth1`, `ppp0`, `ppp1`, and `ppp2` are 172.18.1.0/24, 172.18.3.0/24, 172.18.2.4/30, 172.18.2.8/30, and 172.18.2.12/30, respectively.

Multipoint PPP in a Subnet

Multipoint PPP in a Subnet describes a network architecture that assigns a group of PPP connections to one IP subnet. In effect, this group is analogous to a shared-media LAN. This architecture is well suited for dial-in users. In cases where a LAN is limited in the number of IP addresses available, it's a useful alternative to proxy ARP.

Figure 8-6 illustrates the multipoint PPP in a subnet architecture. It shows a dial-in PPP server with point-to-multipoint PPP connections. Physically, they are still multiple point-to-point connections that connect to PPP users. All IP addresses for PPP belong to the subnet 172.16.0.128/26. It's also possible to create other independent PPP connections in this subnet, as in the case of Node A.

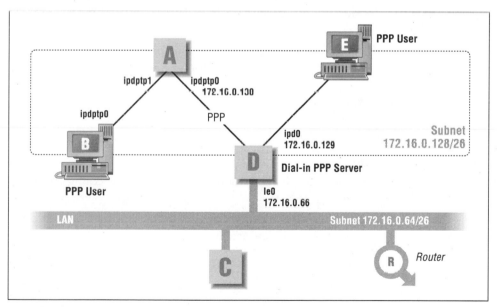

Figure 8-6. Multipoint PPP in a Subnet

Notice that Node B has no direct connection to the dial-in PPP server. It also has no direct connection to Node E. The PPP connection between A and B complicates this architecture somewhat. This is still okay, but you must later manage routing tables for the nodes inside the IP subnet, in order for B to communicate with the D and E nodes.

IP Subnet and IP Addresses

In the multipoint architecture, you must obtain an IP subnet number for use by a contiguous group of PPP connections. This subnet may be an unused one from an existing network number that also serves IP subnets for LANs. Alternatively, you can also obtain a new network number for PPP.

Using fixed-size subnets of an existing network number

In Figure 8-6, there were PPP connections in IP subnet 172.16.0.128/26. The IP addresses available in the subnet are 172.16.0.129 to 172.16.0.190. This subnet for PPP and the subnet shown for the LAN are members of the same class B network number 172.16.0.0. The subnet mask 255.255.255.192 remains consistent throughout this architecture.

Using a new network number

The alternative plan is to assign a new IP network number for PPP, rather than the 172.16.0.128/26 shown. The subnet mask is initially undefined for a new network number. This offers the ability to select a mask that is optimum for your PPP environment. Be careful with the subnet adjacency constraints. We discussed this problem in connection with the PPP in a subnet architecture.

Point-to-Point Interfaces

A multipoint PPP configuration is simply a more general case of a single point-to-point configuration. In Figure 8-6, Nodes A and D are each responsible for managing more than one PPP connection. Thus, you can configure several independent PPP network interfaces for each physical connection. Here is the configuration of Node A, on a Solaris platform:

```
root# ifconfig -a
lo0: flags=849<UP,LOOPBACK,RUNNING,MULTICAST> mtu 8232
        inet 127.0.0.1 netmask ff000000
ipdptp0: flags=8d1<UP,POINTOPOINT,RUNNING,NOARP,MULTICAST> mtu 1500
        inet 172.16.0.130 --> 172.16.0.129 netmask ffffffc0
        ether 0:0:0:0:0:0
ipdptp1: flags=8d1<UP,POINTOPOINT,RUNNING,NOARP,MULTICAST> mtu 1500
        inet 172.16.0.131 --> 172.16.0.132 netmask ffffffc0
        ether 0:0:0:0:0:0
root#
```

The interface names `ipdptp0` and `ipdptp1` represent the PPP connections shown in Figure 8-6. We set the PPP subnet masks to the natural, fixed subnet mask belonging to the 172.16.0.0 network number.

The existence of this subnet mask is especially confusing. If this node actually treats `ipdptp0` and `ipdptp1` as shared medium network interfaces, their subnet masks imply that both can reach any IP address in 172.16.0.128/26. This is a conflict. Therefore, the multipoint PPP in a subnet architecture doesn't work for nodes that behave this way.

On Solaris, the subnet mask for `ipdptp0` and `ipdptp1` doesn't have any real significance for the PPP, since a remote IP address is present. In order for the multipoint PPP in a subnet architecture to work, this Node A must rely on these remote IP addresses for routing. But if Node A advertises routes outside the PPP environment, it must advertise that it's responsible for IP subnet 172.16.0.128/16. This is the IP subnet for PPP.

It's also acceptable to assign the same IP address at the local ends of both `ipdptp0` and `ipdptp1`. You can duplicate PPP addresses this way if you wish to conserve IP addresses and don't need to distinguish different PPP network interfaces with unique addresses.

Point-to-Multipoint Interfaces

Solaris PPP features a unique point-to-multipoint network interface type well suited for the Multipoint PPP architecture. A point-to-multipoint network interface appears almost identical to a LAN network interface. It connects to an IP subnet consisting of many physical PPP connections. This network interface type has a single local IP address and a subnet mask. Therefore, all its PPP connections share the same local IP address.

The dial-in PPP server Node D, in Figure 8-6, has a single point-to-multipoint interface, `ipd0`. `ipd0` serves multiple PPP connections in IP subnet 172.16.0.128/26. The Node D network interface configuration resembles the following:

```
root# ifconfig -a
lo0: flags=849<UP,LOOPBACK,RUNNING,MULTICAST> mtu 8232
        inet 127.0.0.1 netmask ff000000
le0: flags=863<UP,BROADCAST,NOTRAILERS,RUNNING,MULTICAST> mtu 1500
        inet 172.16.0.66 netmask fffffc0 broadcast 172.16.0.127
        ether 8:0:20:9:3d:a9
ipd0: flags=c1<UP,RUNNING,NOARP> mtu 1500
        inet 172.16.0.129 netmask fffffc0
        ether 0:0:0:0:0:0
root#
```

The local IP address for `ipd0` is 172.16.0.129, and a single subnet mask determines the set of reachable destination IP addresses. The proper setting in this example is 0xfffffc0, which is equivalent to 255.255.255.192. This subnet mask really is significant since remote IP address settings are absent.

As PPP users connect to the dial-in PPP server, each user connects with a different IP address in the range 172.16.0.130 to 172.16.0.191. The IP address for the remote PPP endpoint, from the view of all users, is a consistent 172.16.0.129. One difficulty with point-to-multipoint interfaces is that the output of `ifconfig` doesn't show active PPP connections and IP addresses. In fact, many of the regular TCP/IP status utilities don't give a reliable list of users attached to `ipd0`. One method to check if a user is active is to check for his Unix login name on the dial-in PPP server. In Solaris, the `arp` command unexpectedly shows recently active remote IP addresses for `ipd0`, in hexadecimal.

In this chapter:
- *Routing Entries*
- *Using Default Routes*
- *Using Subnet Routes*
- *Using Host-Specific Routes*
- *Dynamic Routing Protocols*

9
Routing to PPP Connections

If the network doesn't know when to use it, a new PPP connection is meaningless. On the Internet, PPP is a conduit for communications with one or more IP addresses at its far end and beyond. A routing table determines which IP datagrams a network node sends through a PPP connection, versus other paths. As administrator, you must set up the routing table at this node and others.

Chapter 4, *TCP/IP*, describes basic TCP/IP routing concepts and routing tables. Chapter 6, *Dial-out PPP Setup*, and Chapter 7, *Dial-in PPP Setup*, introduce some simple routing configurations with default routes. This is fine when PPP serves one user at one IP address. In the more general case, PPP may connect groups of networks, and each network may have an enormous number of destination IP addresses. This chapter shows how to manipulate routing tables for these more complex cases. You may even need to modify the routing tables of nodes that don't have PPP connections. Remember that TCP/IP network nodes route only to a neighbor. In order to forward IP datagrams through PPP, one node may need to relay IP datagrams to another.

In small or simple networks, you can set up routing by manually configuring routing tables. But in more complex cases, routing protocols are the only practical means to dynamically update routing tables throughout a network. TCP/IP routing protocols are topics that can be a subject for an entire book. There exist many of them, each with their strengths and weaknesses. We discuss only the very common Routing Information Protocol here and its problems with PPP.

Routing Entries

A network node, whether it's a computer or a router, is aware of all of its neighbors and can communicate with any one of them. However, if this node wants to send IP datagrams elsewhere, it must consult a local routing table and select the proper neighbor to relay the datagrams to. Presumably, this neighbor has other network connections and can further relay the IP datagram towards its destination.

Consider a general network configuration, such as the one in Figure 9-1. Node A is a member of a large network, 172.16.0.0/16, and manages a PPP connection. The neighbors of A include any node inside 172.16.0.64/24 including C and B. Node A can route IP datagrams to any of its neighbors, depending on the destination IP address embedded in the IP datagrams it receives.

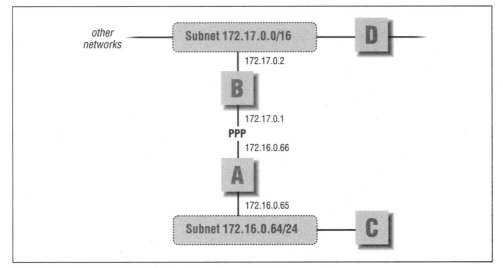

Figure 9-1. General network configuration with PPP connection

The routing table on Node A should resemble the following:

```
user$ /sbin/route -n
Kernel IP routing table
Destination     Gateway         Genmask          Flags Metric Ref    Use Iface
172.17.0.1      0.0.0.0         255.255.255.255  UH    0      0        0 ppp0
10.1.2.69       172.17.0.1      255.255.255.255  UGH   0      0        0 ppp0
172.16.0.64     0.0.0.0         255.255.255.192  U     0      0        4 eth0
172.17.0.0      172.17.0.1      255.255.0.0      UG    0      0        1 ppp0
10.0.0.0        172.17.0.1      255.0.0.0        UG    0      0        0 ppp0
192.168.0.0     172.17.0.1      255.255.0.0      UG    0      0        0 ppp0
192.168.2.0     172.17.0.1      255.255.255.0    UG    0      0        0 ppp0
0.0.0.0         172.17.0.1      0.0.0.0          UG    0      0        0 ppp0
127.0.0.0       0.0.0.0         255.0.0.0        U     0      0        2 lo
user$
```

The routes with 0.0.0.0 in the `Gateway` column represent all the neighboring IP addresses Node A can communicate with. These are network interface routes for `ppp0`, `eth0`, and `lo`, and you don't have to explicitly add them to the table. Some routing tables show the IP address of the node's own network interface in the `Gateway` column, instead of 0.0.0.0.

The routes with an IP address in the `Gateway` column are the ones you must configure by hand or with a routing protocol. These are routes that specify how to forward IP datagrams to nonneighboring destination IP addresses. Most of the routes direct IP datagrams through the PPP connection.

Routing Entry Scope

Every route you install in a routing table can represent many IP address destinations. When you're defining destinations that use a PPP connection, you try to minimize the number of entries in the table. This requires route entries of varying scope, ranging from very specific to very general.

A CIDR routing table includes `Destination` and `Genmask` columns that determine a route's scope. Chapter 4 shows how to interpret these numbers. The `Genmask` is otherwise known as a 32-bit route netmask. Fewer 1 bits in this netmask means the route is wider in scope and represents more destination IP addresses than a mask with more 1 bit.

We can classify routing table entries as follows, from the most general in scope to the most specific:

- The most general route is a "default" route, which causes a node to forward IP datagrams through a common gateway for large numbers of destinations. This is also the route of last resort. If other more specific routes for a destination IP address are nonexistent, the default route applies.

  ```
  0.0.0.0        172.17.0.1      0.0.0.0           UG    0     0        0 ppp0
  ```

- Routes to *supernets* represent IP address destinations belonging to contiguous blocks of network numbers. Here is a route to any class C network number beginning with 192.168:

  ```
  192.168.0.0    172.17.0.1      255.255.0.0       UG    0     0        0 ppp0
  ```

- Routes can represent IP addresses belonging to an individual class A, B, or C network number. One route to any IP address in the 192.168.2.0 class C number and another for the 10.0.0.0 class A number, are as follows:

  ```
  192.168.2.0    172.17.0.1      255.255.255.0   UG    0     0        0 ppp0
  10.0.0.0       172.17.0.1      255.0.0.0       UG    0     0        0 ppp0
  ```

- Routes can represent destination IP addresses in a specific or a contiguous block of IP subnet numbers. The network topology determines whether the route is for one or more IP subnets. A route to an IP subnet in the 10.0.0.0 class A number can be:

  ```
  10.1.2.64      172.17.0.1      255.255.255.192 UG    0     0        0 ppp0
  ```

- The most specific routes are those for a specific IP address. These are also host-specific routes. A route for one destination IP address, 10.1.2.69, is:

```
10.1.2.69      172.17.0.1     255.255.255.255 UGH   0     0        0 ppp0
```

When you build a table of routes for PPP, you are building a complete list of IP address destinations for the traffic that must traverse the PPP connection. But for a routing table to be complete, you may need to include other routes that direct traffic elsewhere, such as to other PPP connections or to neighboring LAN nodes.

The routing table for Node A includes rules such as "send all traffic for the 10.0.0.0 network to PPP" and "send traffic for IP address 10.1.2.69 to PPP." Notice that the default route implements the same rules as the other more specific routes that point to PPP. It's acceptable for routes to overlap with a common set of destination IP addresses. Given a destination, the most specific route is the one that applies. If you choose, you can aggregate these specific routes and replace them with a single default route, because the `Gateway` is the same for all. I nevertheless discuss the more specific PPP routes, in case you have to change the default route to point elsewhere.

A classful routing table omits the `Genmask` column. Nevertheless, an implied route netmask exists for each entry (see Chapter 4). It's not possible to construct a supernet route or a route for a contiguous block of IP subnets in a classful routing table. Instead, multiple network routes are equivalent to a single supernet route. For example:

```
192.168.0.0    172.17.0.1     255.255.0.0     UG    0     0        0 ppp0
```

is equivalent to:

```
user$ netstat -rn
Routing Table:
  Destination           Gateway             Flags  Ref   Use   Interface
-------------------- -------------------- ----- ----- ------ ---------
. . .
192.168.1.0           172.17.0.1            UG     0     0
192.168.2.0           172.17.0.1            UG     0     0
192.168.3.0           172.17.0.1            UG     0     0
192.168.4.0           172.17.0.1            UG     0     0
. . .
192.168.254.0         172.17.0.1            UG     0     0
. . .
user$
```

Specifying the Gateway

Every route you add to a routing table must include a single `Gateway` IP address. For IP datagrams that match the route entry, the `Gateway` address is the neighbor this node forwards IP datagrams to. Since a node may ignore the gateway if the flag is missing, it's important that the "G" flag is present for the route entry.

The `Gateway` IP address must be a neighbor. A common mistake is to specify a nonneighbor, which should result in an error message. Therefore, if Node C in Figure 9-1 has IP datagrams it wants to send through PPP, it must relay the datagrams to Node A at `Gateway` IP address 172.16.0.65. TCP/IP routing doesn't permit Node C to forward directly to PPP with `Gateway` IP address 172.16.0.66 or 172.17.0.1.

To have Node A direct traffic to the PPP connection, you can usually specify either the PPP local or remote end-point IP address as the `Gateway`. I suggest using the remote end-point IP address. In the PPP unnumbered network architecture, a PPP end-point local address can be the same as the address for another network interface. Thus, a route to the local address must identify the correct PPP network interface, to avoid a route ambiguity. Our routing table is still valid if we replace 172.17.0.1 with 172.16.0.66 as the `Gateway` and `ppp0` as the `Interface`.

Our last caution about routing table entries: avoid duplication of routes with conflicting gateway information. It's ambiguous, for example, to install multiple default routes with different `Gateway` IP addresses:

```
0.0.0.0        172.17.0.1     0.0.0.0        UG    0     0     0 ppp0
0.0.0.0        172.17.0.3     0.0.0.0        UG    0     0     0 ppp1
```

At any one time, only one of these routes is active. This can cause mysterious routing problems, especially if some of the duplicate routes are bad.

Static and Dynamic Routes

There are two ways to edit entries in a routing table:

Static

> You must manually install the necessary route entries. On Linux and Unix systems, this requires the use of the `route` command.

Dynamic

> An application program installs, updates, and removes routes based on the information it exchanges with a routing protocol.

Once a route appears in a routing table, its behavior is identical regardless of whether the route is static or dynamic. The static routes you add to routing tables should be the same ones a dynamic routing protocol would add, if you enable dynamic routing.

In complex network topologies, the routes you need to add aren't obvious. Therefore, it's better to depend on dynamic routing to populate routing tables automatically.

Using Default Routes

Dial-up PPP users normally have a standalone PC that initiates a PPP connection. The good news for these users is that routing is trivial and straightforward. Any data a PC sends must leave through a single network connection. This is the routing policy these users must implement. If you make a single PPP connection for a LAN, you can benefit from a similar routing policy. Any data the LAN sends out must leave through a single network node, specifically a router, that manages a PPP connection.

At the edges of the Internet, routing policy requirements are trivial. Thus, dynamic routing protocols are unnecessary. You can easily configure a static route in routing tables and avoid the complexity of establishing dynamic routing.

Figure 9-2 shows a LAN that has one PPP connection exclusively for communications with other networks. Node A manages this connection on behalf of the LAN. Node C and other LAN nodes require a routing policy that forwards IP datagrams with nonneighboring destination IP addresses to the PPP node, Node A. A single default at each node accomplishes this. The routing policy for Node A is to forward all IP datagrams to nonneighboring destination IP addresses through PPP to Node B, again with a default route.

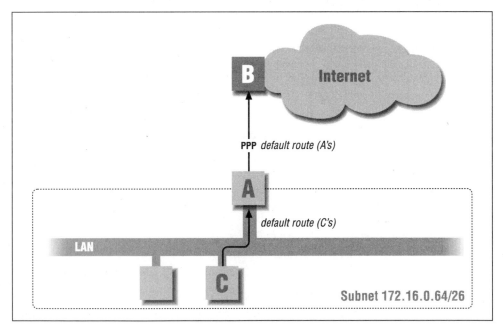

Figure 9-2. Using default routes for PPP

A dial-in PPP user with a PC is a degenerate case of Figure 9-2. By removing the LAN, Node A becomes the equivalent of a standalone PC with a single PPP connection to the Internet.

Configuring a Default Route to a PPP Connection

Only Node A on the LAN in Figure 9-2 can have a default route that points to its PPP connection. Remember that routes can point only to neighboring IP addresses.

Chapter 6 discusses how to establish default routes that point to a PPP connection. Look for a flag, Use default gateway on remote network with Windows NT/98/95, include the option defaultroute with PPP-2.3 or find an equivalent PPP setting that automatically sets up the default route. If the PPP product doesn't add a default route itself, you must edit the routing table. On Linux, the command to add this route is:

```
root# route add default gw 172.17.0.1
```

Other Unix variants require this:

```
root# route add default 172.17.0.1 1
```

Here, the IP address 172.17.0.1 is the far end of Node A's PPP connection.

Configuring a Default Route to a Router

Node C in Figure 9-2 already has the routes it needs for communicating with neighbors on the same LAN. But for communication with foreign destinations, the node requires a single default route that points to Node A. Notice this default route doesn't reference the PPP connection in any way and is thus unrelated to any PPP software.

The procedure for installing this route is similar to the steps necessary for establishing default routes on dial-in PPP servers (see Chapter 7, *Dial-in PPP Setup*). Windows NT/98/95 has a Gateway setting for the TCP/IP properties associated with a LAN adapter. Only one adapter should have the default route. Linux requires the command:

```
root# route add default gw 172.16.0.65
```

Other Unix variants require this:

```
root# route add default 172.16.0.65 1
```

We assume the IP address 172.16.0.65 is the IP address for Node A's LAN network interface.

Distributing Routes

It's not necessary to dynamically distribute routing information to Node A and LAN nodes, as in Figure 9-2. These nodes require only one default route.

However, Node B must accept IP datagrams for all destination IP addresses belonging to its PPP connection and the LAN's IP subnet number. Node B must advertise its responsibility for IP subnet 172.16.0.64/26, as shown in Figure 9-3. One way to advertise this is to configure dynamic routing protocols at Node B and its neighbors. Of course it's possible to configure static routes for 172.16.0.64/26, but this becomes tedious if Node B has many neighbors.

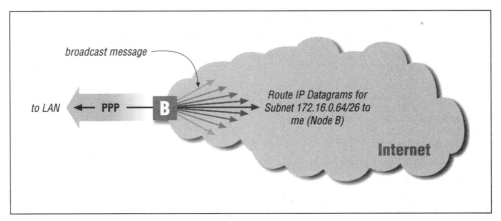

Figure 9-3. Distributing routes to the Internet for a single IP subnet

It's not advisable to set a default route at Node B and its Internet neighbors to represent destination IP addresses in the IP subnet 172.16.0.64/26.

Using Subnet Routes

Several network architectures in Chapter 8, *Network Architectures Incorporating PPP*, incorporate several PPP connections into one IP subnet. To communicate with IP addresses in these subnets, the network nodes surrounding the connection must have routing table entries that specify these subnets as routing destinations. Although it's possible at the periphery of a network to use default routes for this, the nodes embedded in a network and in the vicinity of the PPP connection really need more specific IP subnet routes. In this case, a default route is too general.

A model network with several interconnected IP subnets appears in Figure 9-4. Although some IP subnets are exclusively for PPP connections, this detail is invisible to nodes elsewhere in the network. All that matters are proper routes, regardless of the communication media.

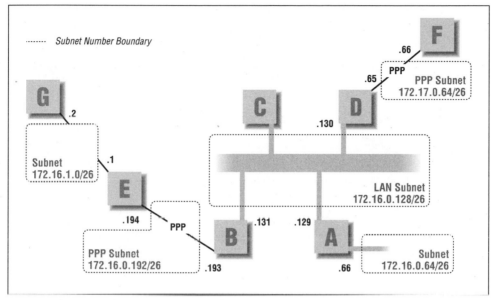

Figure 9-4. Using subnet number routes for PPP

We assume a network architecture where the IP subnets belonging to network number all use a fixed subnet mask. The 172.16.0.0 class B network number shown uses IP subnets with a 26-bit subnet mask. Fixed subnet masks are important when network nodes don't support routing table entries with netmasks or don't support CIDR. With a fixed 26-bit subnet mask, a route to 172.16.0.64 is clearly for a subnet, since this number is invalid as an individual IP address.

Network Number Routes for a PPP Node

In Figure 9-4, Node F maintains a PPP connection that belongs to the IP subnet 172.17.0.64/26. In its routing table, Node F has a network interface route for IP address 172.17.0.65. Although this is a host-specific route, the route represents the reachable destinations in IP subnet 172.17.0.64/26. The next hop neighbor for the other destinations is Node D, at IP address 172.17.0.65.

The routing table that Node F needs is:

```
user$ /sbin/route -n
Kernel IP routing table
Destination     Gateway         Genmask         Flags Metric Ref    Use Iface
172.17.0.65     0.0.0.0         255.255.255.255 UH    0      0        0 ppp0
```

```
172.16.0.0     172.17.0.65    255.255.0.0     UG     0      0      1 ppp0
127.0.0.0      0.0.0.0        255.0.0.0       U      0      0      2 lo
user$
```

Node F is a member of the class B network 172.17.0.0. This number is foreign to the predominant 172.16.0.0 used elsewhere. Node F has no access to information about the IP subnet structure for foreign networks. Therefore, routes to these destinations are less specific and become aggregated into a single route. Route aggregation works as long as all the IP subnets of 172.16.0.0 are all inside a network number boundary and Node F is outside.

Since all the destinations Node F can communicate with are outside its own network, there's no need to reference IP subnets in its routing table.

If the network in Figure 9-4 is an autonomous system with a connection somewhere to the Internet, we may need to add a default route at Node F. Such a route represents all destinations outside the figure. This is useful for passing routing responsibilities up a routing hierarchy. Once IP datagrams reach the Internet backbone, the Internet nodes can no longer depend on default routes. They must maintain network and supernet routes for all possible Internet destinations.

Subnet Routes for a PPP Node

Consider the case for Node E, in Figure 9-4, which maintains a PPP connection. This node already has routes for the IP subnet 172.16.1.0/26. The route for 172.16.0.193 implies the IP subnet 172.16.0.192/26. The next hop neighbor for Node E to reach other destinations is Node B at IP address 172.16.0.193. Here are the routing table entries Node E requires:

```
user$ /sbin/route -n
Kernel IP routing table
Destination    Gateway        Genmask          Flags Metric Ref    Use Iface
172.16.0.193   0.0.0.0        255.255.255.255 UH    0      0      0 ppp0
172.16.1.0     0.0.0.0        255.255.255.192 U     0      0      4 eth0
172.16.0.64    172.16.0.193   255.255.255.192 UG    0      0      1 ppp0
172.16.0.128   172.16.0.193   255.255.255.192 UG    0      0      0 ppp0
172.17.0.0     172.16.0.193   255.255.0.0     UG    0      0      0 ppp0
127.0.0.0      0.0.0.0        255.0.0.0       U     0      0      2 lo
user$
```

The routes to destinations inside the class B network 172.16.0.0 are all subnet routes. Also, they all have 26-bit netmasks. Node E knows about the prevailing subnet mask for 172.16.0.0 because it has a network interface to this network number. The subnet routes specify how to reach other destinations within the boundary of network 172.16.0.0. A single route for 172.16.0.0 is insufficient, since more specific information is needed to locate an IP address within in this network.

Notice there is a 172.17.0.0 class B route to reach Node F. This is a network route because Node E isn't a member of 172.17.0.0. It also has no subnet structure information for this foreign network.

Distributing Routes

Every node in Figure 9-4 requires routing table entries representing all the IP subnet and network numbers in the network architecture. It's not enough to configure routing tables only at Nodes E and F and leave the other nodes untouched.

As administrator, you'll either need to install routes at every node or have a dynamic routing protocol do the work for you. With a dynamic routing protocol, a node can learn the routes it needs from its neighbors.

Node A in Figure 9-4 can learn about new destination IP networks and subnets from its neighbors Nodes B and D. For example:

```
To: 172.16.1.0    (subnet)   Via: 172.16.0.131  Metric: 2  Learned from: B
To: 172.16.0.192  (subnet)   Via: 172.16.0.131  Metric: 1  Learned from: B
To: 172.17.0.0    (net)      Via: 172.16.0.130  Metric: 1  Learned from: D
```

Similarly, the information Node B needs to add to its routing table is:

```
To: 172.16.1.0    (subnet)   Via: 172.16.0.194  Metric: 1  Learned from: E
To: 172.16.0.64   (subnet)   Via: 172.16.0.129  Metric: 1  Learned from: A
To: 172.17.0.0    (net)      Via: 172.16.0.130  Metric: 1  Learned from: D
```

Notice that Node B must know about IP subnet 172.16.1.0 before it can pass this information to its neighboring Node A. The metric shown is the number of routing hops to the destination. If there are multiple routes to a destination, you can pick one from among those with the smallest metrics.

Using Host-Specific Routes

In Chapter 8, the section "Multipoint PPP in a Subnet" discussed one architecture suitable for many PPP connections. In this arrangement, all the IP addresses representing PPP connections belong to a single IP subnet.

Outside this subnet, the network infrastructure considers the PPP connections as a single entity. Network nodes immediately outside the subnet can use a single subnet route for all the IP addresses in use by PPP. However, nodes with connections to the PPP subnet itself may not have access to all its IP addresses as neighbors. Subnet routes are no longer sufficient, and host-specific routing becomes necessary.

Figure 9-5 shows a network with multiple PPP connections in IP subnet 172.16.0.128/26. Nodes E and F can use subnet and network routes, respectively, to reach PPP IP addresses. However, Nodes A, B, C, and D, must use host-specific routes for destinations inside 172.16.0.128/26.

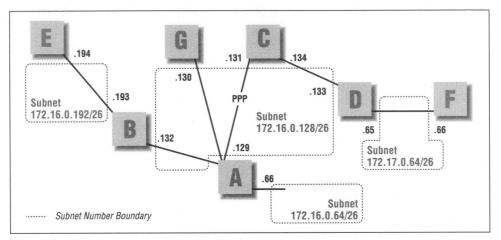

Figure 9-5. Using host-specific routes for PPP

Routes for Nodes Outside the PPP Subnet

The network nodes outside the PPP subnet in Figure 9-5 include E and F. To these nodes, the IP subnet for PPP is like any other subnet. In fact, these nodes can't determine that 172.16.0.128/26 is for PPP. This detail is immaterial anyway.

The routing table for Node E is:

```
user$ /sbin/route -n
Kernel IP routing table
Destination    Gateway        Genmask          Flags Metric Ref    Use Iface
172.16.0.192   0.0.0.0        255.255.255.192 U     0      0        4 eth0
172.16.0.64    172.16.0.193   255.255.255.192 UG    0      0        1 eth0
172.16.0.128   172.16.0.193   255.255.255.192 UG    0      0        0 eth0
172.17.0.0     172.16.0.193   255.255.0.0      UG    0      0        0 eth0
127.0.0.0      0.0.0.0        255.0.0.0        U     0      0        2 lo
user$
```

The earlier section about subnet routing includes further details about the entries in this routing table.

Routes for Nodes Inside the PPP Subnet

In Figure 9-5, the nodes that have network interfaces in the PPP IP subnet require routes for nonneighboring PPP endpoints, in addition to other ordinary subnet and network routes that reference destinations outside the PPP environment. The routing table entries for Node A are:

```
user$ /sbin/route -n
Kernel IP routing table
```

```
Destination     Gateway         Genmask         Flags Metric Ref   Use Iface
172.16.0.130    0.0.0.0         255.255.255.255 UH    0      0       0 ppp0
172.16.0.131    0.0.0.0         255.255.255.255 UH    0      0       0 ppp1
172.16.0.132    0.0.0.0         255.255.255.255 UH    0      0       0 ppp2
172.16.0.64     0.0.0.0         255.255.255.192 U     0      0       4 eth0
172.16.0.133    172.16.0.131    255.255.255.255 UGH   0      0       0 ppp1
172.16.0.134    172.16.0.131    255.255.255.255 UGH   0      0       0 ppp1
172.16.0.192    172.16.0.132    255.255.255.192 UG    0      0       1 ppp2
172.17.0.0      172.16.0.131    255.255.0.0     UG    0      0       0 ppp1
127.0.0.0       0.0.0.0         255.0.0.0       U     0      0       2 lo
user$
```

Only endpoints 172.16.0.130, 172.16.0.131, and 172.16.0.132 are neighbors. These should already appear in the routing table, based on the configuration of the PPP network interfaces on Node A. Host-specific routes have netmasks of 255.255.255.255. A destination IP address must exactly match the route for it to be applicable. All other host-specific routes with the G flag are for communications with nonneighboring IP addresses inside the PPP IP subnet.

The additional 172.16.0.192 and 172.17.0.0 routes are for destinations unrelated to PPP.

Routes for Point-to-Multipoint PPP

If Node D were absent in Figure 9-5, the arrangement of PPP connections would reduce to a single point-to-multipoint topology. Node A would become a common point for all PPP connections. By definition, this node has routes to all PPP endpoints, since the endpoints are all its neighbors. Node A doesn't need any additional routes in its routing table for destinations inside the PPP subnet.

Under this special condition, Nodes B, C, and G can use an aggregate IP subnet route, rather than host-specific routes, to reach all IP address destinations inside the PPP subnet. On Node B, for example, the route for 172.16.0.128/26 covers all PPP endpoint IP addresses:

```
user$ /sbin/route -n
Kernel IP routing table
Destination     Gateway         Genmask         Flags Metric Ref   Use Iface
172.16.0.129    0.0.0.0         255.255.255.255 UH    0      0       0 ppp0
172.16.0.192    0.0.0.0         255.255.255.192 U     0      0       4 eth0
172.16.0.128    172.16.0.129    255.255.255.192 UG    0      0       0 ppp0
172.16.0.64     172.16.0.129    255.255.255.192 UG    0      0       1 ppp0
172.17.0.0      172.16.0.129    255.255.0.0     UG    0      0       0 ppp0
127.0.0.0       0.0.0.0         255.0.0.0       U     0      0       2 lo
user$
```

Whenever Node B wishes to communicate with a member of 172.16.0.128/26, it blindly forwards IP datagrams to Node A. Since every PPP IP address is a neighbor to Node A, it has the knowledge to further route these datagrams.

Distributing Routes

The nodes in Figure 9-5 all require you to populate their routing tables with entries representing all the possible IP address destinations in the figure. The best way to accomplish this task in a large network is to use a dynamic routing protocol so that nodes can learn routes from their neighbors.

If we configure Node A to acquire routes from its neighbors, it should learn the following routes:

```
To: 172.16.0.192  (net)    Via: 172.16.0.132  Metric: 1  Learned from: B
To: 172.16.0.133  (host)   Via: 172.16.0.131  Metric: 1  Learned from: C
To: 172.16.0.134  (host)   Via: 172.16.0.131  Metric: 1  Learned from: C
To: 172.17.0.0    (net)    Via: 172.16.0.131  Metric: 2  Learned from: C
```

The metric is the number of routing hops to the destination and allows Node A to select the best route, in case multiple routes to the same destination exist.

Dynamic Routing Protocols

In complex networks, manually maintaining routing tables on every host and router is impractical and error-prone. Optimum routes aren't obvious, and network topology changes would require updates to many tables. Dynamic routing protocols solve this problem by automatically distributing and updating routing information networkwide with little administrator intervention.

You must install routing software at all the network nodes that participate in a TCP/IP routing protocol. The program at one node communicates with others and exchanges routing data. Routing protocols are categorized as either interior or exterior gateway protocols:

Interior gateway protocols
> A loosely applied term for protocols used in the distribution of routes inside an autonomous system. An autonomous system is a portion of the network assigned to one administrative entity.

Exterior gateway protocols
> A term for protocols that distribute routes between autonomous systems.

Interior gateway protocols include RIP version 1, RIP version 2, IGRP, and OSPF. The exterior ones include EGRP and BGP. The Border Gateway Protocol (BGP) is the current standard for exchanging routes among the large Internet backbone providers.

Routing protocols work by:

- Broadcasting information to neighbors about directly connected IP networks and subnets.

- Listening for updates from neighboring routers. New routes learned are added to the routing tables. Expired routes are eventually deleted.

- Redistributing routes learned from neighboring routers to other neighbors.

The different protocols vary in the amount and type of information they exchange.

Routers are frequently capable of simultaneously supporting several routing protocols. The routes one protocol exchanges may be redistributed with another protocol. This situation can occur at the boundary where both interior and exterior routing protocols are active. It's also common for one protocol, usually RIP-1, to distribute routes to hosts while another distributes routes to routers.

Using the Routing Information Protocol

The Routing Information Protocol version 1 (RIP-1) is perhaps the most widely used routing protocol. Its implementation is available on routers, communication servers, and as the in.routed application program common to many Unix systems. RIP-1 is an interior gateway protocol that implements the exchange of *distance vectors*, as the means for evaluating routes.

Broadcasting routes with RIP

An active in.routed periodically broadcasts a version of its local routing tables to all neighboring IP addresses. A broadcast typically occurs every 30 seconds. The best way to understand the content of a RIP broadcast is to run in.routed with debugging enabled. Consider running in.routed on Node A in Figure 9-5. Its broadcast behavior is as follows:

```
root# /usr/sbin/in.routed -t          # Show in.routed activity
. . .
RESPONSE to 172.16.0.127.0:
        dst 172.16.0.128 metric 1
        dst 172.16.0.192 metric 2
        dst 172.17.0.0 metric 3
. . .
RESPONSE to 172.16.0.132.0:
        dst 172.16.0.130 metric 1
        dst 172.16.0.131 metric 1
        dst 172.16.0.133 metric 2
        dst 172.16.0.134 metric 2
        dst 172.16.0.64 metric 1
        dst 172.17.0.0 metric 3
. . .
RESPONSE to 172.16.0.130.0:
. . .
RESPONSE to 172.16.0.131.0:
. . . ^C
root#
```

RIP broadcasts include destinations and metrics. A destination may represent a network number, a subnet number or a specific IP address. The listening nodes must determine the proper interpretation for a number. Metrics range from 1 to 15 and are the distance vector hop count to the destination, relative to Node A. A 1 indicates the advertising node has a local network interface to the destination. A hop count of 15 represents an unreachable destination. This range limits RIP-1 to network diameters less than 15 hops. You have to use other routing protocols, possibly in conjunction with RIP, to extend this limit.

Notice Node A broadcasts different routes through each of its network interfaces. It doesn't blindly advertise its entire local routing table to every neighbor. In.routed implements *split horizon*. Thus, Node A doesn't rebroadcast information about 172.17.0.0 back to Node C at 172.16.0.131. This improves the ability to expire old routes by not rebroadcasting learned routes back to its source. Another technique is *poison reverse*, which temporarily broadcasts recently expired routes as unreachable, to quickly update RIP listeners.

The routes RIP broadcasts don't include netmasks. This limitation permits RIP to be useful only in networks that use fixed subnet masks per network number. RIP can broadcast IP subnet routes only through network interfaces belonging to the same network number as the route. The assumption is the listener knows the subnet mask to properly interpret the route. If RIP has a subnet route to advertise via network interface in a foreign network number, RIP must convert the subnet route to a network route. This accommodates outside listeners who can't know the prevailing subnet masks for a network number. Consequently, RIP assumes network numbers represent contiguous entities where *subnet adjacency* applies.

Listening for routes with RIP

The second important function of in.routed is to listen for new routes its neighbors broadcast. A listening in.routed basically installs the lowest metric routes for a destination to its local routing table. When two equally desirable routes are available, the listener selects one. RIP must periodically update existing routes, even if nothing changes. If a listener learns a route that disappears from subsequent RIP advertisements, it expires the route from its routing table. Obsolete routes usually last about three minutes.

Controlling the Distribution of Routes

A full-featured RIP implementation gives you the ability to control the specific routes a network node accepts from its neighbors and the routes it broadcasts.

A route broadcast filter may specify interface names, route types, the advertised destinations, or any combination of these. When selecting routes to propagate on the basis of type, the classifications include routes for network interfaces, static routes you install, and dynamic routes a node learns with RIP or other routing protocols. Route filters are useful for security where it's desirable to intentionally omit specific destinations in a RIP broadcast. A more common situation is to suppress RIP activity to PPP connections that service only a single IP address or a single IP subnet for a LAN. Use of RIP is unnecessary at a network edge and can be undesirable. For example, the periodic behavior of RIP can defeat on-demand PPP and disable PPP idle time-outs.

Similar routing access controls can apply when accepting RIP updates from neighboring nodes. As a security precaution, you may want to accept routes only from trusted neighbors. Also, you may wish to accept routes only for certain destinations.

It's unfortunate that the Unix `in.routed` offers very little RIP broadcast filtering and listening control. You can suppress RIP broadcasts to PPP network interfaces on Solaris by configuring the */etc/gateways* file. Many other `in.routed` versions don't have this feature.

```
root# cat /etc/gateways
norip ipdptp0
norip ipdptp1
root#
```

On communication servers such as the Bay Network's Annex, individual PPP interfaces include RIP configurable options:

```
admin : set interface=asy16 rip_advertise none rip_accept none
admin : reset interface=asy16
```

This completely disables RIP for PPP connections on port 16. Furthermore, this server refuses RIP updates from any that a PPP peer may broadcast. Without this feature, PPP users could obtain the unauthorized ability to alter routing tables that propagate to the Internet backbone.

Dedicated network routers tend to offer much more control over RIP behavior in its routing protocol software.

RIP Problems with PPP

`in.routed` is more commonly used on LAN nodes than on network nodes with PPP connections. Thus, many versions of `in.routed` have limitations or problems, when advertising routing information that pertains to PPP connections.

The key `in.routed` problem area is confusion about whether PPP connections require route advertising and whether the routes to advertise are network, subnet, or host-specific. The correct behavior often depends on the network design. A list of possible `in.routed` complications are:

- It should broadcast IP subnet routes, but it broadcasts host-specific routes instead.

- It should broadcast host-specific routes, but it broadcasts IP subnet routes instead.

- It broadcasts extraneous routes.

- It fails to broadcast some necessary routes. For example, host-specific routes for one set of PPP endpoints fail to propagate through other PPP connections.

The best way to determine if `in.routed` is behaving correctly is to observe which routes it learns and which ones it chooses to broadcast. The output of `in.routed -t` can help you determine what's happening at a network node.

Consider, for example, the case of Node A in the network architecture of Figure 9-5. Node A must advertise host-specific routes to its PPP neighbors. It's inappropriate for Node A to advertise the following IP subnet route instead:

```
root# /usr/sbin/in.routed -t
. . .
RESPONSE to 172.16.0.131.0:
        dst 172.16.0.128 metric 1
. . .
root#
```

Advertising a route to 172.16.0.128/26 to the members of the same subnet is useless. The routing information isn't specific enough for an IP datagram to reach its destination, once inside the subnet.

Some route distribution problems may not cause visible network problems. Consider the case of Node E in the network architecture of Figure 9-4. Its `in.routed` could broadcast the following routes to the LAN with IP subnet 172.16.1.0/26:

```
root# /usr/sbin/in.routed -t
. . .
RESPONSE to 172.16.1.63.0:
        dst 172.16.0.193 metric 1
        dst 172.16.0.194 metric 1
. . .
root#
```

What's more desirable is to advertise an IP subnet route, `dst 172.16.0.192 metric 1`. Instead, we see host-specific routes for PPP endpoint IP addresses. `in.routed` should not distribute these routes outside its IP subnet. This can cause other network nodes to carry numerous host-specific routes for every PPP endpoint IP address. If some nodes ignore host-specific routes, then further route propagation fails, and PPP endpoints can become unreachable.

To solve these problems and others, you may need to reconfigure `in.routed` to behave as required. If this isn't possible, consider alternative network designs, other routing protocols, or find an alternative `in.routed` that behaves as you need it.

10

In this chapter:
- *Domain Name System Hierarchy*
- *Using DNS*
- *DNS Records for PPP*
- *Setting up DNS Name Resolution*
- *DNS Servers*

Domain Name System

The Internet routes data based solely on 32-bit IP addresses. While 32-bit numbers are fine for electronic equipment, they are a great inconvenience for people who prefer using names. How many of us know, for example, that O'Reilly & Associates' web server is 204.148.40.9?

Name-resolution maps mnemonic names to IP addresses. This makes the Internet more usable than it would otherwise be. In a small network, a *hosts* file of names and addresses is sufficient. Medium-sized networks may use proprietary services, such as Sun's Network Information Service (NIS) or Microsoft's Windows Internet Naming Service (WINS) to translate names into addresses. The Domain Name System (DNS) accommodates very large, globally distributed networks and is the standard for the Internet. DNS is distributed, and thousands of DNS servers maintain portions of its database. In fact, no one has a complete copy of the DNS database.

When you arrange PPP connections to the Internet or other large TCP/IP networks, you must also set up DNS for their users. Although DNS is unrelated to PPP, it's indispensable for looking up IP addresses for millions of Internet sites. Applications must obtain an Internet site's IP address in order to contact it. A less obvious task is registering PPP user IP addresses in DNS servers. Numerous Internet sites perform a DNS name lookup on the IP addresses of users and deny service if this DNS lookup fails.

This chapter describes how DNS works, how to configure DNS name resolution, and how to register PPP IP addresses in DNS. I omit details about DNS servers. DNS is itself a topic for a book; in fact, O'Reilly's *DNS and Bind*, by Cricket Liu and Paul Albitz, includes DNS server setup information.

Domain Name System Hierarchy

The DNS is organized as a hierarchical tree. There are two important hierarchies for name resolution. The *forward domain* hierarchy translates Internet site names to IP addresses. DNS also includes a separate *reverse domain* hierarchy that translates IP addresses to names.

Forward Domains

Names submitted to DNS servers for translation into IP addresses are the familiar names users enter into web browsers, Telnet, FTP, and other networking programs. Consider this example:

> *www.oreilly.com*

All DNS names consist of multiple words separated with periods. Each word, from right to left, represents successively lower hierarchical levels in the DNS structure. The last word in the chain, *www*, is an entry that belongs to the *oreilly.com* portion of the DNS name space. *oreilly.com* is the domain name registered in the parent *com* domain.

The DNS name space is best represented as a tree, as in Figure 10-1. At the top is *root*; the name of the root is simply a period ".". Internet names that are direct descendants of root are the responsibility of the InterNIC organization. These names represent either geographical or organizational categories. For example: "edu" stands for education, "com," commercial; "net," network providers; "gov," government; "us," United States; etc. The rest of the hierarchy builds from this small set of top level names. DNS servers throughout the Internet each contribute names belonging to subsets of this tree.

Based on this structure, DNS operates as follows:

- All DNS servers are knowledgeable about the root servers. The Internet has at least eight well-publicized root servers.

- A DNS server may be assigned to offer authoritative data for zero, one, or more domains in the tree. There is no relationship between the name of the DNS server itself and its domains.

- Servers authoritative for a domain have immediate knowledge regarding other servers, if any, for its child domains. This is the mechanism that links all the DNS servers on the Internet.

- Most DNS servers that receive queries automatically contact zero, one, or more other servers seeking the information a user application requests.

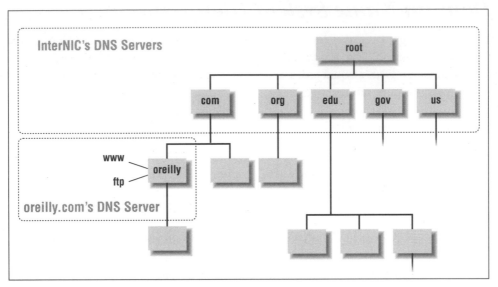

Figure 10-1. DNS forward domain tree

Application programs are responsible for submitting queries to a DNS server. When a user specifies a destination by name, the application seeks a DNS "A" record, which contains an IP address. DNS also maintains other optional records for a name. This includes host information, HINFO, electronic mail exchange, MX, text strings, TXT, and others. Many of these aren't important to a typical PPP user.

Reverse Domains

The DNS hierarchy includes reverse domains that enable computers to translate IP addresses to names. To determine the hostname for address 204.148.40.9, a computer submits a DNS query requesting information for the following DNS name:

```
9.40.148.204.in-addr.arpa
```

Constructing this name requires reversing the individual numbers in the IP address. Again, periods in this name separate the hierarchical levels in the DNS tree. Note the DNS infrastructure simply considers these numbers as character strings. For the IP address 204.148.40.9, we are seeking information about "9" within the domain *40.148.204.in-addr.arpa*. This domain is a member of the parent *148.204.in-addr.arpa* domain, and so forth.

The DNS name space for reverse domains appears in Figure 10-2. Based on the format of IP address names, this hierarchy has a limited number of levels. The InterNIC maintains the DNS name space for the levels immediately below *in-addr.arpa*. They delegate responsibility for the lower hierarchical levels to your DNS server or to an authorized third-party DNS server. This delegation is based on your responsibility for one or more Internet IP address blocks. Like the forward domains, DNS servers can find any information in this tree by following name server referrals beginning at *root.*

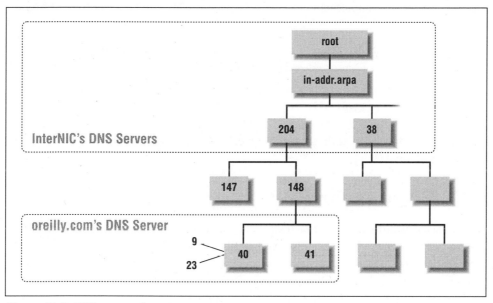

Figure 10-2. DNS reverse domain tree

Applications seeking a name for an IP address query a DNS server for pointer—PTR—records. For example, a PTR record query for *9.40.148.204.in-addr.arpa* returns the canonical name *helio.oreilly.com.* This is the official name of O'Reilly's World Wide Web server. The name, *www.oreilly.com,* is really only an alias for *helio.oreilly.com.*

Using DNS

Once a computer can resolve DNS names, using the service is quite simple. In fact, most users aren't aware that a DNS lookup takes place when they ask for a web page. As an administrator, about all you need to do is make sure that DNS is functioning properly and that the lookups are taking place.

A simple way to check whether DNS is functioning is to execute an application that performs a DNS lookup for a single name. One good program to use is Telnet:

- Try to use Telnet for establishing a connection to a valid IP address. If this fails, there is either a possible network problem or the remote server isn't offering Telnet service.

- Now try to use Telnet for connecting to the same destination by name. If the program hangs, or returns errors indicating "unknown host," DNS lookups may be malfunctioning.

Note that some old implementations of `rlogin` on Unix don't accept IP addresses as destinations.

Another useful utility for checking DNS name resolution is `arp`, normally used to display Ethernet and IP addresses for computer names:

```
user$ /usr/sbin/arp helio.oreilly.com
helio.oreilly.com (204.148.40.9) -- no entry
user$
```

If `arp` displays an IP address for a given DNS name, hostname resolution is functioning.

DNS Records for PPP

You must configure DNS so that users can have access to Internet sites. What is less obvious is that you must also assign and register DNS names for your PPP users. You must install these records on the DNS servers authoritative for your domains. The records for PPP users in the forward domain must be consistent with those appearing in the corresponding reverse domain.

One suggestion for registering PPP users in DNS is to create names reflecting the IP addresses they use, along with any helpful geographical information. If you are responsible for `myisp.net`, for example, you can create DNS records such as these to map each name to an IP address:

```
ppp-166-172-92-103.nj.us.myisp.net.   IN A   166.172.92.103
ppp-166-172-92-104.nj.us.myisp.net.   IN A   166.172.92.104
ppp-166-172-92-105.nj.us.myisp.net.   IN A   166.172.92.105
 . . .
```

The corresponding DNS names in a reverse domain, and the pointer records they map to, are:

```
103.92.172.166.in-addr.arpa.   IN PTR   ppp-166-172-92-103.nj.us.myisp.net.
104.92.172.166.in-addr.arpa.   IN PTR   ppp-166-172-92-104.nj.us.myisp.net.
105.92.172.166.in-addr.arpa.   IN PTR   ppp-166-172-92-105.nj.us.myisp.net.
 . . .
```

A DNS name for a PPP user doesn't need to be consistent with the user's own notion of her name. If users dynamically receive different IP addresses for every new PPP connection, their DNS name changes. You can arrange permanent DNS names for users who have static IP addresses.

Missing DNS Records

As I said earlier, many Internet sites now verify that users are originating requests from IP addresses that have DNS records available. This policy results in service denial if the verification fails. An example of this condition is:

```
user$ ftp 192.48.96.9
Connected to 192.48.96.9.
220 ftp.UU.NET FTP server (Version wu-2.4(3) Fri Nov 25 16:08:40 EST 1994)
ready.
Name (192.48.96.9:root): anonymous
530- Sorry, we re unable to map your IP address 172.16.0.66 to a hostname
530- in the DNS. This is probably because your nameserver does not have
530- matching A and PTR record for your address in its tables, or because
530- your reverse nameservers are not registered. We refuse service to
530- hosts whose names we cannot resolve. If this is simply because your
530- nameserver is hard to reach or slow to respond then try again in a
530- minute or so, and perhaps our nameserver will have your hostname in
530- its cache by then. If not, try reaching us from a host that is in
530- the DNS or have your system administrator fix your servers.
530 User anonymous access denied..
Login failed.
ftp> quit
221 Goodbye.
user$
```

The PPP user requesting FTP service to *ftp.uu.net* originated the request from IP address, 172.16.0.66 (fictitious). Since no DNS name information for this IP address is available in DNS, the FTP server chooses to deny access.

Authenticating with DNS Names

There are several Internet services that critically depend on DNS names for authentication and access control. These services function only for PPP users with proper DNS records.

rlogin, rsh, and rcp are examples of services that depend on DNS for access control. These services enable unauthenticated login and command execution on a remote Unix server. When a user invokes rlogin, the remote server receives an originating IP address. It performs a DNS lookup in the reverse domains to determine the originator's DNS name. The server also checks this name in the DNS forward domains for IP address consistency and as a security measure. If all the DNS information is consistent, and an rlogin trust relationship exists for the DNS name in a *.rhosts* file, the server grants access.

PPP users should never set up trust relationships for rlogin, or any other service, if they don't use a fixed IP address. Ignoring this suggestion opens a security hole. A third party may receive the DNS name and IP address that a user configures a remote server to trust, without password protection.

Setting up DNS Name Resolution

All that is necessary for DNS name resolution is a few IP addresses to send DNS queries to. One DNS server can usually resolve all names available in the entire Internet DNS name space. You're responsible for providing DNS name servers and their IP addresses for PPP users.

Some operating systems can resolve names through multiple name resolution services. In this case, users must include DNS as one of the services the computer uses to resolve names.

PC DNS Name Resolution and Microsoft PPP Extensions for DNS

Microsoft has implemented an extension to the Internet Protocol Control Protocol (IPCP). IPCP normally establishes IP addresses and VJ compression for PPP connections to the Internet or PPP connections to private TCP/IP networks. The Microsoft extension, as RFC-1877 describes, adds the ability to negotiate the following additional items with IPCP:

* Primary and secondary DNS IP addresses

* Primary and secondary NetBIOS name server (NBNS) IP addresses; these are also known as WINS server IP addresses

The intent is to simplify dial-up networking setup for PPP users. You can configure these important IP addresses at the dial-in server. For users with Microsoft software, the server can configure DNS and WINS name resolution on behalf of the user.

This DNS extension is shrouded in controversy. Microsoft has taken past exemptions to PPP numbers registration and exemptions in disclosing extensions to the PPP working groups. In other words, they've abused the PPP protocol and created framework inconsistencies. Although RFC-1877 describes the extension, this document appeared after the fact and after Microsoft already released products with this feature. RFC-1877 is informational only and not on the standards track.

An issue with this extension is that it overlaps with the function of the Dynamic Host Configuration Protocol (DHCP). DHCP can set name server IP addresses for computers with any type of network interface, not just PPP interfaces.

The Microsoft DNS PPP extension is nevertheless a de facto standard. Cisco and several other product vendors support it.

Setting up clients to use the Microsoft DNS PPP extension

Windows NT/98 dial-up networking has a TCP/IP Settings window (Figure 6-9) with DNS settings. These settings apply for a dial-out connection to a specific remote system. To use the Microsoft DNS PPP extension, users simply mark the Server assigned name server addresses option. When Windows NT/98 completes a dial-out PPP connection to the remote system, it asks the remote system for the name server IP addresses to use.

With Windows 98, users can check to see what their active name server IP addresses are with the winipcfg utility. On Windows NT, the equivalent utility is ipconfig:

```
C:\>ipconfig /all
Windows NT IP Configuration
        Host Name . . . . . . . . . : myhost
        DNS Servers . . . . . . . . : 207.25.97.8
. . .
```

If a remote system doesn't implement the Microsoft DNS PPP extension, Windows NT/98 fails to learn anything about name servers. This results in name lookup failures. The workaround is for users to explicitly configure DNS server IP addresses in the TCP/IP Settings window. You must provide this information.

When the Microsoft DNS PPP extension is absent either at the client or server, manually setting DNS server IP addresses is the standard way to set up DNS name resolution. PPP users should fill out both the IP addresses for primary and secondary DNS servers. Windows NT/98 consults a secondary DNS server in the event the primary fails to respond.

Setting up servers to use the Microsoft DNS PPP extension

Windows NT 4.0 RAS in a dial-in PPP server configuration can respond to client requests for name server IP addresses. The RAS server responds with the name server addresses it knows about itself. You can set these addresses with the DNS and WINS Address tabs in Windows NT TCP/IP Properties (Figure 7-6). This window appears in the network control panel.

Linux PPP-2.3 also supports the Microsoft DNS PPP extension on the server side. In other words, PPP-2.3 can supply name server IP addresses for Windows NT/98 dial-in PPP users. However, PPP-2.3 never functions as a client for this information. The PPP-2.3 option that sets name server IP addresses to respond with is ms-dns. This keyword can appear twice for primary and secondary DNS servers in any of PPP-2.3 option files, *.ppprc*, and the pppd command line. For example, here is a pppd command for an incoming call:

```
user$ /usr/sbin/pppd debug modem crtscts 192.168.1.1:192.168.1.2 ms-dns \
192.168.2.2 asyncmap 00000000
```

Here are the IPCP negotiations that PPP-2.3 records, when the dial-in client is Windows NT. Shown are the parts that tell the dial-in client to set its DNS server IP address to 192.168.2.2:

```
May 20 22:30:31 myisp pppd[241]: rcvd [IPCP ConfReq id=0x5 <compress VJ 0f
01> <addr 0.0.0.0> <dns-addr 0.0.0.0> <wins-addr 0.0.0.0> <dns-addr 0.0.0.0>
< 84 06 00 00 00 00>]
May 20 22:30:31 myisp pppd[241]: sent [IPCP ConfRej id=0x5 <wins-addr
0.0.0.0> <dns-addr 0.0.0.0> < 84 06 00 00 00 00>]
May 20 22:30:32 myisp pppd[241]: rcvd [IPCP ConfReq id=0x7 <compress VJ 0f
01> <addr 0.0.0.0> <dns-addr 0.0.0.0>]
May 20 22:30:32 myisp pppd[241]: sent [IPCP ConfNak id=0x7 <addr 192.168.1.2>
<dns-addr 192.168.2.2>]
May 20 22:30:32 myisp pppd[241]: rcvd [IPCP ConfReq id=0x8 <compress VJ 0f
01> <addr 192.168.1.2> <dns-addr 192.168.2.2>]
May 20 22:30:32 myisp pppd[241]: sent [IPCP ConfAck id=0x8 <compress VJ 0f
01> <addr 192.168.1.2> <dns-addr 192.168.2.2>]
```

Linux and Unix DNS Name Resolution

Unlike with PCs, name resolution on Unix is unrelated to its PPP software. Unix clearly separates most of the TCP/IP software layers from PPP. Name resolution is really an application layer service. The name-resolution libraries, which application programs call, can perform DNS lookups as well as lookups with other naming services.

Unix computers with Internet connections require DNS name resolution to be useful. If the computer is also a member of a LAN, other name resolution services may also be active. You, the administrator, must configure DNS for Internet access, yet retain other naming services for a local environment.

Most Unix systems use versions of the Berkeley Internet Name Domain (BIND) libraries. Fortunately, this means DNS configuration is common to many Unix variants. A single configuration file, */etc/resolv.conf*, determines the disposition of DNS queries. This file appears as follows:

```
user$ cat /etc/resolv.conf
domain myisp.net
nameserver 192.52.71.4
nameserver 192.153.156.22
user$
```

If this file is absent, you must create it. Each `nameserver` line contains the IP address of a DNS server. BIND tries each in order until it receives a response. Other options may also appear in */etc/resolv.conf*. However, only the `nameserver` statements are essential.

The `domain` statement is common; it causes BIND to automatically qualify simple DNS name references by appending a default DNS domain. For example, if a user seeks the name *www* when *myisp.net* is the domain default, DNS lookups actually occur first for *www.myisp.net*. Some versions of BIND iteratively append the default domain name and its parent names, to all user-requested DNS names. Unfortunately, this can create both confusion and security problems. A reference to *www.yourisp.net* could result in DNS queries for:

www.yourisp.net.myisp.net

www.yourisp.net.net

www.yourisp.net

If *www.yourisp.net.net* actually exists, users may mistakenly connect to it, rather than the desired *www.yourisp.net*. BIND versions with this behavior may have settings to disable this search feature. Alternatively, you can omit the domain statement in */etc/resolv.conf*.

Name Services Switch

Unix applications may not use DNS, even though the computer has DNS configuration files. Many Unix variants support multiple name resolution services. One of which is DNS. Some other services are the */etc/hosts* file, Network Information Service (NIS) and NIS+. A *name services switch* determines the services applications consult to resolve names. Names are frequently hostnames, but may also include other types of names. The switch file is usually */etc/host.conf, /etc/svc.conf, /etc/ nsswitch.conf*, depending on the Unix variant.

The */etc/host.conf* file is the name services switch for Linux. This file affects lookups pertaining to hostnames. Here is an example:

```
user$ cat /etc/host.conf
order files,bind
multi on
user$
```

This indicates that the file */etc/hosts* is the first place to look for a given name. If the name isn't found, use DNS.

The Solaris */etc/nsswitch.conf* file is its name services switch. Besides hostnames, this file configures sources for usernames, groups, passwords, electronic mail aliases, and other information. Among the multiple lines in this file, the one of concern is the hosts entry:

```
user$ cat /etc/nsswitch.conf
. . .
hosts: files nis dns
. . .
user$
```

As shown, the search sequence for hostnames is */etc/inet/hosts*, NIS, then DNS.

Checking DNS Servers

The DNS query tool, `nslookup`, is useful for checking the DNS servers that appear in */etc/resolv.conf.* This utility is common for Unix, and Microsoft includes it with Windows NT. First, bring up any PPP connection necessary to communicate with the DNS servers. Then, make a `nslookup` query for a known name. For example:

```
user$ /usr/sbin/nslookup www.oreilly.com
Server:  rock.west.oreilly.com
Address:  207.25.97.8

Name:    helio.oreilly.com
Address:  204.148.40.9
Aliases:  www.oreilly.com, www.oreilly.com

user$
```

A response that returns the IP address for the requested name indicates success.

Note that `nslookup` specifically tests DNS servers. This utility doesn't verify whether network applications actually resolve names using DNS. If `nslookup` succeeds, but application programs fail to recognize DNS names, the problem is the name services switch, which determine where applications look up names.

Beware that old versions of `nslookup` are no longer compatible with recent DNS server configurations. Unfortunately, these old versions are still in circulation. In the case of a problem, `nslookup` may behave as follows:

```
user$ /usr/etc/nslookup
*** Can't find server name for address 192.52.71.4: Query refused
*** Can't find server name for address 192.153.156.22: Query refused
*** Can't find initialize address for server : Timed out
Server:  localhost
Segmentation fault (core dumped)
user$
```

This is a `nslookup` specific problem, resulting from DNS inverse queries. Recent DNS servers don't support this query type by default. DNS name resolution still functions despite the failure. Replacing `nslookup` with a more recent version, such as the one with BIND-4.9.7, solves this problem.

DNS Name Resolution with SunOS 4.1.x

Sun's SunOS 4.1.x versions of the Unix operating system are annoyingly unique, in its own way, regarding hostname resolution. Arranging SunOS 4.1.x to use DNS is difficult in comparison to most other Unix platforms. Because many SunOS 4.1.x installations are still active, its unique hostname resolution behavior is described in this section.

By default, SunOS 4.1.x doesn't use DNS for hostname lookups. Furthermore, there is no name service switch for specifying the sources of host information.

SunOS 4.1.x prefers to use only the Network Information Service (NIS) for hostname resolution. If the NIS service isn't active, the fallback is the local */etc/hosts* file. Two options are available for integrating DNS into SunOS 4.1.x. These are:

Arrange NIS to query DNS
> Configure NIS to consult DNS for names it can't find in its own maps

Replace NIS with DNS
> Substitute the hostname resolution routines in shared C libraries with versions that perform DNS lookup

The first option is the simplest and has the fewest side effects on system behavior. This is the vendor-supported option. However, if NIS is undesirable for security or other reasons, you must consider the second, vendor unsupported, option.

When a NIS request arrives for a hostname, the NIS server process `ypserv` performs a DNS query and return the results via NIS. Configuring this behavior requires installing a `YP_INTERDOMAIN` key into the NIS `hosts.byname` and `hosts.byaddr` maps. Enabling the */var/yp/Makefile* line `B=-b` and rebuilding the NIS hosts maps achieves this.

Replacing NIS with DNS requires modifying the computer's shared C library. Most network applications call `gethostbyname` and `gethostbyaddr` library routines in */usr/lib/libc.so.1.9*. You can replace these routines with versions that perform DNS queries. DNS-capable versions of `gethostbyname` and `gethostbyaddr` are available in */usr/lib/libresolv.a*, and third-party versions are available as well. The applications dynamically linking to the revised C library inherit DNS name-resolution ability. A few utilities, including */usr/ucb/rcp* and */usr/etc/mount*, are statically linked (use `ldd` to check). Their name-resolution behavior won't change without replacing the utility itself.

Additional instructions for configuring SunOS 4.1.x to use DNS are available in the Sun Computer Administration Frequently Asked Questions. This FAQ appears regularly in the Usenet group *comp.sys.sun.admin*, and copies are also available at *ftp://rtfm.mit.edu/*. Sun's symptoms and resolutions document, `srdb 4616`, includes directions for rebuilding the shared C library.

DNS Servers

One question that arises is whether a computer with a PPP connection to the Internet or another large network should run DNS name server software. The answer depends on:

* Whether the computer is responsible for any portion of the DNS forward or reverse domain hierarchy. In other words, is the computer authoritative for any DNS domain names?

- Whether the connection is always active and available for other Internet or network users.

If the answers to both are yes, the computer must function as a DNS server. You can configure the DNS server program, usually `in.named` and install authoritative DNS tables with the data to publish for network users. In this scenario, the PPP connection is unlikely to be a telephone line, but a permanent leased line. How to configure DNS servers is outside the scope of our discussion.

The decision to install a DNS server on an individual user's computer with a PPP connection is less clear. Only a DNS caching server is appropriate. A caching server queries other DNS servers to collect information. It doesn't contribute any new data to the DNS hierarchy. DNS caching servers exhibit the following behaviors:

- They have high startup overhead and attempt to query all the DNS root servers at initialization time

- They may recursively query other DNS servers, while seeking the information necessary to fulfill a single request

- They remember answers to previous DNS requests and respond with cached data, as needed

A PPP user's DNS server that performs one lookup may make multiple DNS queries to other DNS servers. Until the server cache builds with enough information for reuse, this is a disadvantage for slow PPP connections. The cache doesn't disappear when the connection terminates, so it can build overtime, but it will disappear if the user shuts the computer down.

Users who choose to install `in.named` on their computer may need to ensure that it doesn't start until after the PPP connection is active. Some `in.named` versions have problems if they can't initially contact DNS root servers. One symptom includes network applications that mysteriously hang, because DNS name resolution is failing. Under these conditions, users must restart their DNS server process. Terminating a DNS server, unfortunately, discards its previously cached data.

When a DNS caching server is more trouble than it's worth, PPP users should simply rely on a remote, but stable Internet DNS server. A DNS server permanently on the Internet isn't dependent on the state of a PPP connection. It can also build its DNS cache without interruption, over long periods of time.

In this chapter:
- *PPP Startup Options for Dial-in Servers*
- *PPP Startup Options for Dial-out Servers*
- *Adjustable LCP Options*
- *Authentication Policy*
- *Adjustable IPCP Options*
- *Setting IP Addresses*
- *Other Adjustable Settings*

11

Customizing and Tuning PPP

Until now, our discussion assumes dial-up PPP for Internet access and straightforward PPP connections for wide-area networks. In typical cases, default settings work reasonably well. But there are many nonstandard and less typical ways to use PPP. The presence of unusual network design constraints may force you to customize and tune your PPP software.

This chapter is the first in a series that describes advanced PPP use and configuration. Later chapters describe authentication tricks, proxies, network address translation, and virtual private networking.

I begin this chapter by describing alternative ways for starting PPP on an existing serial connection. Of course, there are numerous adjustable parameters, and you need to know how and when to set these. One particularly important setting is the IP address. There are many ways PPP can determine and set IP addresses.

PPP Startup Options for Dial-in Servers

With dial-in PPP, you must establish a serial connection before anything can happen. You place a call; a modem attached to the server answers. The server can then respond in several ways:

- Immediate PPP

- Autodetect, automatic serial line protocol detection

- Interactive

Immediate PPP is the simplest to understand. In this case, the dial-in server unconditionally begins PPP communications after answering a call. Authentication, if any, must take place within PPP.

Automatic serial line protocol detection selects among PPP, SLIP, interactive command line, and perhaps other protocols, depending on how the user begins communications. The key benefit is that a single dial-in port serves multiple functions. PPP users, terminal emulation users, and others, can all share the same ports. Autodetection starts PPP if a user first sends a PPP frame. Some autodetecting dial-in PPP servers initially present themselves in interactive mode. This server may respond as follows, after a modem connection:

```
CONNECT 28800/ARQ/V34/LAPM/V42BIS

Welcome
Please Sign-on:
```

PPP users should just send their first PPP frame in response. Users probably don't have the necessary authorization information to proceed in interactive mode anyway.

Servers set to interactive mode produce readable prompts and accept keystroke commands. This mode is oriented to users with a terminal emulator. PPP may start automatically or by user command, following some interactive procedure. Interactive mode can offer users a menu choice of several serial line protocols, one of which is PPP. However, users must manually select or switch to their desired serial line protocol or arrange a chat script to automatically make the selection for them.

Active or Passive PPP

Once PPP starts on a newly established serial connection, it can be either active or passive.

An active PPP endpoint immediately starts sending PPP frames to begin handshaking with its peer. In passive mode, one endpoint waits for the other to send the first frame. Active PPP is the usual behavior for dial-out; both active and passive are common with dial-in PPP servers. An autodetecting dial-in server must operate in passive mode, since it doesn't know the serial line protocol users desire until after the user sends a PPP frame. At least one endpoint must assume the active role to successfully establish the connection.

Whether you can configure active or passive PPP depends on your software. Many products don't offer this setting. For dial-in servers, Solaris PPP is active while Windows NT RAS is passive. PPP-2.3 gives you a choice. The `silent` option changes PPP-2.3 active default behavior to passive.

Communication Servers

Communication servers frequently support several answering modes for incoming dial-in calls. A port setting establishes the desired mode.

On a Bay Network's Annex server, for example, a dial-in port is dedicated to PPP, if set as follows:

```
admin : set port=16 mode ppp
```

The other options include:

```
admin : set port=16 mode auto_detect
admin : set port=16 mode cli
```

The former sets automatic serial line protocol detection, which includes PPP detection. The latter arranges an interactive command line interface, where users can later enter the ppp command or select another communications mode.

Unix

The standard Unix behavior for a serial connection is interactive mode, which begins with a "login" prompt. Many Unix dial-in PPP servers require users to log in first. Afterwards, Unix usually presents the familiar Bourne shell, */bin/sh*, command-line interpreter. This lets the PPP user start PPP by command. You can also replace */bin/sh* in the password file, */etc/passwd*, with a PPP executable. Although this is still interactive mode, PPP starts immediately after the user logs in. This eliminates the need to start PPP by command.

You can also choose to configure a Unix dial-in port with automatic serial line protocol detection or start PPP immediately without the login prompt. Both scenarios require some nontraditional, Unix configuration work.

Automatic serial line protocol detection with mgetty

getty is the common Unix system utility that answers incoming calls. It normally prompts for a username and then invokes */bin/login*. An alternative getty that's available on Linux is mgetty. It also works with Solaris. mgetty can automatically detect several incoming serial line protocols and invoke the proper program for each. For example, if mgetty detects a PPP frame, it can invoke PPP-2.3. Otherwise, for plain-text inputs, mgetty can pass what it receives to */bin/login*.

The basics for obtaining, installing, and configuring mgetty are in Chapter 7, *Dial-in PPP Setup*. To enable automatic PPP detection, you must compile mgetty with the -DAUTO_PPP option. Do this by modifying the mgetty Makefile and appending the auto PPP option to CFLAGS. Next, auto PPP must appear in the login dispatcher file, */etc/default/login.config*. The location of this file may vary depending on the mgetty installation locations. Here is a sample login.config entry that starts PPP-2.3:

```
root# cat /etc/default/login.config
. . .
# Automatic PPP startup on receipt of LCP configure request.
```

```
#  mgetty has to be compiled with "-DAUTO_PPP" for this to work.
#  Warning: Case is significant, AUTOPPP or autoppp won't work!
#  Consult the "pppd" man page to find pppd options that work for you.
#
/AutoPPP/ -    a_ppp   /usr/sbin/pppd debug auth
. . .
```

When mgetty starts PPP-2.3, there is no home directory to consult for a *.ppprc* configuration file. You can therefore create the file */etc/ppp/options.ttyS0* and include PPP-2.3 options specific to a serial interface, rather than a user login name.

Starting PPP immediately

On Solaris, ttymon monitors serial ports for incoming connections. It's the equivalent of getty and mgetty for other Unix platforms. ttymon, like getty, normally prints a login prompt and invokes the traditional */bin/login* to service an incoming connection. However, it's possible to configure ttymon to invoke PPP instead.

The Solaris pmadm utility associates an incoming serial device, such as */dev/term/b*, to an answering program:

```
root# pmadm -a -p zsmon -s ttyb -i root -fu -v 1 -m "`ttyadm -b -c -d
/dev/term/b -l 38400 -s /usr/local/etc/start-ppp -m ldterm,ttcompat -S n
-T vt100`"
root#
```

One important option is –c, which suppresses login prompts ttymon produces by default. This option causes the service, *-s /usr/local/etc/start-ppp*, to execute immediately after ttymon detects an incoming connection. The start-ppp program must first establish Unix environment variables and then call a PPP executable, such as Solaris PPP */usr/sbin/aspppls*. Note Solaris PPP utilizes login information from its environment, to set PPP options that appear in */etc/asppp.cf*.

PCs

Microsoft Windows NT 4.0 RAS for dial-in PPP doesn't offer alternatives methods to respond to incoming calls. When a RAS port receives a dial-in connection, it's for PPP communications only. You can expect most Windows operating systems to behave this way.

PPP Startup Options for Dial-out Servers

There are two ways to initiate a dial-out connection:

Manual dial-out

Users explicitly perform a procedure to initiate dial-out before any applications in their computer can communicate. Users also explicitly terminate the connection.

Automatic dial-out, also known as on-demand PPP

Applications that require PPP communication resources automatically trigger PPP dial-out. The connection can terminate automatically due to inactivity.

Many PPP products support manual control. The only settings in this mode relate to use of chat scripts and terminal windows. For products supporting automatic dial-out, there exist several additional settings to control dial-out and termination behavior. These include idle timers and perhaps redial operations. Idle time-outs can apply to dial-in PPP connections as well.

I already covered manual and on-demand PPP setup procedures for some PPP products in Chapter 6, *Dial-out PPP Setup*. A summary of on-demand PPP settings is in Table 11-1. For PPP-2.3, place settings in one of the configuration files, such as *.ppprc, /etc/ppp/options*. Solaris PPP manages its settings in */etc/asppp.cf*. For Windows NT/98, configuration windows and the registry maintain PPP settings.

Table 11-1. Setting On-Demand PPP

Description	PPP	Default Behavior	How to Set
On-demand PPP	PPP-2.3	Manual dial-out PPP	Set with: demand
	Solaris PPP	Default	
	Windows NT		Set with: Enable auto-dial by location
	Windows 98		Set with: Connect to the Internet using a modem[a]
Idle time-out	PPP-2.3	Disabled	Set with: idle 900 (time in seconds)
	Solaris PPP	120 sec	Set with: inactivity_timeout 120
	Windows NT	20 min (dial-in)	Set registry value name: AutoDisconnect[b] (dial-in) Set with: Idle seconds before hanging up[c] (dial-out)
	Windows 98		Set with: Disconnect a call if idle more than 30 mins[d]
Auto reconnect	PPP-2.3	Disabled	Set with: persist
	Windows NT		Set with: Redial on link failure[c]

[a] This setting is available in the Internet control panel.
[b] Registry key: *HKEY_LOCAL_MACHINE\SYSTEM\CurrentControlSet\Services\RemoteAccess\Parameters*.
[c] See User preferences in Figure 6-15.
[d] See Connection tab in Figure 6-7.

Adjustable LCP Options

When two endpoints first communicate, they begin negotiating PPP options with the Link Control Protocol. Chapter 3, *How PPP Works*, describes how LCP negotiations take place and some of the options that are the subject for negotiations.

In summary, the sender of a PPP option is requesting how it wishes to receive PPP frames. An endpoint has the opportunity to accept, reject, or offer different alternatives to an option it receives. The set of PPP options for each communications direction is independent. From the perspective of one PPP endpoint, each negotiable option may be treated as follows:

- Will request
- Will accept

A *will request* option is one an endpoint actively requests of its peer. *Will accept* determines the disposition of an option, if we receive this option request from the peer. In theory, the will request and will accept should be independent. In practice, PPP implementations may couple them. In other words, telling the software not to request an option may also tell it to reject that option if the peer wants it.

Besides PPP-negotiated options, endpoints must also maintain numerous local counters and timers that control the negotiation process itself and other matters. Counters and timers are another category of options you may choose to adjust.

Address and Control Field Compression

The address and control fields in frames are rarely necessary with dial-up connections (see Chapter 3). When one endpoint sends a request for address and control field compression, it's notifying the peer that it doesn't wish to receive frames with these fields. The peer can accept or decline the request.

According to the PPP specification, address and control field compression is absent by default, unless an endpoint specifically requests it. However, many PPP products actively request this option as its default behavior. This is desirable in most cases, since it reduces communications overhead. Table 11-12 shows how various implementations request address and control field compression.

Table 11-2. Setting Address and Control Field Compression

Description	PPP	Default Behavior	How to Set
Address and control field compression	PPP-2.3	Request and Accept	Disable and reject by setting `noaccomp`
	Solaris PPP	Request and Accept	Disable and reject by setting `lcp_compression` off
	Windows NT	Request and Accept	
	Windows 98	Request and Accept	

Protocol Field Compression

The standard protocol field in PPP frames is two octets. Protocol field compression omits the first octet, if its value is zero. An endpoint requesting this option wants to receive PPP frames from its peer with abbreviated protocol fields.

Protocol field compression is disabled unless an endpoint explicitly requests it. Many PPP products automatically request it, which is normally desirable since it reduces overhead. Table 11-13 summarizes protocol field compression.

Table 11-3. Setting Protocol Field Compression

Description	PPP	Default Behavior	How to Set
Protocol field compression	PPP-2.3	Request and Accept	Disable and reject by setting `nopcomp`
	Solaris PPP	Request and Accept	Disable and reject by setting `lcp_compression` off
	Windows NT	Request and Accept	
	Windows 98	Request and Accept	

Magic Number

Magic numbers help PPP determine serial connection looped-back conditions. An endpoint that successfully requests it must include its own magic number in various PPP frames it sends to its peer. If an endpoint ever receives PPP frames with its own number, a looped back connection is a possibility.

Magic numbers are disabled unless explicitly requested. PPP products frequently request magic numbers by default. This is desirable, unless there are problems with the magic number implementation at either end of the PPP connection. A PPP endpoint that requests magic numbers must also allow its peer to use them. Table 11-4 summarizes the use of magic numbers.

Table 11-4. Setting Magic Number

Description	PPP	Default Behavior	How to Set
Magic number	PPP-2.3	Request and Accept	Disable by setting `nomagic`
	Solaris PPP	Request and Accept	
	Windows NT	Request and Accept	
	Windows 98	Request and Accept	

Asyncmap and Escape

The PPP asyncmap is a will request option. The sender is requesting how it wishes to receive various octets in PPP frames. An asyncmap is a 32-bit mask representing all 32 ASCII control characters. This mask encodes characters that can't be sent "in the clear" due serial connection limitations. Chapter 3 provides extensive detail about how asyncmap works.

The asyncmap value 0xffffffff is the PPP default for asynchronous serial connections. However, many PPP products automatically request 0x00000000. The zero map is the most desirable, since it eliminates half the receiving overhead for ASCII control characters. Most serial connections intended for use with PPP support the zero map.

Serial connections that don't pass certain ASCII control characters require nonzero asyncmaps. Table 11-5 lists the most common characters that present problems. The asyncmap value you must use is the sum of all the masks for all the affected control characters. If a PPP endpoint can't receive Ctrl-Q, Ctrl-S, and Ctrl-], for example, it must inform its peer with asyncmap 0x200a0000.

Table 11-5. Problem ASCII Control Characters in PPP Connections

Character	Purpose	Asyncmap
0x11, Ctrl-Q	Start, for software (Xon/Xoff) flow control	0x00020000
0x13, Ctrl-S	Stop, for software (Xon/Xoff) flow control	0x00080000
0x1d, Ctrl-]	Telnet application, command mode escape	0x20000000

PPP-2.3 also supports an **escape** option for selecting the transmitted characters that require encoding. This feature isn't limited to ASCII control characters. But if the **escape** option does include control characters, it affects the asyncmap values PPP-2.3 will accept from its peer. An **escape 11,13,ff** is useful if PPP-2.3 is aware of problems transmitting Ctrl-Q, Ctrl-S, and 0xff characters, even if the peer doesn't know. Table 11-6 summarizes asyncmap setting.

Table 11-6. Setting Asynchronous Control Character Map

Description	PPP	Default Behavior	How to Set
Asynchronous control character map	PPP-2.3	No request	Disable and reject by setting: `default-asyncmap` Send PPP request by setting: `asyncmap 200a0000`
	Solaris PPP	No request	Send PPP request by setting: `ipcp_async_map 200a0000`
	Windows NT	Request `async-map 00000000`	
	Windows 98	Request `async-map 000a0000`	

MRU and MTU

An endpoint can send a maximum received unit (MRU) option request to its peer, indicating its desire to change the maximum PPP frame size it wishes to receive.

The maximum transmit unit (MTU) option sets the largest PPP frame an endpoint can send to its peer. Since one endpoint's MTU is its peer's MRU, the MTU setting affects how this endpoint behaves in response to a peer's MRU request. If MTU and MRU conflicts arise, the smaller value must prevail, even if one end acknowledges a larger number.

Changing the MRU and MTU can enhance the performance of interactive applications. These applications frequently need to transfer keystroke data in small PPP frames. Maximum-size PPP frames usually carry bulk data. Figure 11-1 illustrates how limiting bulk data to a smaller MTU can help interactive traffic. A small MTU increases the probability for interleaving more interactive data with bulk data. Another reason to change the MTU are cases of frequent transmission errors. Also, some dial-in PPP servers have obscure problems with large IP datagrams and smaller MTU settings may help the situation. Chapter 15, *Troubleshooting*, further discusses these problems.

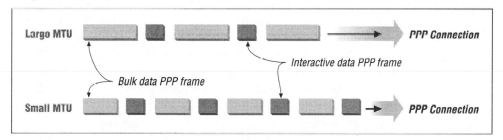

Figure 11-1. Interactive traffic performance with different MTU settings

On slow PPP connections, MRU and MTU may be set as small as 296: 256 bytes of TCP/IP data plus 40 bytes of TCP/IP header. The trade-off with smaller numbers is it increases communications overhead for bulk data.

The procedure to set MRU and MTU varies among PPP products and different computer platforms. Sometimes, PPP controls MRU and MTU settings. In other cases, the network protocol layers in the operating system manages these settings. Table 11-7 shows how to set MRU and MTU.

Table 11-7. Setting Maximum Receive Unit and Maximum Transmit Unit

Description	PPP	Default Behavior	How to Set
Maximum receive unit (MRU)	PPP-2.3	No request	Send PPP request by setting `mru 1500`
	Solaris PPP	Request MRU 1500	Send PPP request by setting `lcp_mru 1500`
	Windows NT	No request Accepts only MRU 1500	
	Windows 98	No request	
Maximum transmit unit (MTU)	PPP-2.3	MTU 1500	PPP peer sets MTU; option to set smaller value: `mtu 1500`
	Solaris PPP	MTU 1500	PPP peer sets MTU; override with `ifconfig`
	Windows NT	MTU 1500	Set registry value name: `MTU`; see text
	Windows 98	MTU 576 (<128 Kbps) MTU 1500 (> 128 Kbps)	Set `IP Packet Size` in `Dial Up Adapter Properties`

Windows 98 doesn't send the MRU option to its peer. The default value of 1500 applies in its receiving direction. In the transmitting direction, Windows 98 sets its MTU to 576 for connections below 128 Kbps, regardless of any larger MRU option the PPP peer requests. Connections above 128 Kbps use MTU 1500. In Windows 98, you can set the MTU for PPP connections by accessing `Control Panel →` `Network → Dial Up Adapter → Properties → Advanced`. The `IP Packet Size`. `Automatic` option sets the Windows 98 default behavior. `Large`, `Medium`, and `Small` correspond to MTU settings of 1500, 1000, and 576, respectively.

The Windows 95 MTU default is 1500 for all dial-up connection speeds. Its MTU pertains to TCP/IP settings bound to a specific dial-up network adapter. Changing it requires adding a value name to one of the following registry keys:

Hkey_Local_Machine\System\CurrentControlSet\Services\Class\netTrans\000n

Each `000n`, where *n* is a digit, represents a different network adapter. You must locate the appropriate *n* for the TCP/IP to dial-up adapter binding. One way is to examine other values in these registry keys. Pay particular attention to the values for `IPAddress` and `IPMask`. The new name to add is `MaxMTU` of type `DWORD`.

The procedure to change the MTU for Windows NT 4.0 is similar to Windows 95. Windows NT maintains global TCP/IP settings in:

HKEY_LOCAL_MACHINE\SYSTEM\CurrentControlSet\Services\Tcpip\Parameters

Network adapter specific TCP/IP settings are in the following registry keys:

> *HKEY_LOCAL_MACHINE\SYSTEM\CurrentControlSet\Services\<Adapter Name>*
> *Parameters\Tcpip*

The dial-up network adapter names for Windows NT are of the form `NdisWan5`, `NdisWan6`, etc. A separate name exists for dial-out and dial-in, even if they both share a single serial interface. You must examine the values associated with these registry keys to determine the correct one to modify. The `Control Panel` → `Network` → `Bindings` → `Remote Access Server Services` → `WINS Client(TCP/IP)` also provides some hints for locating the correct key. The new registry value name to add is `MTU` of type `REG_DWORD`. Restarting Windows NT is necessary to make MTU changes effective.

Counters and Timers

During the PPP negotiations, counters and timers help PPP recover from lost and garbled transmissions, as well as prevent infinite negotiation loops. RFC-1661 requires that counters and timers for the Link Control Protocol to be configurable. Unfortunately, many PPP products fail to document or offer procedures for changing these settings.

The counters and timers for the Link Control Protocol are:

Restart timer
> This timer sets the retransmission delay for an LCP configure-request sent without receiving a response. It also applies to terminate-request messages. The default is three seconds. It's rarely necessary to change this setting. If a peer is slow in responding, you can increase this value.

Maximum terminate
> This counter determines the number of LCP terminate-request messages to send without receiving a response. After sending this many messages, PPP assumes the peer is unable to respond and forcefully disconnects. The PPP default is 2.

Maximum configure
> This counter is the maximum number of LCP configure-request messages to send without receiving a response. The default is 10. Endpoints send a new configure-request with a revised list of options whenever a peer refuses the previous request. Only with rare and very complex PPP negotiations is it necessary to increase this counter. If the peer doesn't respond at all to configure-request, a larger value also increases the time to declare a connection failure.

Maximum failure
> This counter determines the number of LCP configure-nak responses to send before responding with LCP configure-reject. The default is five. Too many

configure-nak responses indicate that negotiations aren't converging for a particular option. Rather than continuing, a configure-reject terminates negotiations for the problem option. The PPP default for that option then applies.

The procedure for setting counters and timers for PPP-2.3 and Windows NT is in Table 11-8. Solaris PPP, Windows 98, and others don't include documented procedures for altering these settings. Thus, it may not be possible to alter them.

Table 11-8. Setting LCP Counters and Timers

Description	PPP	Default Behavior	How to Set
Restart timer	PPP-2.3	3 sec	Set with: `lcp-restart 3`
	Windows NT	3 sec	Set with registry value name: `RestartTimer`[a]
Maximum terminate	PPP-2.3	3	Set with: `lcp-max-terminate 3`
	Windows NT	2	Set with registry value name: `MaxTerminate`[a]
Maximum configure	PPP-2.3	10	Set with: `lcp-max-configure 10`
	Windows NT	10	Set with registry value name: `MaxConfigure`[a]
Maximum failure	PPP-2.3	5	Set with: `lcp-max-failure 5`
	Windows NT	10	Set with registry value name: `MaxFailure`[a, b]

[a] Registry key: *HKEY_LOCAL_MACHINE\SYSTEM\CurrentControlSet\Services\RasMan\PPP*.
[b] The PPP connection fails by exceeding this count; Windows NT doesn't substitute `config-reject` for `config-nak`.

Echo Requests

PPP includes LCP echo-request and echo-response packets to aid in debugging. These features are also useful for keep-alive situations.

Some products can send echo-request messages on a periodic basis. It may track echo-replies to verify that a peer is still alive. If the number of outstanding echo-requests exceeds a threshold, an endpoint can assume its peer is dead and terminate the connection. On some serial connections, this may be the only means for determining if a peer disconnected. These connections are the ones without physical hardware signals to physically signal a disconnect.

Products that don't support echo requests must at least support echo replies, in case its peer sends the requests.

With PPP-2.3, the `lcp-echo-interval` option enables a periodic timer for sending LCP echo-requests. This timer defaults to 10 seconds. If set, the `lcp-echo-failure` option is the threshold for unanswered echo-requests before PPP-2.3 terminates the connection. This counter default is 10.

Authentication Policy

PPP supports authentication with names and secrets. There are numerous authentication methods, which significantly adds to the list of settings you can adjust.

In this section, I discuss only settings that establish authentication policy and behaviors. Chapter 12, *Authentication*, describes how to set up PPP authentication in further detail, including how to set up authentication credentials.

Authenticator

An authenticator is an endpoint that requires its peer to prove its identity with a name and a secret. This is a typical role for a dial in PPP server. Not all PPP software products are capable of the authenticator role.

The standard means for authentication in PPP is CHAP or PAP. There are also several other nonstandard authentication protocols, including Microsoft CHAP and Shiva PAP. During LCP negotiations, the authenticator and its peer must agree on one authentication protocol. If the two parties reach an agreement, the peer later submits its credentials using the agreed-on protocol.

If you are responsible for establishing authentication policy, you can configure the authenticator to accept or reject specific authentication protocols. Table 11-9 shows some of the options various PPP products permit.

Table 11-9. Setting PPP Authenticator Policy

Description	PPP	Default Behavior	How to Set
No authentication	PPP-2.3	Default	Set with: `noauth`
	Solaris PPP	Default	
	Windows NT		Not available
CHAP only	PPP-2.3		Set with: `require-chap`
	Solaris PPP		Set with: `require_authentication chap`
PAP only	PPP-2.3		Set with: `require-pap`
	Solaris PPP		Set with: `require_authentication pap`

Table 11-9. Setting PPP Authenticator Policy (continued)

Description	PPP	Default Behavior	How to Set
CHAP or PAP only	PPP-2.3 Solaris PPP		Set with: `auth` Set with: `require_authentication chap pap`
MS-CHAP, SPAP, or PAP	Windows NT Dial-in only	Default is MS-CHAP only	See Figure 7-8

Authenticating Client

An authenticating client receives an authentication challenge from its peer. If an authenticating client has a set of credentials to use, it can participate in a PPP authentication. Whether the client can respond depends on whether it understands any of the PPP authentication protocols the challenger wants. If it does understand one, policy settings can determine whether authentication proceeds.

Users can restrict the authentication protocols their PPP software uses to respond. Some client-side restriction settings for various PPP products are in Table 11-10.

Table 11-10. Setting PPP Authenticating Client Policy

Description	PPP	Default Behavior	How to Set
No authentication	PPP-2.3 Solaris PPP	 Default	No available credentials
CHAP only	PPP-2.3 Solaris PPP		Only CHAP credentials available, or set with: `refuse-pap` Set with: `will_do_authentication chap`
PAP only	PPP-2.3 Solaris PPP		Only PAP credentials available, or set with: `refuse-chap` Set with: `will_do_authentication pap`
CHAP or PAP	PPP-2.3 Solaris PPP		Any available credentials Set with: `will_do_authentication chap pap`
MS-CHAP, CHAP, SPAP, or PAP	Windows 95; dial-out only		See Figure 6-8
MS-CHAP, CHAP, SPAP, or PAP	Windows NT; dial-out only		See Figure 6-18

Naturally, if authenticating client settings conflict with authenticator requirements, authentication ultimately fails. The connection then terminates. One of the PPP endpoints must change its policy to resolve the matter.

Counters and Timers

Authentication requires several counters and timers that control its procedures. PPP products may allow you to change the values for these.

The PPP specification implies that only one authentication attempt is permitted during connection establishment. If it fails, the connection may terminate immediately without another opportunity to retry. In practice, some PPP products are more lenient and permit multiple authentication attempts. In addition, there may also be a retry delay timer, frequently one second or more.

Some of the general counters and timers that control the PPP authentication process include:

Authentication retries

> Maximum number of retries with invalid authentication credentials. Set this according to your security policy.

Authentication time limit

> Total time permitted to successfully complete authentication. Set this according to your security policy.

Restart timer

> Sets the retransmission delay for resending an authentication request, when there is no response. You can consider increasing this timer for slow peers.

Maximum requests

> This counter limits the number of authentication requests to send without receiving a response. You can consider increasing this counter for slow peers.

These counters and timers and how to set them for various PPP products appear in Table 11-11. The settings available are rather limited for many products, with the exception of PPP-2.3.

Table 11-11. Setting Authentication Counters and Timers

Description	PPP	Default Behavior	How to Set
Authentication retry	PPP-2.3	1	
	Solaris PPP	1	
	Windows NT	2	Set with registry value name: `AuthenticateRetries`[a]
Authentication time limit	PPP-2.3 PAP only	No time limit	Authenticator setting only. Set with: `pap-timeout 0` (time in seconds, 0 is unlimited)
	Windows NT	120 sec	Set with registry value name: `AuthenticateTime`[a]

Table 11-11. Setting Authentication Counters and Timers (continued)

Description	PPP	Default Behavior	How to Set
Authentication maximum requests	PPP-2.3 PAP only	10	Client setting only. Set with: `pap-max-authreq 10`
	PPP-2.3 CHAP only	10	Authenticator setting only. Set with: `chap-max-challenge 10`
Authentication restart timer	PPP-2.3 PAP only	3 sec	Client setting only. Set with: `pap-restart 3`
	PPP-2.3 CHAP only	3 sec	Authenticator setting only. Set with: `chap-restart 3`
Periodic CHAP interval	PPP-2.3	None	Authenticator setting only. Set with: `chap-inteval 60` (time in seconds)

[a] Registry key: *HKEY_LOCAL_MACHINE\SYSTEM\CurrentControlSet\Services\RemoteAccess\Parameters*

Certain counters and timers pertain only to the authenticating client while others pertain to the authenticator. It's the nature of the PPP authentication transaction that determines this. With PAP, the client sends a PAP authentication request packet until the authenticator responses with success or failure. Thus, `pap-max-authreq` and `pap-restart` are a counter and timer for the authenticating client. With CHAP, only the authenticator sends challenges, so `chap-max-challenge` and `chap-restart` apply only to authenticators.

One interesting feature of CHAP is that an authenticator can challenge its peer to reauthenticate on a regular basis. You can enable periodic CHAP in PPP-2.3 with `chap-interval` and a time, in seconds. Beware that many clients understand CHAP only at the beginning of the PPP connection.

Adjustable IPCP Options

PPP negotiates using the Internet Protocol Control Protocol (IPCP) to establish settings applicable for the TCP/IP network layer protocol family. Details regarding how the IPCP negotiation process works are in Chapter 3.

The important TCP/IP settings for PPP connections are VJ compression and IP addresses. Also, several counters and timers control the IPCP negotiation process; and you may need to adjust these.

VJ Compression

VJ compression reduces the overhead with TCP/IP communications. More information about it appears in Chapter 4, *TCP/IP*.

PPP assumes that VJ compression doesn't apply unless an endpoint specifically requests it, and the peer agrees. However, the default behavior for many PPP products is to request this option. This is highly desirable, since using VJ compression increases PPP connection performance without significant drawbacks. However, if VJ compression is broken at either end of a PPP connection, you must disable it.

VJ compression itself includes two settings that control its behavior. These are the number of VJ connection slots and whether VJ "connection number" compression applies.

The VJ compression settings for several PPP products appear in Table 11-12.

Table 11-12. Setting LCP Counters and Timers

Description	PPP	Default Behavior	How to Set
VJ Compression On/Off	PPP-2.3	Request and Accept	Disable and reject by setting: `novj`
	Solaris PPP	Request and Accept	Disable by setting: `ipcp_compression off`
	Windows NT	Request and Accept	Set with registry value names: `RequestVJCompression`[a] `AcceptVJCompression`[a]
	Windows 98		Set with: `Use IP Header Compression`
Maximum connection slots	PPP-2.3	Request 16	Set with: `vj-max-slots 16` (2 to 16)
Connection number compression	PPP-2.3	Request	Disable with: `novjcomp`

[a] Registry key: *HKEY_LOCAL_MACHINE\SYSTEM\CurrentControlSet\Services\RasMan\PPP;* the value is of type `REG_DWORD` with 0 as false and 1 as true.

IP Addresses

IPCP permits an endpoint to send a request to its peer about its desired local IP address. A peer can refuse and include an alternative IP address in its reply. Remember that the peer also initiates and performs the same negotiations. Thus, each PPP endpoint can attempt to establish its own IP address, in addition to its peer's. A successful IPCP address negotiation results in an agreement at both ends to use two IP addresses, one for each end of a PPP connection.

You can establish the following settings that determine an endpoint's IP address negotiation behavior:

- Don't negotiate IP addresses

    This endpoint already has preconfigured, permanent addresses

- A local IP address

  This causes a "will request" to use a specific local IP address. The address request may be 0.0.0.0 if it's unknown

- A remote IP address

  This sets what IP address this PPP endpoint will accept from its peer. In other words, this controls the IP address the peer is permitted to use

- Allow or disallow the peer to change our local IP address

- Allow or disallow the peer to request any IP address for itself

As usual, PPP products don't necessarily offer all these settings. Settings that allow control over the remote IP address of a PPP connection are frequently missing.

Notice there are numerous possible combinations of IP address settings you can independently configure for two communicating PPP endpoints. Whatever the IP negotiation method, it must be consistent between both PPP endpoints. Obviously, if one endpoint wants to acquire its address from a peer that doesn't know how to set the remote address, the connection fails. Similarly, a connection also fails if one endpoint insists on using an IP address that is unacceptable, or in conflict, with its peer.

In common Internet access architectures, a user must acquire all IP addresses, even her own, from the dial-in PPP server. The dial-in server settings have both local and remote IP addresses, and any changes are nonnegotiable. This way, you can ensure that your users receive valid IP addresses compatible with the network infrastructure. You can be more creative when setting IP negotiations for leased lines; the straightforward method is to arrange each PPP endpoint with a hard-coded, nonnegotiable, local IP address.

PPP-2.3

PPP-2.3 happens to support the IP address negotiation settings previously described, except for no negotiation. Therefore, it's a good way to understand how to configure IP address negotiation. Next, we'll see combinations of negotiation settings at two PPP endpoints that are compatible with each other.

First consider two computers, Host A and Host B, each with permanent IP addresses. Thus, each computer sets its own local IP address for its end of the PPP connection. IPCP merely informs each computer as to what its peer uses for its IP address. The pppd startup options are as follows:

```
user$ # Host A        local addr  :remote addr
user$ /usr/sbin/pppd 192.168.1.34:            ...

user$ # Host B        local addr  :remote addr
user$ /usr/sbin/pppd 192.168.1.35:            ...
```

Now let's assume that Host A is the master of IP addresses for a PPP connection between Host A and Host B. When Host A sets IP addresses for both PPP endpoints, the pppd options are:

```
user$ # Host A        local addr   :remote addr
user$ /usr/sbin/pppd 192.168.1.34:192.168.1.35  ...

user$ # Host B
user$ /usr/sbin/pppd noipdefault  ...
```

The noipdefault option means PPP-2.3 must acquire both local and remote addresses for the PPP connection from the peer. Any IP address you explicitly configure for PPP-2.3 isn't negotiable, by default. Thus, a connection can fail if conflicts occur between two endpoints. However, PPP-2.3 allows peers to selectively override its addresses if you use ipcp-accept-local, ipcp-accept-remote, or both.

Configuring other PPP products

In Solaris PPP, you must define both local and remote IP addresses for PPP connections in the ifconfig statements that appear in the */etc/asppp.cf* configuration file. Solaris PPP always allows the peer to reset the remote IP address. The local IP address is nonnegotiable, unless you include the negotiate_address on configuration option.

Windows NT and Windows 98 dial-out PPP offers only Server assigned IP address or Specify an IP address as choices. Both pertain to a local IP address for PPP connections. Windows NT/98 dial-out has no control over remote IP addresses representing the dial-in PPP server.

When operating as a dial-in PPP server, Windows NT RAS normally sets the IP address for both ends of a PPP connection. There exists Allow remote clients to request a predetermined IP address setting that lets Windows NT accept any remote IP address for a PPP connection. Due to the possibility of violating IP address uniqueness in a network, I don't recommend this setting.

Counters/Timers

IPCP negotiation procedures are nearly identical to the procedures for LCP. Each PPP endpoint sends and receives IPCP configure-request, configure-ack, configure-nak, and configure-reject messages when negotiating TCP/IP settings. As with LCP, counters and timers control this process.

Counters and timers for IPCP are analogous to those for LCP. The guidelines to set them are similar to the LCP case earlier. Table 11-13 shows how to set these counters and timers.

Table 11-13. Setting IPCP Counters and Timers

Description	PPP	Default Behavior	How to Set
Restart timer	PPP-2.3	3 sec	Set with: `ipcp-restart 3`
Maximum terminate	PPP-2.3	3 sec	Set with: `ipcp-max-terminate 3`
Maximum configure	PPP-2.3	10 sec	Set with: `ipcp-max-configure 10`
Maximum failure	PPP-2.3	10 sec	Set with: `ipcp-max-failure 10`

Other IPCP Options

Beyond setting VJ compression and IP addresses, IPCP has few adjustable options that affect TCP/IP. One nonstandard Microsoft IPCP option is negotiating DNS and NBNS server IP addresses. If you have PPP products that support this, you may want to adjust it. This was covered in Chapter 10, *Domain Name System.*

Setting IP Addresses

By the time IPCP negotiations take place, PPP endpoints must have specific IP addresses to negotiate with each other. Where do these specific IP addresses come from? You can either explicitly set them beforehand or configure an entire back-end process that derives the specific IP addresses.

In both cases, you must first have an IP address pool available. This pool isn't arbitrary and must be compatible with the TCP/IP network infrastructure surrounding PPP connections. If you don't know the address pool to use for PPP, Chapter 8, *Network Architectures Incorporating PPP*, describes options for establishing this.

Some methods to determine the specific IP addresses for PPP are:

*   Assigning fixed IP addresses with each physical serial connection
*   Assigning IP addresses to the name of the remote computer or user
*   Obtaining unallocated IP addresses from a known IP address pool with DHCP or other IP address allocation service

Not all are available with all PPP products. Some can support several address allocation schemes simultaneously.

The second and third methods in the list dynamically establish IP addresses and may result in different addresses at different times for one physical PPP connection. Thus, when configuring IP address allocation algorithms, you must take precautions to prevent duplicate address conflicts.

Assigning Fixed IP Addresses to Physical Ports

The simplest approach for allocating IP addresses is to assign a permanent one to every physical PPP endpoint. Figure 11-2 illustrates this configuration. The PPP endpoints terminating at a single physical server can share the same IP address.

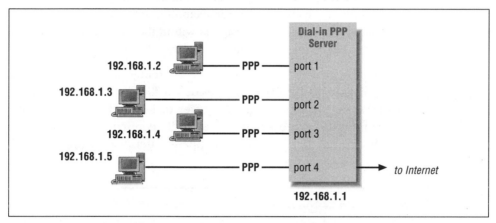

Figure 11-2. Fixed IP addresses per physical PPP connection

There are many benefits with this configuration. The number of IP addresses required is clearly fixed and limited by the number of PPP connections available. Also, once you correctly establish all the addresses, there's no chance of address conflicts.

When all dial-in ports share the same telephone number, users should expect to receive a different address for each PPP session. This happens because they may connect to a different port each time. However, it's also possible to assign unique telephone numbers to each port. A user accessing a specific port can then use the same IP address every time.

If you administer PPP-2.3, you can arrange a specific address for a physical dial-in port by placing the IP address settings in port-specific configuration files. These files are of the form, */etc/ppp/options.ttyS0*. The file suffix is the serial interface device. Solaris PPP and Windows NT don't really support port-specific IP addresses.

Assigning IP Addresses to the Name of a User

A permanent (static) IP address offers users a permanent Internet presence. Other Internet sites worldwide can reliably reference the user's site with a fixed DNS name and IP address. A static IP address is especially important for users running Internet services. Typical examples are a web site, FTP server, an interactive bulletin board, and a mail server. Users who wish to receive SMTP electronic mail directly from Internet sites are in effect running mail servers. PPP users may also need permanent IP addresses to access firewalls and private networks that use IP addresses as a means of access control.

A static IP address also allows disconnecting and reconnecting PPP without interrupting the TCP/IP network layer's status. For example, an FTP file transfer can resume after a disconnect as long as the outage is within the TCP session timeouts that an application program or the operating system has set.

When you configure personal IP addresses, you can arrange a database of user and IP address mappings. This database may reside on the dial-in server itself or may be located elsewhere in the network. Whatever dial-in port a user connects to, the server can consult this database and dynamically configure the connection with a personal IP address. This naturally happens after user authentication. Figure 11-3 illustrates this arrangement.

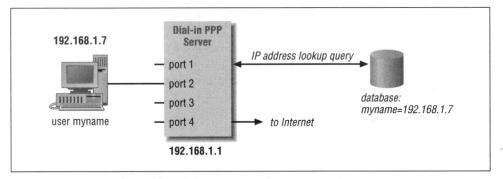

Figure 11-3. Personal IP addresses for PPP users

There are disadvantages and service complications you should consider when users have personal IP addresses. The number of addresses required may greatly exceed the number of dial-in ports. However, arranging personalized addresses for some users and an address pool for others can partially relieve this problem. Another complication occurs if one user establishes two separate PPP connections. Obviously, one address for two connections is a conflict. Finally, a specific IP address isn't portable networkwide. Such an address usually won't function if the user connects to a different dial-in PPP server located elsewhere in the Internet.

With PPP-2.3, the user-specific *.ppprc* configuration file enables setting personal IP addresses. Solaris PPP associates dial-in PPP settings with Unix login names. By definition, Solaris PPP sets IP addresses individually for each user.

Dynamic Host Configuration Protocol

The Dynamic Host Configuration Protocol (DHCP) enables computers to obtain IP addresses and other networking configuration information from a central server. Thus, a dial-in server can consult a DHCP server to obtain IP addresses for PPP. A diagram of this arrangement is similar to the one in Figure 11-3. The DHCP server simply replaces the database.

One feature for DHCP is that it can offer IP addresses to a computer to use for a limited time. This lease time allows DHCP servers to reclaim IP addresses that aren't in permanent use. A PPP connection that is active for a few hours, for example, needs an IP address only for a few hours. DHCP also includes provisions for computers to renew their lease before the original IP address lease expires.

A PPP user that receives an IP address assignment via IPCP never observes or uses DHCP. The dial-in server is responsible for DHCP queries and for requesting address lease renewals on behalf of the PPP user. If for some reason an IP address lease for a PPP connection does expire, the only logical course for the dial-in server is to terminate the user's IP connectivity. It's up to you as administrator to minimize this possibility in your DHCP designs.

Among the popular PPP products, Windows NT 4.0 RAS can consult DHCP to obtain IP addresses for dial-in PPP users. The Use DHCP to assign remote TCP/IP client addresses setting in Figure 7-9 enables this feature.

Other Means of Assigning IP Addresses

Dial-in servers can also assign free IP addresses from one or more fixed address pools. Each server can maintain its own pool and track the list of active and inactive IP addresses. Pools can't overlap between different servers since this raises the possibility of address conflicts. Windows NT supports IP address pools, in this manner, for dial-in.

You can implement any IP address allocation algorithm you wish. On Unix, a program can determine the address to assign using any input criteria. Here is a PPP-2.3 startup script:

```
#!/bin/sh
remoteaddr= /usr/local/bin/get-remote-ip
exec /usr/sbin/pppd 192.168.1.1:$remoteaddr . . .
```

The get-remote-ip program must return an IP address for the remote end of the PPP connection.

Other Adjustable Settings

PPP is extensible and supports numerous enhancements beyond what are described in this chapter. Each enhancement may have additional options, counters, and timers you can adjust. What's available depends on the PPP product.

Two enhancements that control PPP operation and are less visible to users are link quality monitoring and FCS alternatives. Chapter 3 further defines these. Current and upcoming PPP enhancements with benefits more visible to users and administrators include data compression, encryption, callback, and others. Some of these are introduced in Chapter 16, *What's New for PPP?*.

The best resource for information about product-specific PPP settings is written documentation. PPP for Unix frequently includes a list of features and settings in manual pages. For Solaris PPP, consult `man aspppd`. PPP-2.3 includes the manual page in file the *pppd.8*. The descriptions of Windows NT 4.0 RAS registry keys are in the help file for the `rasadmin` utility. After selecting `Help` in the `rasadmin` main window, look for "registry" in the help index.

In this chapter:
- *Password Authentication Protocol*
- *Challenge Handshake Authentication Protocol*
- *Microsoft CHAP*
- *Authenticating Outside PPP*
- *Call Back*
- *Security Tokens*

12

Authentication

Authentication establishes the identity for a computer or its user. This is especially important for dial-in PPP servers open to the public. An identity grants user access to protected network resources and provides accountability regarding user activities and resource usage. Authentication also prevents free and anonymous network access from individuals with possibly malicious intent.

There are many ways to perform authentication, and some are more effective than others. The choice of authentication methods is subjective and depends on the value of the resources you're protecting. More reliable and more secure methods tend to be intrusive and inconvenient. For Internet access, a simple name and password usually suffices. However, private networks may require more sophisticated authentication with one-time passwords.

This chapter discusses how to set up authentication for dial-in PPP. There are two distinct approaches. This first is to start PPP communications immediately after a serial connection is up. An authentication protocol then establishes the identity of the endpoints before useful communications begins. CHAP and PAP were introduced in Chapter 3, *How PPP Works*; their setup is described in this chapter. The second approach is to exchange interactive authentication prompts and replies after the serial connection is up, but before PPP starts. A user authenticates with a terminal emulator or an automatic chat script.

In defining authentication, the term *authenticator*, or *server*, represents a PPP endpoint that's challenging its peer to identify itself. In contrast, an *authenticating client*, or *authenticatee*, sends its credentials to a peer to identify itself. Dial-in PPP servers commonly perform the authenticator role, while dial-in PPP users are authenticating clients. However, PPP allows any endpoint to be authenticator, authenticating client or both simultaneously. Don't confuse these roles; mistakenly configuring two endpoints as authenticating clients disables security.

Password Authentication Protocol

The principle of operation for the Password Authentication Protocol (PAP) is simple. After PPP starts, each endpoint has the opportunity to demand that its peer respond with a name and password. PPP continues as long as the peer agrees to authenticate itself and replies with acceptable credentials. The transactions that take place appear in the section "Password Authentication Protocol" in Chapter 3.

Most PPP products include PAP support, at least in the role of an authenticating client. An authenticating client must provide some means for a user to enter a name and password. Users can enter this information either before the dial-out PPP process begins or at the time the authenticator asks for it.

Products that support the authenticator role frequently maintain a database of valid credentials. You must populate and manage this database. Some simpler products can also function in the authenticator role, but only with one valid name and password pair.

Setting up an Authenticating Client

Low-cost PPP software for dial-out usage generally supports PAP as an authenticating client only. A lot of software for PCs belongs in this category. Its configuration is straightforward: users must locate the authentication window for the remote system they're accessing and fill in a name and password. Some examples of this window include Figure 6-10 and Figure 6-19.

On Linux, Unix, and communication servers. PAP is more difficult to set up, mainly because these systems offer more features and flexibility. There may exist a database of PAP names and passwords. This gives PPP the ability to authenticate with different credentials depending on the remote system.

The database of PAP authentication credentials for PPP-2.3 resides in the file */etc/ppp/pap-secrets*. For a computer, myhost, functioning as an authenticating client, this file resembles:

```
root# cat /etc/ppp/pap-secrets
# Secrets for authentication using PAP
# client        server  secret          IP addresses
username1        ibm     password4       *
username2        psi     password2       *
username3        uunet   password3       *
username1        myisp   password1       *
root#
```

Each row in the *pap-secrets* file contains a PAP name in the client column and a password in the secret column. The credentials in a row apply when this computer interacts with the PPP peer named in the server column. All these names are for PPP use only and aren't necessarily related to hostnames or login names. The server name isn't a part of the PAP authentication process, so users can create any mnemonic to refer to different PPP peers they want to communicate with.

PPP-2.3 functions as an authenticating client as long as it has at least one credential it can use. When users start pppd, they must include a PAP name to use for authenticating. They must also include a server name they previously created, representing the remote system they are communicating with:

```
user$ /usr/sbin/pppd debug /dev/ttyS0 38400 user username1 remotename \
myisp . . .
```

The user option specifies the name to use with PAP authentication. Both the user and remotename options determine the password to send for authentication, according to the information in the *pap-secrets* file. In this example, the credentials myhost sends to a remote system are username1 and password1. Notice password4 isn't applicable, since that's for remotename ibm and not remotename myisp.

You can observe PAP authentication in the PPP-2.3 log file along with any problems that may occur. Examples of PPP traces can be found in the section "Password Authentication Protocol" in Chapter 3.

Setting up an Authenticator

Basic PPP software may not support the authenticator role at all. Some may only support the authenticator role when answering a dial-in call. Windows 98 is one such implementation; users can configure one valid PAP credential (Figure 12-1). Windows 98 ignores the name and cares only about the secret.

On Linux, Unix, Windows NT, and communication servers, a database manages valid PAP names and passwords. Communication servers usually consult other authentication servers responsible for this database. Windows NT uses the same authentication services that apply to Windows NT user accounts.

With PPP-2.3, */etc/ppp/pap-secrets* normally maintains acceptable credentials for the authenticator. This file contains entries in the same form as the one for the authenticating client, myhost, described earlier. For a computer myisp that is an authenticator, PPP-2.3 must inherit an internal name that matches an entry in the server column of *pap-secrets*. By default, this internal name is the same as the hostname, myisp. This identifies the rows in the database with valid PAP credentials PPP peers can use. The credentials themselves are in the client and secret columns. In general, all names in *pap-secrets* are for PPP and may not bear any relationship to host, login, or names for other services.

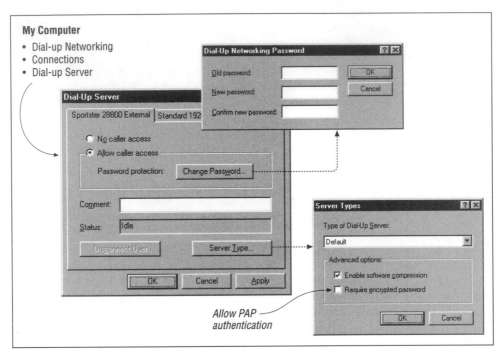

Figure 12-1. Windows 98 dial-up server authentication

When a dial-in user calls, `myisp` first answers the incoming call and then starts PPP with the following options:

```
root# /usr/sbin/pppd debug require-pap name myisp \
172.16.0.69:172.16.0.193 . . .
```

The `require-pap` option is critical and sets the requirement that the peer must authenticate itself with PAP. Otherwise, no authentication is required. The `name` option sets the `pppd` internal name to `myisp`. You must run `pppd` as root, in order to use the `name` option. Otherwise, you can include this option in a PPP-2.3 configuration file, avoiding the root requirement. If we use the *pap-secrets* file shown earlier, `pppd` accepts only `username1` and `password1` as valid. Note that the `remotename` option doesn't apply for authenticators.

Another `pppd` option of interest is `login`. This causes `pppd` to validate PAP credentials with both the *pap-secrets* file and the system password file. Authentication succeeds if credentials are acceptable to both. With the `login` option, the secrets in *pap-secrets* are typically two quotes (`""`) matching any password. Thus, the real PAP name and password validation occurs with the system password file. This allows you to selectively include Unix login credentials for PPP-2.3.

PAP and One-Time Passwords

The Password Authentication Protocol normally supports authentication with reusable names and password. However, some authentication methods use different *one-time passwords* for every sign-on. I don't recommend one-time passwords with PAP. They create special problems with most PPP implementations. Better ways to implement one-time passwords include performing authentication without PPP or using the PPP Extensible Authentication Protocol (EAP).

Consider users with a list of passwords they must use in a sequence. To authenticate with PAP, they must know what the next valid password is. Although inconvenient, they can change a PPP authentication file for each new PPP connection. A more serious problem is after a few authentication successes and failures, it's easy to lose track of what the next valid password should be. PAP also can't provide feedback to help users to determine what their next password is.

Some authentication methods, such as SecurID, require users to look up their password from a credit-card device. This password changes regularly, so users won't know it until they need it. There just isn't enough time to edit a PPP authentication file and initiate a dial-out call, since the password expires within a minute. What is necessary is PPP software that can prompt users for the password precisely at sign-on time. Dynamic password prompting isn't a common PPP software feature. However, Stampede Technologies Remote Office has this ability, and Windows 98 partially supports it. A prompt window appears when the PPP authenticator wants PAP credentials.

Windows 98 attempts authentication first with credentials users supply in the `Dial-Up Networking Connect To` window (Figure 6-10). But by the time the dial-out PPP call completes, those credentials may have expired. If the remote system hasn't disconnected yet, Windows 98 presents a `User Login` window, shown in Figure 12-2, asking the user for authentication credentials in real time. Unfortunately, this window appears only after authentication fails at least once. Thus, this `User Login` feature is limited to dial-in PPP servers that permit multiple authentication attempts.

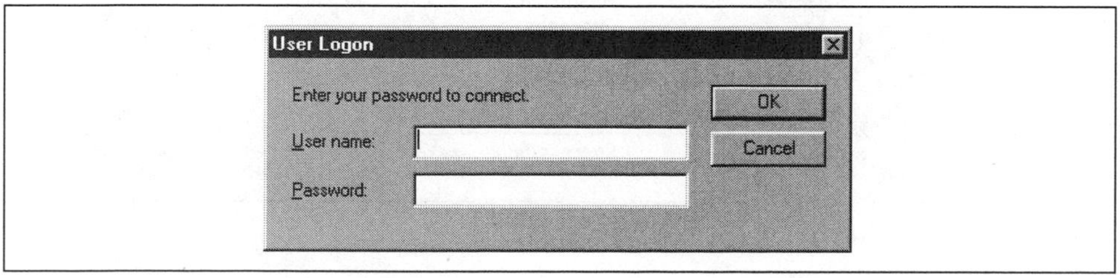

Figure 12-2. Windows 98 user login

Challenge Handshake Authentication Protocol

The Challenge Handshake Authentication Protocol (CHAP) is a common alternative to PAP. From a user perspective, CHAP operates much like PAP. Both require a name and a secret as authentication credentials. In the case of CHAP, this name is a CHAP name and this secret is a CHAP key.

CHAP enables PPP endpoints to prove that they share a common secret CHAP key without having to send the key through a PPP connection. The operating principle for CHAP is a three-way handshake. In summary, the authenticator sends a random challenge. The authenticating client transforms the challenge with a key and the Message Digest 5 cryptographic algorithm and replies with the result. If the authenticator uses the same key and algorithm, it can validate the result and respond with authentication success. The section "Challenge Handshake Authentication Protocol" in Chapter 3 describes CHAP principles in further detail and the PPP transactions that take place.

A minimum CHAP implementation appears in Figure 12-3. In this scenario, CHAP names and keys are fixed. Each endpoint exchanges its name and a string in a challenge and response message. Endpoints may even ignore the names. The response string is the only item necessary to validate the identity of the authenticating client.

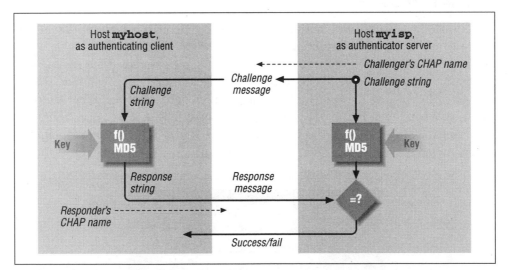

Figure 12-3. CHAP, minimum implementation

A more general implementation includes CHAP names as an authentication credential and uses this name to help both endpoints locate CHAP keys in a database (Figure 12-4). Key databases are important when authentication credentials must differ for every PPP peer. Based on the secret-key lookup procedure in the figure, the authenticator doesn't even know what key to use until the client responds with its CHAP name. Authentication succeeds as long as both endpoints manage to look up the same CHAP key in their databases.

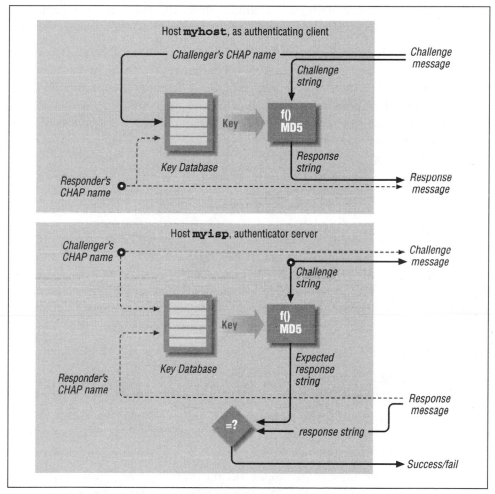

Figure 12-4. Authentication with CHAP key databases

CHAP offers authentication security similar to one-time passwords, as long as the challenge is random and the secret key is secure. CHAP keys should be at least 16 characters, but may be as high as 254.

One important security feature is that the authenticator can periodically send challenges during the course of a PPP session and expect a valid response. This limits exposure time if someone hijacks an existing connection. Unfortunately, many PPP implementations don't support periodic authentication.

Setting up an Authenticating Client

Configuring a CHAP authenticating client is straightforward. Users locate the authentication window for the remote system they wish to access and fill in the proper CHAP name and key. This window is frequently the same, regardless of CHAP, PAP, or another authentication method (see Figure 6-10 and Figure 6-19). It's the authenticator that normally determines how the client must authenticate itself.

Setting up an authenticating client for PPP-2.3 is more difficult, mainly because PPP-2.3 is more flexible in its abilities. PPP-2.3 maintains a CHAP key database file, */etc/ppp/chap-secrets*. Different keys may apply to different authenticators. PPP-2.3 selects keys based on both its own CHAP name and the name of its authenticator. Consider myhost authenticating to a remote system, myisp. The *chap-secrets* file on myhost may resemble:

```
root# cat /etc/ppp/chap-secrets
# Secrets for authentication using CHAP
# client          server  secret                  IP addresses
myname              *        "my-password-xyz#123"  *
root#
```

As the authenticating client, myhost selects all rows in which the client column matches its own CHAP name. The actual key used depends on the CHAP name the authenticator uses. The authenticator's name must match names appearing in the server column. Here, if the local CHAP name is myname, one secret CHAP key applies regardless of the authenticator's CHAP name. Note that strings in *chap-secrets* must be quoted or escaped if they contain special characters.

The PPP startup command string for myhost, when it calls myisp, resembles the following:

```
user$ /usr/sbin/pppd debug /dev/ttyS0 38400 user myname . . .
```

The user option sets the CHAP name myhost uses to identify itself and to find CHAP keys. As long as myhost can find valid credentials for itself, it agrees to PPP peers that demand CHAP authentication.

CHAP authentication transactions appear in the PPP log file. Thus, any CHAP problems would appear in this file. The section "Challenge Handshake Authentication Protocol" in Chapter 3 shows examples of PPP traces with CHAP.

Setting up an Authenticator

On Linux, Unix, and communication servers, you must manage multiple CHAP names and keys in a database. Communication servers can consult an authentication server. Linux and Unix typically use a data file. CHAP keys must be stored as plain text. Thus, it isn't possible to perform authentication with the information in the Unix system password file or any other file that stores passwords in forms that can't be decrypted.

PPP-2.3 maintains authenticator's names and keys in */etc/ppp/chap-secrets*. This is the same file when PPP-2.3 functions in the role of authenticating client. In order for PPP-2.3 to perform the authenticator role, its name must appear in the server column of *chap-secrets*. By default, an authenticator's name is its hostname. Here is the *chap-secrets* file for an authenticator with the CHAP name `myisp`:

```
root# cat /etc/ppp/chap-secrets
# Secrets for authentication using CHAP
# client          server   secret                 IP addresses
username1         myisp    key1                   *
username2         myisp    key2                   *
myname            myisp    "my-password-xyz#123"  *
myisp             myname   key3                   *
root#
```

The three rows in which `myisp` appears in the server column are the valid CHAP credentials authenticating clients may use. Other rows are for other authentication cases. The one with `myisp` in the client column, for example, allows `myisp` to simultaneously function as an authenticating client to a dial-in PPP user with CHAP name `myname`.

If we arrange for a PPP user to call this dial-in server, the `pppd` startup command on `myisp` must include the following options:

```
root# /usr/sbin/pppd debug require-chap name myisp \
172.16.0.69:172.16.0.193 . . .
```

`require-chap` is critical because it causes this server to enforce the CHAP authentication requirement on all its peers. The `name` option sets this server's CHAP name. This is useful if the name used differs from this server's hostname. In order to use the `name` option in the command line, `pppd` must start up with root privileges.

In contrast to PAP, there is no concept of the `remote-name` option. Both authenticating client and authenticator know the CHAP names for each other before they look up keys.

Configuring CHAP for Windows NT 4.0

The Windows NT 4.0 Server Remote Access Service supports PAP, Microsoft CHAP (MS-CHAP), and Shiva Password Authentication Protocol (SPAP) in the authenticator role. PAP is the common PPP standard. The two other authentication methods are nonstandard or proprietary.

Microsoft supports the authenticator role for standard MD5 CHAP, as long as the Windows NT 4.0 service pack 2, or later, is installed. You can either download the service pack from the Microsoft Internet web site or obtain a CD-ROM. Be aware that you must reinstall the service pack after any change that requires the Windows NT 4.0 installation CD-ROM. The service pack may have updated the original installation files.

CHAP authentication is important when non-Microsoft software must dial-in to Windows NT RAS, and when sending passwords in plain text is unacceptable. To enable the MD5 CHAP authenticator in RAS, you must create the following registry key with `regedt32`:

> *HKEY_LOCAL_MACHINE\SYSTEM\CurrentControlSet\Services\RasMan\PPP\CHAP\MD5*

Additional keys beneath the *MD5* registry key correspond to valid CHAP names. Note that all keys appear as folders in `regedt32`. CHAP names in the form `domain\name` must appear in the registry as `domain:name`. The named value `Pw`, of type `REG_SZ`, holds a secret CHAP key. For example:

Key	Named Value	Type	Value
`...\MD5\username1`	Pw	REG_SZ	key1
`...\MD5\username2`	Pw	REG_SZ	key2
`...\MD5\myname`	Pw	REG_SZ	mypassword
`...\MD5\ntdomain:myname`	Pw	REG_SZ	key3

These CHAP credentials apply only to a local RAS server. They are unrelated to Windows NT user account or passwords. When RAS challenges a peer to authenticate, the CHAP name that RAS identifies itself is the null string.

The MD5 CHAP feature is intended only for small numbers of dial-in users. The registry is difficult to manage for large numbers of credentials that may need to be distributed among multiple RAS servers.

Microsoft CHAP

The Microsoft version of CHAP is also known as MS-CHAP or CHAP-80. Windows NT 4.0 RAS supports Microsoft CHAP in the authenticator role. Both Windows NT and 98 can function as authenticating clients with MS-CHAP.

MS-CHAP functions similarly to the standard MD5 CHAP. An important difference is that Data Encryption Standard (DES) substitutes for MD5. In the LCP packet that carries the authentication protocol option (Figure 3-7), MS-CHAP uses the algorithm number 0x80, rather than the standard 0x05. Hence the name CHAP-80.

One problem Microsoft is trying to solve with MS-CHAP is to eliminate the need to store secrets in plain text. Unfortunately, they didn't really enhance security. The MD4 encrypted copy of the secret is analogous to the CHAP key in the standard MD5 CHAP. Therefore, obtaining the encrypted secret itself is all that's necessary to subvert security. Yet, MS-CHAP creates numerous authentication incompatibilities with non-Microsoft software.

If you wish to enable and enforce MS-CHAP authentication in Windows NT 4.0 RAS, you can select **Require Microsoft encrypted authentication** in the RAS **Network Configuration** window (Figure 7-8). This selection is the default. Notice that MS-CHAP authentication is the only way to enable Microsoft PPP data encryption. For dial-in PPP to the Internet, I don't recommend this selection, since it significantly limits PPP software compatibility.

Configuring MS-CHAP for PPP-2.3

PPP-2.3 supports authenticating client ability for MS-CHAP, thanks to the efforts of Eric Rosenquist. This is particularly useful for Linux and Unix users dialing into Windows NT 4.0 RAS, which doesn't accept CHAP or PAP. Administrators for RAS frequently configure it with **Require Microsoft encrypted authentication**, which allows only the nonstandard MS-CHAP authentication.

On Linux, MS-CHAP is already part of PPP-2.3. But with other Unix platforms, you may need to edit the **Makefile** for **pppd** and add compile time options to include MS-CHAP client code. The C compiler options to add are **-DUSE_CRYPT** and **-DCHAPMS**. This works for Unix platforms that include DES encryption libraries. If you don't have DES, you need to obtain it and integrate it into PPP-2.3 according to the instructions in the *README.MSCHAP80* file.

The procedure for configuring and using MS-CHAP is almost identical to the procedure for configuring and using standard MD5 CHAP. The credentials for the authenticating client must appear in its */etc/ppp/chap-secrets* file. Here is the *chap-secrets* file for authentication between PPP-2.3 and a Windows NT RAS server named **ntras**; the server name is just a mnemonic:

```
root# cat /etc/ppp/chap-secrets
# Secrets for authentication using CHAP
# client            server  secret            IP addresses
ntdomain\\ntmyname  ntras   key1              *
root#
```

There is a single entry for the MS-CHAP name, **ntdomain\ntmyname** and the MS-CHAP key, **key1**. All special characters, such as "\", require escaping. It's possible to mix MS-CHAP and CHAP credentials in the same *chap-secrets* file. The authentication process itself determines whether MS-CHAP or CHAP applies to a given credential.

Starting PPP and authenticating to Windows NT RAS requires a `pppd` command like this:

```
user$ /usr/sbin/pppd debug /dev/ttyS0 38400 user 'ntdomain\ntmyname' \
remotename ntras . . .
```

The `remotename` option is necessary, since RAS doesn't identify itself with its MS-CHAP name during the authentication process. Note that if the `user` option is in a configuration file, be sure to escape the "\".

To see whether MS-CHAP authentication actually takes place, you need to consult the PPP logs. Here are some entries that show PPP-2.3 recognizing MS-CHAP and successfully authenticating:

```
Jun  9 22:52:02 myhost pppd[1433]: rcvd [LCP ConfReq id=0x0 <asyncmap 0x0>
<auth chap 80> <magic 0x596a> <pcomp> <accomp>]
Jun  9 22:52:02 myhost pppd[1433]: sent [LCP ConfAck id=0x0 <asyncmap 0x0>
<auth chap 80> <magic 0x596a> <pcomp> <accomp>]
Jun  9 22:52:02 myhost pppd[1433]: rcvd [CHAP Challenge id=0x3
<6e1b81dc400bf566>, name = ""]
Jun  9 22:52:02 myhost pppd[1433]: sent [CHAP Response id=0x3
<00000000000000000000000000000000000000000000000007e7ae22c52fedbcae8c03ea29b1e
0741a43f92e1d6a5d96001>, name = "ntdomain\\ntmyname"]
Jun  9 22:52:02 myhost pppd[1433]: rcvd [CHAP Success id=0x3 ""]
```

In case of authentication failures, Windows NT RAS returns error codes embedded inside a PPP CHAP authentication failure packet. For example:

```
Jun  9 22:50:22 myhost pppd[1415]: rcvd [CHAP Failure id=0x2 "E=691 R=1"]
Jun  9 22:50:22 myhost pppd[1415]: Remote message: E=691 R=1
```

The `E=` is the number representing the error, and the `R=` indicates whether authentication retry is allowed. An authentication failure with bad credentials is `E=691`. Other codes and their meanings are in the Internet-Draft, *Microsoft PPP CHAP Extensions*, available from Internet sites that also maintain RFC document collections. The PPP-2.3 file *README.MSCHAP80* also lists some MS-CHAP error codes.

Authenticating Outside PPP

When a serial connection carries character data for authentication purposes before PPP starts, the authentication happens outside of PPP. During this phase, the data transmitted through the serial connection are human-readable questions and responses. The software necessary to progress through this is either a terminal emulator or an automatic chat script. Once users complete the authentication process, they can start PPP. At this stage, there is no longer any need for PAP, CHAP, MS-CHAP, or other PPP authentication protocols.

Authentication outside PPP enables you to implement exotic authentication methods beyond the capabilities available with standard PAP and CHAP. Now it's possible to prompt an interactive user with random challenges, accept multiple passwords, perform callbacks, and include use of security hardware devices.

In Chapter 6, *Dial-out PPP Setup*, you saw the basics of terminal emulators and chat scripts for initiating PPP. The following sections illustrate advanced methods to use these tools, especially when authentication requires more than a simple name and password.

Authenticating with a Terminal Emulator

A terminal emulator enables users to interact, in real time, with a remote system that wants authentication credentials. The emulator may be an integral part of the PPP software or may be a standalone program.

Built-in terminal emulator

Windows NT/98 PPP and many others support an integrated terminal window. This window may appear during PPP connection establishment (Figure 6-11). It allows users to enter modem commands, respond to one or more authentication prompts, and manually issue all commands necessary to start PPP at a remote system. A special keyboard sequence, a continue button, or equivalent, ends the terminal session and begins PPP at the local end. It's usually up to the user to end the terminal session once the remote system is ready for PPP.

Standalone terminal emulator

PPP software for Linux and Unix usually doesn't integrate terminal emulator functions. Terminal emulators are frequently separate, standalone application programs. They can attach to a serial device, allowing users to dial, manually interact with a remote system, authenticate, and initiate remote PPP. The next challenge is to attach PPP to the same serial device and then disable the terminal emulator.

Minicom and cu are Linux utilities that emulate a terminal. Similar utilities exist on other Unix platforms. Here, cu is used to manually make a serial connection to a remote system:

```
user$ cu -s 19200 -1 /dev/ttyS0
Connected.
at
OK
at dt 1-700-555-4545
CONNECT

Annex Command Line Interpreter   *   Copyright 1991 Xylogics, Inc.

Checking authorization, Please wait...
Enter one-time password:
```

```
annex: ppp
~}#@!}!}!} }8}!}$}%\}"}& }*} } }%}&bNC0}'}"}(}":I~~}#@!}!}!}
```

This interactive sequence includes modem dialing, authenticating with a one-time
password, and issuing the ppp command to start PPP at the far end of this serial
connection:

```
~z
[1]+  Stopped                      cu -s 19200 -l /dev/ttyS0
user$ /usr/sbin/pppd /dev/ttyS0 19200 defaultroute passive
user$ kill %1
user$
```

Next, cu is suspended with the ~z key sequence. This permits starting PPP at our
local endpoint with the pppd command. To prevent serial interface contention
between cu and pppd, cu must be immediately terminated. PPP communications
is active at this point through the dial-up serial connection.

PPP and terminal emulator contention

Separate terminal emulator and PPP programs require users to connect both temporarily to a single serial interface. Unfortunately, serial device-locking semantics
may prevent simultaneous access to it by multiple programs. This can inhibit our
ability to start PPP locally, before we can exit the terminal emulator. A symptom of
this problem is error messages such as:

```
Error 602: The modem is being used by another Dial-Up Networking connection
or another program.
Disconnect the other connection or close the program, and then try again.
```

or:

```
Line in use
```

Simply quitting the terminal emulator frees the serial device but may also hang up
the dial-up connection. What causes modems to hang-up is a state change on the
Data Terminal Ready signal (see Chapter 2, *Serial Interfaces and Modems*) at the
computer's serial interface. This event can be suppressed by:

- Configuring the terminal emulator to leave DTR active, when exiting

- Configuring the modem to ignore the DTR signal

The better solution is the first one. If the emulator won't leave DTR alone, we
must arrange the modem to ignore DTR. Here is an example that works for some
US Robotics modems:

```
at &f1
OK
at &d0
OK
at dt 1-700-555-4545
CONNECT
```

at&f1 loads a factory default template, and at&d0 sets the modem to ignore DTR; at&d2 reverses this. Now we can place a data call as usual, authenticate and start PPP at the remote end. When we exit the terminal emulator, nothing should happen to the dial-up connection. We can now start PPP in its place, attaching to the same serial interface. Be aware that since the terminal emulator can't signal a hang-up, PPP also can't. At the end of the session, manual intervention may be necessary to issue modem commands for hanging up.

Another possible complication when attaching PPP to an active serial interface is that the PPP software itself may attempt to reset the modem. This effectively undoes the work completed with the terminal emulator. We can avoid this by configuring PPP software to use a null modem. Now, since PPP presumes a modem doesn't exist, it doesn't send modem commands that could interfere with an active connection.

Authenticating with Chat Scripts

Chat scripts automate the otherwise repetitive tasks of placing a call, signing on to a remote system, and starting PPP at the remote end. These scripts interact with a remote system just as a person with a terminal emulator would. Scripts consist of a preprogram sequence of responses for all remote system prompts, including authentication. They are very useful for completely unattended operation. A computer can automatically initiate PPP at scheduled times or on demand by network application programs. Some sample chat scripts appear in Chapter 6.

Since chat scripts perform repetitive tasks, they are sufficient only for authentication with reusable credentials. This convenience is also a security drawback. Secrets are frequently part of the chat script. The script must store and transmit them in plain text form. Therefore, anyone with access to a chat script can retrieve and compromise its passwords.

Authentication with nonreusable credentials and call-back security present special problems for chat scripts. In many cases, it may be impossible to use scripts. In the following sections, we will see what some chat script problems are and how to solve some of them.

Call Back

Call-back systems require users to initiate a dial-in connection with a remote system. After the user successfully authenticates, the remote system hangs up the telephone and calls the user back at a designated telephone number. Call back is an enhancement, not a substitute, for an authentication method.

Call-back security depends on the security of the telephone network. In the past, a call to a telephone number guaranteed reaching a fixed destination. Due to recent advances in telephone service, this is no longer true. Call forwarding, when available, enables users to redirect calls for them to alternate destinations. Remote call forwarding is another enhancement that allows users to configure forwarding for their telephone number at any time, from anywhere. If remote call forwarding is abused, you can't guarantee that the return call is reaching the site you intended.

One major disadvantage of call-back security is accommodating mobile users. These users typically originate data calls from telephone numbers they can't predict in advance.

Terminal Emulator

A call-back dialog with a remote system is shown in Figure 12-5. After authentication, this remote system calls the user back and expects the user's modem to answer. In Figure 12-5, an `at a` causes the modem to answer at the appropriate time.

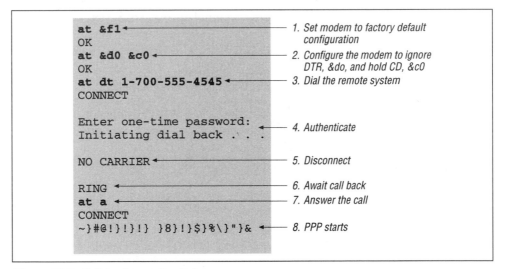

Figure 12-5. Call-back security dialog

Call-back security requires a telephone line disconnect and a reconnect within the same session. Terminal emulators and PPP software frequently assume a dial-up connection has ended or failed when the remote system disconnects. These programs monitor the state of a modem Carrier Detect signal. CD indicates a carrier loss, which may signal terminal emulators to quit. Should this happen in the middle of a call-back procedure, try to configure a modem to hold its CD signal active at all times. This creates the illusion that the dial-up connection is still active, even if it's disconnected and awaiting call back.

After call back, you may need to enter additional commands to answer the call and start PPP at the remote end. Then, we must exit the terminal emulator and start PPP locally. If the terminal emulator insists on resetting the serial interface at this point, configure the modem to ignore DTR. Ignoring DTR insures that the dial-up session remains active after the terminal emulator exits, but before starting PPP.

Chat Scripts

Call-back security presents problems for many chat scripts, causing them to terminate with errors, when the remote system hangs-up prior to call back. One workaround is to have the chat script configure modems to continuously provide the CD signal. This hides carrier loss events from later portions of the script during the call-back procedure.

Some chat programs do accommodate call back. They either ignore the serial interface Carrier Detect signal entirely or support settings necessary to ignore it. These features enable scripts to continue while waiting for the remote system to call back.

Defining a chat script for call back is straightforward. The commands in a script should include:

- Disabling and reenabling serial interface Carrier Detect, if applicable
- Time-out delays, in the order of minutes, while waiting for call back
- Configuring a modem for answer mode

A chat script basically behaves as a user does during a manual call-back procedure with a terminal emulator. A call-back script for PPP-2.3 appears in Figure 12-6. Each line consists of an expect/send string pair or a special script control command. Holding Carrier Detect with **at &c0** or its equivalent is necessary for chat implementations that don't ignore lost carrier. Chat for PPP-2.3 is already call-back compatible and ignores CD when a script is executing.

Security Tokens

Security tokens, or dongle, offer two-factor authentication, meaning that it requires "something you know" in addition to "something you have." Users still must have a traditional name and fixed password, but must also possess a physical device. This device is usually the size of a credit card and computes an additional one-time password. Security-token authentication is quite effective against unauthorized access due to attacks that include password guessing, password capture, and stolen credit-card devices.

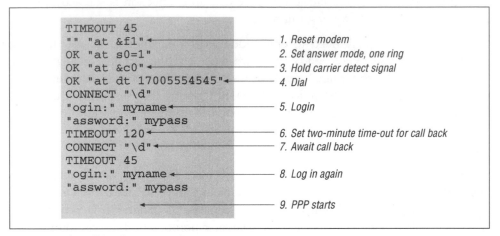

```
TIMEOUT 45
"" "at &f1"          ←———————————   1. Reset modem
OK "at s0=1"                         2. Set answer mode, one ring
OK "at &c0"          ←———————————   3. Hold carrier detect signal
OK "at dt 17005554545" ←————————   4. Dial
CONNECT "\d"
"ogin:" myname       ←———————————   5. Login
"assword:" mypass
TIMEOUT 120          ←———————————   6. Set two-minute time-out for call back
CONNECT "\d"         ←———————————   7. Await call back
TIMEOUT 45
"ogin:" myname       ←———————————   8. Log in again
"assword:" mypass

                     ←———————————   9. PPP starts
```

Figure 12-6. Call-back security chat script

Security token hardware and software products include Security Dynamics, SecurID, and Secure Computing (formerly Enigma Logic) Safeword. Safeword is compatible with hand-held hardware devices from multiple vendors, including the DES Silver card.

The SecurID hand-held device continuously displays new passwords every 30 or 60 seconds. Its authentication process requires users to enter a name, a fixed personal identification number the user memorizes and a dynamic password the device displays (Figure 12-7). Although a dynamic password is valid for up to a full minute, the authentication server only accepts it once. This prevents reuse of a password compromised within the previous minute.

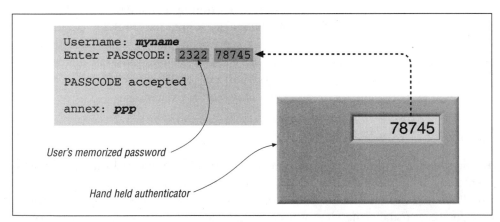

Figure 12-7. Security token authentication

Each SecurID device uses a secret key and the current time as inputs to a crypto-graphic algorithm. This algorithm generates the apparently random passwords the device displays. Both the key and the algorithm are unknown by the holder of the hand-held device.

An authentication server possesses the same information the hand-held devices do and can compute the passwords a given device displays at any given time. To vali-date credentials for many users, the server maintains a database of hand-held device keys, usernames, and user memorized passwords.

Chat Scripts

Chat scripts encode preconfigured dialogs only with remote systems. Unfortu-nately, a fixed script can't accommodate authenticator servers that require unpre-dictable one-time passwords. A script that can prompt users to enter passwords while it executes circumvents this problem. This capability isn't common, so manual authentication with a terminal emulator may be the only other alternative.

Progressive Systems (formerly Morning Star) PPP for Unix supports chat scripts that can invoke other programs as part of a script. This program can interactively obtain password, and other information, from users while the script executes.

Consider a remote dial-in PPP server with SecurID protection, as in Figure 12-7. The Progressive Systems PPP Systems file for the dial-in server named **pppre-mote** resembles the following:

```
user$ cat /etc/ppp/Systems
pppremote Any ACU 38400 17005554545 name: myname CODE: promptuser annex: ppp
user$
```

The script begins expecting the string **name:**, corresponding to the **Username:** prompt. The response is **myname**. For the **PASSCODE:** prompt, this script executes the **promptuser** program, as the backquotes indicate. **Promptuser** obtains a string from an interactive user. This program, for the X Window system, is:

```
#!/bin/sh
DISPLAY=:0
export DISPLAY
xprompt -rlen 20 -re -nograb -p password
```

xprompt is part of the X11R5 distribution. This utility is in directory *contrib/clients/ xprompt*. When **xprompt** exits, the user's response appears on its standard out-put. Once the user configures all items for PPP startup and starts */usr/etc/pppd*, she should receive the **xprompt** display shown in Figure 12-8. At this point, the user enters the one-time password her hand-held device displays and continues.

Figure 12-8. xprompt password prompt

xprompt is also useful for substituting reusable passwords that would otherwise appear in chat scripts, which avoids storing passwords on a user's computer.

In this chapter:
- *Private Network Setup*
- *Application Layer Proxies*
- *Network Address Translation*

13

Private Networks

Home PC users often wonder if several PCs can share a single PPP connection to the Internet for multiple PCs. You, as network administrator, may wonder whether users of one IP address are limited to a single computer. TCP/IP is a packet-oriented protocol capable of multiplexing any number of simultaneous communication sessions, regardless of where the data it carries originates. Therefore, it's possible to connect entire networks to any PPP connection, even if only one IP address is available. This chapter describes methods that achieve this.

The usual way to arrange Internet access for a private network is to first arrange a block of IP addresses for use by all private network devices. A router connects the network to the Internet via a single PPP connection. The Internet service provider must route all TCP/IP packets destined for any of these IP addresses into the connection. Unfortunately, the cost of this service is frequently orders of magnitude greater than the equivalent service for a single computer. This is true even if all computers share a single telephone line with 28.8-Kbps modems.

Low-cost Internet access provides routing to a single IP address at the end of a PPP connection. This address represents the dial-in PPP user's computer. However, nothing can stop users from connecting their computer to a private network, turning their computer into a PPP gateway. Although this private network is invisible to the Internet, the fact that both private network-to-gateway and gateway-to-Internet paths exist means private network-to-Internet communications also exists. What can happen is that a single PPP gateway masquerades as all the other computers in the private network. It communicates with Internet sites on behalf of its private network members using either of these:

- Application layer proxies

- Network Address Translation (NAT)

These techniques are common in Internet firewall designs that intentionally hide networks for security reasons. Our purpose here isn't security. Our private network is hidden only because its IP addresses are invalid for Internet routing.

Private Network Setup

Users with multiple computers create private networks of their own with LAN hardware or with a collection of serial interface cables. In the examples, I assume users have a small LAN. One computer may be designated as the PPP gateway, which manages an Internet PPP connection on behalf of the LAN members. Figure 13-1 illustrates a PC in this role, with both a PPP and LAN network interface.

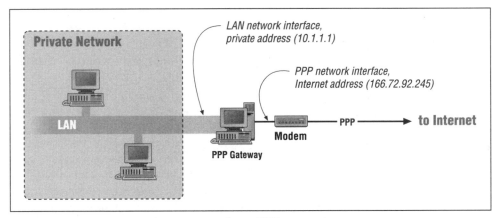

Figure 13-1. Connecting a private network to a PPP connection

The PC responsible for PPP has two IP addresses. The Internet service provider assigns one IP address, 166.72.92.245, for communication with Internet sites. Another address, 10.1.1.1, is used by the PC's LAN interface.

In this situation, it's still possible to route TCP/IP packets from the private network to an Internet site. However, the site won't have routes to reply back to IP addresses inside the user's private network. This is the major obstacle that prevents PPP connection sharing. To bypass this obstacle, you can arrange for all Internet traffic from the private network to appear as if it originates from a single IP address, that of the PPP gateway. In actuality, the traffic content may belong to another PC inside the private network.

Address Allocation for Private Networks

The Internet Assigned Numbers Authority (IANA) has allocated IP address space for use in private networks, including the one in Figure 13-1. Further details are available in RFC-1597. Table 13-1 illustrates the network numbers available. These numbers are usable in networks that either don't have Internet connectivity or achieve Internet connectivity by the means of application proxies, network address translation, or other indirect methods. Any number of independent organizations may use these network numbers without conflict. Consequently, none of these IP addresses are valid for direct use in the public Internet.

Table 13-1. Private IP Address Space (RFC-1597)

	Number Available	Network Number(s)
Class A	1	10.0.0.0
Class B	16	172.16.0.0, 172.17.0.0, . . ., 172.31.0.0
Class C	256	192.168.0.0, 192.168.1.0, . . ., 192.168.255.0

It's critically important for private or hidden networks to use private addressing. Notice in Figure 13-1 that the PPP gateway has a connection to both the Internet and a private LAN. Since the private addresses in RFC-1597 never appear on the Internet, there can never be a conflict, from the PPP gateway's perspective, about whether an IP address is an Internet site or a computer inside the private LAN.

Application Layer Proxies

An application layer proxy requires users inside a private network to first establish a communications session with a proxy server. In Figure 13-1, the PPP gateway is the proxy server. This server then initiates a new session with the desired Internet site. Proxy software then relays traffic between the two sessions until either the user or the Internet site disconnects. As far as the Internet site is concerned, it's communicating with the proxy server. It's unaware that the actual user may be located elsewhere inside the private network. Only the proxy server has the IP address necessary to communicate with Internet sites and another IP address to communicate simultaneously with users in the private network. In total, only one valid Internet IP address is required.

Proxy software at the PPP gateway operates as shown in Figure 13-2. Although a user's client application communicates only with the proxy, the proxy gives users the illusion they are communicating with an Internet site. The proxy appears as a server from the user's perspective, but as a client to Internet sites.

To use a proxy server, users or their client network application programs must be proxy-aware. Either the client software is a modified version that knows how to interact with a proxy server, or users use existing client software in a nonstandard manner to access an Internet site via the proxy server.

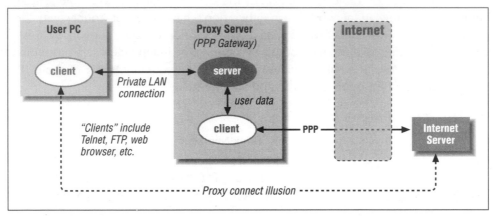

Figure 13-2. Proxy connection

With modified clients, a special Telnet, FTP, or web browser client interacts with a proxy server to connect with an Internet site. There are no procedural changes visible to proxy users. The modified clients handle all proxy details behind the scenes. The unfortunate drawback is that these client programs may be difficult to obtain, especially for numerous computer platforms.

Proxy servers can also function with standard, and existing, network client software. However, user procedures change since many of these clients normally expect to connect directly to an Internet site, rather than to a proxy server. I show later how users interact with a proxy in this arrangement.

Proxy Server Software

Proxy server software is readily available from various Internet sites, as well as from commercial vendors. This software frequently belongs in the category of Internet firewall software. Some commercial vendors are positioning their products for purposes besides firewalls. For example, "Connect your entire LAN to the Internet with one modem" is a pitch for the WinGate product.

Several proxy server products appear in Table 13-2. Most support numerous Internet services including Telnet, FTP, the Web, and others. The Netscape product, however, manages only the Web, although it also supports WWW requests for Gopher and FTP service. Most products listed are available for download as demonstration or evaluation copies. The TIS Firewall Toolkit is supplied in C language source code and is one of the few proxy servers compatible with Linux.

Table 13-2. Proxy Server Software

Product	Platform	Source
WinGate	Windows 95/NT	Deerfield Communications *http://www.deerfield.com/wingate/*
CSM Proxy	Windows 95/NT	Computer Software Manufaktur *http://www.hunterlink.net.au/products/sesame/*
TIS Firewall Toolkit	Various Unix	Trusted Information Systems *http://www.tis.com/*
Netscape Proxy Server	Various PC and Unix	Netscape Communications *http://home.netscape.com/*

User Procedures with Proxies

Users inside the private network connect to the proxy server and then somehow instruct the server to connect them to their desired Internet destination. With standard client programs (Telnet, FTP, etc.), this is a two-step manual procedure on the part of the user.

A user with a Telnet client accessing *archie.internic.net* via proxy server follows. This is a server running the TIS Firewall Toolkit:

```
user$ telnet 10.1.1.1
Trying 10.1.1.1...
Connected to 10.1.1.1.
Escape character is ^] .
PPP telnet proxy (Version V2.0) ready:
tn-gw-> archie.internic.net
Trying 204.159.111.101 port 23...
Connected to archie.internic.net.

         InterNIC Directory and Database Services
 . . .
```

The Telnet client must first connect to the proxy address, 10.1.1.1. A destination prompt appears that enables users to enter their desired destination.

FTP operates similarly. Rather than entering an actual FTP username, the user enters *anonymous@ftp.uu.net*, for example. This informs the proxy where it should connect on behalf of the user:

```
user$ ftp 10.1.1.1
Connected to 10.1.1.1.
220 PPP FTP proxy (Version V2.0) ready.
Name (10.1.1.1:guest): anonymous@ftp.uu.net
331-(----GATEWAY CONNECTED TO ftp.uu.net----)
331-(220 ftp.UU.NET FTP server (Version wu-2.4(4) Mon Jan 6 13:57:37 EST
1997) ready.)
331 Guest login ok, send your complete e-mail address as password.
```

```
Password:
230-
230-                    Welcome to the UUNET archive.
. . .
230 Guest login ok, access restrictions apply.
ftp>
```

Of the popular Internet services, WWW is perhaps the easier one to proxy. Netscape Navigator, Microsoft Internet Explorer, and several others, include proxy compatibility features. In other words, they are already modified clients. Therefore, users can navigate the World Wide Web transparently as if they were directly connected to the Internet. Once users enable the browser's proxy settings, the browser automatically knows to inform the proxy server where it should connect for each request.

Proxy Server Setup, TIS Firewall Toolkit

Proxy server software for PPP gateways are application programs, much like other TCP/IP client and server programs. They don't affect TCP/IP stacks or any network device drivers; thus, their installation and configuration is straightforward. However, you should be aware of possible conflicts between the proxy server and other server programs that may be active on a PPP gateway.

On Unix, `inetd` listens for incoming connection requests for various Internet services including Telnet, FTP, finger, etc. If an incoming request arrives on the Telnet TCP port 23, for example, `inetd` usually invokes the Telnet daemon, `in.telnetd`:

```
user$ cat /etc/inet/inetd.conf
. . .
telnet  stream  tcp    nowait  root    /usr/sbin/in.telnetd    in.telnetd
. . .
```

This `in.telnetd` then passes back the "login" prompt most users observe from a Unix server. A proxy server invokes a Telnet proxy program instead, rather than `in.telnetd`. With the TIS Firewall Toolkit, this is `tn-gw`:

```
user$ cat /etc/inet/inetd.conf
. . .
telnet  stream  tcp    nowait  root    /usr/local/etc/tn-gw    tn-gw
. . .
```

`tn-gw` behaves as described earlier for a user connecting to *archie.internic.net*. You can modify `tn-gw` security behavior with its configuration file, */usr/local/etc/ netperm-table*. To allow Telnet proxy service to any private network client and to allow proxy connections to any destination, the *netperm-table* must include the following:

```
user$ cat /usr/local/etc/netperm-table
. . .
```

```
tn-gw:          permit-hosts *
. . .
```

In general, a proxy server that accepts incoming Telnet connections with `tn-gw` can't accept connections with `in.telnetd` at the same time. Doing so is a conflict, since only one server program can bind to and listen at a specific TCP port. However, the TIS toolkit includes `netacl` as an alternative server program. It can invoke `tn-gw` or `in.telnetd` after it accepts the incoming connection, depending on the client IP address that is requesting Telnet service.

Proxy Issues

Although proxies indirectly provide Internet access for users inside a private network, they still don't offer the equivalent of a direct Internet connection.

Not all Internet services can be proxied. Those that present the most problems are client programs that offer no means of modifying its usage procedure to reference the proxy server. A simple ping, for example, belongs in this category. Furthermore, proxy software is specific to an Internet service, whether it's Telnet, FTP, or the Web. Every service must have a proxy at the PPP gateway, and one may not be available for a new service. If there isn't a proxy for a new multimedia service, for example, the service simply isn't available to users inside a private network.

Another difficult issue arises with user server software that listens for incoming Internet connections. A user running an Internet telephone is an example. Unfortunately, a PC inside a private network is hidden from the Internet and can't accept incoming Internet requests directly. It's possible, but inconvenient, to arrange the proxy server to listen for specific incoming requests and pass the requests to the user. Remember that a proxy server has only a single Internet IP address. Therefore, it can listen only at a specific TCP or UDP port number on behalf of only a single user in the private network.

Network Address Translation

Network address translation (NAT) is a router function that rewrites TCP/IP packets as they traverse through the PPP gateway between the Internet and a private network. The translator modifies IP addresses inside TCP/IP packet headers. Those packets going to the Internet have their source addresses translated to valid Internet IP addresses. Conversely, packets destined to a private network have their destination IP address mapped to the equivalent private network address. Since address translation operates at the IP layer, multiple PCs can share a PPP connection and function without any changes to user procedures or network application client programs. RFC-1631 provides additional details about NAT.

Figure 13-3 illustrates network address translation. In the context of Figure 13-1, the PPP gateway must perform this function, in addition to its role as a TCP/IP router. NAT requires configuring address translation tables. These tables may be static or dynamic depending on the features available in the implementation. PCs inside the private network simply route Internet traffic to the PPP gateway, in a manner identical to a private network with a direct Internet connection. In most cases, these PCs aren't aware that NAT is in use.

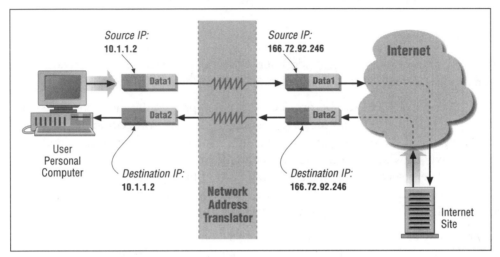

Figure 13-3. Network address translation

There are two address translation methods currently available. Either or both may be used, depending on the availability of Internet IP addresses for a given private network design.

- A private IP address maps to an Internet IP address
- A private IP address and TCP/UDP port pair maps to an Internet IP address and port pair

The second option accommodates a many-to-one mapping of IP addresses. This is the only option for PPP connections that provide a single valid Internet IP address.

Translating IP Addresses

Translating IP addresses from one to another and leaving TCP/UDP port numbers in TCP/IP packet headers untouched is the simpler NAT implementation. Table 13-3 illustrates an example of a static translation table. Each private network IP address maps to a unique Internet address. The NAT modifies only one IP address inside the TCP/IP packet header. The translation occurs for either, but not both, the packet's source or destination IP address, depending on the packet's direction.

Table 13-3. NAT Translation Table, IP Addresses

Private Network (IP Address)	Internet (IP Address)
10.1.1.2	166.72.92.246
10.1.1.3	166.72.92.247
10.1.1.4	166.72.92.248
10.1.1.5	166.72.92.249

NAT tables may also be built dynamically from a pool of assignable Internet IP addresses. This offers the ability to share a small pool of Internet addresses with a larger number of private network addresses. As long as the NAT has a free Internet address at the time of the request, any user in the private network can have Internet access.

For a PPP gateway that performs IP address translation and has a single Internet connection, the ISP must allocate an Internet IP address pool and arrange routing for all of the addresses. Although the PPP gateway has its own address (166.72.92.245), it accepts packets destined to the other IP addresses in the pool. These are the packets NAT rewrites and reroutes to users inside the private network.

Translating IP Address and Port Pairs

A more advanced NAT implementation translates one IP address and port number pair to another unique pair. Table 13-4 illustrates a snapshot of a translation table that may be in effect at a given time on a NAT-enabled PPP gateway. This is a dynamic table, since private network PCs initiating connections to Internet sites dynamically select TCP and UDP source port numbers from its own pool. The NAT creates a mapping to an available Internet address and port number for the duration of the user communication session. Again, NAT translates only the source or destination IP address and port number pair inside a TCP/IP packet. The translation depends on the packet's direction.

Table 13-4. NAT Translation Table, IP Addresses and Ports

Private Network (IP Address and Port)	Internet (IP Address and Port)
IP 10.1.1.2, TCP Port 1025	IP 166.72.92.245, TCP Port 1025
IP 10.1.1.3, TCP Port 1025	IP 166.72.92.245, TCP Port 1026
IP 10.1.1.4, UDP Port 513	IP 166.72.92.245, UDP Port 513
IP 10.1.1.5, TCP Port 32769	IP 166.72.92.245, TCP Port 32769

The benefit of both IP address and port translation is that multiple PCs can simultaneously share a single Internet address. The differences in the port numbers distinguish between packets for different destinations inside the private network. Notice the very similar translation entries in Table 13-4 for users with IP address 10.1.1.2 and 10.1.1.3.

With IP address and port translation, the ISP needs only to provide a single Internet IP address for a PPP gateway. NAT hides all the computers in the user's private network behind the single Internet IP address. Only the PPP gateway administrator knows that the Internet address he is using serves numerous others on her private, and hidden, network.

NAT Software

NAT functionality is available as IP masquerading on Linux. IP Filter, by Darren Reed, is available on the Internet[*] and supports NAT for Solaris and other Unix platforms. These are some readily available source code implementations of NAT.

NAT is also an option for router products available from Cisco Systems, *http://www.cisco.com/*. Checkpoint Software Technologies, *http://www.checkpoint.com/*, offers firewalls with this capability for Windows NT and Unix. There are also several shareware and evaluation NAT products available for Windows NT/98. These products can perform translation either on the basis of IP addresses only, IP address and port pairs, or both.

Since it operates at the lower layers of an operating system TCP/IP stack, NAT software is extremely platform-specific. The "Slirp" package (see the section "PPP Software" in Chapter 5, *Selecting Hardware, Software, and Services*) is an exception. It offers a form of NAT for a private PPP connection to an Internet Unix shell account, rather than the reverse, which we will discuss here.

NAT Setup, Linux

Installing NAT software usually adds to, or alters, the low-level networking software in a computer's operating system. Thus, installation specifics are product- and platform-dependent. Once installed, NAT products include utility programs for maintaining IP address translation tables.

On Linux Slackware 3.4, IP Masquerading requires users to build a Linux kernel with the following networking options (beyond what is necessary for standard TCP/IP support):

- IP forwarding/gatewaying

---

[*] *ftp://coombs.anu.edu.au/pub/net/ip-filter/*

- IP firewalling

- IP masquerading

Notice that IP masquerading is a subcomponent of the available Linux firewall features. Some instructions about how to build a Linux kernel appear in Chapter 6, *Dial-out PPP Setup*. Since this PPP gateway has a LAN network interface, the Linux networking instructions in Chapter 7, *Dial-in PPP Setup*, are also applicable here.

The primary utility for managing Linux IP masquerading is `ipfwadm`. This is the same utility that manages Linux firewall TCP/IP packet-filtering rules for incoming packets, outgoing packets, and packets to forward. Masquerading is a special feature for packet forwarding. If we consider the configuration of a Linux PPP gateway in Figure 13-1, the following are the `ipfwadm` commands enable that IP masquerading:

```
root# # Turn off input packet filtering
root# ipfwadm -I -f        # Flush the input packet filtering rule table
root# ipfwadm -I -p accept# Accept all input packets by default
root# # Turn off output packet filtering
root# ipfwadm -O -f        # Flush the output packet filtering rule table
root# ipfwadm -O -p accept # Send all output packets by default
root# # Configure IP masquerade
root# ipfwadm -F -f        # Flush the packet forwarding rule table
root# ipfwadm -F -p deny # Deny packet forwarding by default
root# ipfwadm -F -a accept -S 10.0.0.0/8 -D 0.0.0.0/0 -W ppp0 -m
root#
```

The last `ipfwadm` command is the important one. This rule accepts TCP/IP packets for forwarding to the `ppp0` network interface. The packets to accept must have a source IP address that matches 10.0.0.0 with an 8-bit mask—in this case, any source IP address beginning with 10 matches. Packets to accept can have any destination, as `-D 0.0.0.0/0` indicates. The `-m` indicates masquerade. Before it forwards the packet to the Internet, Linux rewrites the source IP address to its own and alters the port number. Masquerading in the return direction is automatic.

Linux users can check the status of IP masquerading with the `ipfwadm` extended list, `-l -e`, option:

```
root# ipfwadm -F -l -e
IP firewall forward rules, default policy: deny
 pkts bytes type  prot opt  tosa tosx ifname  ifaddress       source
    destination          ports
 8308  710K acc/m all  ---- 0xFF 0x00 ppp0    any             localnet/8
    anywhere             n/a
root#
```

Positive `pkts` and `bytes` counters indicate that IP masquerading is functioning. Another status command, `ipfwadm -M -l`, shows the current state of the address translation table. Other ways to use `ipfwadm` appear in its manual page; the mini howto document, `IP-Masquerade`; and the IP masquerade FAQ.

The basic NAT concept doesn't function for all Internet services. For this reason, Linux includes specific modules designed to circumvent NAT-related problems with some services. The modules available include FTP, IRC, Quake, Real Audio, Cuseeme, and VDOlive. Users can load these modules, if they need them, on the PPP gateway:

```
root# modprobe ip_masq_ftp
root# modprobe ip_masq_raudio
root# modprobe ip_masq_irc
. . .
```

And finally, Linux also has the IP auto forward patch, `ipautofw`, which accommodates additional Internet services that require the user's client software to send packets on one TCP or UDP port and receive packets on a range of other ports.

NAT Issues

Accessing the Internet with a network address translator is still not the equivalent of a direct connection to the Internet. The side effect of NAT is a collection of Internet services that don't function at all.

NAT technology normally modifies addresses in TCP/IP packet headers. This is insufficient for Internet services that embed IP addresses inside packet data. A good example is FTP, where a client sends its IP address and a port number in a **PORT** command to an Internet FTP server. This information is invalid, once NAT alters the TCP/IP packets. Some NAT implementations can modify IP addresses within TCP/IP packet data, as long as it knows how to interpret the data for the affected service. The Linux `ip_masq_ftp` module, for example, performs this function for FTP. Obviously, a NAT implementation can never know about all the future Internet services that require altering IP addresses embedded in data streams.

NAT configurations that translate port numbers normally assume that a client sending data with one TCP or UDP source port expects to receive replies on the same port number. Unfortunately, this isn't true for some Internet services that may reply with data over a range of ports. When there is no obvious relationship between sending and receiving port numbers, the service is unusable in the presence of a NAT. Again, customizations to NAT, such as Linux `ipautofw`, can accommodate for some of these cases.

Another difficulty arises with services that listen to incoming requests from the Internet. Such services can function as long as address translation tables are static and an Internet IP address and specific port number is available for a listening private network PC. If the tables are dynamic, there is no convenient means for a PPP gateway to know that a PC began listening for incoming requests. Since port numbers are usually fixed for a given service, the number of listeners for one Internet service is limited to the number of valid Internet addresses. This limit may be as low as one.

14

Virtual Private Networking and Tunneling

In this chapter:
- *Virtual Private Network Architectures*
- *Tunneling Protocols*
- *Redirecting Serial Input/Output*
- *Setting up Outgoing PPP Tunnels*
- *Setting up Incoming PPP Tunnels*
- *Routing with Tunnels*
- *Network Security*

PPP isn't limited to use over telephone lines and leased lines. In fact, PPP is compatible with almost any full duplex service that can carry binary data between two endpoints. This includes even the Internet itself. After all, if a computer can open a communication session with an Internet site and transfer a binary file, it can just as easily open a session for a PPP data stream. This advanced use of PPP is the basis for virtual private networks (VPNs).

A traditional private network requires leased lines to connect geographically dispersed LANs. In a virtual private network, the Internet emulates the leased lines, thereby replacing them. This is a significant cost benefit, since the expense for Internet communications is far less than installing and maintaining real leased lines. Another added benefit is the widespread availability of Internet access; anyone who can access the Internet can participate in a VPN. You may be apprehensive about data security, since VPNs use the public Internet for connecting private networks. Fortunately, PPP supports data encryption, which essentially eliminates the privacy threat.

In this chapter, I describe VPNs and the PPP tunneling technologies they depend on. A *tunnel* is what supports a PPP data stream through the Internet. Although there are several tunneling protocols, tunneling is new, and product choices may be limited. Thus, I will discuss the nonstandard Point-to-Point Tunneling Protocol (PPTP) and ad hoc tunneling solutions with raw TCP, Telnet, and `rlogin` utilities.

Later in the chapter, I include information on how to set up VPN connections with several PPP software products.

Virtual Private Network Architectures

A comparison between a private network and a VPN is helpful in understanding the relationships between VPN and tunneling.

Figure 14-1 illustrates a private wide area network architecture with PPP connections for both dial-in users and LAN interconnection. The routers and communication servers in this network each have a physical network interface for PPP and another physical network interface to parts of the private network.

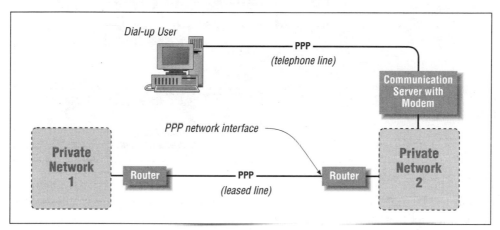

Figure 14-1. Private network with leased and dial-up lines

In the VPN architecture, tunnel connections through the Internet replace both leased and dial-up lines. Yet the tunnels carry PPP within them. Figure 14-2 shows the VPN equivalent for the private network architecture of Figure 14-1.

Leased-Line Replacement

For leased-line replacement between private network 1 and 2, in Figure 14-2, the routers each have a physical network interface for the Internet and an interface that connects to the private network. Routers use their Internet interface and Internet IP addresses solely for establishing a tunnel between them. There exists a logical PPP network interface at the ends of the tunnel. Thus, PPP uses the tunnel as the equivalent of a real serial connection. The logical PPP network interface and the physical private network interface use IP addresses belonging to the private networks.

The routers at the tunnel ends connect the private network only to the tunnel, not the Internet. They also filter out all other undesirable traffic. Since their IP datagrams can never appear on the Internet, computers in the private network thus

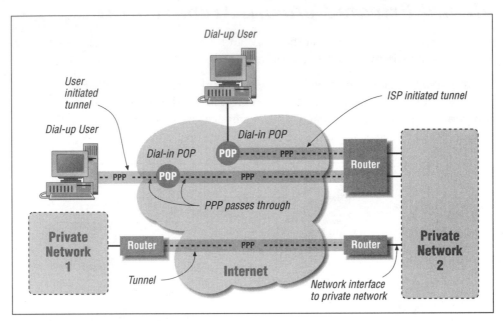

Figure 14-2. Virtual private networking

remain inaccessible to the Internet. Also, these private networks are totally oblivious to the fact that the Internet connects them.

Dial-up Line Replacement

The VPN equivalent for dial-in PPP users is more complex; these users must gain access to the Internet using any means at their disposal. Once users have Internet access, they can set up a tunnel between themselves and the router for the private network. This is shown for the dial-up user on the left in Figure 14-2. This tunnel is equivalent to the telephone line that connects to a communication server in Figure 14-1. However, remote users can access their private network with a local or toll-free call to any ISP, not just a communications server connected directly to the private network. For private network administrators, this eliminates long-distance charges, toll-free lines, dial-in modem pools, and communication servers. All these responsibilities shift to ISPs.

Some ISPs offer VPN value-added services. They can arrange a permanent tunnel between their dial-in Point of Presence (POP) and the router belonging to private network. You can see this with the dial-in user on the right, in Figure 14-2. In this arrangement, dial-in users need only basic PPP software, without tunneling support. The POP automatically encapsulates PPP frames into the tunnel and forwards them to the private network router. This no longer grants users access to other Internet sites, since they no longer have an Internet network interface. The POP forces all user traffic into the tunnel.

Protocol Layers with Tunnels

What may be confusing is the need to send PPP frames through Internet tunnels, when a PPP connection for Internet access may already exist. Remember a tunnel behaves like a leased line or a private dial-up line. This tunnel carries PPP, TCP/IP, and other protocols exclusively for the private network.

Dial-in users may set up a PPP connection to the Internet, a tunnel connection to a private router, and then another PPP connection inside the tunnel. This creates numerous protocol layers user PCs must manage. Figure 14-3 illustrates the relationships between protocols for users dialing into private networks via a tunnel arrangement. Compare this with the protocol layers necessary for dial-in to a private network modem, without the tunnel.

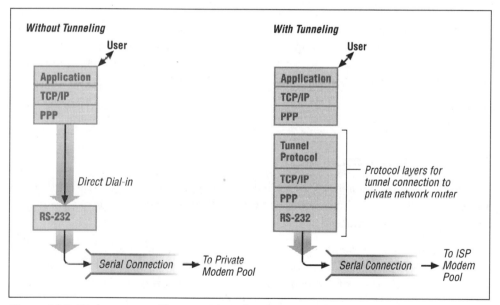

Figure 14-3. Dial-up protocol layers, with and without tunneling

Another name that describes protocol layers for tunneling is "PPP over TCP/IP." If you plan to set up tunnels, you must obtain software that can redirect PPP communications to a protocol stack, rather than a physical interface.

Tunneling Protocols

When you select a tunneling protocol, you must find one that is compatible with the software at both ends of a tunnel. Be careful to understand the idiosyncrasies of protocols not intended as tunnels, so that you can successfully use them with PPP. Keep in mind that the prerequisite for creating a tunnel is preexisting connection to a TCP/IP network.

Almost any service capable of two-way, point-to-point communications can become a tunnel for PPP. The effort required depends on the tunnel's communication characteristics. Bad tunnels are those that alter character codes in transit, but PPP is forgiving and may still function with these tunnels. The requirements for a PPP tunnel are:

- The tunnel must be full duplex. In other words, it must support simultaneous, bidirectional communications.

- Data received must be in the same sequence in which it was sent.

- The tunnel must transport 8-bit character codes.

- The tunnel must be as clean as possible regarding characters it might intercept and insert. PPP is compatible with tunnels that may alter control characters in the range 0x00 to 0x1f. Other character alterations may render the tunnel useless for PPP.

How the tunnel encodes data for actual transmission isn't relevant, as long as it recovers the data properly at the receiving end.

Point-to-Point Tunneling Protocol

The Point-to-Point Tunneling Protocol (PPTP) is specifically designed to provide a tunnel for PPP through the Internet or other TCP/IP networks. PPTP functions in a client/server arrangement.

The PPTP specification defines a control channel for managing a PPTP tunnel. This channel is a TCP connection at port 1723. PPTP sends and receives PPP frames out of band using the IP layer General Routing Encapsulation (GRE) protocol. GRE is IP protocol number 47. Unfortunately, GRE isn't as universal as TCP and UDP. Some network infrastructures refuse to route GRE packets; therefore, these infrastructures can't support PPTP.

Where PPTP is available, some of its capabilities are:

- Management of multiple PPP connections sharing a single PPTP tunnel; PPTP can dynamically add and remove PPP connections in the tunnel

- Congestion and flow control
- Control over PPP dial-out and dial-in modem pools

Many of these capabilities are for tunnels between a dial-up POP and a private network (see Figure 14-2). An ISP communication server, for example, can dynamically route PPP from multiple users to a single tunnel destined to a private network. The same communication server can also receive PPTP requests for modem dial-in and dial-out operations.

PPTP isn't limited to ISP use. In fact, many ISPs don't readily offer tunneling as a service enhancement. Thus, a dial-in PPP user usually must arrange his own PPTP tunnel, directly from his desktop to a private network router. In this case, the ISP simply provides standard Internet access.

Both users and administrators wishing to use PPTP must find PPP software that features PPTP support. The readily available one is Microsoft Windows NT/98. Another important consideration is that PPTP isn't a standard. Although Microsoft initially lead PPTP development, similar activities elsewhere have prompted the industry to develop L2TP as the standard (Chapter 16, *What's New for PPP?*).

Telnet as a Tunnel Protocol

Telnet normally enables users to establish interactive login sessions with remote servers. It sends keystrokes and receives the served responses as characters for display. Over the network, Telnet sends and receives a data stream between two endpoints, exactly suitable for a PPP tunnel.

The Telnet protocol, RFC-854, defines overhead messages and user-data exchange between a client and a server process. Telnet inserts overhead along with characters visible to users or to PPP software. Overhead messages include passing terminal types, environment variables, window dimensions, operating modes, and others. Several Telnet options are critical for its sessions to be compatible with binary PPP. These are:

Character at a time mode
> Telnet must forward characters, one by one, to the remote server immediately. Binary PPP has no concept of a line of characters and won't work with Telnet line mode.

Remote echo
> Any character echo a Telnet client software creates locally corrupts incoming PPP data. Setting remote echo mode prevents this.

Binary mode
> Telnet defaults to ASCII and passes only 7-bit characters. This isn't acceptable for PPP, which requires passing 8-bit characters in binary mode.

Escape character "off"

Telnet clients frequently intercept a special character, normally Ctrl-], for users to escape to a Telnet command prompt. Either this must be disabled or you must configure PPP not to send this character as data.

The first two options are normally outside of user control. However, many Telnet servers negotiate these automatically by default. The critical item to set manually is the binary option. Here is a Telnet session set up for PPP:

```
user$ /usr/local/bin/telnet 172.16.0.66
Trying 172.16.0.66...
Connected to 172.16.0.66.
Escape character is '^]'.

UNIX(r) System V Release 4.0 (solaris)

login: ppp3
Password:
Last login: Mon May 27 12:23:02 from 172.16.0.65
Sun Microsystems Inc.   SunOS 5.6       Generic August 1997
user$ <ctrl-]>
telnet> set binary
Negotiating binary mode with remote host. <ctrl-]>
telnet> set escape off
escape character is 'off'.
exec /usr/sbin/aspppls <ctrl-j>
```

I later show how to connect dial-out PPP to the Telnet client program.

Unfortunately, many versions of Telnet have problems that make them difficult to use with PPP. Some of these bugs are:

- Some older Telnet versions don't support binary and don't recognize the **set binary** command.

- The Telnet escape character may be two characters. If 0x1d is an escape character, the character with the high-order bit set 0x9d may also be an escape character.

- Disabling the Telnet escape character may not actually disable it. Rather, it may just set it to character 0x00 and 0x80.

There is little choice in some of these cases but to upgrade the Telnet software.[*] Alternatively, you can select a different tunneling protocol.

It isn't essential to disable Telnet escape, as long as PPP avoids these characters. Prior to transmission, PPP can encode certain characters as a special sequence. An **escape 0x1d, 0x9d** option with PPP-2.3 encodes Ctrl-] and 0x9d in the transmit-

---

[*] Telnet source code is available from *ftp://ftp.cray.com/* or *ftp://net-dist.mit.edu/*.

ting direction. Many PPP implementations don't feature the user-controllable escape option. In this case, our PPP peer must negotiate an asyncmap of 0x20000000, which sets the equivalent of escape 0x1d at our local PPP endpoint. There's no way to set the equivalent of escape 0x9d with this method, since it's not an ASCII control character.

rlogin as a Tunnel Protocol

rlogin, like Telnet, is also designed for interactive login sessions with remote servers. It too sends and receives data bidirectionally between two endpoints and can function as a tunnel, although some precautions are necessary. Some PPP and rlogin implementations don't work due to character transparency complications.

Here's how to use the rlogin as a PPP tunnel:

```
user$ rlogin -8 -e -l ppp3 solaris
Password:
Last login: Mon May 27 13:11:29 from 172.16.0.65
Sun Microsystems Inc.   SunOS 5.6       Generic August 1997
user$ exec /usr/sbin/aspppls
```

I show later how to connect dial-out PPP to the rlogin client program.

The -8 option is critical. Without this option, the rlogin client passes only 7-bit ASCII characters to the remote server. The -l sets the username for sign-on into remote server solaris. ppp3 is the login name on that server.

The rlogin client, like Telnet, has an escape character. By default, this character is ~; it enables users to forcefully terminate an active session (~.) or temporarily suspend it (~ CTRL-z). Since ~ may be part of PPP data, you must disable rlogin escape with -e, allowing ~ to pass through the tunnel unaltered. PPP can't encode ~, since this is its frame-separating flag character. Thus, rlogin clients that can't change or disable ~ are unsuitable for PPP.

Another difficulty with rlogin is its treatment of 0xff characters. These are flags for an rlogin overhead message that are in band and intermixed with regular user data. A client can send the sequence 0xff, 0xff, s, s, and eight additional characters to the rlogind server, indicating a terminal window size change. Unfortunately, if PPP duplicates this sequence in its own data, rlogind deletes the sequence, corrupting the PPP frame. This is a rare sequence since it's so specific— hence the problem is hard to detect.

One way you can detect this problem is to initiate a regular rlogin session with a remove server, using the PPP connection inside a rlogin tunnel. If the problem is present, the regular rlogin sends the problem sequence in PPP data and mysteriously hangs. The PPP software at far end of the tunnel will complain about **bad fcs** or other errors:

```
16:47:17 007587 ipdptp3 RECEIVE PPP ASYNC 49 Octets {BAD FCS} VJ_UNCOMP_TCP
16:47:22 007588 ipdptp3 RECEIVE PPP ASYNC 69 Octets {BAD FCS} IP_PROTO
16:47:25 007589 ipdptp3 RECEIVE PPP ASYNC 49 Octets {BAD FCS} VJ_UNCOMP_TCP
```

To solve this problem, PPP must send 0xff characters through the **rlogin** tunnel in escaped format. An **escape 0xff** in PPP-2.3 enables this. PPP implementations without this feature aren't suitable for use with **rlogin** tunnels.

TCP Connections

A raw TCP connection can emulate a serial connection and provide a tunnel for PPP. TCP connections are ideal since they cleanly support binary data between two endpoints. Any available TCP port number may be used for this purpose.

The Linux program, **ppptcp**, by Sam Lantinga, enables PPP-2.3 to communicate over a TCP connection, rather than a real serial interface. Another product that inherently supports PPP over TCP is Progressive Technologies PPP for Unix. This package can initiate an outgoing tunnel connection as well as listen for incoming ones.

Other Tunnels

You may wish to develop custom tunnels to carry PPP between two points within an existing network. Custom protocols are useful for overcoming communication limitations that would normally prevent a network from carrying PPP directly.

One example is a network that supports only 7-bit characters. A custom tunnel can encode PPP 8-bit data into a form compatible with 7-bit data, send it, and recover the 8-bit data on reception. Uuencode or base64 are possible data encoding methods. Another possibility is a tunnel protocol that operates over half-duplex communication services. The tunnel protocol can include methods for reversing the communications channel, causing it to emulate a full-duplex connection for PPP.

Redirecting Serial Input/Output

Some PPP implementations support tunneling directly but only with specific tunnel protocols. Most PPP products know how to interact only with serial interfaces. This limitation is a significant obstacle if you wish to establish a connection inside a tunnel through a network, rather than with a real serial interface.

It's sometimes possible, with additional software, to reroute serial input/output into a tunnel. Achieving this depends on the computer operating system. Successfully redirecting serial I/O allows you to reuse PPP software for serial interfaces in tunneling scenarios.

On general-purpose computers, PPP usually interacts with a serial interface device driver (Figure 14-4). By substituting an emulator in the place of this driver, you can intercept and redirect PPP I/O elsewhere. This emulator is sometimes called a *virtual modem* or *modem emulator.* It reroutes PPP frames into another application program that manages a tunnel connection. This tunneling program communicates through either a LAN network interface or an unrelated PPP connection. It sends and receives PPP frames with another Internet site. Meanwhile, the PPP software continues to believe it's communicating with an illusory modem.

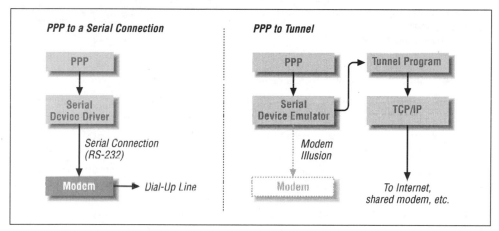

Figure 14-4. Redirecting PPP to a tunnel

Serial I/O redirection is also useful for other software. Terminal emulators, for example, are no longer limited to a serial interface and modem. They can now communicate with network modems or with Internet sites.

Unix

Linux and Unix provide pseudo-terminal (pty) drivers that emulate all the functions of a real terminal device. Pseudo-terminals are really connections to additional programs. Any software communicating with a real terminal can also communicate with a pseudo-terminal equivalent. The programs managing a pseudo-terminal can intercept PPP and redirect it elsewhere.

The utility, `ptysh`, manages a pseudo-terminal device. Its source code and additional information for programmers appears in Appendix B, *Serial Interface Emulation.* `ptysh` initializes a pseudo-terminal device file, such as `/dev/ttyr0` on Linux. When PPP accesses attaches to this device, it interacts with the Bourne shell rather than a real modem. A chat script can then initiate a tunnel connection through a network to establish a PPP connection with a remote system.

Linux and Unix includes several utilities for accessing serial devices. They can also access pseudo-terminals and test serial I/O redirection. On Linux, cu or minicom can verify ptysh and demonstrate how a pseudo-terminal behaves:

```
user$ ./ptysh &
[1] 1055
serial pty: /dev/ttyr0
user$ cu -s 38400 -l /dev/ttyr0
connected
user$ /usr/local/bin/telnet 172.16.0.66
     . . . network connection to remote system . . .
Connection closed by foreign host.
user$ exit
cu: Got hangup signal

Disconnected.
user$
```

In this example, we connect cu to pseudo-terminal device, /dev/ttyr0. ttyr0 responds with a shell prompt as if it were a modem. We then invoke telnet as the tunnel program to a remote system. The exit command we send to the shell is equivalent to a modem disconnect, which in turn ends the cu session. Although programs that interact with serial devices frequently require a line speed, such as 38400, these are meaningless to pseudo-terminals.

Later, I use PPP software to access *dev/ttyr0* rather than the cu utility.

Windows NT/98

Windows NT/98 doesn't appear to have virtual modem software available that can intercept serial I/O and redirect it to a tunneling program of choice.

The closest products that implement serial I/O redirection are those that allow Windows NT/98 to access a modem server. The communication between Windows and the modem server is the equivalent of a tunnel for PPP. Unfortunately, these tunneling protocols are proprietary. Since only modem servers can understand the tunneling protocol, it's difficult to use this tunnel between arbitrary PPP endpoints.

It may be possible with programming effort to implement serial I/O redirection for PPP in a general manner; however, it's not a simple task. Windows NT/98 already supports PPTP tunnels. If other tunneling protocols are important, the best solution may be to select Windows NT/98 PPP software that inherently includes the needed tunneling features.

Setting up Outgoing PPP Tunnels

An outgoing tunnel requires existing networking resources to support the tunnel connection. The physical network connection doesn't matter and can include regular PPP or a LAN network interface card. First, users initiate a tunnel to a remote system. They then establish PPP in the tunnel.

Users must also configure network routing with tunnels, since a tunnel is really a new PPP connection to a new network.

PPTP with Windows 98 and 95

Windows 98 includes PPTP tunneling support. This capability is available if you install **Virtual Private Networking** software components. You can add virtual private networking by selecting **Control Panel** → **Add/Remove Programs** → **Windows Setup** → **Communications**.

The original Microsoft Windows 95 release didn't support PPP tunneling. Since then, Microsoft has released the Windows 95 Dial-up Networking 1.3 upgrade, available from their Internet web site. This upgrade provides client-side support for PPTP and adds numerous other dial-up networking enhancements.

The setup procedures for PPTP on both Windows 98 and 95 are identical.

After you install virtual private networking, Windows 98 creates additional dial-up network adapters that appear in the **Network** control panel (Figure 6-5). The full list of dial-up adapters you should see is:

```
Dial-Up Adapter
Dial-Up Adapter #2 (VPN Support)
Microsoft Virtual Private Networking Adapter
```

There are now two dial-up adapters for virtual private networking. The existing **Dial-Up Adapter** is for a regular PPP connection while the **Dial-Up Adapter #2** supports a PPP connection inside a PPTP tunnel. Both may be active simultaneously. The **Microsoft Virtual Private Networking Adapter** is for PPTP itself.

Even though the Internet supports only TCP/IP, a PPP connection inside a tunnel can carry multiple network layer protocols. Users must bind the network layer protocols they need inside the tunnel to **Dial-Up Adapter #2**. The ones users require depend on the private network the tunnel connects with at the far end. Network protocol choices are:

```
IPX/SPX-compatible Protocol -> Dial-Up Adapter #2 (VPN Support)
NetBEUI -> Dial-Up Adapter #2 (VPN Support)
TCP/IP -> Dial-Up Adapter #2 (VPN Support)
```

Configuring PPP and its PPTP tunnel is nearly identical to configuring a regular connection (see Chapter 6, *Dial-out PPP Setup*). The key difference with tunneling is the `Connect using` field appearing in the dial-out `PPP connection properties` window must reference the `Microsoft VPN adapter`, rather than a real serial interface and a modem.

The properties of a connection named `VPN` with PPTP appear in Figure 14-5. This window includes PPTP settings and is analogous to Figure 6-7 for regular PPP connections. Remember that Windows 98 must already have a network connection before it can establish a tunnel. The VPN server is the IP address for the tunnel's far end. Obviously, the server at 172.16.0.67 must be ready to accept a PPTP connection from this Windows 98 client. Once PPTP is up, dial-up networking automatically establishes PPP inside it. All the PPP settings appear in the `Server Types` tab. This PPP connection is independent from others that may also exist. It has its own network protocols, compression, authentication, and other settings. If the tunnel carries TCP/IP, this PPP connection also requires its own local and remote IP addresses.

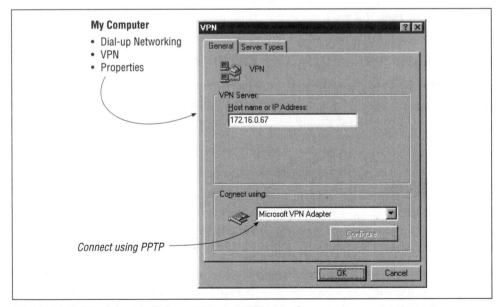

Figure 14-5. Windows 98 dial-out PPP via PPTP tunnel

In order to use the new connection, users must also configure routing for the connection in the tunnel. I cover this later.

TCP Tunnel and Telnet Tunnel with Progressive Systems PPP

Progressive Systems PPP version 1.4 can establish a PPP connection with a remote peer using a raw TCP tunnel in place of a real serial interface. Users must define remote peers in UUCP-style configuration files, much like Solaris PPP (see Chapter 6).

Let's consider an outgoing PPP tunneling arrangement as shown in Figure 14-6. In */etc/ppp/Systems* on the computer `myhost`, redirecting a PPP connection into an outgoing TCP tunnel appears as follows:

```
root# cat /etc/ppp/Systems
# PPP        valid
# remote     connect  connect                phone    chat
# address    times    device        speed    number   script
192.168.1.1  Any      tcp/172.16.0.67/59  -        -
. . .
```

`tcp/172.16.0.67/59` substitutes for a real serial interface, such as */dev/cual*. There are two IP addresses in this configuration file. The first address, 192.168.1.1, refers to the remote end of the PPP connection inside the tunnel. The second address, 172.16.0.67, and TCP port number, 59, is the destination for establishing the TCP tunnel.

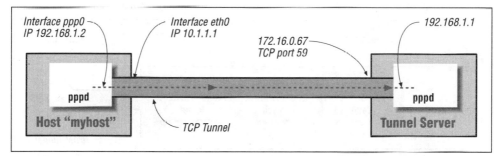

Figure 14-6. Progressive systems PPP, TCP tunneling

Running `pppd` initiates both the tunnel and the PPP connection inside it:

```
user$ #                PPP link    PPP link    run in background
user$ #                local IP    remote IP   initiate connect on demand
user$ /usr/etc/pppd 192.168.1.2:192.168.1.1 auto
```

Since no chat script exists in the `Systems` file, `myhost` expects to communicate with PPP immediately after the tunnel is up. The two IP addresses on the command line are for the connection in the tunnel. One of these addresses, 192.168.1.1, also identifies the entry in the *Systems* file for initiating the connection. These IP addresses are used only with the virtual private network that wants the PPP connection.

Note that as long as the server isn't using the port for other TCP services, you may choose other port numbers besides 59 at the tunnel server.

Progressive Systems PPP also includes a built-in Telnet client for supporting Telnet tunnels. This configuration appears as *telnet/172.16.0.67/23* in the *Systems* file. This PPP knows how to interact with Telnet protocols and performs Telnet negotiations essential for establishing a compatible tunnel with a remote tunnel server. Once a Telnet tunnel is up, Progressive Systems PPP encapsulates and extracts PPP frames from the Telnet protocol, and then interprets the PPP frame contents. Most Unix servers listen for Telnet service on port 23 with the `in.telnetd` daemon. This daemon frequently executes */bin/login*. Therefore, a chat script is necessary in the Systems file to interact with login prompts that first appear in the tunnel connection. This script may also need to initiate PPP software at the remote server.

Telnet Tunnel with PPP-2.3

PPP-2.3 for Linux and Unix insists on communicating with serial devices for outgoing PPP connections. Coercing PPP-2.3 to initiate PPP inside a tunnel requires serial I/O redirection, with the help of the `ptysh` utility. The software relationships necessary for outgoing PPP, through a Telnet tunnel, appear in Figure 14-7.

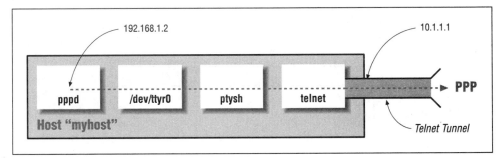

Figure 14-7. Outgoing Telnet tunnel

PPP-2.3 needs to know the serial device to use. On Linux, substitute pseudo-terminal */dev/ttyr0* in place of a serial device, such as */dev/ttyS0*. The `ptysh` utility must first initialize the pseudo-terminal device:

```
user$ /usr/local/bin/ptysh &
[1] 1476
serial pty: /dev/ttyr0
user$
```

Assume myhost has an Internet IP address of 10.1.1.1 and wishes to establish a tunnel to a tunnel server at 172.16.0.67. The local and remote PPP endpoints inside the tunnel have IP addresses 192.168.1.2 and 192.168.1.1, respectively. A PPP-2.3 configuration file on myhost can appear as follows:

```
user$ cd $HOME
user$ cat .ppprc
debug
/dev/ttyr0 19200
connect "/usr/sbin/chat -v -f ./.pppchat"
192.168.1.2:192.168.1.1
escape 1d,9d
user$
```

Notice the presence of the */dev/ttyr0* dial-out device in this configuration file. This file also specifies a chat script, *.pppchat*. The script consists of response and reply strings for starting the Telnet tunnel, logging in to the remote server and invoking PPP as */usr/sbin/aspppls* on the remote server.

```
user$ cat .pppchat
"" ""
"$" "exec /usr/local/bin/telnet 172.16.0.67"
"ogin:" "ppp3"
"assword:" "ppp3"
"$" "^]\c"
"elnet> " "set binary"
"" "exec /usr/sbin/aspppls\n\d\c"
user$
```

When PPP-2.3 connects to */dev/ttyr0*, ptysh responds with a shell prompt, and the chat script starts. This script sets Telnet to binary mode. In this mode, the tunnel server needs a line-feed terminator (\n) for the exec */usr/sbin/aspppls*, rather than the usual carriage return, suppressed with \c. A small delay, \d, allows time for PPP to initialize at the remote end, prior to the start of PPP negotiations. escape 1d,9d in the local PPP options prevents PPP-2.3 from sending the Telnet escape character through the tunnel.

A user can now start pppd on myhost, which initiates both the Telnet tunnel and the PPP connection:

```
user$ /usr/sbin/pppd
```

The tunnel connection progress appears in the PPP-2.3 log file, as follows:

```
user$ cat /var/log/local2
Apr  7 22:34:18 myhost chat[124]: send (^M)
Apr  7 22:34:18 myhost chat[124]: expect ($)
Apr  7 22:34:18 myhost chat[124]: ^M
Apr  7 22:34:19 myhost chat[124]: user$ -- got it
Apr  7 22:34:19 myhost chat[124]: send (exec /usr/local/bin/telnet
172.16.0.67^M)
Apr  7 22:34:19 myhost chat[124]: expect (ogin:)
Apr  7 22:34:19 myhost chat[124]:  ^M
Apr  7 22:34:19 myhost chat[124]: user$ exec /bin/telnet 172.16.0.67^M
```

```
Apr  7 22:34:19 myhost chat[124]: Trying 172.16.0.67...^M
. . .
Apr  7 22:34:22 myhost chat[124]: $ -- got it
Apr  7 22:34:22 myhost chat[124]: send (^])
Apr  7 22:34:22 myhost chat[124]: expect (elnet> )
Apr  7 22:34:22 myhost chat[124]:  ^M
Apr  7 22:34:22 myhost chat[124]: telnet> -- got it
Apr  7 22:34:22 myhost chat[124]: send (set binary^M)
Apr  7 22:34:22 myhost chat[124]: send (exec /usr/sbin/aspppls^J\d)
. . .
```

This chat script interacts with the Unix shell in the same way other scripts interact with modems.

The PPP connection progress appears in the PPP-2.3 log file, as follows:

```
user$ cat /var/log/daemon
Apr  7 22:34:17 myhost pppd[123]: pppd 2.3.5 started by myname, uid 2001
Apr  7 22:34:24 myhost pppd[123]: Serial connection established.
Apr  7 22:34:25 myhost pppd[123]: Using interface ppp0
Apr  7 22:34:25 myhost pppd[123]: Connect: ppp0 <--> /dev/ttyr0
. . .
```

At this point, users must set up routing to take advantage of the new PPP connection.

Setting up Incoming PPP Tunnels

Tunnel servers usually function as routers for a private network. They must listen for incoming tunnel connections and start PPP when answering. Its PPP software must process PPP frames, extract network layer protocols, and relay these protocols into the private network. Thus, tunnel servers frequently have at least two physical network interfaces and many additional logical network interfaces for PPP connections inside tunnels.

PPTP with Windows NT 4.0 Server

Microsoft Windows NT 4.0 Server features a tunnel server for authorized users that wish to access to a private network. The Remote Access Service supports incoming PPP connection from the Point-to-Point Tunneling Protocol (PPTP), along with the usual incoming connection from dial-in ports.

PPTP is typically used with the Internet. Thus, Windows NT must already have TCP/IP connectivity to the Internet and connectivity to a private network. The physical connections may be of any type, including regular PPP connections. Here, we assume Windows NT has separate LAN network interfaces for the Internet and private network, respectively.

Since PPTP is a TCP/IP application protocol, it must appear in the **Protocols** tab under the Windows NT Network control panel (Figure 14-8). PPTP is absent initially, but you can **Add** it. The only **Properties** for PPTP is the number of VPN devices. Each simultaneous PPTP user requires one device. If you wish to enable PPTP, add it to RAS as if it were another dial-in connection. This procedure is similar to adding dial-in ports, as shown in Chapter 7, *Dial-in PPP Setup*.

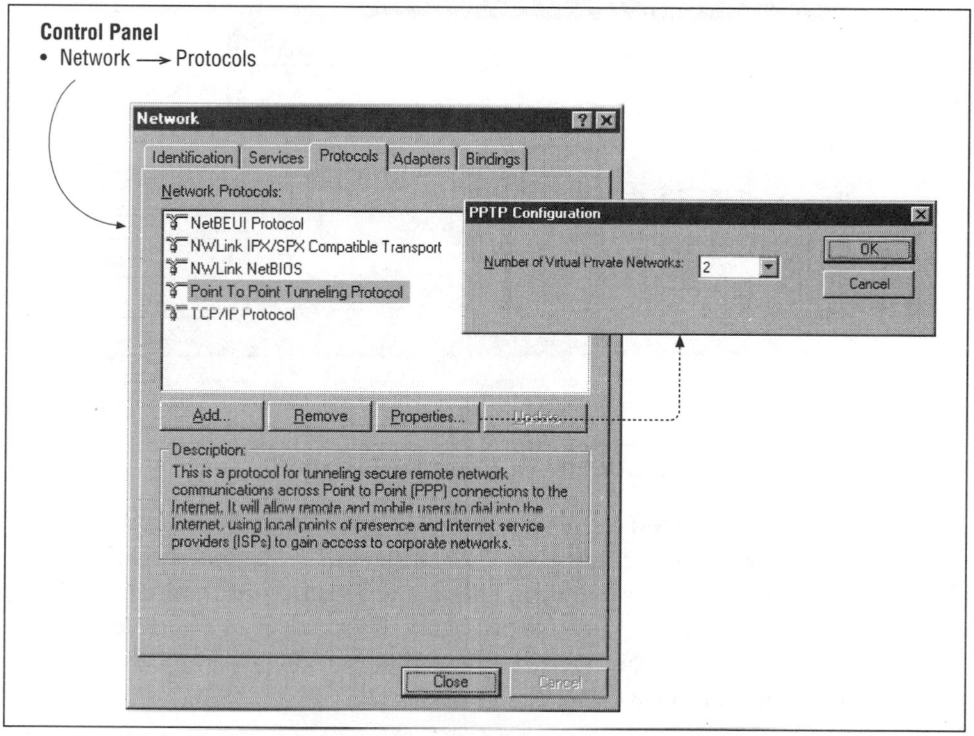

Figure 14-8. Windows NT PPTP Configuration

If any VPN devices appear in the **Remote Access Setup** window, RAS listens for incoming PPTP. Figure 14-9 shows this window. You can use the **Add** button to add VPN ports. Like real dial-in ports, the **Configure** button can set VPN ports to receive incoming PPTP calls. Since a VPN carries a PPP connection within it, the **Network** button establishes applicable PPP and network protocol parameters for that connection. Configure network protocols the same way you would real dial-in ports.

Windows NT RAS accepts incoming PPTP and the PPP connection inside it from any physical network interface. In a secure VPN configuration, the RAS server's Internet interface should allow only PPTP connections. Windows NT includes a PPTP filter that can block access to other services that may otherwise be available

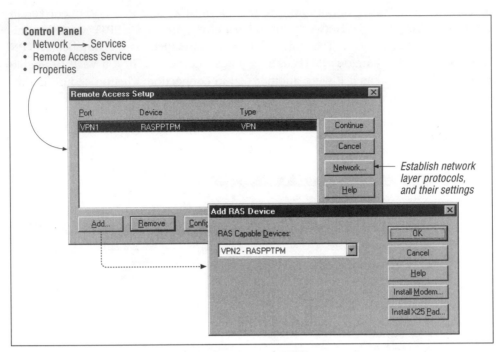

Figure 14-9. Windows NT Remote Access Setup with PPTP ports

at the Internet network interface. You can enable this feature with the `Network` →
`Protocols` → `TCP/IP` → `Properties` → `IP Address` → `Advanced` configuration
window. Select the proper network interface and check `Enable PPTP Filter-`
`ing`. Note that PPTP filtering also blocks `ping`. This feature is available for only
LAN network interfaces. If the Internet connection is really a dial-up line instead,
`Enable PPTP Filtering` isn't available.

TCP Tunnel and Telnet Tunnel with Progressive Systems PPP

Progressive Systems PPP for Unix can listen for and accept incoming PPP connections in a tunnel without unusual PPP software configuration. It allows the Internet daemon, `inetd`, to hand off incoming tunnel connections directly to it. The
configuration lines in */etc/inetd.conf* and */etc/services* that arrange this hand-off are:

```
user$ cat /etc/inetd.conf
# service end-point              wait                    program
# name    type      protocol status uid  program        arguments
ppptcp    stream    tcp       nowait root /usr/etc/pppd  pppd 192.168.1.1:
. . .
user$ cat /etc/services
ppptcp    57/tcp
. . .
```

Here, we configure `inetd` to listen at TCP port 57, which appears as `ppptcp` in the `services` file. Once an incoming connection arrives, `inetd` invokes Progressive Systems PPP as */usr/etc/pppd* to service the connection. The arguments to `pppd` set the local IP address of the virtual PPP connection to 192.168.1.1. The PPP peer sets the remote IP address. This tunnel is raw TCP connection data. It's not compatible with an inbound tunnel connection from a Telnet client.

As it turns out, Performance Systems PPP includes a built-in Telnet server and can accept incoming Telnet tunnels. The alternative `inetd.conf` configuration for this is:

```
user$ cat /etc/inetd.conf
# service end-point        wait                   program
# name    type    protocol status uid  program   arguments
ppptelnet stream  tcp       nowait root /usr/etc/pppd pppd 192.168.1.2: telnet
. . .
```

And in the `services` file:

```
user$ cat /etc/services
ppptelnet 59/tcp
. . .
```

This arranges `inetd` to hand off incoming Telnet connections on port 59 to Progressive Systems PPP. The `telnet` argument instructs `pppd` to interpret the Telnet protocol and remove its overhead before interpreting the data within as PPP frames.

Telnet Tunnel with Solaris PPP

With dial-in PPP, Solaris PPP attaches to the terminal device associated with its interactive login session. Solaris PPP can't distinguish whether the login session that invokes it originates from a network connection or from a real dial-in connection. Those incoming connections that originate from a network are essentially tunnels that can carry PPP frames.

For incoming network connections, `inetd` must invoke a program that manages a pseudo-terminal device for the PPP software. The good news is that Unix already includes programs that behave this way. When `in.telnetd` receives an inbound Telnet request, it allocates a pseudo-terminal, such as */dev/pts/0*, for */bin/login*. This begins a session that can start PPP. PPP communicates through the same pseudo-terminal device. As long as the Telnet tunnel remains up, `in.telnetd` relays PPP serial I/O between the tunnel and the PPP software, `aspppls`. Figure 14-10 illustrates this situation.

Notice that the tunnel server imposes interactive steps the PPP peer must follow before the server can start its PPP software. The PPP peer is the computer initiating the Telnet tunnel. It's responsible for a chat script that automatically responds

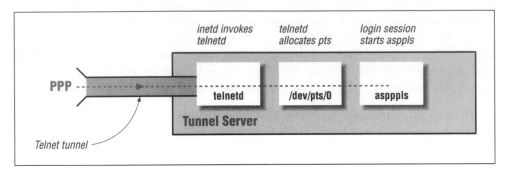

Figure 14-10. Solaris PPP, incoming Telnet tunnel

to the tunnel server's prompts. Here is the interactive login transcript for a peer interacting with the tunnel server **solaris**:

```
UNIX(r) System V Release 4.0 (solaris)

login: ppp3
Password:
Last login: Sun May 26 00:28:03 on term/b
Sun Microsystems Inc.    SunOS 5.5       Generic November 1995
user$ tty
/dev/pts/0
user$ exec /usr/sbin/aspppls
```

You can arrange for the tunnel server to forego the login and password steps and start PPP immediately. This greatly simplifies the steps peers must follow to get PPP up and running. You can achieve this by obtaining in.telnetd source code and modifying it so in.telnetd invokes aspppls directly, instead of /bin/ login. The disadvantage of this approach is that the tunnel server no longer provides true Telnet service, which may be useful for other purposes.

Note that it's usually not possible to have inetd invoke PPP directly, unless the PPP software supports it. inetd provides a network socket interface to the programs it invokes, rather than a terminal device interface. PPP almost always expects a terminal device and can malfunction if it encounters a network socket instead.

Routing with Tunnels

Computers managing tunnels in VPN architectures usually have PPP or LAN connections to the Internet. The Internet supports the tunnel connection, which encapsulates a private network PPP connection inside. The two ends of the tunnel use real Internet IP addresses. However, the PPP connection inside uses IP addresses that are meaningful only for private network communications. It's critical that Internet IP addresses don't conflict with those inside the private network.

When routing IP datagrams, a computer with a tunnel connection must distinguish datagrams destined to the Internet from those destined to private network. You can better understand tunnel routing by assuming your Internet connection and private network PPP connection are entirely separate, each having their own network interfaces. Figure 14-11 illustrates this. The "logical PPP connection" really traverses the Internet on a tunnel connection between IP addresses 10.1.1.1 and 172.16.0.67. IP addressing and routing guidelines for a PPP connection in a tunnel are similar to a real physical PPP connection.

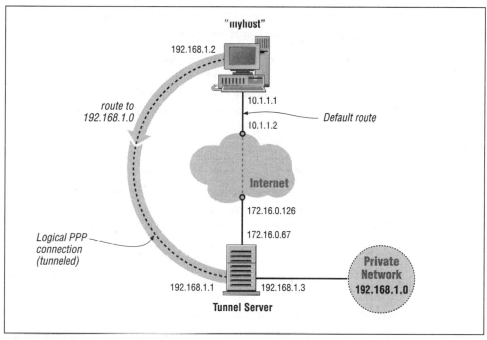

Figure 14-11. Routing with tunnels

Tunnels secure private networks from the Internet. Since tunneling clients and servers have both Internet and the private network connections, they must not behave as traditional routers. This is critical for maintaining private network security. In other words, the private network and its tunneled PPP connection must never see IP datagrams with Internet addresses. Arranging private network IP addresses that are invalid to the Internet prevents this problem, although active IP datagram filtering is a more proactive and secure solution.

Tunnel Clients

Standalone tunnel clients are usually PCs with an Internet dial-in connection. Computers at the edge of the Internet commonly establish a default route to the ISP.

Consider myhost with a PPP connection to the Internet, as shown in Figure 14-11. Its default route is as follows, on Linux:

```
root# route add default gw 10.1.1.2
```

This arranges myhost to route by default all traffic to the next hop IP address in the route command. This address, 10.1.1.2, is the PPP network interface belonging to the ISP. All Internet sites contacting myhost must use its real Internet address, 10.1.1.1.

Establishing a tunnel is technically similar to establishing any other TCP connection. This default route supports tunnel communications between myhost at IP address 10.1.1.1 and the tunnel server at Internet address 172.16.0.67.

Simply creating a PPP connection inside a tunnel doesn't substantially alter the routing behavior for myhost. Without any additional changes, most private network IP address destinations appear as any other Internet destination. The default route incorrectly sends IP datagrams for the private network to the ISP. To rectify this problem, create a more specific route for the destination IP addresses of the private network:

```
root# route add -net 192.168.1.0 netmask 255.255.255.0 gw 192.168.1.1
```

This routing entry overrides the default route for IP datagrams with destination addresses in the 192.168.1.0 network. More specifically, myhost routes datagrams for destinations in the range 192.168.1.0 to 192.168.1.255 through the PPP connection in the tunnel. If there are other network numbers belonging to the private network, users must add routes for these too. Note that when myhost communicates with the private network, its originating IP address is 192.168.1.2. This address grants myhost membership in the private network. In contrast, when myhost communicates with Internet sites, its originating IP address is 10.1.1.1.

A second routing configuration for tunneling clients is arranging its default route for private network communications, rather than for Internet communications. Users can establish a specific route first for communications with the tunnel server:

```
root# route add -host 172.16.0.67 gw 10.1.1.2
```

A default route forwards IP datagrams to most other IP address destinations into the tunnel:

```
root# route add default gw 192.168.1.1
```

Inverting the default route entry this way is convenient if the private network is large and has numerous network numbers. A single default route covers all private network destinations. Unfortunately, this default route inappropriately represents most Internet destinations too. Thus, myhost now sends its own Internet traffic into the tunnel. Without more specific routes pointing to the 10.1.1.2 ISP address, communications between myhost and most Internet sites won't be possible. But then, maybe this is desirable for security reasons.

Tunnel Servers

A tunnel server relays IP datagrams between a private network and tunnel connections through the Internet. Unlike a real router, a tunnel server doesn't relay IP datagrams directly between its private network interface and its Internet interface. The tunnel server itself does communicate with Internet sites, but only to set up tunnels.

In simple configurations, a tunnel server's routing is similar to those for tunnel clients. There is a default route to the Internet to support tunnel connections. And, there are routes that specify how to route IP datagrams arriving from inside a tunnel to destinations inside the private network. There may also exist specific routes to forward IP datagrams into a tunnel.

On a tunnel server (Figure 14-11) with an Internet PPP connection, a LAN network interface to the private network, and a PPP tunnel through the Internet, its network interfaces should resemble the following, on Linux:

```
user$ ifconfig eth0
eth0      Link encap:Ethernet  HWaddr 00:60:B0:A1:3D:13
          inet addr:192.168.1.3  Bcast:192.168.1.255  Mask:255.255.255.0
          UP BROADCAST RUNNING MULTICAST  MTU:1500  Metric:1
. . .
user$ ifconfig ppp0
ppp0      Link encap:Point-to-Point Protocol
          inet addr:172.16.0.67  P-t-P:172.16.0.126  Mask:255.255.0.0
          UP POINTOPOINT RUNNING NOARP MULTICAST  MTU:1500  Metric:1
. . .
user$ ifconfig ppp1
ppp1      Link encap:Point-to-Point Protocol
          inet addr:192.168.1.1  P-t-P:192.168.1.2  Mask:255.255.255.0
          UP POINTOPOINT RUNNING NOARP MULTICAST  MTU:1500  Metric:1
    . . .
```

Interface ppp1 is the PPP connection inside a tunnel; ppp0 is the regular PPP connection for Internet access. Some important entries in this server's routing table are:

```
user$ netstat -rn
Kernel IP routing table
Destination     Gateway         Genmask         Flags   MSS Window  irtt Iface
172.16.0.126    0.0.0.0         255.255.255.255 UH      1500 0         0 ppp0
192.168.1.2     0.0.0.0         255.255.255.255 UH      1500 0         0 ppp1
192.168.1.0     0.0.0.0         255.255.255.0   U       1500 0         0 eth0
127.0.0.0       0.0.0.0         255.0.0.0       U       3584 0         0 lo
0.0.0.0         172.16.0.126    0.0.0.0         UG      1500 0         0 ppp0
user$
```

Most of these routes Linux defines automatically, since the destinations are directly connected to this tunnel server. The exception is the default route, which you must add. Note that the tunnel client at 192.168.1.2 uses an address belonging to the IP subnet for the Ethernet interface eth0. This requires proxy ARP too, described in Chapter 8, *Network Architectures Incorporating PPP*.

Tunnel servers are likely to participate in more complex network topologies than this example. There may be many clients accessible through one tunnel, rather than one. The private network Ethernet interface may also be the access point to an enterprise consisting of many IP subnets and networks. All these require additional routes. If routing tables are nontrivial, the tunnel server needs to use dynamic routing protocols.

Although a tunnel server traditionally listens and accepts incoming tunnel connections, it can also function as a client and initiate a tunnel connection to other servers. Once the server establishes the tunnel and a PPP connection within it, routing and IP addressing issues remain the same for either arrangement.

Network Security

As we have seen, tunneling can access networks that aren't directly accessible with normal means. An important security concern is data privacy, especially when a public network transmits the data. Data encryption can address this issue.

Like many other useful services, PPP tunnels can also be abused. They can provide network connectivity under circumstances where connections shouldn't exist. Since users of PCs can arrange tunnels with the right software, this can easily lead to network security breaches.

Encryption

In a VPN, tunnels through the Internet replace long-distance leased lines and telephone lines. Since tunnels connect private networks, the data traversing it may be confidential and may require safeguarding from unauthorized retrieval and tampering.

The Internet makes no attempt to provide data security. Communications between two sites may require half a dozen or more intervening ISPs. Each provider, and perhaps some of their customers, have the opportunity to eavesdrop on data in transit. Another major problem is the pervasiveness of shared-medium LAN technologies in the Internet. A LAN member can observe all LAN traffic, including traffic not intended for it. This is the basis of numerous sniffer attacks that collect clear-text passwords traversing a LAN.

The tunnel that supports a PPP connection inside is generally not responsible for data encryption, since PPP features encryption extensions. PPP encryption can be used in tunnels, as well as for real serial connections. It encrypts both the header and the data portion of network layer datagrams, using a growing list of encryption algorithms. To enable encryption, both endpoints of a tunnel must use PPP software with encryption capability. The endpoints must also understand and agree to use a particular algorithm. One PPP product with encryption support is Windows NT. Numerous others don't offer encryption. Chapter 16 describes PPP encryption in greater detail.

A custom tunnel protocol can encrypt data on behalf of PPP, even if the PPP connection in the tunnel can't. This is a feature of the **ppptcp** package, compatible with PPP-2.3 on Linux.

Abuse

As a network security administrator, you must be aware that any two-way communication service may be adapted to carry PPP. This includes communications through the most secure Internet firewalls. As long as a communication channel exists between two points, forming a PPP tunnel is simply a matter of coordination, and possibly programming effort, between the users at both endpoints.

Once a tunnel is active, it's a covert private line. Potentially, the endpoints could be a PC inside a secure private network and an insecure Internet site. Incoming and outgoing connection requests pass freely through the tunnel, despite security restrictions firewalls may enforce. If the computers at the tunnel endpoints function as routers and advertise routes, the tunnel becomes a much more serious security concern. Now, any one in the insecure network may have unrestricted connectivity to any computer in the secure private network, courtesy of the tunnel connection.

Detecting unauthorized tunnels is difficult. Although PPP data formats are clear, tunnel connections may arbitrarily encode the data they transmit. Monitoring data traversing through a tunnel is meaningless. The data may represent anything and is determined solely by the programs generating the data. Symptoms that suggest a PPP tunnel may exist include the following:

- Have routing tables inherited entries to destinations that should be unreachable?

- Are there interactive sessions that appear active for unusual lengths of time?

Preventing tunnels is a policy problem, not a technical one. Perhaps users are bypassing overly restrictive security policies. Short of disconnecting physical communication lines, or denying users access to all communication services, few technical precautions can prevent tunnel connections.

15

Troubleshooting

In this chapter:
- *Troubleshooting Approaches*
- *Trace and Activity Logs*
- *Checking the Serial Connection*
- *Checking Modems*
- *Chat Script Problems*
- *PPP Failures*
- *Checking TCP/IP*

A PPP connection is useful only in conjunction with many layers of hardware and software. Malfunctions at any layer cause communication failures. You can prevent problems with careful design, configuration, and testing. But still, problems are inevitable.

Troubleshooting requires knowledge and skill in topics that include serial interfaces, modems, TCP/IP, and of course PPP itself. You need to be familiar with the equipment responsible for a PPP connection, whether it is a computer, communications server, or router. Also you need to understand the relationships of the connection you are troubleshooting with the rest of the network infrastructure. Unfortunately, it's difficult to have all this knowledge at hand. Although a methodical approach to troubleshooting is best, you may still need to discover, by trial, error, and debugging, the information about a PPP setup in an unfamiliar environment.

In this chapter, I present various problems that can occur. Various problem symptoms, tools, and techniques are described that can assist you in isolating PPP connection faults. Each symptom may have many causes. Thus, one symptom can appear in many sections of this chapter.

Troubleshooting Approaches

The first important troubleshooting step is determining whether a problem with PPP actually exists. This isn't as easy as it sounds. The obvious symptoms are web browsers and other applications that misbehave or fail to communicate with a server.

The first question to ask is: does the application operate correctly with other servers, especially nearby* ones, using the server's IP address? A "yes" is a good indication that the problem isn't PPP. Application problems with some Internet sites are frequently unrelated to the PPP connection. It may be the result of an overloaded site, network congestion, or a network failure elsewhere. Also notice the phrase "using its IP address." If an application hangs or fails while it accesses an Internet site by name, but works with an IP address, then DNS is the frequent culprit. DNS name resolution may be disabled, the DNS server addresses may be misconfigured, or a DNS server outage may exist.

If PPP fails to stay up or if communications operate poorly or fail to all IP addresses that depend on PPP, a PPP fault is likely. The traffic application programs send shouldn't affect the operating condition of PPP. If they do and cause stalls or disconnects, a PPP problem is likely.

The troubleshooting approach I suggest is to diagnose the hardware and software layers that can affect PPP. These layers are:

- The serial interface and its physical connection
- Modems and telephone lines
- PPP itself
- TCP/IP or other applicable network layer protocols

Determining the area may be as simple as interpreting error messages or consulting a log file. However, many error messages are misleading or may have multiple causes. If you can't isolate the problem area, I suggest a bottom-up approach. This means testing the lowest communications layer, the serial interface, and working up towards the application program.

Trace and Activity Logs

In order to diagnose the problems, it's essential to obtain PPP trace and activity logs. The logs should show details about how your PPP software is interacting with its serial interface and modem. The same logs should show and interpret the exchange of PPP frames between endpoints. It's not necessary to record all PPP frames. The most important ones to capture are LCP, authentication, NCP, and other overhead frames. These are all for connection management and don't carry user data.

---

* "Nearby" means a minimum number of network hops. Servers maintained by your ISP are usualy nearby.

Enabling PPP trace and activity logging is product-specific. The dial-up PPP setup chapters include details about how to obtain traces from several PPP software products. A summary of these details and the location of PPP log files is in Table 15-1.

Table 15-1. Obtaining PPP Trace and Activity Logs

	Log File	How to Enable PPP Logging
PPP-2.3	*/var/log/local2*[a] */var/log/dae-mon*	Configure syslog `local2.debug` and `daemon.debug` to write the log file Include `debug` as `pppd` option
Solaris PPP	*/var/adm/log* */asppp.log*	Include `debug_level` 8 as PPP option in file */etc/asppp.cf*
Windows 98	*c:\windows* *\ppplog.txt*	Set `Record a log file for this connection`; or in `Control Panel` → `Network` → `Dial-Up Adapter` → `Properties` → `Advanced`, set `Record a log file` to `Yes`
Windows NT	*c:\winnt* *\system32* *\ras\ppp.log*	Set registry value *HKEY_LOCAL_MACHINE* *\SYSTEM\CurrentControlSet\Services\RasMan* *\PPP\Logging* to *DWORD 1*

[a] The Unix syslog facility can direct PPP-2.3 debug messages to any filename or a remote server. The configuration file, */etc/syslog.conf*, sets up syslog.

For some software, it may be difficult, if not impossible, to obtain trace and activity logs. If you're resourceful, you can perform diagnostics using the following methods:

- Connect your computer to a peer computer or communication server that uses a version of PPP that can trace frames.

- Modify your operating-system environment to intercept, record, and analyze data passing through serial interface device drivers.

- Tap the electrical signals at the serial interface directly and connect them to an RS-232 analyzer or to another serial interface on the same computer with PPP monitoring software.

These techniques are beyond the resources and skills of most people. If none of these are available, you can rely only on messages your PPP software displays for users. Unfortunately, these messages are often unspecific or cryptic for troubleshooting purposes. Another option is to try a different PPP product with better diagnostic features.

Checking the Serial Connection

Serial interfaces communicate over a connecting cable, usually to another serial interface on a modem or a computer. The two interfaces must have matching communication settings, such as speed, flow control, and modem control, to successfully transfer data.

On personal computers, a serial interface also requires unique hardware IRQ and I/O address resources. The operating system's IRQ and I/O address settings for a serial interface must be consistent with that of the actual hardware.

All these variables are potential sources for problems. Some symptoms of a serial connection problem are:

- Gross communication failure. The serial interface refuses to send or receive any characters.

- Poor serial interface performance. Sending characters and receiving responses that should be immediate may instead take 15 seconds or more.

- The serial connection garbles or looses data.

With gross failures, you should verify that the serial hardware is working. If the problem appears to be data corruption, the cause may be flow control, modem control, or data transparency issues.

Does the Serial Interface Work?

If a serial interface appears to be totally dead, the first areas you should check are physical wiring and power:

- Is the serial interface turned on? Is it enabled? Many portable PCs disable power to serial interfaces as a battery-saving feature. To use it, a setup program or utility must turn the interface on.

- Computers may have multiple serial interfaces. Be sure to connect the right one.

- A line tester can check to see if electrical signals are present at the serial interface connector. Also check the mating cable. The transmit or receive signals must be active; modem and flow control signals should be also.

- A null modem adapter or a null modem cable may be necessary. Most computer to computer connections are DTE-to-DTE and require a null modem. A computer to modem connection, namely DTE to DCE, requires a straight-through cable.

The electrical signals active on an unconnected serial interface and cable determine whether you need a null modem. Figure 15-1 illustrates the test. Only one of the TD and RD signals (DB 25 pins 2 and 3) should be active at a single connector. If the same pins are active at both the PC connector and the cable, then insert a null modem adapter to avoid electrical signal contention. If a null modem doesn't resolve the signal contention, there is an interface or a cable problem. Usually, the fault is a cable that is wired for purposes besides serial interfacing.

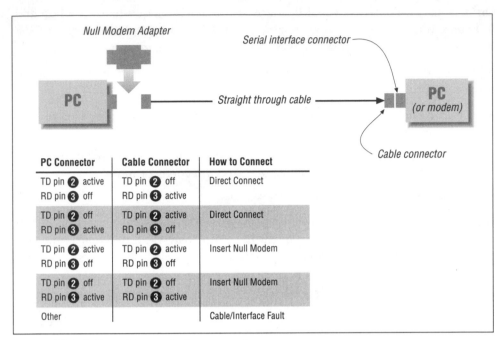

Figure 15-1. Null modems and when to use them

Checking Data Transfer

You can use a terminal emulator to configure an RS-232 serial interface and verify its ability to transfer data. Serial interface settings between two devices must be consistent. For two computers with a null modem connection, you must manually configure each computer's serial interface. But if a computer connects to a modem, most modems automatically adapt to match the setting of the computer.

The following RS-232 settings are for testing:

Speed
 Set to a fixed value and within the limits of the two connected devices.

Parity
 Set this to "none."

Data bits
 Set to 8 bits.

Flow control
 Disable all flow control by setting it to "none."

Modem control

> Disable all modem control. Modems should ignore DTR and assert the CD signal; computers should assert DTR, but ignore the CD signal.

Windows NT/98 Hyperterminal prompts for settings after you define a new connection. Be sure to select **Connect using: Direct to Com #**, even if the interface has an attached modem. Don't use the control panel to configure serial interfaces. Many Windows communication programs, including terminal emulators and PPP, simply override the control panel settings.

On Linux systems you can use **minicom** or **cu** to configure and connect to a serial interface. Unix systems include the **cu** utility, and some versions include **tip**, useful for the same purpose. Some Unix variants may have separate dial-in and dial-out device names for the same physical serial interface. Be sure you select the dial-out device, if such a distinction exists. On Linux:

```
user$ cu -s 38400 --parity=none --nostop -1 /dev/ttyS0
Connected.
at
OK
. . .
```

The **nostop** option disables software flow control.

Linux systems may refuse a **cu** connection. This can happen if a dial-in service is active, or if the permissions on the serial device file is incorrect. The cryptic errors from cu under these conditions include:

```
cu: open (/dev/ttyS0): Permission denied
cu: /dev/ttyS0: Line in use
```

Similarly, **tip** can return obscure errors such as:

```
tip: unknown host /dev/cua1
all ports busy
```

If any of these messages appear chronically, you may need clear lock files, usually in */var/locks* or */var/spool/locks*. Otherwise, reconfigure or reset permissions for the serial interface device file. Sometimes, serial interface drivers can end up in a state that requires a reboot in order to reset them.

When establishing serial interface speeds, be sure the settings are compatible for the device. Some serial interfaces have 28.8- and 14.4-Kbps speeds, even though many 28.8-Kbps modems don't support it. Many Sun workstations don't support speeds higher than 38.4 Kbps with their onboard serial interface hardware. Try to use standard values, such as 57.6 or 38.4 Kbps.

Modem control signals are sometimes difficult to configure. You can try to ignore these, unless the interface refuses to function. If modem control default behaviors interfere with testing, try configuring modems to ignore DTR and assert CD. Some modems have DIP switches to set this option. Others require software commands. Computers should ignore CD and assert DTR for testing, but setting this is platform-dependent. Many computers already behave as needed, even if they don't offer explicit modem-control settings.

If you can successfully send and receive characters through a serial interface, you verify its data-transfer ability. An **OK** or **ERROR** modem response following an **at** command indicates your serial interface is functioning. For two interconnected computers, both can run terminal emulators. Keystrokes on the keyboard of one computer should appear on the display of the other.

Poor Serial Interface Performance

One common serial interface misconfiguration symptom on PCs with Linux is poor serial interface performance. Serial interfaces wired to a Hayes compatible modem should respond immediately with the OK string following a simple **at** command. **minicom** and **cu** are useful for checking delays in real time. A chat script log can also aid diagnostics:

```
Apr 26 02:50:46 myhost chat[1447]: send (at^M)
Apr 26 02:50:46 myhost chat[1447]: expect (OK)
Apr 26 02:51:05 myhost chat[1447]: at^M^M
Apr 26 02:51:05 myhost chat[1447]: OK
Apr 26 02:51:05 myhost chat[1447]: -- got it
```

If the delay is excessive, as it is here (19 seconds), then this is a telltale sign that an IRQ conflict exists between the serial interface and other hardware device, or an inconsistency exists between what Linux believes is the serial interface IRQ and the actual hardware IRQ setting.

You can resolve these problems by checking BIOS settings, jumpers, and perhaps plug and play settings, to determine or reassign serial interface IRQs. The **setserial** utility reports and sets what Linux believes to be the hardware resources for a serial device. If **setserial** shows incorrect information then you must correct it, as follows:

```
root# /sbin/setserial /dev/ttyS0
/dev/ttyS0, UART: 16550A, Port: 0x03f8, IRQ: 4
root# /sbin/setserial /dev/ttyS0 irq 3
root#
```

On PCs, it's critical to set serial interface IRQ and I/O addresses correctly. If you neglect this, PPP may later report LCP-Configure timeouts and other errors that can mislead you into believing a PPP problem exists, when in fact a serial interface problem exists.

Flow Control Problems

Flow control temporarily stops communications when a computer or modem is too busy to accept new data. If flow control asserts inappropriately or doesn't function at all, it can cause sporadic and otherwise bizarre communication failures. Some symptoms that may result are:

- Communications errors or failures, but only with large quantities of data.

- The serial interface hardware reports high numbers of "overrun" errors.

- Frequent retransmissions, resulting in poor PPP connection throughput.

- Communication deadlocks. This may be a permanent condition, or one that results when PPP data content inappropriately stops communications.

- Erratic, or no response from the peer when sending PPP frames. Frame corruption errors when receiving PPP frames. Such errors include "Bad FCS," "short message," and others identical to those that transmission bit errors cause.

- PPP is without problems while negotiating with the Link Control Protocol, but doesn't respond afterwards.

Flow control faults are often difficult to isolate, test, and resolve. Unrelated problems with data transparency can also cause many of these symptoms.

A dial-up PPP setup usually has four serial interfaces in its communications path. At the local end, a computer and its modem have two serial interfaces in total. Remotely, the two interfaces belong to a modem and a communication server.

You can determine if a flow control problem exists anywhere along a serial connection by using a terminal emulator. First, you can manually sign on to a far-end communication server or a computer. Then try to exchange a few large text files. If the transfer shows lost characters, flow control is absent or is failing:

```
myisp>?
Exec commands:ppletalk Remote Access
  atmsig           Execute Atm Signalling Commands
. . .
  exit             Exit from the EXEC
  help      lat connection
nd version information from            router
  mstat            Show statistics after multiple multicast traceroutes
  mtrace      tion
  ping             Send echo messagesppp            Start IETF Point-to-
Point Protocol (PPP)
  resume           Resume an active network connection
  --More--          --          show            Show running system
information  slip            Start Serial-line IP (SLIP)
```

This isn't a 100% reliable test. If all appears normal, it's still possible the affected equipment wasn't busy enough to assert flow control at the time. Also, you can't use this test with dial-in PPP servers that support only PPP communications.

Hardware flow control wiring

If a serial interface successfully transfers data without flow control, but deadlocks once hardware flow control is active, it has a problem with RTS and CTS signals. Perhaps the connecting cable or null modem omitted the wiring for these signals. A serial interface may interpret unconnected signals as either "not ready" or "ready." A not-ready assumption blocks communications. A permanent ready assumption effectively disables hardware flow control.

Overruns

Another local flow control fault indicator is "overruns" reported by the serial interface. Overruns occur when a UART (see Chapter 2, *Serial Interfaces and Modems*) overwrites its data buffer before a CPU has a chance to read its contents. This can happen if flow control fails to stop arriving data when the CPU is busy. Some Unix versions indicate this error as follows:

```
Dec 25 13:07:16 myhost vmunix: zs1: silo overflow
```

Zs1 is the serial interface controller on a Sun workstation. With Windows 98, overrun statistics appear in its PPP log file, at the end of a PPP session:

```
C:\WINDOWS>type ppplog.txt
. . .
09-10-1998 17:34:59.90 - Overrun Errors          0
. . .
```

Some PPP software doesn't report overrun errors. Another observable side affect of overrun problems is PPP frame corruption during reception.

You can resolve overrun problems by inspecting and correcting RTS and CTS signal usage with hardware flow control, or XOFF and XON character usage with software flow control. Unfortunately, even if there are no flow control problems, overruns can still occur with buffer-limited UARTs. In this case, you can lower the speed of the serial interface or replace the UART with high speed models that feature larger receiver buffers.

Software flow control characters

Software flow control uses the XOFF (Ctrl-S, ASCII code 19) and XON (Ctrl-Q, ASCII code 17) characters to restart and stop communications, respectively. PPP may wish to include these characters as data in PPP frames, which is the main cause of PPP software flow control problems. Although you can configure PPP to avoid Ctrl-S and Ctrl-Q characters in its PPP frames, I recommend you instead avoid using software flow control.

In the erroneous presence of software flow control, PPP operates without problems as long as you send and receive PPP frames without Ctrl-S and Ctrl-Q characters. But once a Ctrl-S appears in a PPP frame, it forces a communications deadlock until a Ctrl-Q arrives. The serial connection also removes these characters from PPP frames, causing frame corruption. Therefore, a mixture of PPP frames with and without these magic characters results in erratic communication behaviors. This can cause obscure situations where the ping utility fails, but Telnet functions erratically. Applications may work but mysteriously fail a short moment later.

One way to check whether software flow control is present is to establish an interactive login session with a remote server. The GNU emacs editor usually maps Ctrl-S as the incremental search forward command. Striking this character while running emacs should produce the prompt:

```
-----Emacs: *scratch*          (Lisp Interaction Isearch)--All-------------
I-search:
```

If Ctrl-S doesn't produce the I-search response, the serial connection has intercepted Ctrl-S for flow control. A Ctrl-Q should release the communications deadlock.

There are two approaches for resolving software flow control problems. The first is to configure all serial interfaces in a connection to use hardware flow control instead of software. On modems, you must issue initialization strings to disable software flow control. For computers and communication servers, the operating system or PPP software settings determine the state of software flow control.

If your serial connection really requires software flow control, the second approach is to avoid Ctrl-S and Ctrl-Q characters. A PPP endpoint can encode these problem characters in the transmitting direction if it receives a request from the peer for the asyncmap 0x0000a000. Similarly, an endpoint that successfully requests this option from its peer never receives Ctrl-S and Ctrl-Q in plain form. It's best to arrange Ctrl-S and Ctrl-Q encoding with PPP for both directions of a software flow-controlled serial connection.

PPP software that negotiates the asyncmap 0x00000000 option aren't compatible with software flow control. If you can't change this behavior for a product, then you can't use it with software flow control.

Modem Control Problems

Modem control signals help a computer determine and control the current state of its physical serial connection. If these control signals are incorrect, or ignored, the following problem symptoms can result:

- Communication deadlocks. This can result when one device refuses to communicate with another because one believes the other isn't online.

- A computer fails to disconnect after the end of a PPP communications session. In other words, a computer fails to signal its modem to hang up the telephone.

A modem can refuse to interact with a computer if the computer doesn't assert its DTR modem control signal. You can use an RS-232 line tester to determine whether this is the case. The DTR signal may be absent due to a hardware limitation. Otherwise, you may have a serial interface configuration error or cable problem. If you're unable to repair the DTR signal itself, then configure DTR override at a modem. This requires either setting modem DIP switches or issuing the proper modem initialization commands.

Communicate failures can also occur due to missing CD or DSR signals. If CD is missing, you can configure CD override at the modem to enable communications.

Without CD, PPP software can't detect that a modem has disconnected. Therefore, you may need to manually terminate your PPP software. PPP supports LCP echo requests as a workaround. LCP echo requests require a reply by the peer, and if several requests go unanswered, your PPP software can conclude that the peer disconnected. PPP-2.3 supports LCP echo requests with the `lcp-echo-interval` and `lcp-echo-failures` options.

Without DTR, a computer can't use this signal to request a modem to hang up. Normally, a modem automatically disconnects when it loses carrier with its peer. Some peer modems may fail to drop carrier at the end of a PPP session. You must then manually initiate the disconnect with modem commands, rather than with a hardware signal. This requires you to send a "command mode escape" sequence to your modem, then the hang-up command. Some PPP software products already know this procedure. For those that don't, first terminate PPP, then use a terminal emulator to regain control of your modem:

```
user$ cu -s 38400 -1 /dev/ttyS0
Connected.
+++
OK
ath
OK
~.
Disconnected.
user$
```

Power cycling a modem also forces it to disconnect, although this isn't an elegant solution.

Transparency

Transparency describes the set of characters a serial connection carries without interception or modification. Ideally, all 256 8-bit characters codes should transparently pass through a serial connection. When some don't, it can become a serious problem. Some symptoms of transparency problems are:

- PPP complains that the serial connection isn't 8-bit clean.

- The serial connection frequently and unexpectedly disconnects. Or the serial connection mysteriously hangs, and no further data transfer is possible.

- PPP unexpectedly reports a looped-back serial connection.

- Erratic, or no response from the PPP peer, when sending PPP frames; PPP frame corruption errors, when receiving PPP frames. Such errors include "Bad FCS," "short message," and others identical to those that transmission errors can cause.

- PPP has no problems negotiating with the Link Control Protocol, but PPP doesn't respond afterwards.

Seven- and eight-bit clear connections

PPP requires an 8-bit clean serial connection. This means the connection must pass all 8 bits in characters as data during transmission. All intervening serial devices must have 8-bit, no parity, and 1 stop bit settings. If any device operates with 7-bit characters, the connection irreparably corrupts 8-bit binary data in PPP frames.

If a serial connection isn't 8-bit clean, your PPP software may not receive any PPP frames from its peer. If PPP frames do arrive, your PPP software may not recognize it or may complain about corrupted data. Here is an example:

```
Bad PPP frame: 7e 7f 7d 23 40 21 . . .
```

Notice the data doesn't include any character codes greater than 0x7f. This suggests that the eighth most significant bit of every character was stripped. PPP-2.3 reports a "not 8-bit clean" situation in its log:

```
Dec 26 21:17:11 myhost pppd[238]: Serial link is not 8-bit clean:
Dec 26 21:17:11 myhost pppd[238]: All received characters had bit 7 set to 0
```

PPP doesn't function with 7-bit serial connections. The resolution is to reconfigure all intervening serial devices to support 8-bit characters. Many PPP implementations automatically set their serial interfaces for 8 bits. But if you dial into a communication server never intended for PPP, its default behavior may be for 7-bit characters. You can attempt to temporarily configure a remote communication server for 8-bit data before using it for PPP. On a Cisco platform:

```
myisp>show terminal
. . .
Baud rate (TX/RX) is 38400/38400, even parity, 1 stopbits, 7 databits
Status: Ready, Active, No Exit Banner
```

```
    Capabilities: Hardware Flowcontrol In, Modem RI is CD,
       Output non-idle
    Modem state: Ready
    Special Chars: Escape  Hold  Stop  Start  Disconnect  Activation
                    ^^x     none   -     -      none
    Timeouts:        Idle EXEC      Idle Session    Modem Answer  Session   Dispatch
                     0:10:00         never                        none      not set
    . . .
myisp>terminal flowcontrol hardware in
myisp>terminal flowcontrol hardware out
myisp>terminal databits 8
myisp>terminal parity none
myisp>terminal telnet transparent
myisp>terminal escape-character break
<BREAK> is the escape character
myisp>telnet ppp.myisp.net
    . . .
```

At the same time, you can correct flow control and other settings before connecting to the dial-in PPP server, *ppp.myisp.net.*

Changing serial interface settings for remote equipment isn't elegant. This "on the fly" reconfiguration workaround isn't always successful, since there may exist an inaccessible, intervening serial device that's also not 8-bit clean.

I suggest that you always configure equipment to be 8-bit binary data compatible. Even non-PPP users utilizing file-transfer protocols, such as X/Y/Zmodem, require an 8-bit binary clean connection.

Intercepted characters

Serial devices and software that form a serial connection may watch the data stream for various "magic" characters, which trigger special functions. We already discussed Ctrl-S and Ctrl-Q for software flow control and the problems they can cause. The same serial devices could intercept additional characters for other special purposes.

Intercepted characters are a problem because PPP may try to use these characters for actual data. When the communication path between two endpoints isn't completely character-transparent, the serial connection can either disconnect, not respond, loop back, or cause data corruption, depending on the content of frames. Unlike data transmission errors, character-transparency problems are frequently repeatable. A notable pattern is a line disconnect or the inability for PPP to recover after repeated retransmissions of the exact same data. This can result in communication hangs after LCP negotiations, file transfer that hangs at the same point in the file, consistent hangs with rlogin, or similar problems with user activity.

The best resolution for transparency problems is to disable all special characters for all your serial devices and communication programs. Table 15-2 shows common escape sequence characters, their purpose, and how to disable them.

Table 15-2. Escape Sequences

Character	Program and Device	Sequence	Purpose	Disabling
0x2b, "+"	Modems	pause, +++, pause	Command mode escape	at s2=128
0x1d, Ctrl-]	Telnet, Unix	Ctrl-]	Command mode escape	Telnet -E
0x7e, "~"	rlogin, Unix	~.	Disconnects from remote host	rlogin -E
0xff	rlogin	0xff, 0xff, "s", "s", ...	Client-to-server window size (rows and columns) message	
0x1e, Ctrl-^	Telnet, Cisco	Ctrl-^, "x"	Command mode escape	term escape none
0x1d, Ctrl-]	Telnet, Annex	Ctrl-]	Command mode escape	stty tesc u
0x7e, "~"	tip, Unix	~.	Drop connection and exit	
0x7e, "~"	cu, Unix	~.	Drop connection and exit	

If you can't disable all escape characters, you can try to configure PPP to avoid them. PPP is forgiving for serial connections that intercept ASCII control characters with codes below 0x20. The asyncmap option selects the set of control characters PPP encodes into two character sequences, prior to transmission. Further information about asyncmap appears in Chapter 3, *How PPP Works.*

If you're not sure what characters aren't transparent, set **asyncmap ffffffff** at both ends of the connection. This causes PPP to encode all ASCII control characters and should resolve most common character-transparency problems. If transparency problems exist for noncontrol characters, PPP-2.3 features the **escape** option, which can encode some characters using sequences of other characters. Note that PPP can't encode the tilde (~) character. Thus, serial connections not transparent for ~ aren't suitable.

Only the Link Control Protocol works

The Link Control Protocol is special in the sense that it avoids ASCII control characters in literal form during communications. In other words, during LCP, the effective asynchronous control character map is **ffffffff** for both PPP endpoints. Once LCP completes, the negotiated asyncmap determines what control characters each endpoint can receive in literal form.

If the negotiated asyncmaps following LCP are incompatible with the transparency characteristics of the serial connection, then frame corruption and frame discards are inevitable. This can lead to symptoms of PPP deafness and bad FCS complaints. More specifically, deafness can cause a PPP endpoint to become non-responsive to authentication requests or responses. The same can also happen with IPCP and other NCPs. This problem tends to exhibit itself only after LCP. I show examples that have the same symptoms in the section "Asyncmap default error," later in this chapter.

To resolve the "only LCP works" problem, it is necessary to determine whether asyncmap settings for both endpoints of a PPP connection are correct. Again, if you're not sure what control characters are not transparent, then set the asyncmap to ffffffff.

Testing character transparency

One way to test whether you have transparency problems is to set up a PPP connection and use it to transfer binary data files. The files should include all possible 8-bit character codes. Make sure you disable PPP data compression and encryption while testing. This ensures that PPP transmits and receives data in its actual form.

If PPP errors, communications hangs, or other problems result during the transfer, a character-transparency problem exists. The point of failure during the transfer is the data sequence that's causing trouble.

One way to prepare a PPP test file containing all 8-bit codes is:

```
user$ awk 'BEGIN { for($i=0;$i<256;$i++) { printf("%c",$i); } }' > \
ppptest
user$ awk 'BEGIN { for($i=0;$i<256;$i++) { printf("%c",$i); } }' >> \
ppptest
user$ echo '~. ~.  ~.' >> ppptest
user$ echo -e '\177ss12345678.\177ss12345678..\177ss12345678' >> \
ppptest
user$ echo '+++ +++  +++' >> ppptest
```

The awk utility can generate all the 8-bit character codes. Include several copies of common escape sequences in the test file, in case PPP splits a sequence between two PPP frames.

Next, use a file-transfer utility, such as ftp, to send and receive the *ppptest* file.

Checking Modems

Modems transmit and receive digital data over the standard telephone service; problems with telephone service are common and recurring. However, the many current and legacy standards for modem communications cause incompatibilities among different modem models.

When troubleshooting modems, the external models are more helpful. These have status indicators that show data transmission, reception, telephone off hook, and other states. For modems with internal audible speakers, it helps to listen in on the dialing and connect process. Modems dialing out should echo command strings they receive and offer verbose feedback. You can set these options as follows for Hayes compatible modems:

```
    Enable echo
at e1
OK
    Enable speaker
at m1
OK
    Enable verbose response (modem dependent)
at q0 v1
OK
```

You can manually control and troubleshoot a modem with a terminal emulator. It's difficult to troubleshoot modem problems with automatic dialers. However, some PPP software includes "manual dial," "interactive mode," "terminal window," which are useful for overriding auto-dialers.

Modem Negotiation

After a modem dials a telephone number, it negotiates rates, protocols, compression, and error correction with a peer modem. These parameters are unrelated to those PPP uses. Naturally, dialing or negotiations may fail, resulting in the following common symptoms:

- The modem fails to dial out for outgoing data calls or to answer incoming data calls.

- The modem disconnects shortly after contacting another modem.

The first potential problem is dialing out. Modems can either "tone" or "pulse" dial telephone numbers. You must use pulse dialing if your telephone service is without the touch-tone feature:

```
    Dial Touch-Tone
at dt 17005551212
NO CARRIER
    Dial Pulse
```

```
at dp 17005551212
CONNECT
```

If a modem is answering telephone calls, it operates in answer mode instead of the usual originate mode. An answering modem sequentially generates different carriers, until the originating end responds to one it recognizes. Dial-in PPP servers frequently require modems set to autoanswer mode. Linux mgetty and Windows NT RAS doesn't require autoanswer because they monitor the modem directly for RING indications and issue the at a answer command.

A modem set to autoanswer mode shouldn't generate response strings, such as CONNECT. These could be mistaken, by a computer or communication server, to be data from a remote user:

```
    Enable answer mode, answer in one ring
at s0=1
OK
    Disable response strings (modem dependent)
at q1
OK
```

A third class of problems is modulation incompatibilities. This occurs, for example, if one modem wishes to use the old V.FC standard, but another requires V.34. There are many other obsolete model modulation standards including V.terbo, U.S. Robotics HST, Telebit PEP, etc. Besides incompatible modulation, there may be disagreements among modem compression, such as V.42bis verses MNP5, or error correction, such as V.42 verse MNP4. Conflicts normally cause connection failures, but sometimes a successful connection refuses to pass data. Some modems report disconnect reasons, which is very helpful for determining compatibility problems:

```
at i6
. . .
Disconnect Reason is DISC received

OK
```

Disconnect reasons are often cryptic and may require you to have extraordinary expertise with modem technology to interpret. But without this status information, you must resolve problems with trial and error.

Some ways to resolve modem incompatibilities are:

*   If a modem has configurable modulation, compression, and error correction protocols, disable all proprietary protocols in favor of the standard ones.
*   Configure the modem to specifically connect at lower carrier rates. This may change the modulation protocol to a version that's compatible with both ends.
*   Disable modem data compression and try reconnecting.

- Disable error correction and try reconnecting. But be aware that a peer modem may require error correction before it's willing to connect.

The modem commands necessary for each of these actions vary. You may need to consult your modem documentation to determine the appropriate command strings.

Line Quality, Line Noise

The quality of a telephone line is the single most important factor that determines how well modems perform. Modems are much more sensitive to line noise, interference, and other telephone-service impairments than people are. Even during a single telephone call, line quality may vary. This directly affects how quickly data transfers can occur.

The symptoms of poor line quality problems are:

- A modem spontaneously disconnects.

- Random PPP frame corruption errors, when receiving PPP frames. Such errors include "Bad FCS," "short message," and others. Poor or no response when sending PPP frames.

- Poor communications throughput. A modem constantly asserts flow control thereby slowing down communications.

Initial modem connect speed

Perhaps the most obvious indication of telephone line quality is the initial connection speed. High carrier rates (28.8 Kbps or greater) require exceptionally clean telephone service:

```
CONNECT 28800/ARQ/V34/LAPM/V42BIS
```

These rates aren't as common as one hopes. If two compatible high-speed modems frequently connect at rates significantly lower than their capacity, a poor line is the likely problem. These are the items to check:

- Try placing the call again. You may receive a better connection with a new call.

- Try calling a different number. If connect rates are consistently low, the problem lies with the local side of the telephone call.

- Attach a telephone set to the line, dial a "1", and listen. The line should be quiet. There shouldn't be significant buzzes, scratching noises, or cross talk from other telephone users.

- Disconnect your inside telephone wiring from the "Network Interface" and attach a test telephone set to the line. Perform the listening test again. If abnormalities still exist, the telephone company is responsible. Otherwise, the fault lies within inside house wiring. Your wiring may have a loose connection, be too close to power lines, etc.

Modem retraining

Let's assume a modem initially connects at a high carrier rate. As the line quality varies, speed fall back and fall forward may occur. This temporarily establishes a new rate that's compatible with current line quality. But with more extreme changes in line quality, "retraining" temporarily suspends communications. During retraining, the modem performs a channel probe, which analyzes the communications characteristics of the telephone line. This helps establish a new communications strategy consistent with the new characteristics of the line. In extreme cases, especially with V.FC, retraining can require a minute or more. If this happens frequently, it effectively blocks the line for useful data. Here are suggestions for this condition:

- Disconnect and reconnect

- If the problem persists, configure the modem for an artificially low carrier rate and disable retraining

Modem error correction

When modem error correction is active, it's responsible for detecting and retransmitting corrupted data. But in the presence of transmission errors, communication stalls occur during retransmission, since a modem is busy and can't process new data. There is retransmission limit of about 12 that causes a modem to disconnect. Like retraining, retransmissions block data transfers. Again, you can try reconnecting, or reconnecting at lower carrier rates.

Modem error correction is unavailable with some modulation protocols and may be defeated with most others. It's not absolutely necessary to enable modem error correction. PPP can function without error correction, since it can still detect and discard bad PPP frames. Network layer protocols can initiate retransmissions, recovering from data lost in transit. When modems don't correct errors, PPP software reports errors when receiving a bad frame. Some error messages are:

```
ppp_async: short message (%d)
ppp_async: short input packet (%d)
ppp_async: FCS Error
ppp_async: missed ALLSTATIONS (0xff), got 0x%x
ppp_async: missed UI (0x3), got 0x%x
ppp_async: bad protocol high byte %x
ppp_async: bad protocol low byte %x
ppp_async: too many chars in input buffer %d
```

Be careful not to confuse these with serial interface problems. Bad PPP frames due to telephone line problems don't generate overrun errors. Furthermore, transmission errors are random and don't repeat for the same frame. These PPP errors aren't a critical problem, unless they occur frequently. You can try to adjust MRU and MTU parameters, which can help performance in the presence of transmission errors.

Adjusting MRU and MTU

Maximum receive unit (MRU) and maximum transmit unit (MTU) define the largest PPP frames to receive and send, respectively, through the connection. When frequent transmission errors are present and modem error correction is disabled, MRU and MTU should be set to small values; smaller frames have less chance of becoming corrupted. Also, less data requires retransmission when errors occur.

The default MRU and MTU for PPP is 1500. A reasonable alternate value is 576. When a PPP endpoint establishes a PPP connection, it negotiates the maximum size for PPP frames it wishes to receive.

Fragmentation of incoming IP datagrams

Fragmentation of large IP datagrams presents a problem with small MRUs. A distant remote site may generate a large datagram during an FTP download, for example. The network must "fragment" the datagram to smaller pieces and encode them into several frames. Figure 15-2 illustrates this process. If a frame carrying one of the fragments is lost or damaged, TCP/IP requires retransmitting all fragments. Thus, the loss of one PPP frame requires retransmitting many other frames, defeating the advantage of small MRUs.

Some remote sites use Path MTU Discovery (RFC-1191) and first send probes to determine the smallest MRU in your receiving path. The initial probe may cause communication delays. All IP datagrams from the site, after the probe, can then fit into a small MRU, avoiding the fragmentation problem.

Another way to control fragmentation is to alter the TCP maximum segment size (MSS) you are willing to receive. Two communicating sites can announce MSS options at the beginning of a TCP connection. If an MSS setting exists, you can set it to the smallest MRU in your receiving path, minus 64.[*] This should prevent fragmentation in those IP datagrams you receive that contain TCP segments.

In general, you don't always have control over IP datagram sizes you receive from a remote Internet site.

---

[*] MSS = MTU – (the size of the IP header) – (the size of the TCP header). Since headers can vary in size, 64 is a guideline, but 40 is the smallest number you should use.

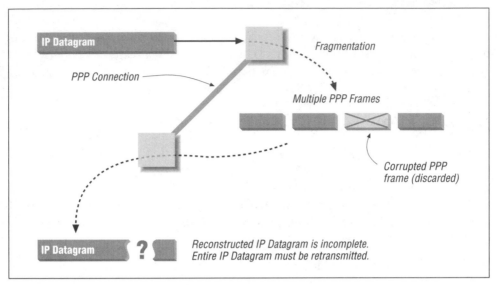

Figure 15-2. TCP/IP IP datagram fragmentation

Fragmentation of outgoing IP datagrams

In the transmitting direction, the MTU limits the maximum outgoing PPP frame size. You may be able to reset your MTU locally, even if your peer wants a different MRU. An MTU smaller than the default 1500 can help if you are frequently retransmitting outgoing IP datagrams.

The fragmentation problem can still apply to large outgoing IP datagrams. Some computers automatically limit IP datagram sizes to the MTU setting. Others use path MTU discovery. And some don't allow you to control outgoing IP datagram sizes at all.

Chat Script Problems

Any number of problems can cause chat scripts to fail. When they fail, the obvious symptom is that the connection fails to start. Network communications subsequently fail.

Chat script failures are frequently obvious when you examine the script's behavior, either in real time or as recorded in log files. Two common symptoms are that a chat script terminates with an error or that it hangs.

One important event to look for is whether a chat script issued the final command, at the appropriate time, to start PPP. Here is a transcript:

```
Nov 6 20:45:43 myhost chat[2993]: expect (assword:)
Nov 6 20:45:43 myhost chat[2993]: Password: -- got it
```

```
Nov 6 20:45:43 myhost chat[2993]: send (mypass^M)
Nov 6 20:45:43 myhost chat[2993]: expect (%)
Nov 6 20:45:43 myhost chat[2993]:  ^M
Nov 6 20:45:43 myhost chat[2993]: Last login: Mon Nov  4 21:45:48 from myhost^M
Nov 6 20:45:44 myhost chat[2993]: Sun Microsystems Inc. SunOS 5.6 Generic August 1997
Nov 6 20:46:28 myhost chat[2993]: $
Nov 6 20:46:28 myhost chat[2993]: alarm
Nov 6 20:46:28 myhost chat[2993]: Failed
Nov 6 20:46:28 myhost pppd[2989]: could not set up connection
Nov 6 20:46:28 myhost pppd[2989]: Exit.
```

The command necessary to start PPP at this peer is */usr/sbin/aspppls*, which our chat script never sends. The script timed out waiting for a % prompt from the remote system, which responds with a $ instead.

This and other chat script problems are:

- The remote peer responds to commands in a manner inconsistent with the expectations of the chat script.

- An unanticipated error occurs, and the remote peer returns an error message the script wasn't configured to handle.

- The remote peer expects command strings to be terminated with a character besides the default carriage return character, shown as ^M in the preceding transcript.

- The remote peer expects to interact during a chat script with a specific serial-interface parity setting.

The resolution for the first two problems is straightforward. You need to modify the chat script as appropriate, depending on the problem the transcript shows. A terminal emulator can help you determine what commands and responses you must include in a chat script for interacting with a remote peer.

Command-Line Termination Problems

A chat script can hang and fail to receive a response if a remote peer expects a nonstandard command-line termination character. Many chat scripts send a carriage-return character at the end of a command, but this may not be the correct character for a specific peer. A Unix server in binary mode, for example, expects a line-feed character, instead of the carriage return. Thus, you must modify the script accordingly. UUCP dialers and PPP-2.3 chat send a line feed if \n is part of its send string. Some equivalents for other script languages are \012 as octal code, $n or $010 as decimal code.

Parity Problems

If a chat script appears correct, but still hangs, there may be a serial-interface parity problem. Parity problems exhibit themselves in mysterious ways. Received responses may not match what the script expects even though they appear correct in a transcript. A peer may respond unexpectedly to a command or password string you are sure is correct. A terminal emulator may not show any problem at all, yet the script still hangs or fails. If you think you may have this problem, try to configure chat to send 7-bit characters and zero parity and ignore the most significant eighth bit when receiving characters.

One chat implementation with parity control is Solaris PPP. Solaris PPP uses UUCP for connecting with remote PPP peers. You can set parity to zero in chat scripts by including a null expect string and a P_ZERO response string, as part of a script. An example of this, in the file */etc/uucp/Systems*, is as follows:

```
root# cat /etc/uucp/Systems
. . .
#Host  Time Device Speed Phone       Chat sequence, expect/send pairs
myisp  Any  ACU    38400 17005551212 "" P_ZERO ogin: ppp3 assword: mypass
. . .
```

The P_ZERO directive indicates the chat script must send all strings that follow with zero parity. This parity setting is effective after the modem connects. Without this directive, the default is P_EVEN, which can cause complications with many remote peers.

Very few chat languages offer parity control. Thus, to minimize problems with diverse chat implementations, you and your users should set all serial interfaces at both ends of a connection to 8N1 at all times. All command interpreters should accept 8-bit characters and ignore the most significant bit. All replies should also use 8-bit characters but with zero set for the most significant bit.

PPP Startup Problems

When a chat script completes, the script issues a final command string or receives a final response string. At this point, the peer should have its PPP software active and be ready for PPP communications. Sometimes, PPP startup fails, even though the chat script succeeds. The symptoms of this condition include:

- PPP reports a looped-back serial connection. All traffic sent to the peer resembles the same information received.

- PPP complains that the serial connection isn't 8-bit clean.

- The peer fails to respond to any PPP frames and the connection terminates after a chat script successfully completes.

- PPP software reports it can't recognize frames from the data it receives from its peer. This occurs after the chat script ends.

- A chat script sent a few extraneous characters at the end, and now the peer doesn't expect to communicate with PPP.

I now describe the loopback, no response, and invalid frame problems in greater detail. The solutions for all the problems in this list are similar and are discussed at the end of this section.

Looped-Back Serial Connection

Once a PPP connection is up, the first frames exchanged are the LCP configure packets. If there is a remote PPP startup problem, the serial connection may become looped back. This condition appears in the following trace:

```
Oct 24 23:05:29 myhost pppd[24815]: sent [LCP ConfReq id=0x1 <mru 1500>
<asyncmap 0x0> <magic 0x617dc6f0> <pcomp> <accomp>]
Oct 24 23:05:30 myhost pppd[24815]: rcvd [LCP ConfReq id-0x1 <mru 1500>
<asyncmap 0x0> <magic 0x617dc6f0> <pcomp> <accomp>]
. . .
Oct 24 23:05:30 myhost pppd[24815]: sent [LCP ConfNak id=0x1 <magic
0x1f323f93>]
Oct 24 23:05:30 myhost pppd[24815]: rcvd [LCP ConfNak id=0x1 <magic
0x1f323f93>]
. . .
Oct 24 23:05:30 myhost pppd[24815]: sent [LCP ConfReq id=0x2 <mru 1500>
<asyncmap 0x0> <magic 0x253e03b5> <pcomp> <accomp>]
. . .
Oct 24 23:05:30 myhost pppd[24815]: The line appears to be looped back.
```

This sequence repeats about 10 times before the connection terminates. Magic numbers help determine loop-back conditions. Notice all magic numbers sent exactly match those received.

Sometimes, a loop back can also produce a misleading error about a serial-connection character-transparency problem:

```
Oct 24 23:04:42 myhost pppd[24802]: Serial link is not 8-bit clean:
Oct 24 23:04:42 myhost pppd[24802]: All received characters had bit 7 set to 0
```

When a chat script completes, it sends a PPP start command to a peer, accepts a CONNECT response from a modem, or accepts some other response string. A small time delay may be necessary before the peer is ready for the first PPP frame. If you send the initial frame with an LCP configure-request too quickly, some of the characters in the frame can cause the PPP at the peer to abort, before it has time to initialize. Similarly, a modem can disconnect if it receives characters too soon after its CONNECT response.

The loop-back error results because we are now sending PPP frames into a command line interpreter (CLI), instead of a PPP peer. This interpreter may belong to the remote peer, a modem, or another intervening device. Most CLIs echo back characters. CLIs also expect to interact with people, rather than with binary PPP. Thus, the characters some CLIs echo back may have the eighth bit stripped, yielding the "serial link isn't 8-bit clean" error, instead of a "loop back" error.

No PPP response

Another possible behavior when PPP fails to start at the peer is a "no response" condition. Here we send and resend PPP LCP configure-requests, but the peer never responds. The connection terminates, usually after 10 LCP configure requests:

```
Nov  4 21:46:55 myhost pppd[27189]: Connect: ppp0 <--> /dev/ttyS0
Nov  4 21:46:55 myhost pppd[27189]: sent [LCP ConfReq id=0x1 <mru 1500>
<asyncmap 0x0> <magic 0x617c4b1e> <pcomp> <accomp>]
 . . .
Nov  4 21:47:22 myhost pppd[27189]: sent [LCP ConfReq id=0x1 <mru 1500>
<asyncmap 0x0> <magic 0x617c4b1e> <pcomp> <accomp>]
 . . .
Nov  4 21:47:25 myhost pppd[27189]: LCP: timeout sending Config-Requests
Nov  4 21:47:25 myhost pppd[27189]: Connection terminated.
```

The cause of this problem may be similar to the serial-connection looped-back case. Our first LCP configure-request may have terminated PPP at the peer before it had a chance to initialize.

Other explanations include the possibility that PPP startup failed outright at the peer. The remote peer could have responded with a text error message, but after the chat script sent the final PPP startup command.

Unrecognized PPP frames

PPP software expects to receive PPP frames from a peer after the chat script completes. But if your software receives text instead, it may complain about its inability to recognize PPP frames.

This condition can happen if the peer generates text before the first PPP frame. An example of this, on a Cisco communication server, is:

```
myisp>ppp default
Entering PPP mode.
Async interface address is unnumbered (Ethernet0)
Your IP address is 192.168.3.2. MTU is 1500 bytes
Header compression will match your system.

~~ }#.!}!}!} }4} }&} }*} } }%}&}3º( } } }{}   ~~ }#.!}!} } }4} }&} }*} }
}%}&}3~
```

The final command a chat script issues is `ppp default`. However, the remote peer first responds with informational messages before an actual PPP frame. This can confuse some PPP software and possibly cause the PPP connection to fail.

Resolving PPP startup problems

If you suspect a PPP startup problem at the remote peer, the resolution is to modify your chat scripts. The loop back, no response, and unrecognizable PPP frame symptoms usually require some changes at the end of a chat script. Here are some items to consider checking and changing:

- Verify that the chat script correctly invokes PPP before it terminates. If text messages precede the first PPP frame you receive from a peer, arrange the chat script to wait for these messages before terminating.

- Have the chat script wait for a real PPP frame from the peer before it terminates. A "~" character always appears in a PPP frame.

- You can simply wait for the peer to send you the first PPP frame. This ensures that the peer PPP is already active before you send it binary data.

- Include a chat-script delay following the final command the script issues. This gives time for the peer to start its PPP software.

- Make sure the end of a chat script doesn't send extra characters, particularly carriage-return characters.

Generally, chat scripts should interact with a remote peer and read all the characters the peer sends up to, but excluding, the first character that belongs to the first PPP frame. In the preceding communications server dialog with the `ppp default` command, a chat script should read the `"system."` string. It may be insufficient to simply end a script after sending `ppp default`. Thus, the end of a PPP-2.3 chat script can resemble the following:

```
"myisp>" "ppp default"
"system." "\c"
```

After this script receives `"system."`, it sends nothing in response. The `\c` escape code suppresses an implied carriage return at the end of the send string. This escape code is especially important with PPP-2.3 and UUCP chat scripts if your remote peer uses autodetection to determine whether to start PPP communications. Without this escape code, the chat script sends a carriage-return character at the time your PPP software should send its first PPP frame. This can confuse PPP autodetection. As a result, your peer may then mistakenly start a command-line interpreter, instead of PPP.

After a chat script completes, PPP-2.3 immediately sends its first PPP frame, which can cause PPP startup to abort with some peers. You should add a delay at the end of the script by modifying the last line as follows:

```
"myisp>" "ppp default"
"system." "\d\c"
```

The \d represents a time delay, on the order of one second. This should give the peer sufficient time to initialize before the first PPP frame is sent.

Rather than insert a chat script delay, PPP-2.3 can passively wait for the first PPP frame from a peer. This prevents any initial PPP frame transmissions that can cause problems with some peers:

```
user$ /usr/sbin/pppd debug /dev/ttyS0 38400 silent . . .
```

An alternate way to set up a chat script without using the delay directive is to have the chat script itself wait for the first PPP frame. Instead of waiting for the string **"system."** Our script can wait for the ~ character instead. This character always appears in the first PPP frame:

```
"myisp>" "ppp default"
"~" "\c"
```

By the time the ~ arrives, the peer is ready for PPP communications, and a chat script delay is no longer necessary. But if the chat script reads the first character in a PPP frame, PPP-2.3 must miss the first frame. This shouldn't be a concern because PPP frame retransmissions are common at startup.

What happens if the PPP peer is operating in passive mode and requires you to send the first frame before communications begin? Now there is no way for a chat script to know when the peer is ready to receive the first frame. In this case, adding delays into a chat script before sending a PPP frame is the best way to prevent potential problems.

PPP Failures

A PPP connection, soon after it starts, transitions through several states before it is useful for user traffic. These states include connection establishment, in which PPP endpoints negotiate PPP options with LCP, authentications in which they share authentication credentials, and networkings where they negotiate network layer protocol options. Chapter 3 describes the states in further detail.

Each step in this process can be a source of problems. Although PPP products can display helpful error messages directly to users, these messages are often not informative:

```
Connection failed
```

In many cases, it's essential to examine trace and activity logs, in order to pinpoint how PPP is failing. PPP-2.3, for example, records most of its messages in log files.

Link Control Protocol Problems

During a negotiation process, there are bound to be disagreements, renegotiations, and compromises. PPP negotiations with LCP are no exception. The most common problems with LCP are the irreconcilable differences that remain between PPP endpoints after too many negotiation attempts. Some symptoms are:

* Endless LCP negotiation loops between two PPP endpoints.

* One PPP endpoint refuses to compromise on a nondefault PPP option or value and terminates the PPP connection.

Certain options and values may be nonnegotiable, depending on the configuration. Authentication is commonly nonnegotiable, but this may be true of other options as well. Consider a dial-in PPP server an ISP maintains. You can dial-in and decline authentication, which is the default. Obviously, this isn't acceptable to the dial-in server, and further renegotiations won't reconcile the matter. Therefore, the PPP connection must fail.

Here is a log file that shows an LCP negotiation failure. This log shows what happens when **myhost** rejects some options the peer requests.

```
Nov 13 20:46:07 myhost pppd[24263]: Connect: ppp0 <--> /dev/ttyr0
. . .
Nov 13 20:46:07 myhost pppd[24263]: rcvd [LCP ConfReq id=0x16 <mru 1500>
<asyncmap 0x0> <auth chap 05> <magic 0xc5aa2d07> <pcomp> <accomp>]
. . .
Nov 13 20:46:08 myhost pppd[24263]: sent [LCP ConfRej id=0x16 <auth chap 05>]
. . .
Nov 13 20:46:08 myhost pppd[24263]: rcvd [LCP ConfReq id=0x17 <mru 1500>
<asyncmap 0x0> <auth upap> <magic 0xc5aa2d07> <pcomp> <accomp>]
. . .
Nov 13 20:46:08 myhost pppd[24263]: sent [LCP ConfRej id=0x17 <auth upap>]
. . .
Nov 13 20:46:08 myhost pppd[24263]: rcvd [LCP TermReq id=0x18]
Nov 13 20:46:08 myhost pppd[24263]: sent [LCP TermAck id=0x18]
Nov 13 20:46:08 myhost pppd[24263]: Modem hangup
Nov 13 20:46:08 myhost pppd[24263]: Exit.
```

myhost first receives an LCP configure request that includes the option `auth chap` 5. The second configure request includes the option `auth upap`. These options are for CHAP and PAP authentication, respectively. myhost rejects both, prompting the peer to disconnect.

In other situations, over 10 configure requests may occur before a disconnect. This limit is reasonable behavior that should prevent infinite negotiation loops. However, negotiation loops are possible under certain conditions and with some PPP software.

You can resolve LCP negotiation problems as follows:

- Configure the appropriate endpoint to stop requesting the offending options. Use PPP defaults to avoid the option altogether.

- Configure the other endpoint to accept the offending option.

Returning to the preceding example, LCP can succeed if `myhost` accepts one of the two authentication options the peer wants. Alternatively, LCP can succeed if the peer doesn't require authentication. The former resolution is the most likely. This means you must configure PPP at `myhost` to perform authentication.

When LCP succeeds, `myhost` sends an `LCP ConfAck` in response to an `LCP ConfReq` it received earlier from the peer. `myhost` must also receive an `LCP ConfAck` for one `LCP ConfReq` it sent earlier to its peer. Configure rejects and negative acknowledgments are a normal part of LCP negotiation, as long as both endpoints eventually reach an agreement.

Authentication Problems

One of the PPP connection states is *authenticate*, which allows two endpoints to authenticate to each other. You can configure authentication for either or both endpoints. Furthermore, the authentication protocol for each endpoint can differ.

When authentication is required, several problems can result. Some symptoms are:

- One endpoint fails to recognize one or more authentication options and rejects authentication outright. The connection subsequently terminates.

- Authentication fails due to invalid credentials. In other words, a name or a secret is invalid.

- Unauthorized communications error occurs while establishing TCP/IP or other network layer protocols.

Notice that these symptoms occur in the establish, authenticate, and network states of the connection, respectively.

Authentication problems tend to be more frequent with full-featured PPP software, such as PPP-2.3. PPP-2.3 offers almost every possible PPP authentication arrangement. The trade-off for this flexibility is a greater chance of configuration errors and confusion.

Authentication roles confusion

One of the most common errors is configuring authentication for the wrong direction of the PPP connection. Consider the case when you dial into an ISP and authenticate with PAP. PPP-2.3 automatically authenticates itself to a peer, at the peer's request, as long as it has authentication credentials to submit. There is no need to explicitly include special options for this to happen.

You may incorrectly start PPP-2.3 as follows, believing `require-pap` or `auth` causes authentication to occur:

```
user$ /usr/sbin/pppd debug /dev/ttyS0 38400 require-pap . . .

user$ /usr/sbin/pppd debug /dev/ttyS0 38400 auth . . .
```

The `require-pap` option sets PPP-2.3 to require its peer to authenticate itself, with PAP. In other words, you become an authenticating server. This isn't the same as authenticating yourself to the peer, as an authenticating client does. PPP log files may indicate LCP negotiation failures. If not, errors may be deferred until one endpoint attempts to establish network layer protocols. The latter condition appears as follows:

```
Nov 17 21:59:27 myhost pppd[312]: sent [LCP ConfReq id=0x1 <mru 1500>
<asyncmap 0x0> <auth upap> <magic 0xf0d2c620> <pcomp> <accomp>]
Nov 17 21:59:27 myhost pppd[312]: rcvd [LCP ConfRej id=0x1 <auth upap>]
. . .
Nov 17 21:59:27 myhost pppd[312]: sent [LCP ConfReq id=0x2 <mru 1500>
<asyncmap 0x0> <magic 0xf0d2c620> <pcomp> <accomp>]
Nov 17 21:59:27 myhost pppd[312]: rcvd [LCP ConfAck id=0x2 <mru 1500>
<asyncmap 0x0> <magic 0xf0d2c620> <pcomp> <accomp>]
. . .
Nov 17 21:59:27 myhost pppd[312]: peer refused to authenticate
Nov 17 21:59:27 myhost pppd[312]: sent [LCP TermReq id=0x3]
. . .
Nov 17 21:59:27 myhost pppd[312]: rcvd [IPCP ConfReq id=0x12 <compress VJ 0f
01> <addr 172.16.0.193>]
Nov 17 21:59:27 myhost pppd[312]: io(): Received non-LCP packet when LCP not
open.
Nov 17 21:59:27 myhost pppd[312]: rcvd [LCP TermAck id=0x3]
. . .
```

LCP successfully negotiates no authentication. However, myhost later realizes that the peer refused to authenticate and terminates the connection.

Authentication protocol conflicts

The common standard PPP authentication protocols are CHAP and PAP (see Chapter 12, *Authentication*). It's unfortunate that some software supports only PAP. If you have software with this limitation, you will encounter LCP negotiation failures or unauthorized communications failure with a peer that requires CHAP. Your peer could allow the simpler PAP, but some administrators perceive PAP to be less secure and refuse to allow it. The solution to this problem is to upgrade your PPP software.

Another cause of problems are PPP software products that require proprietary PPP authentication protocols. Windows NT 4.0 RAS may be set to accept only Microsoft's variation of CHAP, also known as MS-CHAP and MS-CHAP-80. Standard CHAP and MS-CHAP aren't compatible. If you attempt to access a Windows NT dial-in PPP server, you may encounter the following:

```
Nov 17 17:00:51 myhost pppd[259]: rcvd [LCP ConfReq id=0x1 <mru 1500>
<asyncmap 0x0> <auth chap 80> <magic 0x6bec5b87> <pcomp> <accomp>]
. . .
Nov 17 17:00:51 myhost pppd[259]: sent [LCP ConfNak id=0x1 <auth chap 05>]
. . .
```

`auth chap 80` isn't the same as the standard `auth chap 05`. This leads to an LCP negotiation disagreement and a disconnect. The best solution is to disable proprietary authentication protocols in favor of the standard ones. This provides broader compatibility with standards-compliant software. Requiring your user population to use PPP software with proprietary features is poor practice. The few PPP products that support a proprietary feature may all have other serious deficiencies, or missing features.

Invalid authentication credentials

If your PPP authentication credentials are incorrect, the usual error message you receive is "name or password incorrect." Sometimes authentication failures appear in PPP log files, rather than on-screen:

```
Nov 17 22:47:59 myhost pppd[346]: sent [CHAP Challenge id=0x1
<f3e7ab4a3ddf6a57779a0fe3779828121eb5b4834f2bd0248308660568f2144b9e58a38b>,
name = "hostaname"]
. . .
Nov 17 22:47:59 myhost pppd[346]: rcvd [CHAP Response id=0x1
<eb951a86536596d55598574a9bba2152>, name = "hostbname"]
Nov 17 22:47:59 myhost pppd[346]: ChapReceiveResponse: received name field:
hostbname
Nov 17 22:47:59 myhost pppd[346]: sent [CHAP Failure id=0x1 "I don't like
you.  Go 'way."]
. . .
Nov 17 22:47:59 myhost pppd[346]: CHAP peer authentication failed
Nov 17 22:47:59 myhost pppd[346]: sent [LCP TermReq id=0x2]
. . .
```

Depending on the behavior of your software and the peer, you may have another opportunity to authenticate, or the connection may drop.

Checking authentication credentials is straightforward for PPP software that only supports one set of credentials. Just verify that authentication is active and that the appropriate software configuration files or windows have the correct information. The situation is more complex with software that maintains authentication credential tables. PPP-2.3 has two tables, each for different authentication protocols. The table format enables PPP-2.3 to act as an authenticator server, an authenticating client, or both.

As authenticator, one potential PPP-2.3 error is missing CHAP or PAP authentication names. If it can't locate a secret corresponding to its peer's name, PPP-2.3 can't validate credentials its peer submits. Consequently, PPP either never starts or terminates prematurely after an authentication failure. Consider a computer with the hostname myhost that has the CHAP name hostaname. A table of CHAP credentials is as follows:

```
root# cat /etc/ppp/chap-secrets
# Secrets for authentication using CHAP
# client      server      secret             IP addresses
hostbname     hostaname   "hostb-secret"          *
root#
```

In the authenticator role, hostaname must appear in the server column. This name identifies valid CHAP names and the corresponding CHAP keys a peer may use. The hostxname string in the following pppd command is an error; this string should be hostaname instead:

```
root# /usr/sbin/pppd debug /dev/ttyS0 38400 name hostxname require-chap
pppd: peer authentication required but no authentication files available
root#
```

A peer responding to an authentication challenge includes its own CHAP name. This name must appear in the client column of the chap-secrets file. If the CHAP name is missing, another error occurs. If the peer claims its CHAP name to be hostxname, instead of hostbname, the following error occurs:

```
Nov 17 22:52:43 myhost pppd[355]: ChapReceiveResponse: received name field:
hostxname
Nov 17 22:52:43 myhost pppd[355]: No CHAP secret found for authenticating
hostxname
Nov 17 22:52:43 myhost pppd[355]: sent [CHAP Failure id=0x1 "I don't like
you.  Go 'way."]
```

The authenticating client role for PPP-2.3 operates differently. PPP-2.3 can start without error, even if no authentication credentials are available. But without credentials, PPP-2.3 refuses to authenticate itself, if the peer asks. This defers the PPP connection failure until the peer requests authentication options in LCP. Additional details about how to configure PPP-2.3 as an authenticating client appear in Chapter 12.

Network Control Protocol Problems

The NCP establishes one or more network layer protocols to use with a connection. At least one network layer protocol is required for a PPP connection to be useful. NCP problems, if any, occur after LCP and authentication succeeds. The usual symptom of an NCP problem is that PPP reports failures establishing one or more network layer protocols. The PPP connection may terminate.

PPP connections that support networks for PCs are more prone to NCP errors simply because they may need several different network layer protocols; Windows NT/98 supports NetBEUI, TCP/IP, and IPX/SPX, for example.

If your PPP software requests a network layer protocol the peer doesn't recognize, an error results. PPP may ignore the error or terminate the connection. If Windows 98 is unable to negotiate any protocol, you will see the following:

```
Dial-Up Networking could not negotiate a compatible set of network protocols
you specified in the Server Type settings.  Check your network configuration
in the Control Panel then try the connection again.
```

Other PPP products may report:

```
Login Failed: Protocol Rejected
```

Unfortunately, error messages are often not specific enough to isolate the exact problem. Here is an error indication from a log file:

```
Nov 19 22:38:42 myhost pppd[567]: rcvd [proto=0x802b] 01 04 00 12 02 08 02 6f
6f 84 64 80 03 06 00 02 03 00
Nov 19 22:38:42 myhost pppd[567]: Unknown protocol (0x802b) received
Nov 19 22:38:42 myhost pppd[567]: sent [LCP ProtRej id=0x6 80 2b 01 04 00 12
02 08 02 6f 6f 84 64 80 03 06 00 02 03 00]
 . . .
Nov 19 22:38:47 myhost pppd[567]: rcvd [LCP TermReq id=0x2]
 . . .
```

The specific problem here is that **myhost** failed to recognize the protocol (0x802b) the peer requested. This value corresponds to the IPX Control Protocol (see Appendix A, *PPP Assigned Numbers*). The reply by **myhost** is an LCP protocol reject. Unfortunately, this rejection was unacceptable to the peer, which eventually sent an **LCP TermReq** to disconnect PPP.

To prevent NCP protocol rejects, you must disable all attempts to establish networking protocols the PPP peer doesn't understand. Connections to the Internet require only TCP/IP. Private network may require other networking protocols, but you should enable only the protocols you need, and only if the PPP peer supports them.

Internet Protocol Control Protocol Problems

IPCP is a specific NCP for establishing TCP/IP and TCP/IP parameters. It negotiates IP addresses and VJ compression. Establishing IP addresses is critical since communication is impossible without them. This is also a source of potential problems:

- PPP fails to acquire either local or remote IP addresses. TCP/IP remains inoperative or the connection terminates.

- One endpoint refuses to accept either the local or remote IP address the peer wants.

In order to troubleshoot IP address negotiation failures, you need to understand which endpoint is responsible for setting the IP addresses at ends of the connection. Either endpoint may set one or both IP addresses. For connections to the Internet, the ISP usually sets both endpoint addresses. These addresses are usually nonnegotiable.

Unresolved null IP address

When IPCP asks the PPP peer to provide IP addresses, the peer may have none to provide. Consider a computer, myhost, that accepts incoming dial-in PPP calls. This computer behaves as many ISP dial-in PPP servers do. The peer requests myhost to provide it local address. This activity appears as follows:

```
Nov 24 02:44:10 myhost pppd[721]: rcvd [IPCP ConfReq id=0x0 <compress VJ 03
00> <addr 0.0.0.0>]
Nov 24 02:44:10 myhost pppd[721]: sent [IPCP ConfRej id=0x0 <addr 0.0.0.0>]
. . .
Nov 24 02:44:10 myhost pppd[721]: rcvd [IPCP ConfReq id=0x1 <compress VJ 03
00>]
Nov 24 02:44:10 myhost pppd[721]: sent [IPCP ConfAck id=0x1 <compress VJ 03
00>]
. . .
Nov 24 02:44:10 myhost pppd[721]: ipcp: up
Nov 24 02:44:10 myhost pppd[721]: Could not determine remote IP address
Nov 24 02:44:10 myhost pppd[721]: ipcp: down
Nov 24 02:44:10 myhost pppd[721]: sent [IPCP TermReq id=0x2]
```

myhost receives an IPCP ConfReq with a null IP address, 0.0.0.0. This special address indicates myhost should reply with a real IP address in a IPCP ConfNak. Since myhost has no information, it replies with IPCP ConfRej instead. Next, the peer no longer requests an IP address at all. Later, myhost discovers there is no address for the peer end of the PPP connection, and TCP/IP terminates.

Resolving missing IP addresses requires configuring PPP software with the missing information, at either end of the connection.

Some PPP products can negotiate and set an address only at the local end of their connection. These products can't set the IP address of their peer. If only one IP address setting is available in a configuration window, it would be for the local end of the PPP connection.

Full functionality PPP software, such as PPP-2.3, can negotiate IP addresses for either or both ends of a PPP connection. PPP-2.3 offers the local-addr:remoteaddr option to set IP addresses:

```
user$ #                     device    speed local addr :remote addr
user$ /usr/sbin/pppd debug /dev/ttyS0 38400 172.16.0.65:172.16.0.193 ...
```

Since a connection requires only two IP addresses, conflicts arise if both PPP endpoints have independent notions of their local and remote IP addresses. Such conflicts can cause an IPCP negotiation failure. Therefore, the safest setup strategy is to configure no more than two IP addresses among two endpoints.

Nonnegotiable IP address conflict

Another problem case occurs when one endpoint requests an IP address that is unacceptable to the peer. If this endpoint refuses to compromise, no negotiation agreement is possible, and the connection may drop. An `IPCP ConfReq` and `IPCP ConfNak` negotiation loop may appear in PPP traces, since one endpoint refuses to change its IP address to a value acceptable to its peer:

```
Nov 24 03:57:27 myhost pppd[852]: rcvd [IPCP ConfReq id=0x1 <addr
172.16.0.193> <compress VJ 0f 01>]
Nov 24 03:57:27 myhost pppd[852]: sent [IPCP ConfNak id=0x1 <addr
172.16.0.194>]
. . .
Nov 24 03:57:27 myhost pppd[852]: rcvd [IPCP ConfReq id=0x5 <addr
172.16.0.193> <compress VJ 0f 01>]
Nov 24 03:57:27 myhost pppd[852]: sent [IPCP ConfNak id=0x5 <addr
172.16.0.194>]
. . .
Nov 24 03:57:27 myhost pppd[852]: rcvd [IPCP ConfReq id=0x6 <addr
172.16.0.193> <compress VJ 0f 01>]
Nov 24 03:57:27 myhost pppd[852]: sent [IPCP ConfRej id=0x6 <addr
172.16.0.193>]
. . .
```

Here, `myhost` wants its peer to use IP address 172.16.0.194. However, the peer insists on 172.16.0.193 instead. A `IPCP ConfRej` occurs after five negotiation attempts, which later terminates the PPP connection.

If two endpoints disagree about an IP address, simply revise their IP address configurations to agree. Alternatively, you can configure one endpoint to compromise during IP address negotiations or configure one endpoint to learn IP addresses from its peer. It's not always clear whether a set IP address is negotiable.

With PPP-2.3, IP address settings are nonnegotiable, unless additional options specify otherwise:

```
user$ #                         device    speed local addr :remote addr
user$ /usr/sbin/pppd debug /dev/ttyS0 38400 172.16.0.65:172.16.0.193 \
ipcp-accept-local ipcp-accept-remote . . .
```

The `ipcp-accept-remote` option lets the peer negotiate an IP address different from the remote address in the command line. Similarly, `ipcp-accept-local` lets the peer set the local address to something else. If you have no IP address information, use:

```
user$ /usr/sbin/pppd debug /dev/ttyS0 38400 noipdefault
```

The `noipdefault` option indicates there is no default local address. The peer must establish it. The absence of a remote address means the peer must establish this too.

Bad IP addresses

IPCP can happily negotiate any IP address, including invalid ones. As long as both endpoints agree, the connection succeeds.

If an IP address is inappropriate or incompatible with the network infrastructure, the integrity of an active PPP connection remains unaffected. However, the connection simply won't carry traffic useful for users. A bad IP address is really a TCP/IP problem, rather than a PPP problem.

Compression Control Protocol Problems

PPP optionally supports CCP, which enables negotiations for data compression. For data compression to be active, both endpoints must understand CCP and agree on a compression algorithm. If either fails, PPP communications continue without data compression.

CCP transactions can appear in the PPP log files. The `CCP ConfReq` requestor wishes to decompress the traffic it receives, according to the algorithm in the request. A peer that doesn't understand CCP simply rejects it:

```
Nov 19 22:38:21 myhost pppd[567]: sent [CCP ConfReq id=0x1 <bsd v1 12>]
. . .
Nov 19 22:38:21 myhost pppd[567]: rcvd [LCP ProtRej id=0x1 80 fd 80 fd 01 01
00 07 15]
Nov 19 22:38:21 myhost pppd[567]: lcp_rprotrej.
Nov 19 22:38:21 myhost pppd[567]: lcp_rprotrej: Rcvd Protocol-Reject packet
for 80fd!
. . .
```

Here, `myhost` sends a CCP request with `bsd v1 12` as the compression algorithm. The peer responds, causing a `protocol-reject packet for 80fd!` error. The 80fd is the protocol number for CCP.

In another failure scenario, both endpoints understand CCP, but don't share any compression algorithms in common. Additional negotiations occur, but with CCP configure requests and rejects:

```
Jan  4 19:04:49 myhost pppd[1398]: rcvd [CCP ConfReq id=0x1 < 12 06 00 00 00
01> < 11 05 00 01 04>]
Jan  4 19:04:49 myhost pppd[1398]: sent [CCP ConfRej id=0x1 < 12 06 00 00 00
01> < 11 05 00 01 04>]
. . .
Jan  4 19:04:49 myhost pppd[1398]: rcvd [CCP ConfReq id=0x2]
Jan  4 19:04:49 myhost pppd[1398]: sent [CCP ConfAck id=0x2]
. . .
```

```
Jan  4 19:04:49 myhost pppd[1398]: rcvd [CCP TermReq id=0x3]
Jan  4 19:04:49 myhost pppd[1398]: fsm_rtermreq(CCP): Rcvd id 3.
Jan  4 19:04:49 myhost pppd[1398]: CCP terminated at peer's request
Jan  4 19:04:49 myhost pppd[1398]: sent [CCP TermAck id=0x3]
 . . .
```

Here, a Windows 98 peer wants compression with either Microsoft PPC (0x12) or Stac LZS (0x11). Eventually, both endpoints agree to the "null" compression algorithm. Later, CCP terminates, and PPP continues without data compression.

When CCP results in no compression algorithm agreements, CCP must terminate. If a PPP implementation fails to follow the correct termination sequence, negotiation loops can result. Consequently, the PPP connection may fail. One incorrect sequence, for example, is responding to a CCPConfReq with a CCP_TermReq. The problem is that CCP_TermReq requires CCP to be active, and not in the negotiating state.

For endless CCP negotiations, one resolution is to disable CCP entirely. You can achieve this with PPP-2.3 using the noccp option:

```
user$ /usr/sbin/pppd debug /dev/ttyS0 38400 noccp
```

Another notable problem is PPP connection termination that immediately follows any form of CCP rejection. In this situation, one of the PPP endpoints requires mandatory use of the PPP compressed datagram feature. WinNT 4.0 exhibits this behavior when RAS requires Microsoft encryption.

Compatibility Problems

PPP has evolved since the release of its early specification document, RFC-1171. Since then, several changes have been made that can create compatibility problems between older and current PPP software. Basic PPP connection management is unchanged since its inception. However, there are several important IPCP revisions:

- The current procedure for negotiating IP address replaces an older procedure.

- Several ambiguities and errors were corrected for negotiating Van Jacobson compression.

Of the two, the most critical compatibility item is negotiating IP addresses. Since it's an optional capability, VJ compression is less critical. If VJ compression incompatibility does cause a problem, you can disable it.

IP addresses

Negotiating IP addresses with early IPCP requires sending configure requests with configuration option type 1 (see Chapter 3 and RFC-1172). This is the "IP addresses" option. The sender is notifying its peer of the local and remote IP addresses it desires. Both PPP endpoints exchange this notification and await feedback. In total, there are initially up to four outstanding IP addresses. IPCP negotiations must continue until the PPP endpoints agree to two IP addresses.

Software that still understands the "IP addresses" IPCP option may show the following in the PPP log files:

```
Nov 24 03:37:17 myhost pppd[761]: rcvd [IPCP ConfReq id=0x29 <addrs
172.16.0.193 172.16.0.69> <compress VJ 0f 01>]
```

The newer IPCP configuration option type 3, IP address (see RFC-1332), supersedes option type 1. As this singular name implies, a PPP endpoint notifies only its peer about the local IP address it desires. Both endpoints still exchange this option. Thus, initial IPCP negotiations begin with two IP addresses, rather than the earlier four. This better insures that both endpoints can reach agreements about IP addresses.

As shown in PPP log files, the IP address IPCP option appears as follows:

```
Nov 24 03:37:17 myhost pppd[761]: rcvd [IPCP ConfReq id=0x26 <compress VJ 0f
01> <addr 172.16.0.193>]
```

An incompatibility results if one endpoint understands only the newer IP address option while its peer understands only the older IP addresses option. Whenever an endpoint fails to understand an IPCP option, it must respond with an IPCP configure reject:

```
Nov 26 05:25:32 myhost pppd[1062]. rcvd [IPCP ConfReq id=0x52 <compress VJ 0f
01> < 03 06 ac 10 00 c1>]
Nov 26 05:25:32 myhost pppd[1062]. sent [IPCP ConfRej id=0x52 < 03 06 ac 10
00 c1>]
    . . .
```

Here, myhost failed to understand the newer IPCP type 3, length 6 (03 06) option. It may even complain about receiving IPCP configuration option 3. This alone may not result in a fatal error. The peer may support backward compatibility and later negotiate using the older IP addresses option. If not, IP address negotiations fail.

If you have IP address negotiation incompatibilities, the best resolution is to upgrade all PPP software to versions that understand the current IPCP option type 3. Another alternative is to install software with backward compatibility. The former is preferable since the use of the old IP addresses option is deprecated.

Van Jacobson compression

Requests for Van Jacobson compression appear in IPCP packets as *IP compression protocol* option type 2. Van Jacobson is only one of many possible IP compression protocols. Thus, the IP compression protocol option includes additional fields that identify VJ and VJ-specific parameters (see Chapter 3).

The standard protocol number for VJ is 0x002d as it appears in RFC-1332. However, an earlier RFC-1172 indicates this number to be 0x0037. The information in RFC-1172 is believed to be a typographical error. Unfortunately, there may exist PPP software that uses different IP compression protocol numbers to refer to the same VJ protocol. Another area of ambiguity relates to VJ-specific compression parameters. The early RFC-1172 implies that you can negotiate VJ with a "short" four-octet configuration option field within IPCP. This only allows requesting the VJ protocol, without parameters. RFC-1332 later corrects this by requiring a length six configuration option. The length increase accommodates VJ parameters `max-slot-id` and `comp-slot-id`. As a result of the initial ambiguity, some PPP software may negotiate with the short VJ configuration option, while others may use the `regular-length` option.

Three VJ negotiation permutations can occur. The method that is the current standard appears as:

```
Nov 19 22:31:23 myhost pppd[554]: rcvd [IPCP ConfReq id=0x0 <compress VJ 03
00> <addr 0.0.0.0>]
```

`Compress` is the name corresponding to IPCP configure option 2. VJ is a symbolic name for the number 0x002d. The `max-slot-id` and `comp-slot-id` values follow. If `myhost` receives an IPCP configure request with the incorrect VJ protocol number 0x0037 and recognizes it, the following may appear in the PPP log files:

```
Nov 26 05:17:10 myhost pppd[1026]: rcvd [IPCP ConfReq id=0x48 <compress old-
VJ> <addr 0.0.0.0>]
```

The preceding `old-VJ` request is also a short request. This is exactly consistent with RFC-1172. It's also possible to receive a short request that uses an up-to-date VJ protocol number. A PPP endpoint that chooses to accept the short VJ option assumes 0x0f and 0x01 as the values for `max-slot-id` and `comp-slot-id`, respectively.

In the event of an incompatibility, the PPP endpoint that receives a VJ compression request it can't understand must return a `IPCP ConfRej`:

```
Nov 27 20:25:10 myhost pppd[1175]: rcvd [IPCP ConfReq id=0x60 <compress 0x37>
<addr 0.0.0.0>]
Nov 27 20:25:10 myhost pppd[1175]: sent [IPCP ConfRej id=0x60 <compress 0x37>]
. . .
```

Here, `myhost` receives the short VJ option with the incorrect VJ protocol number, 0x0037. There is no symbolic interpretation for 0x37 because `myhost` doesn't recognize this number. A peer with VJ backward compatibility may try other VJ compression numbers. If all attempts fail, VJ compression isn't used.

You can best resolve VJ compression compatibility problems by upgrading your PPP software to releases that comply with current standards. Alternatively, use software offering backward compatibility. PPP-2.3 and others automatically recognize old forms of VJ. With Performance Systems PPP, backward compatibility requires the explicit `rfc1172-vj` or `rfc1172-typo-vj` options. This enables recognition of the short VJ option with the current or incorrect VJ protocol number, respectively.

Bugs

Any software with any degree of complexity inevitably has programming errors, defects, or bugs. PPP software is no exception. PPP is already complex and extensible with additional, complex features. It's unfortunate that a number of popular PPP software products have their share of defects.

PPP bugs tend to be difficult to isolate and diagnose. You need a close understanding of PPP to identify errors. Few problems occur when two PPP endpoints use the same software. Bugs, if any, tend to become evident when two different PPP products must communicate. Some bugs are serious enough to cause connection failures.

In the event of a PPP software bug, the solutions available to you are:

- Install patches and software upgrades, if available. Otherwise, complain to the software vendor regarding the bug.

- Apply a workaround, if possible. This includes disabling the affected PPP features.

- Replace the offending software with a competing product that is more robust and reliable.

- If you have PPP software that includes source code, such as PPP-2.3, you might try to repair the bug yourself. Please let the software authors know too.

It's impossible to anticipate all possible PPP software bugs. A few examples of some interesting ones are included in this chapter.

Asyncmap default error

A PPP endpoint must maintain a transmitter asynchronous control character map. This map determines the character codes to "escape" prior to transmission through a serial connection. For asynchronous RS-232 serial connections, the PPP default clearly requires endpoints to send all ASCII control characters in escaped format. However, LCP negotiations can later change this.

Some PPP software incorrectly assumes it can send ASCII control characters in plain form, without negotiating this setting. Other implementations incorrectly assume that asyncmap is consistent for both communications directions, regardless of negotiations. These bad assumptions cause compatibility problems with PPP software that correctly implements the PPP asyncmap rules.

The symptoms of asyncmap default errors are deafness behaviors on the part of one or both endpoints. Complaints about bad PPP frames or unescaped characters are also possible. These symptoms occur after successful LCP negotiations. Here's an example of deafness during the PPP authentication state:

```
Apr 26 03:46:30 myhost pppd[1678]: sent [LCP ConfReq id=0x1 <magic
0x600cb70a> <pcomp> <accomp>]
Apr 26 03:46:31 myhost pppd[1678]: rcvd [LCP ConfAck id=0x1 <magic
0x600cb70a> <pcomp> <accomp>]
Apr 26 03:46:31 myhost pppd[1678]: rcvd [LCP ConfReq id=0x1 <mru 1500>
<asyncmap 0xa0000> <auth pap> <pcomp> <accomp>]
Apr 26 03:46:31 myhost pppd[1678]: sent [LCP ConfAck id=0x1 <mru 1500>
<asyncmap 0xa0000> <auth pap> <pcomp> <accomp>]
Apr 26 03:46:31 myhost pppd[1678]: sent [PAP AuthReq id=0x1 user="myname"
password="mypass"]
Apr 26 03:46:34 myhost pppd[1678]: sent [PAP AuthReq id=0x2 user="myname"
password="mypass"]
Apr 26 03:46:37 myhost pppd[1678]: sent [PAP AuthReq id=0x3 user="myname"
password="mypass"]
Apr 26 03:46:40 myhost pppd[1678]: sent [PAP AuthReq id=0x4 user="myname"
password="mypass"]
. . .
Apr 26 03:47:02 myhost pppd[1678]: No response to PAP authenticate-requests
```

Either myhost ignored and discarded the authentication result, or the peer ignored the authentication request.

Deafness during IPCP may appear as follows, for a peer that ignores the IPCP ConfAck:

```
Apr 26 10:09:45 myhost pppd[2189]: rcvd [IPCP ConfReq id=0x2 <addr
192.168.1.65> <compress VJ 0f 01>]
Apr 26 10:09:45 myhost pppd[2189]: sent [IPCP ConfAck id=0x2 <addr
192.168.1.65> <compress VJ 0f 01>]
Apr 26 10:09:48 myhost pppd[2189]: rcvd [IPCP ConfReq id=0x3 <addr
192.168.1.65> <compress VJ 0f 01>]
Apr 26 10:09:48 myhost pppd[2189]: sent [IPCP ConfAck id=0x3 <addr
192.168.1.65> <compress VJ 0f 01>]
Apr 26 10:09:51 myhost pppd[2189]: rcvd [IPCP ConfReq id=0x4 <addr
192.168.1.65> <compress VJ 0f 01>]
Apr 26 10:09:51 myhost pppd[2189]: sent [IPCP ConfAck id=0x4 <addr
192.168.1.65> <compress VJ 0f 01>]
. . .
```

The PPP endpoint that receives PPP frames, and discards them due to asyncmap problems, may show the following:

```
00:26:43 003048 ipdptp1 RECEIVE {Unescaped characters} PPP ASYNC 133 Octets
IP_PROTO
00:26:44 003049 ipdptp1 RECEIVE {Unescaped characters} PPP ASYNC 133 Octets
IP_PROTO
00:26:45 003050 ipdptp1 RECEIVE {Unescaped characters} PPP ASYNC 133 Octets
IP_PROTO
```

The result of asyncmap bugs include endless negotiation loops, or a PPP connection that terminates and fails.

There are several possible workarounds for this problem. You can arrange one PPP endpoint to explicitly negotiate an asyncmap of 0xffffffff, or another value, with the faulty peer. In more severe cases, try to force the use of the PPP default asyncmap for both directions of a PPP connection. Here are specific suggestions for PPP-2.3:

asyncmap ffffffff

This causes an explicit request for the PPP default asyncmap, just in case the peer may have wrong ideas about the default if the PPP asyncmap request is absent.

asyncmap 0

If the peer blindly, and incorrectly, assumes you negotiate asyncmap 0, this request should force consistency between the endpoints.

asyncmap a0000

This matches the asyncmap request the peer sent, in case the peer incorrectly assumes that asyncmap must be consistent for both PPP communications directions.

default-asyncmap

This disables and rejects all asyncmap negotiations. The PPP endpoints must use the PPP default asyncmap of ffffffff for both communication directions.

Hopefully, these can establish consistent PPP asyncmap settings at both ends of a connection. By explicitly negotiating asyncmap, the faulty PPP endpoint no longer has to make incorrect assumptions about the asyncmap setting.

Failure to recognize valid PPP frames

There are several ways to encode PPP frames, even for frames with identical content. These differences exist because an endpoint can send character codes above 32 in "escaped" format. Unfortunately, if certain character codes are escaped, faulty PPP software may fail to recognize valid PPP frames.

PPP-2.3 offers the escape option for pppd. Enabling this feature can trigger problems with faulty peers. Suppose we flag character code 0xff to be escaped, as in:

```
user$ /usr/sbin/pppd debug /dev/ttyS0 escape ff . . .
```

All 0xff characters in a PPP frame become 0x7d 0xdf. A faulty receiver may expect 0xff literally but ignore its escaped equivalent in the address field of a full PPP frame. The receiver then discards the frame. It may report "Missed all stations," other obscure messages, or no error at all. Needless to say, the connection fails.

The way to resolve this problem is to avoid escaping noncontrol characters in PPP frames. To do this, all hardware and software components that form the serial connection between two endpoints must transparently pass all noncontrol character codes. If any component alters noncontrol character codes, you must reconfigure it.

Magic numbers, improper use

Here is a record of a problem that causes a connection to fail consistently, after 20 minutes:

```
PPP[8021] RCV CONFACK ID=02 LEN=16 IPCP(002D0F01) IPADDR(C0A83E6F)
PPP[8021] state = opened
PPP[C021] RCV ECHOREQ ID=1C LEN=8 data B6 04 00 00
PPP[C021] SND ECHOREP ID=1C LEN=8 data B6 04 00 00

 . . .
PPP[C021] SND ECHOREP ID=2D LEN=8 data B6 04 00 00
PPP[C021] RCV ECHOREQ ID=2E LEN=8 data B6 04 00 00
PPP[C021] SND ECHOREP ID=2E LEN=8 data B6 04 00 00
PPP[C021] RCV ECHOREQ ID=2F LEN=8 data B6 04 00 00
PPP[C021] SND ECHOREP ID=2F LEN=8 data B6 04 00 00
PPP[C021] RCV TERMREQ ID=30 LEN=4
PPP[C021] SND TERMACK ID=30 LEN=4
PPP[C021] state = stopping
PPP[C021] state = stopped
```

Here, we receive an LCP echo request periodically from the peer to verify that the PPP connection is still active. There is an echo reply response to all of them. Mysteriously, a terminate request occurs after the 21st response.

This PPP connection terminates because of invalid use of magic numbers. PPP requires each endpoint to identify itself with its own magic number in echo request and response LCP packets. As shown previously, the echo reply uses its peer's magic number, B6 04 00 00, rather than its own.

One workaround for this problem is to avoid it. Configure all PPP endpoints not to send LCP echo requests and anything else with magic numbers. Alternatively, disable the magic number option. If this isn't feasible, then the PPP software at the misbehaving endpoint requires a patch, upgrade, or replacement.

PPP options for the wrong communications direction

LCP negotiations establish options independently for each direction of a PPP connection. This is also true for the TCP/IP settings IPCP establishes. When an endpoint sends a request for Van Jacobson compression, for example, it indicates its ability to receive VJ-compressed PPP frames. This endpoint may not send VJ compressed frames unless its peer requests it.

Some PPP software incorrectly assumes that the options for its receiving direction automatically apply for its transmitting direction as well. Consider this VJ compression request sequence:

```
Nov 30 12:46:14 myhost pppd[1417]: sent [IPCP ConfReq id=0x1 <addr
172.16.0.193>]
Nov 30 12:46:14 myhost pppd[1417]: rcvd [IPCP ConfAck id=0x1 <addr
172.16.0.193>]
. . .
Nov 30 12:46:14 myhost pppd[1417]: rcvd [IPCP ConfReq id=0x8b <compress VJ 0f
01> <addr 172.16.0.194>]
Nov 30 12:46:14 myhost pppd[1417]: sent [IPCP ConfAck id=0x8b <compress VJ 0f
01> <addr 172.16.0.194>]
. . .
```

Here, myhost may send VJ-compressed PPP frames because the peer requests it. The peer doesn't have the same privilege because myhost didn't indicate its ability to receive VJ-compressed PPP frames. If the PPP peer is faulty and myhost receives VJ-compressed PPP frames anyway, myhost must discard it. You may see errors resembling the following:

```
Nov 30 13:13:40 myhost vmunix: VJU rejected
Nov 30 13:13:40 myhost vmunix: VJC rejected
Nov 30 13:13:40 myhost vmunix: VJU rejected
Nov 30 13:13:43 myhost last message repeated 2 times
Nov 30 13:13:46 myhost vmunix: VJC rejected
```

Unfortunately, the faulty peer doesn't receive indications about its error. The connection remains up but is unusable.

It's obvious that the peer requires a software patch, upgrade, or replacement. One workaround is to disable all use of VJ and all attempts to negotiate it. Windows NT/98 includes a checkbox Use IP header compression to control VJ compression. Performance Systems PPP has the novjcomp option, Solaris PPP requires ipcp_compression off, and PPP-2.3 has the novj option.

Checking TCP/IP

The TCP/IP family of protocols carry data from an originating source to a final recipient. In contrast, PPP is for communications through a serial connection and relays data through only one network hop. TCP/IP settings determine when data traveling through a PPP connection can reach its destination.

TCP/IP problems are often related to routing. In other words, one or more intermediate recipients of IP datagrams fail to forward them correctly towards their destination. Some symptoms of TCP/IP faults are:

- You can't communicate with any destination IP address; yet the PPP connection is up.

- You can only communicate with the IP address of the PPP peer. Applications such as web browsers, Telnet, FTP, and others function but only with this IP address.

Figure 15-3 illustrates your responsibility for TCP/IP routing. This figure shows a common network architecture that uses PPP connections for dial-in. Dial-in servers relay data between the connection and a LAN network interface. A PPP user can't successfully communicate with a destination site if any of the six routing paths fail.

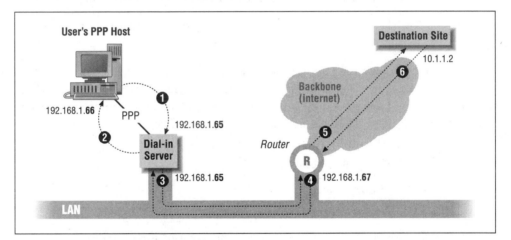

Figure 15-3. Dial-up service and its TCP/IP routes

The IP datagrams that follow paths 1, 3, and 5 have destination IP addresses representing the remote Internet site. In contrast, IP datagrams following paths 6, 4, and 2 have destination IP addresses representing the PPP user. When troubleshooting, begin with the routes closest to the PPP user and work your way towards the Internet.

Diagnostic Tools

Almost every network node supporting TCP/IP includes basic diagnostic utilities. The most common and useful tools include `ping` and `traceroute`. In addition, applications such as Telnet can also be useful for troubleshooting. Figure 15-4 illustrates how each utility behaves for troubleshooting purposes.

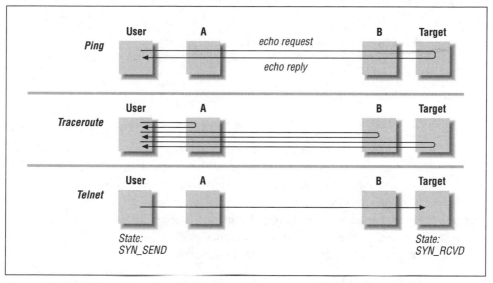

Figure 15-4. TCP/IP diagnostic utilities: ping, traceroute, and Telnet

The `ping` utility generates TCP/IP ICMP echo requests and awaits "echo replies." Don't confuse this with LCP echo requests and replies, which only test connections. `ping` can check the round-trip paths to a destination IP address anywhere in the network. When it succeeds, every routing hop to and from the destination is working. This includes User to A, A to B, B to Destination, Destination to B, etc. A ping error indicates a problem to the destination. However, no response indicates faults at the destination or somewhere in the return path:

```
user$ ping 192.168.2.12          # A successful ping
192.168.2.12 is alive
user$ ping 10.1.1.2              # A problem "to" the destination
ICMP Net Unreachable from gateway 192.168.1.67 (192.168.1.67)
 for icmp from myhost (192.168.1.66) to 10.1.1.2
^C
user$                            # A problem at the destination,
user$ ping 192.168.13.13         # or its return path
no answer from 192.168.13.13
user$
```

`ping` is only indirectly useful for hop-by-hop troubleshooting. Be careful to understand that a successful ping from User to A, and then A to Destination, doesn't imply that User to Destination works. In each case, the combination of originating and destination IP addresses are different.

The `traceroute` utility sends UDP packet probes, which elicit responses from intermediate network nodes in the path to a destination IP address. This helps isolate a routing problem, particularly in cases of missing returning routes. A

response indicates the round-trip route from an originating node up to the report-
ing node is functioning.

```
user$ traceroute -n prep.ai.mit.edu
traceroute to prep.ai.mit.edu (18.159.0.42), 30 hops max, 40 byte packets
 1  128.180.1.254  2 ms  2 ms  2 ms
. . .
14  18.168.0.11  30 ms  40 ms  20 ms
15  18.159.0.42  59 ms  47 ms  130 ms
```

Both `ping` and `traceroute` depend on round-trip routes to function in order for
you to receive diagnostic feedback. However, the Telnet program is useful for testing one way routes to a destination IP address. Normally, this is an application for
signing on to a remote Internet server. If Telnet functions normally, no problem
exists to diagnose. However, if you don't receive a `connection established` or
`connection refused` response, the destination server administrator can determine if the server actually receives the Telnet connect request. We assume the
destination is prepared to accept the Telnet connection.

```
user$ telnet 10.1.1.2
Trying 10.1.1.2...
telnet: Unable to connect to remote host: Connection timed out
user$
```

Let's assume Telnet originates at 192.168.1.66, representing the PPP user. Before
the `connection timed out` error occurs, the administrator for 10.1.1.2 can check
the TCP/IP network connection status:

```
user$ netstat -an
Active Internet connections (including servers)
Proto Recv-Q Send-Q  Local Address      Foreign Address       (state)
tcp        0      0  10.1.1.2.23        192.168.1.66.32778    SYN_RCVD
. . .
```

This server reports it is receiving a Telnet request on port 23 from the user's IP
address. This is a half-open connection, as the `SYN_RCVD` state indicates. The fact
that the server receives the request indicates successful one way routing from the
user to the destination. However, the connection remains half-open because
acknowledgments aren't returning to the user. Eventually, after a time-out interval
on the order of one minute or more, the incomplete connection clears.

Another class of useful diagnostic tools are *protocol analyzers*, which are also
known as *sniffers*. They can monitor, capture, and interpret IP datagrams on a
LAN. Some can also watch PPP frames and the IP datagrams inside that traverse a
serial connection. Protocol analyzers are usually dedicated equipment. However,
Unix frequently offers protocol analyzer functions with `tcpdump`, `snoop`, `ether-
find`, or other utilities like them.

IP Forwarding Enabled?

A dial-in PPP server that receives IP datagrams for destination addresses other than its own must forward the datagrams. The server is really a router. It routes and forwards datagrams from one network interface to another. Communication servers and routers perform *IP forwarding* by default. However, IP forwarding is an explicit feature you must enable on general-purpose computers. If disabled, these servers silently discard IP datagrams that aren't destined to their own IP addresses. This may appear as a PPP failure.

IP forwarding is a setting in the network code in many operating systems. The procedure to enable it is operating system-specific. Chapter 7, *Dial-in PPP Setup*, describes how to enable IP forwarding for several dial-in PPP servers. A summary of these details is in Table 15-3.

Table 15-3. Enabling IP Forwarding

Operating System	How to Enable IP Forwarding
Linux	Set with: `echo "1" > /proc/sys/net/ipv4/ip_forward` Check with: *cat /proc/sys/net/ipv4/ip_forward*
Solaris	Set with: `ndd -set /dev/ip ip_forwarding 1` Check with: *ndd -get /dev/ip ip_forwarding*
Windows NT 4.0 Server	Set and check with: `Control panel` → `Networking` → `Protocols` → `TCP/IP` → `Routing` → `Enable IP Forwarding`

Verifying IP forwarding

A protocol analyzer can help you verify if IP forwarding is functioning. A dial-in PPP server must first have proper TCP/IP routing table entries set to forward IP datagrams. Also, the server itself must be able to ping its network neighbors.

When the user in Figure 15-3 uses **ping**, her IP datagrams should appear on the LAN, even if the **ping** goes unanswered. A LAN protocol analyzer utility shows this:

```
root# tcpdump -n -i eth0 icmp
tcpdump: listening on eth0
12:09:55.519037 192.168.1.66 > 10.1.1.2: icmp: echo request
. . .
```

Here, the dial-in PPP server is forwarding IP datagrams from the PPP connection to the LAN. Be careful when using **tcpdump** and other equivalent utilities on the dial-in PPP server itself; some may have limitations when tracing IP datagrams its own LAN network interface transmits.

Routing Problems with the PPP Connection

TCP/IP routing tables at both PPP endpoints must reference the IP addresses of their PPP connection. Without the proper references, IP datagrams would never traverse a PPP connection.

PPP user (path 1)

Most PPP users have a single PPP connection for all their network communications. This requires a user to route all outgoing IP datagrams through path 1 in Figure 15-3. A computer that behaves this way must have a concept of a default route. Chapter 9, *Routing to PPP Connections*, includes details for arranging this route.

Consider a PPP user's computer with the following PPP connection. On Linux, the PPP network interface configuration resembles:

```
user$ /sbin/ifconfig -a
. . .
ppp0      Link encap:Point-to-Point Protocol
          inet addr:192.168.1.66  P-t-P:192.168.1.65  Mask:255.255.255.224
. . .
```

The correct default route in the routing table should resemble:

```
user$ route -n
Kernel IP routing table
Destination     Gateway         Genmask          Flags Metric Ref    Use Iface
192.168.1.65    0.0.0.0         255.255.255.255 UH    0      0        2 ppp0
127.0.0.0       0.0.0.0         255.0.0.0        U     0      0        3 lo
0.0.0.0         192.168.1.65    0.0.0.0          UG    0      0        0 ppp0
user$
```

Output formats vary. Thus, 0.0.0.0 may appear as shown or as the string `default`. The `Gateway` address for the default route must be an endpoint of the PPP connection. If an IP address ambiguity exists because `ppp0` is an unnumbered interface, `ppp0` must appear in the `Iface` column. The default route `Genmask`, if it exists, is 0.0.0.0.

You can verify that PPP is carrying outgoing IP datagrams by generating some traffic to an Internet destination. The `ping` utility, at the PPP user's computer, is useful for this purpose:

```
user$ ping -s 10.1.1.2
```

The ping may not generate a response if there are problems with routes besides path 1 in Figure 15-3. However, you should still observe:

• Modem indicators should show outgoing traffic. In particular, note the send data indicator.

- PPP traffic statistics should increase. With PPP-2.3, the pppstats utility shows this. On Linux, ifconfig also shows traffic for a PPP network interface.

- Some PPP log files show IP datagrams at high debug levels. Solaris PPP can show the following, in /var/adm/log/asppp.log:

```
11:32:32 005697 ipdptp3 SEND PPP ASYNC 89 Octets IP_PROTO
11:32:33 005698 ipdptp3 SEND PPP ASYNC 89 Octets IP_PROTO
11:32:34 005699 ipdptp3 SEND PPP ASYNC 89 Octets IP_PROTO
```

- Some operating systems allow protocol analyzer utilities to trace IP datagrams through PPP network interfaces:

```
root# tcpdump -n -i ppp0 icmp
tcpdump: listening on ppp0
12:54:00.669037 192.168.1.66 > 10.1.1.2: icmp: echo request
12:54:00.669037 192.168.1.66 > 10.1.1.2: icmp: echo request
. . .
```

An indication of activity on the PPP connection confirms that path 1 of Figure 15-3 is functioning correctly. If communications with Internet destinations are still failing, the problem lies with the other routing paths.

Dial-in PPP server (path 2)

PPP users, by definition, are already neighbors of the dial-in PPP server. Thus, the server should already know how to route IP datagrams to the user's IP address. This is path 2 in Figure 15-3. No routing table configuration is necessary.*

Testing the dial-in server's route to the PPP user is straightforward. Consider a server that has the following PPP connection:

```
user$ /sbin/ifconfig -a
. . .
ppp0      Link encap:Point-to-Point Protocol
          inet addr:192.168.1.65  P-t-P:192.168.1.66  Mask:255.255.255.224
. . .
```

The IP address of the PPP user is 192.168.1.66. A ping to this address from the server should produce traffic through the PPP connection:

```
user$ ping -s 192.168.1.66
```

Modem indicators, traffic counts, and other monitoring tools should all show activity on the PPP connection, even if the ping produces no response.

---

* If the PPP connection is really a gateway to other networks, the dial-in PPP server requires additional routes for these networks.

Other items to check

After you verify TCP/IP routing, two-way communications between the PPP user and the dial-in server should succeed. This confirms paths 1 and 2 in Figure 15-3. If there are still problems, here are some additional areas to check:

- Make sure that both PPP endpoints have consistent notions of their IP address assignments. Sometimes, IPCP can succeed even though both endpoints don't achieve IP address agreements.

- If `ping` works, but Telnet, FTP, and other applications hang, there may be problems with VJ compression. Disable VJ at both PPP endpoints and try again.

Routing Problems with the LAN

Both the dial-in PPP server and router in Figure 15-3 must have routes that direct IP datagrams to each other, via the LAN. Improper or missing routes can cause failures for paths 3 and 4.

Dial-in PPP server (path 3)

A dial-in PPP server that doesn't know where to send IP datagrams for an Internet destination may cause unreachable errors, from a PPP user's point of view. Sometimes, users may observe time-outs or won't receive errors messages at all:

```
user$ ping 10.1.1.2
ICMP Host Unreachable from gateway 192.168.1.65
 for icmp from 192.168.1.66 to 10.1.1.2
^Cuser$
user$ telnet 10.1.1.2
Trying 10.1.1.2 ...
telnet: connect: Host is unreachable
telnet> quit
user$
```

These errors show that the dial-in server at 192.168.1.65 is missing routes for destination 10.1.1.2. In other words, path 3 is broken in Figure 15-3.

IP datagrams with destinations on the Internet must go from the server to the router. This requires the server to have routes referencing the router's IP address:

```
user$ route -n
Kernel IP routing table
Destination     Gateway         Genmask          Flags Metric Ref    Use Iface
. . .
0.0.0.0         192.168.1.67    0.0.0.0          UG    0      0        0 eth0
user$
```

This server can acquire routes with TCP/IP routing protocols, administrator configuration, or other means. Whatever the means, there must exist route entries for all accessible destination IP addresses. The routes don't necessarily have to be the 0.0.0.0 default route. Numerous network and subnet numbers can also appear in the `Destination` column, each with a different router in the `Gateway` column. These routes are in addition to others that handle IP datagrams going to the users' IP addresses.

A quick way to verify if the route to a router is functioning is to access an Internet site. When the dial-in PPP server attempts to use a neighboring router on a LAN, you should be able to observe the following:

- If the routing table includes `Ref` or `Use` columns, the numbers for appropriate routing entries that point to the router should increase.

- The dial-in PPP server learns the hardware MAC address for the router's network interface:

```
user$ arp -a
Address          HWtype  HWaddress          Flags Mask        Iface
192.168.1.67     ether   08:00:20:09:3D:A9  C     *           eth0
user$
```

- tcpdump or other protocol analyzers show IP datagrams on the LAN that has originating IP addresses either from the dial-in PPP server itself or from the PPP user.

Corrupted routes

A corrupted routing table might look like this:

```
user$ netstat -rn
Routing tables
Destination         Gateway           Flags   Refcnt  Use     Interf
127.0.0.1           127.0.0.1         UH      1       554     lo0
192.168.1.32        192.168.1.67      UGH     0       0       le0
192.168.1.64        192.168.1.67      UGH     0       0       le0
192.168.1.96        192.168.1.67      UGH     0       0       le0
192.168.1.128       192.168.1.67      UGH     0       0       le0
192.168.1.160       192.168.1.67      UGH     0       0       le0
. . .
```

Routes to IP subnets incorrectly became host-specific routes, as the H flag indicates. The 32 IP addresses for each of the original subnet route entries became a route to a single, reserved IP address. Some Unix platforms behave this way if they become confused about the subnet mask for a network number. In this case, the network number is the Class C, 192.168.1.0.

```
user$ ifconfig -a
le0: flags=63<UP,BROADCAST,NOTRAILERS,RUNNING>
        inet 192.168.1.65 netmask ffffffe0 broadcast 172.16.0.64
lo0: flags=49<UP,LOOPBACK,RUNNING>
        inet 127.0.0.1 netmask ff000000
ppp0: flags=10<POINTOPOINT>
```

```
        inet 192.168.1.65 --> 192.168.1.66 netmask ffffff00
user$
```

Note the inconsistency between the netmask settings for the `le0` and `ppp0` network interfaces. The one for `ppp0` is incorrect. It must be set to 0xfffffe0 to prevent this server from misinterpreting entries in its routing table. Not all dial-in PPP servers have this problem.

Router (path 4)

In addition to routes representing Internet destinations, the router in Figure 15-3 must also have routes to forward IP datagrams toward PPP users. This route is path 4 in Figure 15-3. If this path fails, PPP users can communicate only with the dial-in PPP server and other servers on the 192.168.1.64/27 LAN. Since the return path is broken, other destination IP addresses result in time-out errors.

What causes the router to relay IP datagrams into the dial-in server may be one of the following:

- Explicit routes with the IP addresses of PPP users as the `Destination` and the dial-in PPP servers IP address as the `Gateway`

- A Proxy ARP arrangement; the router believes PPP user IP addresses are its own network neighbors

You can test explicit routes to PPP users by originating IP datagrams on the router. The `ping` utility is useful for this purpose. If the routes work, the router learns the MAC address of the dial-in PPP server's LAN network interface. IP datagrams in transit to PPP users also appear on protocol analyzers attached to the LAN.

If the IP addresses for PPP users belong in the IP subnet shared by the router and the dial-in PPP server, Proxy ARP applies. This is the arrangement shown in Figure 15-3. When the router has IP datagrams for a PPP user, it broadcasts ARP packets on the LAN to determine the user's MAC address. Remember, the router assumes PPP users are its neighbors. It is the responsibility of the dial-in PPP server to respond with its own MAC address. You can verify this at the router, as follows:

```
user$ ping 172.16.0.65              # The dial-in PPP server
172.16.0.65 is alive
user$ arp 172.16.0.65               # MAC address of dial-in PPP server?
172.16.0.65 (172.16.0.65) at 8:0:20:9:3a:e2
user$ ping 172.16.0.67              # The PPP user
no answer from 172.16.0.67
user$ arp 172.16.0.67               # MAC address of PPP user?
172.16.0.67 (172.16.0.67) at 8:0:20:9:3a:e2
user$
```

If the command to determine the PPP user's MAC address returns "no entry," a fault exists with Proxy ARP at the PPP dial-in server. Chapter 8, *Network Architectures Incorporating PPP*, describes how to set up Proxy ARP.

Internet Routing

To complete all the paths between PPP users and Internet sites, the Internet in Figure 15-3 must have routes to all possible destination IP addresses. More importantly, explicit or wild-card routes must exist for destination IP addresses of PPP users. There may be a dozen or more intervening routers in paths 5 and 6, each with their own routing tables.

Dynamic routing protocols distribute routes for all but the smallest networks. These protocols, like any others, must be configured correctly. You must arrange Internet routing for all network numbers you assign for PPP connections. This procedure varies, but the basic idea requires you to coordinate with the administrators of the closest router that globally advertises network numbers. On the Internet, major service providers usually exchange routes with the Border Gateway Protocol.

traceroute can test routes to and from an Internet site. Each response from traceroute verifies round-trip paths to successive intermediate routers. From a PPP user perspective, a failed traceroute may show:

```
user$ traceroute -n prep.ai.mit.edu
traceroute to prep.ai.mit.edu (18.159.0.42), 30 hops max, 40 byte packets
 1  128.180.1.254   3 ms   2 ms   2 ms
 2  128.180.6.11    2 ms   3 ms   2 ms
 3  206.245.159.21  14 ms   9 ms  27 ms
 4  137.39.34.65    46 ms  23 ms  15 ms
 5  137.39.40.131   11 ms  13 ms  21 ms
 6  * * *
 7  * * *
^C
user$
```

There may be a problem following the fifth router. At that point, either a route to the destination, 18.159.0.42, is missing, or the return route to the user's IP address is missing. This can also be the result of a transient network failure or a route distribution failure.

Internet problems are outside the control of most users and dial-in server administrators. You can take action only if you manage the routers at the point of failure. Otherwise, you need to report the problem to the responsible parties.

Other TCP/IP Problems

Numerous mystery problems can still remain when PPP connections support TCP/IP networking. Some of these are:

- Communications deadlocks and stalls; communications to a site may work fine at the beginning, but suddenly stop a short time later

- Bulk file downloads that work fine, but bulk file uploads that stall

- Sporadic, poor, or inconsistent performance

These are particularly difficult problems to resolve once you eliminate serial hardware, flow control, modems, PPP, and TCP/IP routing faults as the cause.

TCP/IP includes numerous parameters that can greatly affect its behavior and performance. These include counters, timers, thresholds, limits, packet sizes, and window sizes. Some operating systems allow you to adjust these settings. Because every site and every intervening router have their own settings and limits, there are hundreds of combinations that can affect performance.

Some TCP/IP settings you may want to try adjusting are:

- TCP Maximum Segment Size (MSS)

- Receive window (RWIN)

- MTU and MRU

I described MTU and MRU settings earlier and suggested some values to try. There is also a dependency between MSS and MRU/MTU. Trial and error is the common method for finding suitable settings. One setting may give different performance results with different Internet sites.

In this chapter:
- *Communication Services*
- *Network Layer Protocols*
- *PPP Extensions*
- *Developments Relating to PPP*
- *Product Obsolescence*

16

What's New for PPP?

Computer and data networking technologies change almost daily, and you may wonder whether PPP could become obsolete shortly. PPP is highly extensible and can accommodate enhancements that enable it to remain current with the state of networking technology. As long as the point-to-point communications paradigm continues, PPP should remain in active use for many years to come.

As new data communications services develop, a *proposal* also frequently develops as a technique that enables the new service to carry PPP. By supporting PPP, a service instantly adds the ability to carry the wide range of networking protocol families PPP itself supports. Then as PPP evolves, so does the underlying service. PPP extensions add support for new protocol families or further expand communications options. Data encryption and multilink are examples of some protocol-independent extensions. There are also new developments that don't affect the PPP specification, but do affect how you can use it. L2TP is one example, which lets PPP traverse the Internet via a tunnel connection.

In this chapter, we'll see some recent and future communications services that can carry PPP. I'll give examples of less common network protocols PPP supports, and some protocol-independent PPP extensions. There is much development activity, and it's impossible to describe all recent events or correctly anticipate future PPP enhancements.

An important resource for tracking developments is the PPP Extensions Working Group that is part of the Internet Engineering Task Force (IETF). This group, as well as others, publishes Internet drafts and Request For Information (RFC) documents. These documents cover PPP proposals, current standards, and some informational nonstandards.

Communication Services

Throughout this book, we focused on PPP over standard telephone lines. However, many other communications technologies, both analog and digital, exist. Chapter 5, *Selecting Hardware, Software, and Services*, describes basic leased lines and switched communication services as carriers for PPP. But PPP isn't limited to these; standards are already in place allowing packet services and multiplexed circuit services, to also carry PPP.

Frame Relay

Frame relay is a service built with packet-switching technology. Its concept is a virtual circuit, a stream of frame relay "frames" that share a common data link connection identifier (DLCI). The DLCI is a field in the frame-relay header that represents a preestablished end-to-end route through the frame-relay network. Frames in a virtual circuit can encapsulate PPP frames belonging to a PPP connection. RFC-1973 describes the encapsulation procedure to do this. Figure 16-1 illustrates "VC 1" assigned for PPP use. The other virtual circuits may be for other PPP connections, or for purposes unrelated to PPP.

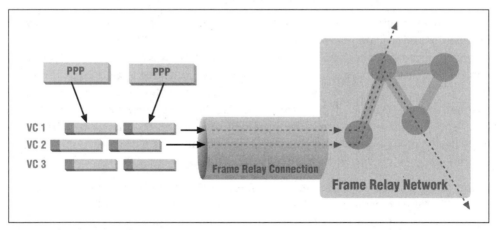

Figure 16-1. PPP over frame relay (packet service)

Frame relay statistically multiplexes virtual circuits. In other words, these virtual circuits dynamically share the communications bandwidth available in the access line, as well as resources inside the network itself. As long as other virtual circuits are idle, PPP can utilize much or little of a line's transmission capacity. An important frame-relay feature is its flexibility for managing and controlling virtual circuit resources. It's possible to reserve, limit, or provide on-demand bandwidth, on a per circuit basis.

Notice a single physical serial connection to a frame-relay network can multiplex large numbers of PPP connections within it. This characteristic is particularly valuable for those of you who would otherwise arrange point-to-point leased lines to many destinations. Subscribers to frame relay service can eliminate multiple subscriptions for leased lines and eliminate redundant serial interface hardware. This frequently results in a substantial cost savings in comparison with PPP connections over many leased lines.

Frame relay's predecessor, X.25, is another packet service that can also carry PPP (RFC-1598). The popularity of frame relay is due in part to its availability at DS1 speeds and above. In contrast, X.25 is a more complex packet protocol that requires more processing inside its service infrastructure. This limits its speed and performance.

Broadband ISDN

One emerging new technology is Broadband Integrated Services Digital Network (B-ISDN). This high-bandwidth service uses Synchronous Optical NETwork (SONET) lines to carry asynchronous transfer mode (ATM) fixed size cells. SONET operates at 150 Mbps and above. Each ATM cell is a 53-octet packet, consisting of 48 octets of data and 5 octets of header.

The low overhead for cell switching promises extremely high performance. ATM can multiplex voice, video, data, and other traffic types onto individual virtual circuits. The adaptation layer standards define procedures for encoding each traffic type into ATM cell streams. In the future, B-ISDN will carry high-speed PPP as well.

ISDN

The Integrated Services Digital Network (ISDN) is a telecommunications service offering a specific number of multiplexed circuits. Its declining cost, increased availability, and the Internet, are some reasons for the recent ISDN penetration into the large residential and business markets. Many products now available support PPP over ISDN.

An ISDN basic rate interface (ISDN-BRI) service is a single two-wire line that offers digital transmission at 144-Kbps capacity. Using time division multiplexing (TDM), the 144 Kbps is broken down into two 64-Kbps bearer channels (B channels) and one 16-Kbps data channel (D-channel): 2B+D. Each bearer channel can carry data or voice in digital format. The D-channel carries signaling for call setup and dialing functions but can also support low-speed packet data. Figure 16-2 shows a PPP connection on one channel of an ISDN-BRI service. RFC-1618 specifies how to encode and transmit PPP over ISDN.

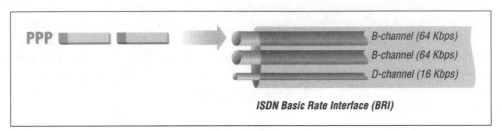

Figure 16-2. PPP over ISDN (multiplexed circuits)

Time-division multiplexing creates permanent independent channels by reserving a fixed bandwidth for each. The two B-channels function as two separate telephone lines, sharing a common wire. Resources dedicated to one B-channel normally can't be shared with others. However, there are channel-bonding proposals that combine several B-channels into a larger one at the bit level. Bonding modifies ISDN-BRI service into one that provides a single 128-Kbps and a 16-Kbps channel. However, bonding deployment is very limited.

The popularity of ISDN, and its service limitations, has motivated several extensions to the PPP specification to better exploit this technology:

* Multilink PPP

* Bandwidth Allocation Protocol (BAP)

Without special accommodation, a PPP connection on a B-channel is 64 Kbps. Multilink PPP enables users to establish several independent connections to the same destination and load balance their traffic among the connections multiplying the effective line speed. The BAP extension allows on-demand additions and deletions of B-channels participating in a logical PPP session. I describe both later in the "PPP Extensions" section.

Other PPP Carriers

Even basic leased-line service is evolving and should continue its ability to carry PPP. Leased-line advances primarily increase communications speeds. The latest services are SONET with standard speeds in integral multiples of 50 Mbps. RFC-1619 specifies how to encode PPP on SONET lines.

Modem technology for use with standard dial-up telephone service is also advancing. The traditional analog modem supports data speeds to approximately 33 Kbps. However, new modems are emerging that connect directly to the telephone service digital infrastructure. With V.90 technology, ISPs can now offer 56-Kbps service to compatible modems still attached to regular analog telephone lines.

Wireless is another future technology that can support PPP connections. This includes the cellular telephone network that connects laptop computers, personal digital assistants, and other portable equipment to the Internet. Also, satellite services have become available for users to download Internet data at high speeds. Uploading still occurs over standard telephone services. Next-generation satellite services maay be able to transmit and receive data.

Network Layer Protocols

The primary purpose of PPP is transporting multiprotocol datagrams through point to point connections. PPP already supports numerous protocols; the most common belong to the TCP/IP and IPX/SPX families. Less common ones are OSI, DecNET, SNA, and many others. One notable addition is IP version 6, the probable successor to IP version 4 that's part of TCP/IP.

The standard PPP framework includes a protocol field in the frame header. This field identifies the nature of the data the frame carries. PPP is easily extensible for new network protocols. The additions necessary to introduce a new network layer protocol are:

* Define the PPP encapsulation standards for the new network layer protocol. Assign a PPP protocol number to this standard. For example, IP is 0x0021 (see Appendix A, *PPP Assigned Numbers*).

* Define a new control protocol in the PPP Network Control Protocol (NCP) family. A control protocol establishes parameters, if any, before PPP carries the network layer protocol's first datagram. For example, IPCP is PPP protocol number 0x8021 (see Appendix A).

A rash of new network layer protocols is unlikely in the future. Much recent work in data networking concentrates on TCP/IP and its successors. This is the Internet standard and is the most universally available on computer and data-communications equipment.

PPP isn't limited to network layer protocols; it can also encapsulate protocols belonging to other layers in the OSI model. There now exist standards for *bridging* (see RFC-1638), which encodes data link layer protocols into PPP frames. Ethernet, FDDI, and token ring are examples. At the physical layer is a nonstandard, informational proposal for the Serial Data Transport Protocol (see RFC-1963). SDTP arranges PPP connections to emulate a hardwired serial connection, complete with flow control and handshake signals. One reason to use PPP this way is that it offers compression and encryption.

The existence of PPP specifications for new physical, data link, and network protocols doesn't mean that PPP products support them. The protocols you can use are determined by your hardware, software, and network infrastructure.

PPP Extensions

PPP includes multiple provisions for extending its capability. New numbers may be assigned for the protocol field in PPP frames for purposes besides network layer data. Also, each existing protocol PPP can encapsulate frequently has protocol-specific fields that can inherit new numbers for new purposes. Variations to extend PPP based on new protocol numbers and other methods are as follows:

- An enhanced PPP communications mode can have a PPP protocol number. For example, there is a number assignment for data compression and data encryption.

- A new PPP connection management feature can have its own PPP protocol field number. This is an overhead protocol. Examples include authentication, Link Quality Monitoring (LQM), and the Bandwidth Allocation Protocol (BAP).

- New codes in the option fields for existing PPP protocol, particularly the PPP Link Control Protocol (LCP), can extend PPP capabilities.

One interesting aspect of PPP is its ability to encapsulate its own PPP frames. In other words, PPP in PPP supports enhanced PPP communication modes. This feature can alter intermediate PPP frames in a useful manner and send them inside a normal frame. Compression, encryption, and multilink PPP all take advantage of this technique.

Link Control Protocol (LCP) Extensions

PPP begin with LCP, which negotiates PPP options. Each option has an assigned number in LCP, and more may be added. LCP extensions add option numbers representing options PPP endpoints establish at the beginning of a session.

New option numbers

Some examples of recent LCP additions are options that pertain to multilink PPP. These include Multilink Procedure, Multilink MRRU, Multilink Short Sequence Number Header, and Multilink Endpoint Discriminator.

Many existing options also have subfields that can inherit new values. One example is the CHAP authentication option, which includes an algorithm field. One standard value is 5 for MD5, but others can appear in the future.

Vendor LCP extensions

LCP now includes the provision for vendors to add their own negotiable PPP options (RFC-2153). As we saw in Chapter 3, *How PPP Works*, standard PPP options have unique assigned numbers in the PPP LCP specification. A new number, zero "0", is available for vendor-specific PPP extensions. Vendors can choose to keep their unique extensions proprietary and unpublished.

In PPP LCP frames carrying vendor-specific options, vendors include an Organizationally Unique Identifier (OUI), plus additional vendor-maintained codes that identify their extended options. The OUI is based on IEEE 802 vendor assignments and prevents contention among the PPP working group and multiple vendors augmenting PPP. The first three octets in MAC addresses are the OUI. Manufacturers of Ethernet and other LAN hardware already have their own identifier. However, software and other entities that don't have an OUI may apply for a PPP-specific one that begins with the 0xcf prefix.

Compression/Encryption

Compression's obvious benefit is that it increases the effective throughput of limited speed connections, such as 28.8-Kbps modems with telephone lines. Encryption offers data security in case of PPP session eavesdropping or interception by third parties. The PPP specification has extensions for compressing and encrypting data. Both operate independently and transparently for all the data PPP carries. In other words, compression and encryption are invisible to network layer software and user applications.

PPP implements compression, encryption, or both by encapsulating a transformed copy of a regular PPP frame. Figure 16-3 illustrates this procedure. When both compression and encryption are active, PPP must perform compression first. Intermediate PPP frames are similar but not identical to normal frames actually transmitted through a serial connection. These frames omit flags, address, control, and FCS fields. The protocol field in intermediate PPP frames remains intact prior to compression. This identifies the nature of the data after the receiver recovers it.

Chapter 3 already discusses the PPP Compression Control Protocol (CCP) and shows some negotiation procedures that attempt to establish data compression between two endpoints. Encryption operates similarly but uses the Encryption Control Protocol (ECP). The applicable standards are RFC-1962 and RFC-1968, respectively.

The PPP compression protocol and its corresponding control protocol support many compression algorithms, each with its own assigned number. This list is extensible as compression technology evolves. Many algorithms are already defined (Table 16-1), and many are proprietary. As a result, when different PPP

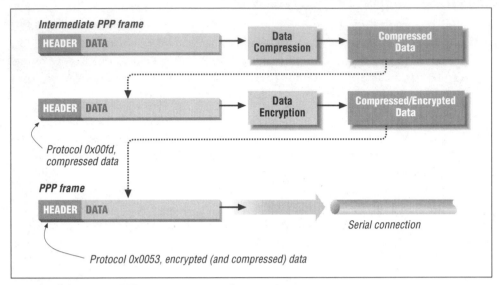

Figure 16-3. PPP in PPP, compression and encryption

implementations try to negotiate compression, they may fail to understand an algorithm in common. A more complete list of PPP compression algorithms is in Appendix A.

Table 16-1. PPP Compression Algorithms (Partial List)

Algorithm	Reference	PPP Software
LZS-DCP Compression Protocol	RFC-1967	
Stac LZS Compression Protocol	RFC-1974	
Magnalink Variable Resource Compression	RFC-1975	
BSD Compression Protocol	RFC-1977	PPP-2.3
Predictor Compression Protocol	RFC-1978	
Deflate Protocol	RFC-1970	PPP-2.3
Gandalf FZA Compression Protocol	RFC-1993	
Microsoft Point-to-Point Compression Protocol (MPPC)	RFC-2118	Windows NT/98

The PPP encryption protocols also support numerous encryption algorithms, including DES (RFC-1969). A more complete listing appears in Appendix A.

With compression and encryption, both ends of a connection must agree to use a common algorithm for encoding and decoding. The algorithms for each communication direction are independent. If two PPP implementations don't have two common algorithms, it's not fatal. Compression, encryption, or both are simply unavailable for the session.

Multilink PPP

The multiple channels available with ISDN services motivated the development of multilink PPP, as documented in RFC-1990. Regular PPP operates with a single point-to-point connection. For users of ISDN-BRI, a single connection is 64 Kbps, less than half the ISDN bit-rate capacity.

Multilink PPP arranges several independent connections between a fixed pair of endpoints to function logically as one. By combining two 64-Kbps calls placed on two ISDN B-channels, multilink PPP can achieve the equivalent of 128-Kbps service. This technique isn't limited to ISDN. Any number of PPP connections of varying speeds and different link types may be bundled together. Thus, it's possible to create one logical PPP session with dial-up modem lines, channels from ISDN-PRI service, a leased line, and other point-to-point services. However, a bundle must still connect between the same two endpoints.

The multilink procedure encodes PPP fragments within PPP frames. Each link in a bundle begins as an independent and standalone connection. Later negotiations establish the multilink option and uniquely identify the bundle a physical connection participates in. Once the bundle is active, the multilink procedure fragments, sequences, and reassembles logical PPP frames. Figure 16-4 illustrates this procedure. Frames containing fragments have the protocol field value 0x003d. A logical frame size is limited by a negotiated maximum received reconstructed unit (MRRU). This value may be very large, since each fragment may have sizes within the MRU established for individual connections. However, practical upper limits do exist due to resources necessary to sort and assemble fragments, as well as detect their loss.

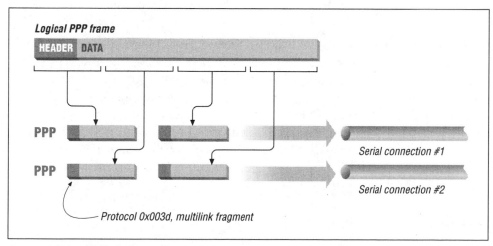

Figure 16-4. Multilink PPP

Multilink is a recent extension. It raises difficult design issues for network adminis-trators with multiple communication servers in large dial-up installations. If a user establishes two calls to a common telephone number, but different servers answer each call, one server usually can't coordinate a multilink session with another. You could reserve dial-in ports and assign special telephone numbers as a workaround. However, dedicating resources for multilink is an inefficient use of physical resources.

Multichassis PPP (MCPPP), also known as multichassis multilink PPP (MMP), is an emerging PPP enhancement that allows splitting multilink bundles among several communication servers. MCPPP uses PPP tunneling technology, such as L2TP. A L2TP tunnel between servers passes the members of a bundle to a master server. This master can then aggregate traffic from all the members of a single bundle. Multichassis PPP is yet to become a draft standard, but some remote access prod-ucts are available now that offer this feature.

Bandwidth Allocation Protocol (BAP)

The Bandwidth Allocation Protocol (BAP) is an enhancement for multilink PPP. BAP offers the ability to dynamically add or remove connections that are a part of a PPP multilink bundle. This is particularly useful for ISDN users.

ISDN-BRI users arranging multilink PPP frequently assign all available B-channels to achieve a 128-Kbps logical PPP session. These users can still receive indications about an incoming telephone call, since ISDN has a D-channel for signalling pur-poses. However, online users can't answer incoming calls without freeing a B-channel. If BAP is available, users can dynamically remove one B-channel from their PPP session without interrupting it. They can then answer and place voice telephone calls as needed. Later, BAP can reinstate this B-channel back into the PPP session.

To initialize bandwidth-allocation features, PPP endpoints must successfully nego-tiate with the Bandwidth Allocation Control Protocol (BACP). The BACP protocol number is 0xc02b. Then, during the PPP session, the BAP protocol manages requests and responses pertaining to PPP connections participating in multilink bundles. It passes call, callback, link drop, and call status messages for the individ-ual connections in a bundle. PPP frames that carry BAP have 0xc02d in their pro-tocol fields. RFC-2125 describes additional details about the transactions that must occur, the data required for each message, which PPP connections to send BAP-and other information.

Call Back

In a PPP call-back configuration, users initiate a short PPP connection that arranges the peer to call them back at a predetermined or user-specified telephone number. Some reasons for using call back include reversing telephone charges and security.

Call back with LCP

Since call back occurs at the beginning of a new PPP session, LCP includes the call-back option type and related settings. RFC-1570 further describes this. After endpoints agree to call back, authentication occurs as needed, and the connection terminates. One endpoint then initiates the call-back procedure to the other.

The call-back scenarios available include the following:

- Call back to a user-specified telephone number

- Call back to an administrator-defined telephone number associated with the user

- Call back to an administrator-defined list of telephone numbers associated with the user; the user sends a "location identifier" in her PPP request indicating the call-back location

Some call-back settings aren't fully defined in the RFC. In particular, the information in dialing string and location identifier messages are dependent on the PPP software and its call-back hardware implementation. This dependency can create interoperability problems.

Another item to consider is call back negotiations that occur before PPP authentication. Anyone can anonymously determine they've reached a call-back PPP dial-in server before they've identified themselves. Furthermore, the two PPP endpoints must exchange callback information, including telephone numbers, prior to authentication. This could be a security issue.

Call Back Control Protocol (CBCP)

The interoperability and possible security issue with LCP call back prompted Microsoft to develop the PPP Call Back Control Protocol (CBCP). This is currently not an official standard, even though CBCP has several PPP-assigned numbers.

CBCP still requires endpoints to negotiate its use with the standard LCP call-back option type. A new call-back operation field number determines that CBCP applies later in the PPP session.

PPP frames that carry CBCP occur after PPP authentication. This defers most details of call-back negotiations until after PPP endpoints have authenticated themselves. Thus, exchanging call-back telephone numbers, for example, no longer occurs anonymously. Although CBCP functions much like other PPP on-going connection management protocols, it exchanges messages only at the beginning of the PPP session, rather than during the course of a session. The PPP protocol number for CBCP is 0xc029.

The call-back scenarios available with CBCP are similar to those available with standard LCP call back. But CBCP adds the ability to negotiate call-back delay, in seconds.

PPP Extensible Authentication Protocol

One recent PPP extension is the Extensible Authentication Protocol (EAP). The protocol number for EAP is 0xc227. Endpoints that wish to use it must successfully understand EAP during LCP negotiations. Prior to EAP, authentication outside of PPP is necessary for less common, or unusual authentication methods. We already saw in Chapter 12, *Authentication*, that one-time passwords are difficult for use with PAP.

EAP is a general authentication protocol. While EAP is active, endpoints can exchange numerous requests and replies of various types. Some of these types are Identity, Notification, Nak (response only), One Time Password, and others. At the end, the authenticator sends a success or failure EAP packet. EAP supports user prompting through multistep authentication processes. Thus, it can accommodate situations including password expiration notification and authentication challenge strings.

Additional information about EAP appears in RFC-2284. To you as administrator, EAP is available only if the PPP software you use features it.

Other Extensions

Creating new protocol numbers for PPP, adding options to LCP, and defining new subfield numbers in existing PPP protocols, all extend PPP with new features.

The Internet Assigned Numbers Authority is responsible for the central registration of PPP numbers (see Appendix A). With the exception of PPP extensions that use organizationally unique identifiers (OUI), all other extensions should be registered with IANA before deployment. This preserves the PPP framework and avoids compatibility issues and conflicts among different PPP implementations in the industry.

Developments Relating to PPP

There exist many initiatives in the data communications industry to develop technologies that support or depend on the availability of PPP. These don't affect the PPP specification; however, they do enhance its usefulness.

One emerging effort is virtual private networks (VPN). VPNs use PPP in ways not originally envisioned. Another effort of interest for administrators of dial-in PPP servers is the remote authentication dial in user service (RADIUS).

Virtual Private Networks

Virtual private networking interconnects two networks, using PPP connections through the Internet rather than a real serial connection. These networks can communicate using networking protocols PPP carries. Individual users rather than networks can also use PPP tunnels through the Internet as a means of accessing resources of a private network.

Several tunneling protocols are emerging. Chapter 14, *Virtual Private Networking and Tunneling*, discusses PPP tunneling at length. Included are examples of the Point-to-Point Tunneling Protocol (PPTP) and other ad hoc protocols not originally intended for tunneling. PPTP is one tunneling protocol, primarily developed by Microsoft. A major competing contender is Cisco System's Layer Two Forwarding (L2F) protocol, which achieves similar goals. Since then, the two working groups responsible for these protocols have combined their efforts to develop a single standard VPN and tunneling protocol. The Layer Two Tunneling Protocol (L2TP) is the result of the combined effort.

Products supporting PPTP and L2F will phase out in favor of those compliant with L2TP. Newer networking products are likely to feature backward compatibility with the older tunneling protocols. Even L2TP itself is evolving. Revisions to L2TP are inevitable before it becomes a standard. Thus, products incorporating early versions of L2TP may require regular updates until the standards stabilize.

RADIUS

Remote authentication dial in user service is a standard (RFC-2138) originally developed by Livingston Enterprises for their remote access products. It's a client/server protocol between dial-in servers and a central database server. The database can authenticate users and retrieve user-specific access and configuration information. One central database in the RADIUS model supports geographically disperse dial-in pools, all with wide area network connections. You can maintain all your user records on one server and can grant users access to several, or all, of your dial-in pools.

RADIUS is useful for all types of dial-in services in addition to PPP. RADIUS provides backend support for standard PPP authentication, PAP and CHAP. After authentication, a RADIUS server returns specific configuration information a dial-in server can apply specifically to a PPP session:

* Authorization of network layer protocols the user can communicate with

- An IP address assignment, for TCP/IP networking

- Access control lists, if any, limiting users to specific network resources

There are other contending protocols that operate similarly to RADIUS. One example is Cisco's TACAS+. There are other proprietary protocols also.

Product Obsolescence

The PPP core standard defines a minimum set of capabilities for all implementations. All the enhancements in this chapter and future ones are optional. Thus, new products can include any combination of these enhancements, if any at all. It's unlikely for any single product to support all of PPP's capabilities. Although there exist standards for a new PPP feature, a feature's success still depends on the demands of the computer and data networking market.

Different generations of PPP software products should remain compatible over time. This remains true until industry "best practices" impose a mandatory PPP enhancement older products don't understand or support. As data communications progress, there will be new communication technologies that can carry PPP, and there will be numerous new extensions to PPP. To take advantage of new extensions requires new or updated PPP software and perhaps communications hardware. These are the main causes for PPP product obsolescence. Other reasons for PPP products to become obsolete include changes in a computer or operating system.

If you're seeking to upgrade or replace your PPP products, you must evaluate new products. Here are the things to consider for new PPP products:

- Hardware and operating system compatibility

- Physical compatibility with the communication services you plan to use for PPP

- Network, data link, and physical layer, protocol requirements. Transferring data with TCP/IP and Appletalk, for example, requires a PPP implementation that supports both

- Support for specific PPP options, or feature enhancements

- What features your PPP peer supports. For example, users with multilink PPP software can't use the multilink feature unless their service provider also supports it.

Although products often become obsolete, PPP itself should remain an active technology in the foreseeable future.

A

PPP Assigned Numbers

The Point-to-Point Protocol defines frames with many numeric fields. Chapter 3, *How PPP Works*, describes these fields and their relationships inside a PPP frame. All fields have unique number assignments for representing a PPP overhead message, a feature number, a network protocol, the active compression algorithm, the active encryption algorithm, and others. As PPP technology evolves, additional number assignments are added.

The Internet Assigned Numbers Authority (IANA) is the central organization responsible for maintaining the registration of unique numbers for specific PPP fields. IANA also reviews applications for new PPP numbers. The Information Sciences Institute (ISI) of the University of Southern California (USC), *http://www.isi.edu/*, is the home of IANA.

You don't normally need to be aware of assigned numbers. However, these numbers are important to know in the following circumstances:

- Developers must use standard assigned numbers. This insures compatibility among different PPP implementations.

- Assigned numbers indicate the state of PPP technology. New PPP developments frequently appear as assigned numbers before products become available to support them.

- Troubleshooters dissecting and interpreting PPP frames need to know the meaning of various numbers.

The PPP field assignments change reasonably often. The latest assignments are available online from IANA at:

http://www.isi.edu/in-notes/iana/assignments/ppp-numbers/

This document, as of April 30, 1998, appears as follows:

```
POINT-TO-POINT PROTOCOL FIELD ASSIGNMENTS

PPP DLL PROTOCOL NUMBERS

The Point-to-Point Protocol (PPP) Data Link Layer [146,147,175]
contains a 16 bit Protocol field to identify the the encapsulated
protocol.  The Protocol field is consistent with the ISO 3309 (HDLC)
extension mechanism for Address fields.  All Protocols MUST be
assigned such that the least significant bit of the most significant
octet equals "0", and the least significant bit of the least
significant octet equals "1".

Assigned PPP DLL Protocol Numbers

Value (in hex)    Protocol Name

0001              Padding Protocol
0003 to 001f      reserved (transparency inefficient)
0021              Internet Protocol version 4
0023              OSI Network Layer
0025              Xerox NS IDP
0027              DECnet Phase IV
0029              Appletalk
002b              Novell IPX
002d              Van Jacobson Compressed TCP/IP
002f              Van Jacobson Uncompressed TCP/IP
0031              Bridging PDU
0033              Stream Protocol (ST-II)
0035              Banyan Vines
0037              reserved (until 1993)
0039              AppleTalk EDDP
003b              AppleTalk SmartBuffered
003d              Multi-Link                                 [RFC1717]
003f              NETBIOS Framing
0041              Cisco Systems
0043              Ascom Timeplex
0045              Fujitsu Link Backup and Load Balancing (LBLB)
0047              DCA Remote Lan
0049              Serial Data Transport Protocol (PPP-SDTP)
004b              SNA over 802.2
004d              SNA
004f              IPv6 Header Compression
0051              KNX Bridging Data                             [ianp]
0053              Encryption                                   [Meyer]
0055              Individual Link Encryption                   [Meyer]
0057              Internet Protocol version 6                 [Hinden]
006f              Stampede Bridging
0071              Reserved                                       [Fox]
0073              MP+ Protocol                                 [Smith]
007d              reserved (Control Escape)                  [RFC1661]
007f              reserved (compression inefficient)         [RFC1662]
0081              Reserved Until 20-Oct-2000                    [IANA]
```

```
0083            Reserved Until 20-Oct-2000          [IANA]
00c1            NTCITS IPI                          [Ungar]
00cf            reserved (PPP NLPID)
00fb            single link compression in multilink [RFC1962]
00fd            compressed datagram                 [RFC1962]
00ff            reserved (compression inefficient)

02xx-1exx       (compression inefficient)

0201            802.1d Hello Packets
0203            IBM Source Routing BPDU
0205            DEC LANBridge100 Spanning Tree
0207            Cisco Discovery Protocol            [Sastry]
0209            Netcs Twin Routing                 [Korfmacher]
0231            Luxcom
0233            Sigma Network Systems
0235            Apple Client Server Protocol        [Ridenour]
0281            Tag Switching - Unicast             [Davie]
0283            Tag Switching - Multicast           [Davie]

4001            Cray Communications Control Protocol  [Stage]
4003            CDPD Mobile Network Registration Protocol [Quick]
4021            Stacker LZS                         [Simpson]
4023            RefTek Protocol                     [Banfill]

8001-801f       Not Used - reserved                 [RFC1661]
8021            Internet Protocol Control Protocol
8023            OSI Network Layer Control Protocol
8025            Xerox NS IDP Control Protocol
8027            DECnet Phase IV Control Protocol
8029            Appletalk Control Protocol
802b            Novell IPX Control Protocol
802d            reserved
802f            reserved
8031            Bridging NCP
8033            Stream Protocol Control Protocol
8035            Banyan Vines Control Protocol
8037            reserved till 1993
8039            reserved
803b            reserved
803d            Multi-Link Control Protocol
803f            NETBIOS Framing Control Protocol
8041            Cisco Systems Control Protocol
8043            Ascom Timeplex
8045            Fujitsu LBLB Control Protocol
8047            DCA Remote Lan Network Control Protocol (RLNCP)
8049            Serial Data Control Protocol (PPP-SDCP)
804b            SNA over 802.2 Control Protocol
804d            SNA Control Protocol
804f            IP6 Header Compression Control Protocol
8051            KNX Bridging Control Protocol               [ianp]
8053            Encryption Control Protocol                 [Meyer]
8055            Individual Link Encryption Control Protocol [Meyer]
8057            IPv6 Control Protovol                       [Hinden]
```

```
806f            Stampede Bridging Control Protocol
8073            MP+ Control Protocol                           [Smith]
8071            Reserved                                        [Fox]
807d            Not Used - reserved                         [RFC1661]
8081            Reserved Until 20-Oct-2000                     [IANA]
8083            Reserved Until 20-Oct-2000                     [IANA]
80c1            NTCITS IPI Control Protocol                   [Ungar]
80cf            Not Used - reserved                         [RFC1661]
80fb            single link compression in multilink control [RFC1962]
80fd            Compression Control Protocol                [RFC1962]
80ff            Not Used - reserved                         [RFC1661]

8207            Cisco Discovery Protocol Control             [Sastry]
8209            Netcs Twin Routing                       [Korfmacher]
8235            Apple Client Server Protocol Control       [Ridenour]
8281            Tag Switching - Unicast                       [Davie]
8283            Tag Switching - Multicast                     [Davie]

c021            Link Control Protocol
c023            Password Authentication Protocol
c025            Link Quality Report
c027            Shiva Password Authentication Protocol
c029            CallBack Control Protocol (CBCP)
c02b            BACP Bandwidth Allocation Control Protocol   [RFC2125]
c02d            BAP                                         [RFC2125]

c081            Container Control Protocol                      [KEN]
c223            Challenge Handshake Authentication Protocol
c225            RSA Authentication Protocol                 [Narayana]
c227            Extensible Authentication Protocol          [RFC2284]
c229            Mitsubishi Security Info Exch Ptcl (SIEP)      [Seno]
c26f            Stampede Bridging Authorization Protocol
c281            Proprietary Authentication Protocol             [KEN]
c283            Proprietary Authentication Protocol       [Tackabury]
c481            Proprietary Node ID Authentication Protocol     [KEN]
```

It is recommended that values in the 02xx to 1exx and xx01 to xx1f ranges not be assigned, as they are compression inefficient.

Protocol field values in the 0xxx to 3xxx range identify the network-layer protocol of specific datagrams, and values in the 8xxx to bxxx range identify datagrams belonging to the associated Network Control Protocol (NCP), if any.

Protocol field values in the 4xxx to 7xxx range are used for protocols with low volume traffic which have no associated NCP.

Protocol field values in the cxxx to exxx range identify datagrams as Control Protocols (such as LCP).

PPP LCP AND IPCP CODES

The Point-to-Point Protocol (PPP) Link Control Protocol (LCP),
the Compression Control Protocol (CCP), Internet Protocol Control
Protocol (IPCP), and other control protocols, contain an 8 bit
Code field which identifies the type of packet. These Codes are
assigned as follows:

```
Code         Packet Type
----         -----------
   0         Vendor Specific                          [RFC2153]
   1         Configure-Request
   2         Configure-Ack
   3         Configure-Nak
   4         Configure-Reject
   5         Terminate-Request
   6         Terminate-Ack
   7         Code-Reject
   8       * Protocol-Reject
   9       * Echo-Request
  10       * Echo-Reply
  11       * Discard-Request
  12       * Identification
  13       * Time-Remaining
  14       + Reset-Request                            [RFC1962]
  15       + Reset-Reply                              [RFC1962]


  * LCP Only
  + CCP Only
```

PPP LCP CONFIGURATION OPTION TYPES

The Point-to-Point Protocol (PPP) Link Control Protocol (LCP)
specifies a number of Configuration Options which are distinguished by
an 8 bit Type field. These Types are assigned as follows:

```
Type         Configuration Option
----         --------------------
   0         Vendor Specific                          [RFC2153]
   1         Maximum-Receive-Unit
   2         Async-Control-Character-Map
   3         Authentication-Protocol
   4         Quality-Protocol
   5         Magic-Number
   6         DEPRECATED (Quality-Protocol)
   7         Protocol-Field-Compression
   8         Address-and-Control-Field-Compression
   9         FCS-Alternatives                         [RFC1570]
  10         Self-Describing-Pad                      [RFC1570]
  11         Numbered-Mode                            [RFC1663]
  12         DEPRECATED (Multi-Link-Procedure)
  13         Callback                                 [RFC1570]
  14         DEPRECATED (Connect-Time)
  15         DEPRECATED (Compound-Frames)
  16         DEPRECATED (Nominal-Data-Encapsulation)
  17         Multilink-MRRU                           [RFC1717]
```

```
18        Multilink-Short-Sequence-Number-Header     [RFC1717]
19        Multilink-Endpoint-Discriminator           [RFC1717]
20        Proprietary                                     [KEN]
21        DCE-Identifier                            [SCHNEIDER]
22        Multi-Link-Plus-Procedure                     [Smith]
23        Link Discriminator for BACP                [RFC2125]
24        LCP-Authentication-Option                   [Culbert]
25        Consistent Overhead Byte Stuffing (COBS)    [Carlson]
26        Prefix elision                              [Bormann]
27        Multilink header format                     [Bormann]
```

IPV6CP CONFIGURATION OPTIONS

IPV6CP Configuration Options allow negotiation of desirable IPv6
parameters. IPV6CP uses the same Configuration Option format defined
for LCP, with a separate set of Options. If a Configuration Option is
not included in a Configure-Request packet, the default value for that
Configuration Option is assumed.

```
1         Interface-Token                            [RFC2023]
2         IPv6-Compression-Protocol                  [RFC2023]
```

PPP ECP CONFIGURATION OPTION TYPES

A one octet field is used in the Encryption Control Protocol (ECP)
to indicate the configuration option type [RFC1968].

ECP Option	Configuration Type	
0	OUI	[RFC1968]
1	Deprecated (DESE)	[Fox]
2	3DESE	[Kummert]
3	DESE-bis	[Fox]
4-255	Unassigned	

PPP CCP CONFIGURATION OPTION TYPES

A one octet field is used in the Compression Control Protocol (CCP)
to indicate the configuration option type [RFC1962].

CCP Option	Configuration Type	
0	OUI	[RFC1962]
1	Predictor type 1	[RFC1962]
2	Predictor type 2	[RFC1962]
3	Puddle Jumper	[RFC1962]
4-15	unassigned	
16	Hewlett-Packard PPC	[RFC1962]
17	Stac Electronics LZS	[RFC1974]
18	Microsoft PPC	[RFC2118]
19	Gandalf FZA	[RFC1962]
20	V.42bis compression	[RFC1962]
21	BSD Compress	[RFC1977]

22	unassigned	
23	LZS-DCP	[RFC1967]
24	MVRCA (Magnalink)	[RFC1975]
25	DCE	[RFC1976]
26	Deflate	[RFC1979]
27-254	unassigned	
255	Reserved	[RFC1962]

The unassigned values 4-15 are intended to be assigned to other
freely available compression algorithms that have no license fees.

PPP SDCP CONFIGURATION OPTIONS

A one octet field is used in the Compression Control Protocol (CCP)
PPP Serial Data Transport Protocol (SDTP) to indicate the option type
[RFC1963].

SDCP Option	Configuration Element	
1	Packet-Format	[RFC1963]
2	Header-Type	[RFC1963]
3	Length-Field-Present	[RFC1963]
4	Multi-Port	[RFC1963]
5	Transport-Mode	[RFC1963]
6	Maximum-Frame-Size	[RFC1963]
7	Allow-Odd-Frames	[RFC1963]
8	FCS-Type	[RFC1963]
9	Flow-Expiration-Time	[RFC1963]

Note that Option Types 5-8 are specific to a single port and require
port numbers in their format. Option Types 6-8 are specific to the
HDLC-Synchronous Transport-Mode.

PPP AUTHENTICATION ALGORITHMS

A one octet field is used in the Challenge-Handshake Authentication
Protocol (CHAP) to indicate which algorithm is in use [RFC1994].

Number	Name	
0	Reserved	[RFC1994]
1	Reserved	[RFC1994]
2	Reserved	[RFC1994]
3	Reserved	[RFC1994]
4	Reserved	[RFC1994]
5	CHAP with MD5	[RFC1994]
128	MS-CHAP	[Crocker]

PPP LCP FCS-ALTERNATIVES

The Point-to-Point Protocol (PPP) Link Control Protocol (LCP)
FCS-Alternatives Configuration Option contains an 8-bit Options field

which identifies the FCS used. These are assigned as follows:

```
Bit    FCS
----   ----------
 1     Null FCS
 2     CCITT 16-Bit FCS
 4     CCITT 32-bit FCS
```

PPP MULTILINK ENDPOINT DISCRIMINATOR CLASS

The Point-to-Point Protocol (PPP) Link Control Protocol (LCP)
Multilink Endpoint Discriminator Option includes a Class field which
identifies the address class, These are assigned as follows:

```
Class   Description
-----   -----------
  0     Null Class                                    [RFC1717]
  1     Locally Assigned                              [RFC1717]
  2     Internet Protocol (IPv4)                      [RFC1717]
  3     IEEE 802.1 global MAC address                 [RFC1717]
  4     PPP Magic Number Block                        [RFC1717]
  5     Public Switched Network Director Number       [RFC1717]
```

PPP LCP CALLBACK OPERATION FIELDS

The Point-to-Point Protocol (PPP) Link Control Protocol (LCP) Callback
Configuration Option contains an 8-bit Operations field which
identifies the format of the Message. These are assigned as follows:

```
Operation   Description
---------   -------------------------
    0       Location determined by user authentication.
    1       Dialing string.
    2       Location identifier.
    3       E.164 number.
    4       X.500 distinguished name.
    5       unassigned
    6       Location is determined during CBCP negotiation.
```

PPP IPCP CONFIGURATION OPTION TYPES

The Point-to-Point Protocol (PPP) Internet Protocol Control Protocol
(IPCP) specifies a number of Configuration Options which are
distinguished by an 8 bit Type field. These Types are assigned as
follows:

```
Type      Configuration Option
----      --------------------
  1       IP-Addresses (deprecated)                   [RFC1332]
  2       IP-Compression-Protocol                     [RFC1332]
  3       IP-Address                                  [RFC1332]
  4       Mobile-IPv4                                 [RFC2290]
```

```
129          Primary DNS Server Address                [RFC1877]
130          Primary NBNS Server Address               [RFC1877]
131          Secondary DNS Server Address              [RFC1877]
132          Secondary NBNS Server Address             [RFC1877]
```

PPP ATCP CONFIGURATION OPTION TYPES

The Point-to-Point Protocol (PPP) Apple Talk Control Protocol (ATCP)
specifies a number of Configuration Options [RFC-1378] which are
distinguished by an 8 bit Type field. These Types are assigned as
follows:

```
Type         Configuration Option
----         --------------------
  1          AppleTalk-Address
  2          Routing-Protocol
  3          Suppress-Broadcasts
  4          AT-Compression-Protocol
  5          Reserved
  6          Server-information
  7          Zone-Information
  8          Default-Router-Address
```

PPP OSINLCP CONFIGURATION OPTION TYPES

The Point-to-Point Protocol (PPP) OSI Network Layer Control Protocol
(OSINLCP) specifies a number of Configuration Options [RFC1377] which
are distinguished by an 8 bit Type field. These Types are assigned as
follows:

```
Type         Configuration Option
----         --------------------
  1          Align-NPDU
```

PPP BANYAN VINES CONFIGURATION OPTION TYPES

The Point-to-Point Protocol (PPP) Banyan Vines Control Protocol (BVCP)
specifies a number of Configuration Options [RFC1763] which are
distinguished by an 8 bit Type field. These Types are assigned as
follows:

```
Type         Configuration Option
----         --------------------
  1          BV-NS-RTP-Link-Type
  2          BV-FRP
  3          BV-RTP
  4          BV-Suppress-Broadcast
```

PPP BRIDGING CONFIGURATION OPTION TYPES

The Point-to-Point Protocol (PPP) Bridging Control Protocol (BCP)
specifies a number of Configuration Options which are distinguished by

an 8 bit Type field. These Types are assigned as follows:

```
Type      Configuration Option
----      --------------------
  1       Bridge-Identification
  2       Line-Identification
  3       MAC-Support
  4       Tinygram-Compression
  5       LAN-Identification
  6       MAC-Address
  7       Spanning-Tree-Protocol
```

PPP BRIDGING MAC TYPES

The Point-to-Point Protocol (PPP) Bridging Control Protocol (BCP)
contains an 8 bit MAC Type field which identifies the MAC
encapsulated. These Types are assigned as follows:

```
Type      MAC
----      -----------
  0       Reserved
  1       IEEE 802.3/Ethernet    with cannonical addresses
  2       IEEE 802.4             with cannonical addresses
  3       IEEE 802.5             with non-cannonical addresses
  4       FDDI                   with non-cannonical addresses
 5-10     reserved
  11      IEEE 802.5             with cannonical addresses
  12      FDDI                   with cannonical addresses
```

PPP BRIDGING SPANNING TREE

The Point-to-Point Protocol (PPP) Bridging Control Protocol (BCP)
Spanning Tree Configuration Option contains an 8-bit Protocol field
which identifies the spanning tree used. These are assigned as
follows:

```
Protocol  Spanning Tree
--------  ---------------
  0       Null - no spanning tree protocol supported
  1       IEEE 802.1D spanning tree protocol
  2       IEEE 802.1G extended spanning tree protocol
  3       IBM source route spanning tree protocol
  4       DEC LANbridge 100 spanning tree protocol
```

PPP INTERNETWORK PACKET EXCHANGE CONTROL PROTOCOL (IPXCP)

IPXCP CONFIGURATION OPTIONS

```
Option    Description                          Reference
------    -----------                          ---------
   1      IPX-Network-Number                   [RFC1552]
   2      IPX-Node-Number                      [RFC1552]
   3      IPX-Compression-Protocol             [RFC1552]
```

```
          4        IPX-Routing-Protocol              [RFC1552]
          5        IPX-Router-Name                   [RFC1552]
          6        IPX-Configuration-Complete        [RFC1552]
```

IPX COMPRESSION PROTOCOL VALUES

```
     Value           Protocol                      Reference
     -----           --------                      ---------
       2        Telebit Compressed IPX               [Fox]
      235       Shiva Compressed NCP/IPX             [Fox]
```

IPX-ROUTING-PROTOCOL OPTIONS

```
     Value           Protocol                      Reference
     -----           --------                      ---------
       0        No routing protocol required      [RFC1552]
       1        RESERVED                          [RFC1552]
       2        Novell RIP/SAP required           [RFC1552]
       4        Novell NLSP required              [RFC1552]
       5        Novell Demand RIP required        [RFC1582]
       6        Novell Demand SAP required        [RFC1582]
       7        Novell Triggered RIP required    [Edmonstone]
       8        Novell Triggered SAP required    [Edmonstone]
```

NBFCP Configuration Options

NBFCP Configuration Options [RFC 2097] allow modifications to the
standard characteristics of the network-layer protocol to be
negotiated. If a Configuration Option is not included in a
Configure-Request packet, the default value for that Configuration
Option is assumed.

NBFCP uses the same Configuration Option format defined for LCP,
with a separate set of Options.

Current values are assigned as follows:

```
          1        Name-Projection
          2        Peer-Information
          3        Multicast-Filtering
          4        IEEE-MAC-Address-Required
```

PPP EAP REQUEST/RESPONSE TYPES

A one octet field is used in the Extensible Authentication Protocol
(EAP) to indicate the function and structure of EAP Request and
Response packets [RFC2284].

```
  Type     Description
  ----     -----------
    1      Identity                             [RFC2284]
    2      Notification                         [RFC2284]
    3      Nak (Response only)                  [RFC2284]
```

```
    4       MD5-Challenge                          [RFC2284]
    5       One Time Password (OTP)                [RFC2289]
    6       Generic Token Card                     [RFC2284]
    7
    8
    9       RSA Public Key Authentication          [Whelan]
   10       DSS Unilateral                           [Nace]
   11       KEA                                      [Nace]
   12       KEA-VALIDATE                             [Nace]
   13       EAP-TLS                                 [Adoba]
   14       Defender Token (AXENT)               [Rosselli]
```

PPP VENDOR SPECIFIC OUI OPTIONS

There are some provisions in some PPP message formats for vendor
specific options to be identified by the Organisationally Unique
Identifier (OUI), namely the first three octets of a Vendor s Ethernet
address assigned by IEEE 802 [RFC1968. RFC2153]. These are listed in
the ethernet-numbers file (see
http://www.iana.org/in-notes/iana/assignments/ethernet-numbers).

REFERENCES

. . .

PEOPLE

[Adoba] Bernard Adoba <aboba@internaut.com>, December 1997.
[Banfill] Robert Banfill <r_banfill@reftek.com>, July 1997.
[Blunk] Larry Blunk, <ljb@merit.edu>, December 1995, 1997.
[Bormann] Cartsen Bormann <cabo@tzi.org>, March 1998.
[Carlson] James Carlson, <jcarlson@andr.ub.com>, January 1998.
[Crocker] Ken Crocker, <kcrocker@Exchange.Microsoft.com>, March 1996.
[Culbert] Ken Culbert, <ken@funk.com>, October 1996.
[Davie] Brice Davie, <bsd@cisco.com>, January 1997.
[Edmonstone] Richard Edmonstone, <richarde@spider.co.uk>, July 1996.
[Fox] Karl Fox, <karl@ascend.con>, January 1997.
[Hinden] Bob Hinden, <hinden@ipsilon.com>, March 1996.
[ianp] <ianp@knxunix.knx.co.uk> November 1994.
[KEN]   <ken@funk.com>
[Korfmacher] Oliver Korfmacher, <okorf@netcs.com>, April 1995.
[Kummert] Holger Kummert, <kummert@nentec.de>, August 1997.
[Meyer] Gerry Meyer <gerry@spider.co.uk> December 1994.
[Nace] William Nace <wanace@missi.ncsc.mil>, December 1997
[Quick] Frank Quick <fquick@qualcomm.com>
[Ridenour] Howard Ridenour, <RIDENOUR1@applelink.apple.com>, February 1995.
[Rosselli] Michael Rosselli, <mrosselli@axent.com>, January 1998.
[Sastry] Arun Sastry, <asastry@cisco.com>, April 1995.
[Schneider] Kevin Schneider <kevin@adtran.com>
[Seno] Shoichiro Seno, <senos@kousoku.isl.melco.co.jp>, April 1995.
[Simpson] Willian Allen Simpson, <bsimpson@morningstar.com>, March 1995.
[Smith] Kevin Smith, Kevin@Smith.ascend.com, January 1996.
[Stage] Erling B. Stage <ebs@craycom.dk> October 1994.
```
```

[Solomon] Jim Solomon, <solomon@comm.mot.com>, Feburary 1997.
[Narayana] Badari Narayana <badari@ca.SJF.Novell.COM>
[Tackabury] Wayne Tackabury, <wayne@cayman.cayman.com>, January 1995.
[Ungar] Alan Ungar, <AUngar@farradyne.com>, April 1995.
[Whelan] William Whelan, <bwhelan@nei.com>, December 1997.

[]

I omit the references section, which contains a citation for all the RFC documents mentioned. The documents themselves are readily available at many RFC repositories; for more information, see *http://www.rfc-editor.org.*

B

Serial Interface Emulation

PPP normally communicates through physical RS-232 serial interfaces, modems, and telephone service. But sometimes serial communication is desirable through an existing network connection or through intervening software. Chapter 14, *Virtual Private Networking and Tunneling*, shows how the Internet can behave as a serial connection for connecting private networks. This connection actually carries PPP frames. In effect, we have PPP over TCP/IP.

Most PPP software expects to communicate with serial interfaces only. Arranging this software to communicate through an Internet connection instead is a challenge. This requires intercepting serial I/O from PPP and redirecting it to TCP/IP communication programs. Linux and Unix includes operating system services and resources that can arrange this redirection. Unfortunately, redirecting serial I/O is more difficult, if not impossible, with Microsoft Windows, communication servers, and router equipment.

This appendix describes Unix serial interface resources and provides C language source code for the `ptysh` utility. This utility is useful for redirecting serial I/O into programs that communicate with TCP/IP connections. The description we present here for `ptysh` is for programmers that wish to understand how this utility functions. Chapter 14 describes how to use this utility with PPP connections.

Unix Serial Interface Devices

The Unix operating system and its variants such as Linux, provide terminal devices and pseudo-terminal devices. The former provides access to real serial interface device drivers; while the latter emulates a serial interface device in software.

Terminal Devices

Unix applications, including PPP, UUCP, and terminal emulator programs, access a physical serial interface by opening a terminal device. Terminal devices, also known as tty devices, have filenames including */dev/ttyS1* on Linux, and */dev/cua/b* on Solaris. After an application opens a terminal device file, various `ioctl` operations establish serial interface operating parameters. Data reads and writes to the device file appears as data the serial interface receives and sends, respectively.

Pseudo-Terminal Devices

Unix also supports pseudo-terminals, which emulate terminal devices. A pseudo-terminal behaves exactly as a real terminal device to any Unix applications that access it. However, it's a connection to another Unix process, rather than to a physical serial interface. Pseudo-terminals have device filenames similar to those of real terminals. Examples include */dev/ttyr0* on Linux and */dev/pts/0* on Solaris.

A PPP, UUCP, terminal emulator, or other application that expects to access a terminal device can just as easily access a pseudo-terminal instead, without modification. Before a pseudo terminal is available for use, a third-party Unix process must initialize the pseudo-terminal and attach to it. Once a PPP, UUCP, or other application begins reading and writing to a pseudo-terminal, the third-party Unix process becomes responsible for processing all of this application's serial I/O. This process may perform any operation on serial I/O data and perhaps redirect it to yet another TCP/IP application. Figure 14-4 shows this with PPP.

In summary, pseudo-terminals permit serial I/O with a Unix process, rather than with a real serial interface.

ptysh

The **ptysh** utility manages several pseudo-terminal devices and connects one of them to a Bourne shell, */bin/sh*, hence its name. This utility gives Unix application programs the ability to interact with the shell, in place of a real serial interface and modem. These applications must now send Unix commands to the shell, rather than modem command strings to a modem. Shell commands allow chat scripts to launch other programs that can transform serial I/O data or provide TCP/IP network communications. The relationship between **ptysh**, PPP, and Unix pseudo-terminal devices appears in Figure B-1. Pseudo-terminal device names in the figure belong to Unix System V variants.

Users must start **ptysh** before PPP software can use its pseudo-terminal device. **ptysh** obtains pseudo-terminals by opening */dev/ptmx*. Each open creates a master and slave pty device, analogous to two ends of a data pipe. */dev/pts/2* is the

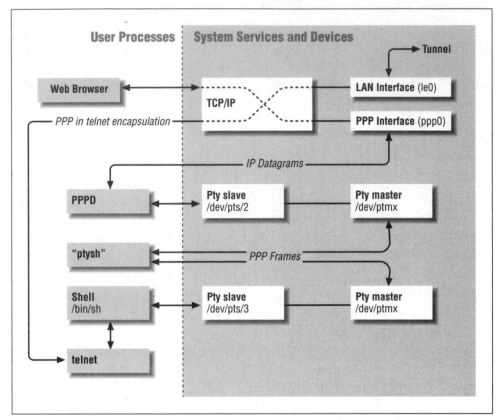

Figure B-1. PPP connection via Unix emulated serial interface

slave that appears as a terminal device to PPP software. `ptysh` must also obtain a second master and slave pair to communicate with the shell and Telnet, since these programs also expect to interact with terminals. After establishing all the software connections in Figure B-1, `ptysh` simply relays data between the PPP process, the shell, and the Telnet process until one of these processes disconnects.

Pseudo-terminal implementations differ considerably among Unix variants. Thus, I present separate code examples for Unix System V and Linux. The Linux version is also compatible with Unix BSD variants.

ptysh for Unix System V

`ptysh` for Unix System V obtains pseudo-terminals on demand. Thus, the pseudo-terminal device file PPP software must attach to may change for every PPP session. Obviously, additional programming effort can correct this limitation.

When **ptysh** starts, it reports the pseudo-terminal it creates for PPP to use:

```
user$ ./ptysh &
serial pty: /dev/pts/3
user$
```

PPP software can now access this device filename as its dial-out serial interface. Since **ptysh** won't initially respond when a PPP connects to it, a chat script must send a carriage-return character first. This wakes up **ptysh**, which presents a shell prompt.

The **ptysh** sample code below is intended only as an example. It's not robust enough for critical production use. As written, the code is incomplete regarding error checking and may unexpectedly terminate when an invoking user logs off:

```
/*
ptysh.c   "Pseudo Terminal Shell"

For UNIX System V variants (Sun Microsystem s Solaris 2.5).
Compile with "cc -o ptysh ptysh.c"


Author: Andrew Sun
Revision: January 10, 1998


Description:

This program enables the /bin/sh command interpreter to
emulate a "terminal device".  Tip, cu, the UUCP environment,
and PPP normally interact with serial interfaces via terminal
device files, such as /dev/cua/b.  Rather than limiting these
applications to physical serial interfaces, "ptysh" enables them
to interact with the shell (/bin/sh), and with TCP/IP communication
programs, including telnet and rlogin.


Usage:

Once ptysh is active, an application accessing the serial pty
device it reports will interact with /bin/sh.  At this point,
an application s chat script can "exec telnet" or "exec rlogin"
to establish communications over a network.
*/

#include <stdio.h>
#include <errno.h>

#include <sys/types.h>
#include <sys/stat.h>
#include <fcntl.h>

#include <stropts.h>
```

```
#include <poll.h>

char *ptsname(int fildes);

main(argc,argv)
int argc;
char *argv[];
{

int shellpid;

char iobuf12[2000], iobuf21[2000];
char *iobuf12p, *iobuf21p;
int iofdcnt, iowrcnt, iordcnt12, iordcnt21;

int fd1m, fd1s, fd2m, fd2s;
char *slavename;

struct pollfd fds[2];
unsigned long nfds;
int timeout;

for (;;) {

/* Create serial interface ptys */
if ( (fd1m = open("/dev/ptmx", O_RDWR)) < 0 ) {
    perror("open serial pty master"); exit(1);
}
    grantpt(fd1m); unlockpt(fd1m);
if ( (slavename = ptsname(fd1m)) == NULL ) {
    perror("can t determine serial pty"); exit(1);
}
    printf("serial pty: %s\n", slavename);
if ( (fd1s = open(slavename,O_RDWR)) < 0 ) {
    perror("open serial pty slave"); exit(1);
}
    ioctl(fd1s, I_PUSH, "ptem");
    ioctl(fd1s, I_PUSH, "ldterm");

/* Detect "open" for serial pty slave */
fds[0].fd = fd1m;
fds[0].events = POLLIN;
nfds = 1; timeout = -1;
poll(fds, nfds, timeout);
close (fd1s);/* Application has serial pty slave now */

/* Create shell ptys */
if ( (fd2m = open("/dev/ptmx", O_RDWR)) < 0 ) {
    perror("open shell pty master"); exit(1);
}
    grantpt(fd2m); unlockpt(fd2m);
if ( (slavename = ptsname(fd2m)) == NULL ) {
    perror("can t determine shell pty"); exit(1);
}
```

```
        /* printf("shell pty: %s\n", slavename); */

    /* Invoke /bin/sh as a subprocess */
    if (! (shellpid = fork()) ) {
        close (fd1m);
        close (fd2m);
        setsid();
        if ( (fd2s = open(slavename,O_RDWR)) < 0 ) {
            perror("open shell pty slave"); exit(1);
        }
        ioctl(fd2s, I_PUSH, "ptem");
        ioctl(fd2s, I_PUSH, "ldterm");
        dup2 (fd2s, 0);/* stdin */
        dup2 (fd2s, 1);/* stdout */
        dup2 (fd2s, 2);/* stderr */
        system ("stty sane");
        execl ("/bin/sh", "sh", (char *) 0);
    }

    iordcnt12 = 0;/* I/O read character count, fd1m to fd2m */
    iordcnt21 = 0;/* I/O read character count, fd2m to fd1m */

    for (;;) {

    fds[0].fd = fd1m; fds[1].fd = fd2m;
    fds[0].events = fds[1].events = 0;
    nfds = 2; timeout = -1;
    if (iordcnt12) {
        fds[1].events |= POLLOUT;
    } else {
        fds[0].events |= POLLIN;
    }
    if (iordcnt21) {
        fds[0].events |= POLLOUT;
    } else {
        fds[1].events |= POLLIN;
    }

    iofdcnt = poll(fds, nfds, timeout);
    if ( iofdcnt < 0 )
        if ( errno == EINTR ) continue;
        else {
            perror("poll"); exit(1);
        }

    if ( fds[0].revents & POLLIN ) {

        /* Read from fd1m data to be written to fd2m */
        iobuf12p = iobuf12;
        iordcnt12 = read (fd1m, iobuf12, 2000);
        if ( iordcnt12 <= 0 ) break;
    }
    if ( fds[0].revents & POLLOUT ) {
```

```
        /* Write to fd1m with data read from fd2m */
        iowrcnt = write (fd1m, iobuf21p, iordcnt21);
        if ( iowrcnt <= 0 ) break;
        iordcnt21 -= iowrcnt;
        iobuf21p += iowrcnt;
    }
    if ( fds[1].revents & POLLIN ) {

        /* Read from fd2m data to be written to fd1m */
        iobuf21p = iobuf21;
        iordcnt21 = read (fd2m, iobuf21, 2000);
        if ( iordcnt21 <= 0 ) break;
    }
    if ( fds[1].revents & POLLOUT ) {

        /* Write to fd2m with data read from fd1m */
        iowrcnt = write (fd2m, iobuf12p, iordcnt12);
        if ( iowrcnt <= 0 ) break;
        iordcnt12 -= iowrcnt;
        iobuf12p += iowrcnt;
    }


    }
    close (fd1m);
    close (fd2m);
    sleep(3);/* Delay for pty close */
    wait();
    }


    }
```

ptysh for Linux

The pseudo-terminal facility on Linux consists of many independent master and slave pty device pairs in the */dev* directory. Programs obtaining a pseudo-terminal must search for an available master pty device. I omit this search logic. ptysh simply assumes the */dev/ptyr0* master pty is available. This master manages the */dev/ttyr0* slave device, for PPP software to use. The */dev/ptyr1* and */dev/ttyr1* files are the master and slave ptys, respectively, that ptysh uses to communicate with a Linux shell.

ptysh doesn't manage permissions or ownerships for pseudo-terminal device files. Therefore, you may need to set */dev/ptyr0*, */dev/ptyr1*, */dev/ttyr0*, and */dev/ttyr1* to be world-readable and writable.

When ptysh successfully starts, it reports creating pseudo-terminal */dev/ttyr0*:

```
user$ ./ptysh &
serial pty: /dev/ttyr0
user$
```

PPP software can now access */dev/ttyr0* as its dial-out serial interface. This pseudo-terminal device doesn't respond until a chat script sends a character first, such as a carriage return.

This ptysh code is a sample only and not suitable for critical production use. It doesn't check for all error conditions, aborts if specific pseudo-terminal devices are busy, and may terminate if an invoking user logs off. If ptysh is waiting for a connection, any user can attach to */dev/ttyr0* and obtain a shell with permissions matching the ptysh process itself. This is a security deficiency and requires additional programming to correct.

```
/*
ptysh.c  "Pseudo Terminal Shell"

For Linux Slackware 3.4
Compile with "cc -o ptysh ptysh.c"


Author: Andrew Sun
Revision: January 17, 1996, January 10, 1998, June 1, 1998


Description:

This program enables the /bin/sh command interpreter to
emulate a "terminal device".  Tip, cu, the UUCP environment,
and PPP normally interact with serial interfaces via terminal
device files, such as /dev/cua1.  Rather than limiting these
applications to physical serial interfaces, "ptysh" enables them
to interact with the shell (/bin/sh), and with TCP/IP communication
programs, including telnet and rlogin.


Usage:

Once ptysh is active, an application accessing the serial pty
device /dev/ttyr0 will interact with /bin/sh.  At this point,
an application s chat script can "exec telnet" or "exec rlogin"
to establish communications over a network.
*/

#include <stdio.h>
#include <errno.h>

#include <fcntl.h>
#include <sys/termio.h>

#include <sys/types.h>
#include <sys/time.h>
```

```
main(argc,argv)
int argc;
char *argv[];
{

int shellpid;

char iobuf12[2000], iobuf21[2000];
char *iobuf12p, *iobuf21p;
int iofdcnt, iowrcnt, iordcnt12, iordcnt21;

int fd1m, fd2m, fd2s;
fd_set readfds, writefds;

for (;;) {

/* Create serial interface ptys */
if ( (fd1m = open("/dev/ptyr0",O_RDWR)) < 0 ) {
    perror("open serial pty master /dev/ptyr0");
    exit(1);
}
    printf("serial pty: %s\n", "/dev/ttyr0");

/* Detect "open" for serial pty slave */
FD_ZERO (&readfds);
FD_ZERO (&writefds);
FD_SET (fd1m, &readfds);
/* FD_SET (fd1m, &writefds); *//* Remove this if wait for open fails */
while ( select (64, &readfds , &writefds, (fd_set *) 0, NULL) < 1 )
    ;

/* Create shell ptys */
if ( (fd2m = open("/dev/ptyr1",O_RDWR)) < 0 ) {
    perror("open shell pty master /dev/ptyr1");
    exit(1);
}
    /* printf("shell pty: %s\n", "/dev/ttyr1"); */

/* Invoke /bin/sh as a subprocess */
if (! (shellpid = fork()) ) {
    close (fd1m);
    close (fd2m);
    setsid();
    if ( (fd2s = open("/dev/ttyr1",O_RDWR)) < 0 ) {
        perror("open shell pty slave /dev/ttyr1");
        exit(1);
    }
    dup2 (fd2s, 0);/* stdin */
    dup2 (fd2s, 1);/* stdout */
    dup2 (fd2s, 2);/* stderr */
    system ("stty sane");
    execl ("/bin/sh", "sh", (char *) 0);
}
```

```
iordcnt12 = 0;/* I/O read character count, fd1m to fd2m */
iordcnt21 = 0;/* I/O read character count, fd2m to fd1m */

for (;;) {

FD_ZERO ( &readfds );
FD_ZERO ( &writefds );
if (iordcnt12) {
    FD_SET (fd2m, &writefds);
} else {
    FD_SET (fd1m, &readfds);
}
if (iordcnt21) {
    FD_SET (fd1m, &writefds);
} else {
    FD_SET (fd2m, &readfds);
}

iofdcnt = select (64, &readfds, &writefds, (fd_set *) 0, NULL);
if ( iofdcnt < 0 )
    if ( errno == EINTR ) continue;
    else {
        perror("select"); exit(1);
    }

if ( FD_ISSET (fd1m, &readfds) ) {

    /* Read from fd1m data to be written to fd2m */
    iobuf12p = iobuf12;
    iordcnt12 = read (fd1m, iobuf12, 2000);
    if ( iordcnt12 <= 0 ) break;
}
if ( FD_ISSET (fd1m, &writefds) ) {

    /* Write to fd1m with data read from fd2m */
    iowrcnt = write (fd1m, iobuf21p, iordcnt21);
    if ( iowrcnt <= 0 ) break;
    iordcnt21 -= iowrcnt;
    iobuf21p += iowrcnt;
}
if ( FD_ISSET (fd2m, &readfds) ) {

    /* Read from fd2m data to be written to fd1m */
    iobuf21p = iobuf21;
    iordcnt21 = read (fd2m, iobuf21, 2000);
    if ( iordcnt21 <= 0 ) break;
}
if ( FD_ISSET (fd2m, &writefds) ) {

    /* Write to fd2m with data read from fd1m */
    iowrcnt = write (fd2m, iobuf12p, iordcnt12);
    if ( iowrcnt <= 0 ) break;
    iordcnt12 -= iowrcnt;
    iobuf12p += iowrcnt;
```

```
    }

    }
close (fd1m);
close (fd2m);
sleep(3);/* Delay for pty close */
wait(NULL);
    }

    }
```

Index

A

ACCM (see asyncmap)
activity logs, 330
Address Resolution Protocol (see ARP)
admintool utility, configuring Solaris login
    service, 174
application layer proxies, 291–292
ARP (Address Resolution Protocol), 77–78
ARP tables
    listing contents of, 77
    Proxy ARP, 196
    Split Subnet, 199
arp utility
    checking DNS, 236
    editing ARP tables, 178
    listing ARP table contents, 77
ARPAnet, history of PPP and, 3–4
asppp program, 123–126, 177–178
asyncmap (async control character
    map), 32–34, 43, 98
    asyncmap default, 367
    setting options, 251–252
authentication, 114, 269
    CHAP, 276–277
    counters and timers, 259
    dial-in PPP, 157
        authentication servers, 160
        Windows NT, 183, 187
    DNS names, 237
    options offered by PPP software, 98–99
    outside PPP, 281–283
    PAP, 270–272
    policy, 257–260
    problems with, 356–359
    protocol option, 44
    protocols, 49–53
    security-token, 285–288
    supported by Windows 98, 135
    (see also individual authentication
        protocols)
autodetection, of PPP frames, 35

B

bandwidth-to-user ratios, 93
BAP (Bandwidth Allocation Protocol), 392
BIND (Berkeley Internet Name
    Domain), 240
B-ISDN (Broadband Integrated Services
    Digital Network), 385
bit timings, of TD line format, 14–16
breakout boxes, 13

C

Call Back Control Protocol (CBCP), 393
call-back systems, 392–394
    authentication, 284–285
    security, 284
carrier rate, 22
CBCP (Call Back Control Protocol), 393
CCP (Compression Control Protocol), 58,
    135, 363–364
CD (Carrier Detect) control signal, 18

CHAP, 51–52, 260, 274–275
   authenticating clients, 276
   authenticators, 276–277
CHAP-80 (see MS-CHAP)
chap-secrets file, 276–277
chat
   configuration, 112–113
   dial-up process and, 115
   invoking with pppd, 112
chat scripts, 112
   authenticating with outside PPP, 283
   call-back systems, 285
   as feature of PPP software, 96–97
   problems with, 348–354
   UUCP, 120–122
CIDR tables, 79–216
classful routing tables, 80–82
classless interdomain routing (see CIDR
      tables)
code-reject LCP error packet, 46
communications servers, 158
   authenticating clients, PAP, 270
   CHAP authentication, 276
   dial-in PPP on, 156, 246
   LAN settings, 160
   PAP authentication, 271–272
   as PPP hardware platform, 89–90
   Proxy ARP, setting up, 195
   RIP options, 229
compiling PPP (see dial-in PPP; dial-out
      PPP)
compressed datagram, 28, 58–59, 66
Compressed SLIP (CSLIP), 5
compression, 389–390
   of fields in PPP frames, 250
   issues on Windows 98, 135
   (see also VJ compression)
Compression Control Protocol, 58, 135, 363
configure utility, compiling PPP, 108
connection states, 35–36
   network, 53–58
control packets, 35
CSLIP (Compressed SLIP), 5
CTS control signal, 17
cu utility
   checking serial interface, 333
   connecting to pseudo-terminal
         devices, 312
   testing chat scripts, 122

D

data bits, number of, 15
data communications equipment
         (DCE), 12–13
Data Set Ready (DSR) control signal, 18
data terminal equipment (see DTE)
Data Terminal Ready (DTR) control
         signal, 18
datagrams (see IP datagrams)
DB serial interface connectors, 11
DCE (data communications
         equipment), 12–13
DDS (Digital Data Service), 85
default routes, 218–219
Devices and Dialers files, 120–122
DHCP (Dynamic Host Configuration
         Protocol), 179
   IP addresses, 267
   MS PPP extensions, 238
dial-in PPP, 156–157
   authentication, 157, 269–288
   configuration
      asppp, 177–178
      DNS IP addresses, 238
      LAN interface settings, 160
      ports, 161–165
      pppd, 169–171
      RAS, 144
      Solaris login service, 174
      Windows NT network
            interface, 179–180
   Linux, 167–169
   Proxy ARP, 193–194
   RAS, 178, 181–187
   security
      Linux, 160, 170
      Solaris, 177
   software features, 96
   Solaris, 174–176
   startup options, 245–248
   verification, 165
   Windows NT, 180, 183, 187, 189
dial-out PPP, 104
   compilation, Linux, 109–110
   configuration
      asppp, 123–124
      chat, 112–113, 120–122
      pppd, 113–114

RAS, 144
Windows 98, 133–137
establishing connection
Linux, 115–116
Solaris, 125–127
Windows 98, 137–140
Windows NT, 150–152
initiation, commands for, 105–106
installation
Linux, 107–109
Solaris, 117–118
Windows 98, 128–129
Windows NT, 144–145
setting up (general), 106
software features, 96–97
startup options, 249
termination, 117
Solaris, 127
dial-up adapter
Windows 98, 129, 131–133
Windows NT, 255
dial-up line connections, 87–88
dial-up networking (see DUN)
Digital Data Service (DDS), 85
DIN serial interface connector, 11
DNS, 232–235
authentication, 237
checking functioning of, 235–236
dial-in PPP on Windows NT and, 180
dial-out PPP on Windows 95/98
and, 136
DNS servers, 243
Linux and, 116
missing records, 237
name resolution on various
platforms, 238–242
operation of, 233
registering PPP users, 236
Solaris and, 127
User Datagram Protocol (UDP) and, 64
Domain Name System (see DNS)
dongle (see security token)
DTE (data terminal equipment), 13, 22, 28
DUN (dial-up networking), 128
Windows 95/98, 128, 140–142
Windows NT, 152–154
Dynamic Host Configuration Protocol
(DHCP), 179
IP addresses, 267
MS PPP extensions, 238

dynamic routes, 217
dynamic routing protocols, 226–231

E

EAP (Extensible Authentication
Protocol), 273, 394
echo requests, 256
encryption, 389–390
tunneling, 326–327
Windows 98 and, 136
errors
correction, 59
detection, 116
error packets, 46–47
Ethernet addresses, 76–77
eventvwr utility, viewing dial-in PPP
connections, 187
Extensible Authentication Protocol
(EAP), 273, 394
exterior gateway protocols, 226

F

FCS (frame check sequence), 31, 45, 59
File Transfer Protocol (FTP), 64
flow control, 16–17, 59
checking, 335–337
dial-in PPP, on communications
servers, 161
fragmentation, 347
frame check sequence (FCS), 31, 45, 59
frame relay, 384–385
frames
fields in, 30–35
setting compression, 251
VJ compression and, 66
LCP packets and, 37
unrecognizable, 352, 369
FTP, TCP and, 64
full duplex communications, 14

G

GND (ground reference), 14

H

hardware flow control, 17
host-specific routes, 223–226
Hyperterminal program, 23, 333

I

IANA (Internet Assigned Numbers
        Authority), 65, 290, 397
ICMP (Internet Control Message
        Protocol), 64
IETF (Internet Engineering Task Force), 5
ifconfig utility
    commands establishing PPP, 123
    detecting errors at serial interface, 116
    installing Solaris dial-in PPP
            interfaces, 177
    MAC address reporting, 76
in.routed program, implementing
        RIP, 227–231
installation of PPP (see dial-in PPP or dial-
        out PPP)
Integrated Services Digital Network
        (ISDN), 385–386
interior gateway protocols, 226
International Standards Organization
        (ISO), 7
Internet
    history of, 4
    PPP software on, 94
    routing, 78, 82
        problems with, 381
    (see also tunneling protocols)
Internet Assigned Numbers Authority
        (IANA), 65, 290, 397
Internet Control Message Protocol
        (ICMP), 64
Internet Engineering Task Force (IETF), 5
Internet Protocol Control Protocol (see
        IPCP)
interrupt requests (IRQs), 92
    sharing, 111
IP addresses, 69–74, 79
    assigning, 265–267
        to private networks, 290
    conflicts with, 362
    depletion of, workarounds for, 73
    determining specific addresses for
            PPP, 264
    DHCP and, 267
    dial-in PPP, 156
        communications servers, 163
        Windows NT, 183–184
    DNS and, 234
    Ethernet, 76–77
    Gateway, 216–217

    MAC addresses, 75–78
    network architectures and, 194–210
    PPP gateways and, 290
    PPP in a Subnet, 205
    routing, 216
    settings, 261–263
    special-purpose, 74–75
    translating with NAT, 296–298
IP datagrams, 60–62
    format, 62–63
    forwarding, 375
    fragmentation, 347
    Linux, 167
    routing, 79, 213–217
    Solaris, 173
IPCP (Internet Protocol Control
        Protocol), 54–57
    counters and timers, 263
    IP addresses, 261–263
    MS PPP extensions, 238
    PPP software and, 99
    problems with, 360–363
    VJ compression, 69, 260
IRQs (interrupt requests), 92
    sharing, 111
ISDN (Integrated Services Digital
        Network), 385–386
ISO (International Standards
        Organization), 7
ITU V.42/LAPM modem correction
        standard, 27

L

LANs (local area networks)
    Linux and, 166–167
    PPP gateways and, 290
    routing, problems with, 378–381
    Solaris and, 118, 172–173
    subnet mask for, 160
    subnets and, 72
LCP (Link Control Protocol), 30, 35
    counters and timers, 255–256
    echo requests, 256
    extensions, 388–389
    packets, 37–48
        PPP options and, 42–45
    problems with, 355–356
leased line connections, 85–86
line formats, 14–16
Link Control Protocol (see LCP)

link termination, reasons for, 45
Linux
    capturing messages with
            syslog, 111–112
    CHAP authentication, 276
    configuration
        chat, 112–113
        network, 116
        pppd, 113–114
    dial-in PPP on, 167–169
    DNS and, 116, 240–241
    IP forwarding, 167, 375
    LANs, 166–167
    MS-CHAP, 279
    NAT setup on, 298–300
    PAP authentication, 270–272
    PPP, 94, 107–112
        dial-in, 247
        establishing connection, 115–116
        negotiation example, 40–42
        pseudo-terminal devices, 311–312
        routing, 217
        serial interface, checking, 333
    TCP/IP and, 167
    terminal programs for, 23
local area networks (see LANs)
longest match algorithm, 80

M

MAC (media access control)
            addresses, 75–78
magic number option, 44
magic numbers
    improper use of, 370
    setting, 251
maximum receive unit (MRU), 97, 347–348
    setting, 253–255
maximum transmission unit (MTU), 63, 97,
            347–348
    setting, 253–255
media access control (MAC)
            addresses, 75–78
mgetty utility, 168–169
    enabling automatic PPP
            detection, 247–248
modems, 21, 23–25
    bandwidth, 93–94
    compression, 28
        Windows 98, 135

    connecting and configuring, 22–25
    control signals, 18–19
    dial-in PPP, 157
        communications servers, 161
        Windows NT, 181, 187
    error detection and correction, 27, 346
    modulation, 25–27
    number of users per, 92
    setting up
        Windows 98, 129–131, 133–134
        Windows NT, 146–150
    throughput, 93–94
    troubleshooting, 337, 343–348
MRU (maximum receive unit), 97, 347–348
    setting, 253–255
MRU option, 43
MS-CHAP, 183
    for PPP v2.3, 279–280
    Windows NT RAS, 279
MS DNS PPP extension, 239
MS-DOS 6.22, and PPP, 91
MTU (maximum transmission unit), 63, 97,
            347–348
    setting, 253–255
multilink PPP, 391–392
multiplexing, 62
Multipoint PPP in a Subnet, 191, 209–212
musrmgr utility, creating Windows NT user
            accounts, 185

N

name services switch, 241
NAT (network address
            translation), 295–301
NCP (Network Control Protocol), 99
    packets, 36
    problems with, 359–360
    protocols, 54
        (see also IPCP)
negotiation process of PPP, 38
netconfig utility
    configuring networks with Slackware
            Linux, 110
    setting up files for DNS, 116
netmasks, 79–80
    in routing tables, 216
network adapter, for dial-in PPP on
            Windows NT, 179

network address translation
        (NAT), 295–301
network architectures
    choosing, 190–193
    (see also individual architectures)
network layer protocols, 387–388
none flow control option, 17
nslookup, checking DNS servers, 242
null modems, 13
    cables, 11
    Windows 98 and, 142
    Windows NT and, 154, 189

O

octet stuffing, 32–33
on-demand PPP, 126–127
    Windows 98 and, 140
    Windows NT and, 151–152
One PPP Link per Subnet, 191
OSI (Open Systems Interconnect), 6–8

P

packet switching, 3
packet switching service, 85
PAP (Password Authentication
        Protocol), 49–51, 270–272
pap-secrets file, 270–272
parity bits, 16
PCs
    CHAP authentication, 276
    dial-in PPP on, 248
    DNS name resolution, 238–240
    modem control signals and, 19
    PAP authentication, 270–272
    PPP
        dial-in, 156
        hardware platforms, 89, 91–92
        history of, 2–3
    resource conflicts and, 92
    routing, 218
    RS-232 interface, 11–12
    Solaris for, 119
    TCP/IP and, 99
Phonebook (Windows NT), 146–150
ping
    Internet Control Message Protocol
        (ICMP) and, 64
    troubleshooting PPP, 373–374

Plain Old Telephone Service (POTS), 87
pmadm utility, servicing incoming
        connections, 248
point-to-multipoint interfaces
    Multipoint PPP in a Subnet, 211–212
    routing, 225–226
    Solaris, 211
point-to-point interfaces, Multipoint PPP in
        a Subnet, 210–211
point-to-point protocol (see PPP)
point-to-point serial connections, 1, 4
Point-to-Point Tunneling Protocol (see
        PPTP)
ports, 11
    configuration, example of, 161–165
    port numbers, 64–65
    translating port pairs with NAT, 297–298
POTS (Plain Old Telephone Service), 87
PPP, 6, 35
    assigned numbers, 397–409
    compatibility problems, 364–367
    compression, Windows 98, 135
        (see also VJ compression)
    connection states, 35–36
        authentication, 49–53
        network, 53–58
    dial-in/dial-out (see dial-in PPP; dial-out
        PPP)
    dial-up services, 88
    DNS, 236, 238, 243
    extensions, 388–394
    features lacking, 59
    frames, 30–35, 37
    gateways to private LANs, 290
    hardware platforms for, 89–92
    history of, 2–5
    leased line serial connection and, 86
    MS-DOS 6.22 and, 91
    MTU and, 63
    Multilink PPP, 87
    negotiation, 38, 40–42
    octet stuffing, 32–33
    options, 43–45
    OSI reference model and, 7–8
    product obsolescence, 396
    RIP-1, problems with, 229
    software, 94–102
    subnets and, 73–74

terminal emulators, contention
    with, 282–283
termination, transaction example, 46
Unix software and, 90
v2.3
    authentication, 257–260, 270–272,
      276–280, 285
    on the Internet, 107
    IP addresses, 262–263
    IPCP options, 261–264
    LCP options, 250–257
    logging, 330
    manual pages, 268
    MS-CHAP, 279–280
    on-demand PPP settings, 249
    Proxy ARP, 195
    VJ compression and (see VJ
      compression)
    VPNs and, 395
    Windows 3.x and, 91, 128
    (see also dial-in PPP or dial-out PPP)
PPP in a Subnet, 205–209
pppd program, 112–117
    authentication and, 271–272
    configuration, 169–171
    verification, 171–172
ppplog.txt file, 140
pppstat utility, 116
PPTP (Point-to-Point Tunneling
    Protocol), 306–307
    incoming tunnels, 318–320
    outgoing tunnels, 313–314
Progressive Systems PPP
    incoming tunnels, 320–321
    outgoing tunnels, 315–316
protocol field compression option, 44
protocol field of PPP frames, 30–32, 35
protocol-reject LCP error packet, 46
Proxy ARP, 157, 178, 191, 193
    configuration, 195–196
      Split Subnet, 199–200
    IP addresses and subnets, 194–195
proxy servers, 291–295
pseudo-terminal devices, 311–312
PSN (packet-switching nodes), 3
ptysh utility
    managing pseudo-terminal
      devices, 311–312, 411–412
    for Unix System V, 412–413

Q

quality protocol option, 44

R

RADIUS (remote authentication dial in
    user), 395
RAS (remote access service), 143–146,
    186–187
    dial-in PPP, 178, 181–187
rasadmin utility
    administering RAS, 186
    Windows NT RAS registry keys, 268
RD (received data) signals, 14
remote access servers (see communications
    servers)
remote access service (see RAS)
remote authentication dial in user service
    (RADIUS), 395
resequencing, PPP and, 59
resource conflicts, PCs and, 92
RFCs
    accessing, xii
    FCS computational algorithm, 31
    FCS standards, 45
    IP address options, 56
    IPCP standards, 54
    LCP counters and timers standards, 255
    MS PPP extensions, 238
    multilink PPP, 391
    PAP and CHAP standards, 49
    PPP standards, 5, 29, 35
    RADIUS, 395
    SLIP standards, 5
    VJ compression standards, 66
Ring Indicator (RI) control signal, 18
RIP (Routing Information Protocol), 180
RIP-1 (Routing Information Protocol
    v1), 227–229
rlogin, as a tunneling protocol, 309–310
route command, editing routing tables, 217
routers, as PPP hardware platform, 89–90
routing, 78, 82, 224, 229
    default routes, 116, 124, 126, 218–219
    host-specific routes, 223
    for point-to-multipoint, 225–226
    problems with, 376–381
    protocols, 226–231
      (see also individual protocols)
    Solaris, 173

routing (*continued*)
    static routes, 218
        Split Subnet, 200–201
    subnet routes, 220–223
    tables, 213–217
        (see also CIDR tables)
    with tunnels, 322–326
    Windows NT, 188
Routing and Remote Access Upgrade, 188
Routing Information Protocol (RIP), 180
Routing Information Protocol v1 (RIP-
        1), 227–229
RS-232 interface, 11–13, 22, 84
    Linux and, 111
    octet stuffing and, 35
    PPP drivers, 109
RTS control signal, 17

S

SAC (Service Access Controller), 174
security
    call-back systems, 284–285
    dial-in PPP
        Linux, 160, 170
        Solaris, 177
    dial-up services and, 88
    routing, 229
    tunneling, 326–327
security token, 285–288
serial connections, 85–88
    checking, 331, 338–342
serial interface, 10–11
    checking, 331–334
    detecting errors at, 116
    dial-in PPP, 157, 174
        Windows NT, 181
    emulation, 410
    Solaris, 119
    Windows 98, 129–131
serial I/O, redirecting, 310–312
Serial Line Internet Protocol (SLIP), 4–5
Service Access Controller (SAC), 174
set up/shut down PPP (see dial-in PPP or
        dial-out PPP)
single octet code field in PPP frames, 37
Slackware v3.4 Linux (see Linux)
SLIP (Serial Line Internet Protocol), 4–5
software flow control, 17

Solaris
    authentication, 257–260
    chat scripts, 350
    configuration
        asppp, 123–124
        IP addresses, 263
    IP forwarding, enabling, 375
    IPCP options, 261–264
    LANs, 118, 172–173
    LCP options, 250–257
    LCP protocol-reject example, 47
    logging, 330
    point-to-multipoint interfaces, 211
    PPP
        configuring OS for, 118–120
        dial-in, 174–176, 247–248
        dial-out, 249
        establishing connection, 125–127
        installing, 117–118
        manual pages, 268
        termination, 127
    Proxy ARP, setting up, 196
    routing, 173
    serial interface devices, 119
    tunneling, 321–322
    (see also Unix)
Split Subnet, 191, 197, 201
    configuration, 199–201
    IP addresses and subnets, 197–199
start bits and stop bits, 14
static address pool, 183–184
static routes, 217–218
straight-through cables, 11
stty utility, setting Unix serial I/O
        options, 20
subnet masks, 71, 210
    fixed, 221
    for LAN interface, 160
    Proxy ARP, 195
    Split Subnet, 199
    variable length subnet masks
        (VLSM), 72
subnet routes, 220–224
subnets, 70–74, 79
    network architectures and, 194–210
SunOS 4.1.x, DNS name resolution, 242
switched services, 87–88
syslog, capturing messages on
        Linux, 111–112

Systems file, 120–122, 124
sys-unconfig utility, configuring LANs, 173

T

TCP (Transmission Control Protocol), 64
  incoming tunnels, 320–321
  outgoing tunnels, 315–318
TCP/IP, 73, 99
  datagrams and, 5
  diagnostic tools, 372–374
  dial-up PPP and, 160
  Ethernet addresses, 76–77
  history of PPP and, 3
  IP addresses, 69–75
  Linux, 110
  MAC addresses (see MAC addresses)
  network architectures (see network
    architectures)
  port numbers and, 64–65
  protocols, family of, 63–64
  routing, 78, 119, 213
    protocols, 82, 167
    Split Subnet and, 197
  Solaris, 117, 119
  Unix software and, 90
  VJ compression and (see VJ
    compression)
  Windows 98, 129, 136–137
TD (transmitted data) signals, 14–16
Telnet, 307–309
  checking DNS, 235–236
  incoming tunnels, 320–322
  outgoing tunnels, 315–318
  troubleshooting PPP, 374
terminal emulators, 281–285
terminal servers (see communications
    servers)
trace logs, 330
traceroute utility, sending UDP packet
    probes, 373
Transmission Control Protocol (see TCP)
transmission line formats (see line formats)
transmitted data (TD) signals, 14–16
transparency, 338–342
troubleshooting PPP, 328–382
  Solaris, 178
  Windows 98, 132
ttymon utility, servicing incoming
    connections, 248

tunneling, 305
  custom tunnels, 310
  incoming PPP, 318–322
  outgoing PPP, 313–318
    Progressive Systems PPP, 315–316
  protocols, 100, 306–310
    (see also individual protocols)
  routing and, 322–326
  security, 326–327

U

UART (Universal Asynchronous
    Receiver/Transmitter), 19–20
UDP (User Datagram Protocol), 63–64
  troubleshooting PPP, 373
Unix
  authenticating clients, PAP, 270
  CHAP authentication, 276
  checking DNS servers with
    nslookup, 242
  dial-in PPP on, 247–248
  DNS name resolution, 240–241
  MAC addresses and, 76
  MS-CHAP, 279
  PAP authentication, 271–272
  port numbers, 65
  proxy servers and, 294
  pseudo-terminal devices, 311–312, 411
  RIP-1 and, 229
  routing, 217
  serial device driver settings, 20–21
  serial interface, checking, 333
  servers, as PPP hardware
    platform, 89–91
  setting serial I/O options, 20
  terminal devices, 411
Unnumbered (network architecture), 191,
    201
  IP addresses, 204
User Datagram Protocol (UDP), 63–64
  troubleshooting PPP, 373
user-to-modem ratios, 92

V

V.42bis modem compression standard, 28
virtual private networking (see VPNs)
VJ compression, 66–69, 260
  problems with, 365–367
  Windows 98 and, 137

VLSM (variable length subnet masks), 72
VPNs (virtual private networking)
    architectures, 303–305
    capabilities in PPP software, 100
    PPP and, 395

W

Web, 64, 94
Well Known Ports and Registered Ports, 65
Windows 3.x, 91, 128
Windows 95, 91
    DNS and, 136
    DUN, 128
    PPP software and, 94
    tunneling, outgoing, 313–314
Windows 98, 23, 91
    authentication, 135, 271, 273
    determining UART type, 19
    dial-out PPP, on-demand PPP
        settings, 249
    DNS and, 136
    DUN, 128–129
    encryption, 136
    establishing PPP connection, 137–140
    installing PPP, 128–129
    IP addresses, 263
    IPCP options, 261–264
    LCP options, 250–257
    logging, 330
    port numbers, 65
    redirecting serial I/O on, 312
    setting up
        clients for MS DNS PPP
            extension, 239
        null modems, 142–143
        PPP, 133–137
        serial interface and
            modems, 129–131, 133–134
    TCP/IP, 129, 136–137
    troubleshooting PPP, 132
    tunneling, outgoing, 313–314

Windows NT, 65
    authentication, 257–260
    client for MS DNS PPP extension, 239
    dial-in PPP on, 179–181, 248
    dial-out PPP, on-demand PPP
        settings, 249
    DUN scripts, 152–154
    establishing PPP connection, 150–152
    installation, of PPP, 144–145
    IP addresses, 263
    IPCP options, 261–264
    LCP options, 250–257
    logging, 330
    network adapter for, 179
    null modems, 154
    on-demand PPP, 151–152
    PAP authentication, 271–272
    Phonebook, 146–150
    PPP software and, 94
    RAS, 187, 263
        CHAP, 277
        MS-CHAP, 279
        Proxy ARP, 195
        setting up servers for MS DNS PPP
            extension, 239
    redirecting serial I/O on, 312
    routing, 188
    terminal program for, 23
Windows NT Server
    IP forwarding, enabling, 375
    tunneling, incoming, 318–320
winipcfg utility, listing addresses and
        gateways on Windows 98, 140
Winsock API, 128
wireless technology, 387
World Wide Web (see Web)

X

XOFF and XON, 17

About the Author

Andrew Sun's experience with computers dates back to the early 1980s. He is an electrical engineer by training, with an MSEE degree from Stanford University.

Andrew has many years of experience in the telecommunications industry and has performed engineering work for emerging broadband ISDN and ATM products. He currently engineers IT infrastructures, and his areas of expertise include networking, firewalls, email with SMTP, DNS, Usenet, Solaris administration, and of course, dial-up remote access.

Andrew continues to experiment with diverse computer platforms and networks.

Colophon

Our look is the result of reader comments, our own experimentation, and feedback from distribution channels. Distinctive covers complement our distinctive approach to technical topics, breathing personality and life into potentially dry subjects.

The animal on the cover of *Using and Managing PPP* is a turtle, one of many species of terrestrial or aquatic reptile with a bony shell as part of their skeleton protecting the back and underside. All turtles can (to varying degrees) pull the head, neck, tail, and legs into the shell. The dorsal part of the shell is called the carapace; the ventral is the plastron. Turtles have a layer of sensitive skin between the bony plates and horn of the shell; they can feel what touches their shell. The appearance and size of the shell varies greatly with the species. Turtle species range in size from about 11 cm to 2 meters. Aquatic species usually have webbed feet and use their lungs as air or swim bladders, causing air to flow into different parts of the lung.

Turtles have a small but highly developed brain; they are generally somewhat mute and hear poorly, but have an excellent sense of smell. They are capable of learning and have significant memories. Their external sexual characteristics are difficult to distinguish. Some species live for around 100 years; many also have the capability to regenerate or heal severe wounds.

Turtles appear worldwide on land and in oceans with temperate to warm environments. All turtles are hatched from eggs, and all turtle eggs are laid on land. The shape of eggs and number in each batch varies with species. Many species hibernate when the temperatures become too low (or too high). They are slow growers, and their shells display rings showing uneven growth periods, much like the rings of a tree trunk.

Mary Anne Weeks Mayo served as production editor for *Using and Managing PPP*; Mary Anne also served as copyeditor, Sheryl Avruch was the production manager; Ellie Fountain Maden and Marleis Roberts provided quality assurance. Chris Reilley created the illustrations using Macromedia FreeHand 8. Mike Sierra provided FrameMaker technical support. Nancy Crumpton wrote the index and provided production services.

Edie Freedman designed the cover of this book, using a 19th-century engraving from the Dover Pictorial Archive. The cover layout was produced with Quark XPress 3.32 using the ITC Garamond font. Whenever possible, our books use RepKover™, a durable and flexible lay-flat binding. If the page count exceeds RepKover's limit, perfect binding is used.

The inside layout was designed by Nancy Priest and implemented in FrameMaker 5.5 by Mike Sierra. The text and heading fonts are ITC Garamond Light and Garamond Book. This colophon was written by Nancy Kotary.

More Titles from O'Reilly

Network Administration

Virtual Private Networks

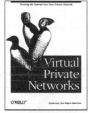

By Charlie Scott, Paul Wolfe & Mike Erwin
1st Edition February 1998
184 pages, ISBN 1-56592-319-7

This book tells you how to plan and build a Virtual Private Network (VPN), a collection of technologies that creates secure connections or "tunnels" over regular Internet lines. It starts with general concerns like costs and configuration and continues with detailed descriptions of how to install and use VPN technologies that are available for Windows NT and UNIX, such as PPTP and L2TP, the AltaVista Tunnel, and the Cisco PIX Firewall.

DNS and BIND, 3rd Edition

By Paul Albitz & Cricket Liu
3rd Edition September 1998
502 pages, ISBN 1-56592-512-2

DNS and BIND discusses one of the Internet's fundamental building blocks: the distributed host information database that's responsible for translating names into addresses, routing mail to its proper destination, and many other services.
The third edition covers BIND 4.9, on which most commercial products are currently based, and BIND 8, which implements many important new features and will be the basis for the next generation of commercial name servers.

TCP/IP Network Administration, 2nd Edition

By Craig Hunt
2nd Edition December 1997
630 pages, ISBN 1-56592-322-7

A complete guide to setting up and running a TCP/IP network for practicing system administrators. Beyond basic setup, this new second edition discusses the Internet routing protocols and provides a tutorial on how to configure important network services. It now also includes Linux in addition to BSD and System V TCP/IP implementations.

sendmail, 2nd Edition

By Bryan Costales & Eric Allman
2nd Edition January 1997
1050 pages, ISBN 1-56592-222-0

sendmail, 2nd Edition, covers sendmail Version 8.8 from Berkeley and the standard versions available on most systems. This cross-referenced edition offers an expanded tutorial, solution-oriented examples, and new topics such as the #error delivery agent, sendmail's exit values, MIME headers, and how to set up and use the user database, *mailertable*, and *smrsh*.

Cracking DES

By Electronic Frontier Foundation
1st Edition July 1998
272 pages, ISBN 1-56592-520-3

The Data Encryption Standard withstood the test of time for twenty years. *Cracking DES: Secrets of Encryption Research, Wiretap Politics & Chip Design* shows exactly how it was brought down. Every cryptographer, security designer, and student of cryptography policy should read this book to understand how the world changed as it fell.

The Networking CD Bookshelf

By O'Reilly & Associates, Inc.
1st Edition March 1999
Features CD-ROM
ISBN 1-56592-523-8

Network administrator alert! Six bestselling O'Reilly Animal Guides are now available on CD-ROM, easily accessible with your favorite Web browser: *TCP/IP Network Administration, 2nd Edition*; *sendmail, 2nd Edition*; *sendmail Desktop Reference*; *DNS and BIND, 3rd Edition*; *Practical UNIX & Internet Security, 2nd Edition*; and *Building Internet Firewalls*. As a bonus, the new hardcopy version of *DNS and BIND* is also included.

Network Administration

Managing IP Networks with Cisco Routers

By Scott M. Ballew
1st Edition October 1997
352 pages, ISBN 1-56592-320-0

This practical guide to setting up and maintaining a production network covers how to select routing protocols, configure protocols to handle most common situations, evaluate network equipment and vendors, and setup a help desk. Although it focuses on Cisco routers, and gives examples using Cisco's IOS, the principles discussed are common to all IP networks.

Protecting Networks with SATAN

By Martin Freiss
1st Edition May 1998
128 pages, ISBN 1-56592-425-8

SATAN performs "security audits," scanning host computers for security vulnerabilities. This book describes how to install and use SATAN, and how to adapt it to local requirements and increase its knowledge of specific security vulnerabilities.

Networking Personal Computers with TCP/IP

By Craig Hunt
1st Edition July 1995
408 pages, ISBN 1-56592-123-2

This book offers practical information as well as detailed instructions for attaching PCs to a TCP/IP network and its UNIX servers. It discusses the challenges you'll face and offers general advice on how to deal with them, provides basic TCP/IP configuration information for some of the popular PC operating systems, covers advanced configuration topics and configuration of specific applications such as email, and includes a chapter on on integrating Netware with TCP/IP.

Managing Mailing Lists

By Alan Schwartz
1st Edition March 1998
288 pages, ISBN 1-56592-259-X

Mailing lists are an ideal vehicle for creating email-based electronic communities. This book covers four mailing list packages (Majordomo, LISTSERV, ListProcessor, and SmartList) and tells you everything you need to know to set up and run a mailing list, from writing the charter to dealing with bounced messages. It discusses creating moderated lists, controlling who can subscribe to a list, offering digest subscriptions, and archiving list postings.

Managing Usenet

By Henry Spencer & David Lawrence
1st Edition December 1997
512 pages, ISBN 1-56592-198-4

Usenet, also called Netnews, is the world's largest discussion forum, and it is doubling in size every year. This book, written by two of the foremost authorities on Usenet administration, contains everything you need to know to administer a Netnews system. It covers C News and INN, explains the basics of starting a Netnews system, and offers guidelines to help ensure that your system is capable of handling news volume today—and in the future.

How to stay in touch with O'Reilly

1. Visit Our Award-Winning Web Site

http://www.oreilly.com/

★ "Top 100 Sites on the Web" —*PC Magazine*
★ "Top 5% Web sites" —*Point Communications*
★ "3-Star site" —*The McKinley Group*

Our web site contains a library of comprehensive product information (including book excerpts and tables of contents), downloadable software, background articles, interviews with technology leaders, links to relevant sites, book cover art, and more. File us in your Bookmarks or Hotlist!

2. Join Our Email Mailing Lists

New Product Releases

To receive automatic email with brief descriptions of all new O'Reilly products as they are released, send email to:
listproc@online.oreilly.com
Put the following information in the first line of your message (*not* in the Subject field):
subscribe oreilly-news

O'Reilly Events

If you'd also like us to send information about trade show events, special promotions, and other O'Reilly events, send email to:
listproc@online.oreilly.com
Put the following information in the first line of your message (*not* in the Subject field):
subscribe oreilly-events

3. Get Examples from Our Books via FTP

There are two ways to access an archive of example files from our books:

Regular FTP

- ftp to:
  ftp.oreilly.com
  (login: anonymous
  password: your email address)
- Point your web browser to:
  ftp://ftp.oreilly.com/

FTPMAIL

- Send an email message to:
  ftpmail@online.oreilly.com
  (Write "help" in the message body)

4. Contact Us via Email

order@oreilly.com
To place a book or software order online. Good for North American and international customers.

subscriptions@oreilly.com
To place an order for any of our newsletters or periodicals.

books@oreilly.com
General questions about any of our books.

software@oreilly.com
For general questions and product information about our software. Check out O'Reilly Software Online at **http://software.oreilly.com/** for software and technical support information. Registered O'Reilly software users send your questions to: **website-support@oreilly.com**

cs@oreilly.com
For answers to problems regarding your order or our products.

booktech@oreilly.com
For book content technical questions or corrections.

proposals@oreilly.com
To submit new book or software proposals to our editors and product managers.

international@oreilly.com
For information about our international distributors or translation queries. For a list of our distributors outside of North America check out:
http://www.oreilly.com/www/order/country.html

O'Reilly & Associates, Inc.
101 Morris Street, Sebastopol, CA 95472 USA
TEL 707-829-0515 or 800-998-9938
      (6am to 5pm PST)
FAX 707-829-0104

O'REILLY®

International Distributors

UK, EUROPE, MIDDLE EAST AND AFRICA (EXCEPT FRANCE, GERMANY, AUSTRIA, SWITZERLAND, LUXEMBOURG, LIECHTENSTEIN, AND EASTERN EUROPE)

INQUIRIES

O'Reilly UK Limited
4 Castle Street
Farnham
Surrey, GU9 7HS
United Kingdom
Telephone: 44-1252-711776
Fax: 44-1252-734211
Email: josette@oreilly.com

ORDERS

Wiley Distribution Services Ltd.
1 Oldlands Way
Bognor Regis
West Sussex PO22 9SA
United Kingdom
Telephone: 44-1243-779777
Fax: 44-1243-820250
Email: cs-books@wiley.co.uk

FRANCE

ORDERS

GEODIF
61, Bd Saint-Germain
75240 Paris Cedex 05, France
Tel: 33-1-44-41-46-16 (French books)
Tel: 33-1-44-41-11-87 (English books)
Fax: 33-1-44-41-11-44
Email: distribution@eyrolles.com

INQUIRIES

Éditions O'Reilly
18 rue Séguier
75006 Paris, France
Tel: 33-1-40-51-52-30
Fax: 33-1-40-51-52-31
Email: france@editions-oreilly.fr

GERMANY, SWITZERLAND, AUSTRIA, EASTERN EUROPE, LUXEMBOURG, AND LIECHTENSTEIN

INQUIRIES & ORDERS

O'Reilly Verlag
Balthasarstr. 81
D-50670 Köln
Germany
Telephone: 49-221-973160-91
Fax: 49-221-973160-8
Email: anfragen@oreilly.de (inquiries)
Email: order@oreilly.de (orders)

CANADA (FRENCH LANGUAGE BOOKS)

Les Éditions Flammarion ltée
375, Avenue Laurier Ouest
Montréal (Québec) H2V 2K3
Tel: 00-1-514-277-8807
Fax: 00-1-514-278-2085
Email: info@flammarion.qc.ca

HONG KONG

City Discount Subscription Service, Ltd.
Unit D, 3rd Floor, Yan's Tower
27 Wong Chuk Hang Road
Aberdeen, Hong Kong
Tel: 852-2580-3539
Fax: 852-2580-6463
Email: citydis@ppn.com.hk

KOREA

Hanbit Media, Inc.
Sonyoung Bldg. 202
Yeksam-dong 736-36
Kangnam-ku
Seoul, Korea
Tel: 822-554-9610
Fax: 822-556-0363
Email: hant93@chollian.dacom.co.kr

PHILIPPINES

Mutual Books, Inc.
429-D Shaw Boulevard
Mandaluyong City, Metro
Manila, Philippines
Tel: 632-725-7538
Fax: 632-721-3056
Email: mbikikog@mnl.sequel.net

TAIWAN

O'Reilly Taiwan
No. 3, Lane 131
Hang-Chow South Road
Section 1, Taipei, Taiwan
Tel: 886-2-23968990
Fax: 886-2-23968916
Email: benh@oreilly.com

CHINA

O'Reilly Beijing
Room 2410
160, FuXingMenNeiDaJie
XiCheng District
Beijing, China PR 100031
Tel: 86-10-86631006
Fax: 86-10-86631007
Email: frederic@oreilly.com

INDIA

Computer Bookshop (India) Pvt. Ltd.
190 Dr. D.N. Road, Fort
Bombay 400 001 India
Tel: 91-22-207-0989
Fax: 91-22-262-3551
Email: cbsbom@giasbm01.vsnl.net.in

JAPAN

O'Reilly Japan, Inc.
Kiyoshige Building 2F
12-Bancho, Sanei-cho
Shinjuku-ku
Tokyo 160-0008 Japan
Tel: 81-3-3356-5227
Fax: 81-3-3356-5261
Email: japan@oreilly.com

ALL OTHER ASIAN COUNTRIES

O'Reilly & Associates, Inc.
101 Morris Street
Sebastopol, CA 95472 USA
Tel: 707-829-0515
Fax: 707-829-0104
Email: order@oreilly.com

AUSTRALIA

WoodsLane Pty., Ltd.
7/5 Vuko Place
Warriewood NSW 2102
Australia
Tel: 61-2-9970-5111
Fax: 61-2-9970-5002
Email: info@woodslane.com.au

NEW ZEALAND

Woodslane New Zealand, Ltd.
21 Cooks Street (P.O. Box 575)
Waganui, New Zealand
Tel: 64-6-347-6543
Fax: 64-6-345-4840
Email: info@woodslane.com.au

LATIN AMERICA

McGraw-Hill Interamericana
Editores, S.A. de C.V.
Cedro No. 512
Col. Atlampa
06450, Mexico, D.F.
Tel: 52-5-547-6777
Fax: 52-5-547-3336
Email: mcgraw-hill@infosel.net.mx

O'REILLY®